THE LEGEND OF
KINGDOM HEARTS

The Legend of Kingdom Hearts Volume 1: Creation. Genesis of Hearts
by Georges Grouard
is published by Third Éditions
10 rue des arts, 31000 Toulouse, France
contact@thirdeditions.com
www.thirdeditions.com

Follow us:

🐦 : @Third_Editions
f : Facebook.com/ThirdEditions
👤 : Third Éditions
📷 : Third Éditions

Publishing Directors: Nicolas Courcier and Mehdi El Kanafi
Publishing Assistants: Damien Mecheri and Clovis Salvat
Text: Georges "Jay" Grouard
Proofreading: Valentin Angrand
Editing: Claire Choisy and Thomas Savary
Layout: Julie Gantois
Classic cover: Johann Blais
Collector cover: Frédéric Tomé
Translated from French by Michael Ross, ITC Traductions

This educational work is Third Éditions' tribute to the *Kingdom Hearts* video games.

The author presents an overview of the history of the *Kingdom Hearts* games
in this one-of-a-kind volume that lays out the inspirations, the context, and the content of these titles
through original analysis and discussion.

English edition, copyright 2019, Third Éditions.
All rights reserved.
ISBN 978-2-37784-250-6
Legal submission: December 2019
Printed in the European Union by Grafo.

GEORGES "JAY" GROUARD

THE LEGEND OF
KINGDOM HEARTS

VOLUME 1: CREATION

Genesis of Hearts

03rd. THIRD
éditions

In memory of my dearest Val,
who passed away shortly after finishing
work on this book.
We are 'connected', my friend.
You will live on in my heart forever.
Sleep well.
We will meet again.

THE LEGEND OF
KINGDOM HEARTS

VOLUME 1: CREATION

Genesis of Hearts

PREFACE

H EY THERE, reader, welcome to this book dedicated to *Kingdom Hearts*.

I hope you don't mind me using this informal tone. I figured I would use this preface to establish a rapport between you and me. Don't worry, the rest of the book is more serious. But this isn't about me, or about you for that matter. We must both make way for the real star: *Kingdom Hearts*. Every now and then, we'll pause for a second to check in with each other before we keep going. Since we'll be together for more than 400 pages in this first volume, I should warn you about something: I'm pretty neurotic. That means that certain things are non-negotiable. For example, there will be no bibliography in this book because, having made a career in journalism, I never cite my sources. I have my reasons—it's just part of my DNA. Please, just go with it.

So, I'm going to lay down a style guide for this book. My way of seeing things. I hope that you'll share that view, or at least that you'll learn to appreciate it.

POINT 1 — I'M OBSESSED WITH BEING ACCURATE.

Everything in this book has been verified more than ten times using multiple sources. If I have a doubt about the accuracy of something, I say so clearly using conditional phrasing or appropriate adverbs. As such, everything you read in this book is perfectly accurate, even if it goes against, more or less, what you already know.

Point 2 — I only have partial confidence in my writing.

I'll spare you the details, but I'm a bit like Tetsuya Nomura. A pathological super-perfectionist. In fact, certain passages in this book were rewritten more than twenty times. And the final version you have in your hands went through about 27 versions before being submitted to the editor. It's probably because of my lack of talent and because I like to waste time and money.

Point 3 — I only have relative confidence
in people's statements.

As a journalist by trade, I can assure you that interviews are not the be-all and end-all. Developers may be under pressure (from spokespeople in the room), read a written statement, or recite from memory. Or they might just have to go to the bathroom or want to have a smoke and thus speed up the conversation. These factors are all enemies of facts. By cross-referencing information given over the years, you'll eventually find the truth. This is true even though you may find numerous contradictions that then need to be cross-referenced to remove all doubt, checking whether a statement is likely true or not. Also, with experience, you learn to read between the lines. For example, when a publisher puts out a press release saying that a director is unable to finish their game for medical reasons, it's often false. You should be particularly skeptical if the director in question doesn't say a word, or worse, if they show you an X-ray of their right lung to prove that it's true.

Point 4 — I have a passion for credits.

Above all, creating a video game is a group effort. While in the 1980s it took anywhere from 10 to 60 people to create a game, this number increased into the hundreds by the end of the 20th century. This is a fact to bear in mind, as it's indicative of the technical evolution of games, which has had direct consequences for smooth game development.

You have to understand that people are important—vital even. It's people who make games. They imagine them, design them, write them. They realize the vision. People have the technical skills to program, model, animate, and package all of that on cartridges/CDs/Blu-rays. As such, I spend a lot of time reading the credits and analyzing them. Consequently, in this book, you will have to put up with a constant barrage of Japanese names and mini-biographies. In my view, this is essential. This information says a lot about a game, a series, its creator, its publisher, and how it was conceived. Just to give you an idea, when a publisher delegates production to one or more contractors, they have specific reasons for doing so. A game creator can get fed up, tired, overworked, and those feelings can start to show through in their work. By looking at the number of people involved and the way the development team is managed, you can discover the real ambitions of the producer and/or how polished their game is.

I promise, I won't use excessive name-dropping. All of these mentions are just part of my obsessiveness.

POINT 5 — I'M (KIND OF) AN OBSESSIVE-COMPULSIVE PURIST.

This is probably the worst of my faults. I'm often astounded by the poor quality of translations, when it comes to games, expressions, and individual words, even including complete mistranslations by people attempting to "adapt." For example, I find it infuriating that many people have never played a correctly translated version of *Final Fantasy VI* (by the way, the best is the GBA version). The worst is when translations are thoroughly dishonest and influenced by factors with complete disregard for the art of the video game and the story it's trying to tell.

How is it, for example, that publishers can severely censor words or even themes used by the game creators, under the pretext that it won't sit well with an American audience or will be an obstacle to distribution?

Furthermore, in this book, the names of characters or important words tied to the universe will be in the original language: Japanese or English. In the case of *Kingdom Hearts*, we will refer to the *Final*

Mix versions, since their creator considers them to be the only definitive versions. If I cite something from before the final versions, it will always be to mention the first occurrence, i.e. a game released in Japan with a Japanese release date. Finally, even though, when it comes down to it, people don't really give a crap, I give a lot of importance to the roles, positions, and titles of the people involved. It is important to understand exactly what they do. This is particularly true today with a video game industry that has professionalized, and thus become more hierarchical. This will help you understand that: 1.) making a video game used to be cooler, 2.) it was also less of a pain in the butt, 3.) no, a producer does not have the same influence as a director. Also, it is important to respect the technical terms from within the video game industry. Of course, I could waste time trying to dumb-down the language... but what good is a standardized lexicon used by every developer on the planet if we're not going to use it? I might as well just teach you to use video game terms the right way instead of just turning a blind eye under the pretext of, well, nothing actually.

POINT 6 — I HAVE AN ECCENTRIC WRITING STYLE.

It's nothing serious. It's just that I have a particular way of manipulating language, either going for just the bare bones, to the point of having sentences with no verbs, or using run-on sentences with embedded clauses within embedded clauses (the Russian doll technique), or trying to bring you straight to the point, or even using word play. Perhaps that last sentence even demonstrates some of those points. That's the beauty of language. You'll learn to appreciate my style. I'm less annoying than Agnès from the game *Bravely Default*. I promise. It may be a bit jarring, but I like to use punctuation. Here, there, and everywhere! You will see strange symbols like *;* quite often. And for good reason: a sentence can often have more than one meaning.

I'm serious about this, I've done tests. And for some bad readers (yes, it's not just bad writers out there), these things can go right over their heads. It's a generational thing.

POINT 7 — I AM A GAMING ADDICT.

Like Setzer Gabbiani. Even life and, in particular, writing are like games to me. What's more, you will be my guinea pig, subjected to experiments whether you like it or not. Don't worry, it won't hurt a bit. This book is not just a string of sentences to be read. It is a living text. It has nothing to do with me: it's the magic of Disney. This being said, a bit of advice: never forget what the subject is—*Kingdom Hearts*—and how it's addressed. The series lays out a world of pure imagination in which you can lose yourself in order to better find yourself. It's only logical then that a book dedicated to this series should do the same. I do so through puzzles, word play, word choice, and even deception. And while I'm at it, I'll deliberately lie to you just to see if you're following me, and then I'll scold you for not paying enough attention. Everything is on the table.

POINT 8 — IT MAY SEEM LIKE I DIGRESS.

In several instances, you may wonder why this thing or that thing is discussed in this book as it has—seemingly—nothing to do with *Kingdom Hearts*. Don't forget Point 7. With few exceptions (after all, I'm only human), the pen is mightier than the sword and narration can spin a formidable spiderweb.

Now that you know me a little better, I would like to let you in on a secret: the second you bought this book, you became my friend. No, not because you helped me pay my rent. Or at least, that's not the only reason. I'd like to thank you from the bottom of my heart for giving me this opportunity. That's not just a cliché. This is a real pleasure for me. It's an extraordinary experience that you've made possible for me—to write about *Kingdom Hearts*. One of the most unusual works of pop culture of the 21st century; probably the most comprehensive, the most on-point, the most poetic, and one of the most significant, with a real purpose behind it. In fact, several. I had the immense privilege of playing the role of biographer for this series throughout my months of work. Along the way, I got a boost to my ego as I am (now) the de-facto authority on *Kingdom Hearts*.

So, thank you for that. I hope that I can live up to your expectations and do right by *Kingdom Hearts* and its creators.

THE LEGEND OF
KINGDOM HEARTS

VOLUME 1: CREATION

Genesis of Hearts

CHAPTER I — THE ARCHITECT

ARCHITECT

Common noun, from the Greek word αρχιτεκτων (*architektôn*, master builder).

An architect is a professional who plans the creation, and sometimes the embellishment, of a structure or building and who supervises the execution of this work. The architect works on the orders of a project owner who asks them to design and build a building according to an aesthetic style and particular technical rules.

The first known (or recognized) architect—at least from a Western perspective—lived nearly three thousand years BCE. His name was Imhotep, chancellor to the pharaoh Djoser of Lower Egypt, high priest at Awnu (Heliopolis in Greek), physician, but also, and above all, a sculptor and architect. He was responsible for the funerary complex at Saqqara, which includes, among other things, the oldest step pyramid[1] in the world (an intermediate style between the mastaba[2] and the flat-faced pyramid[3]) and two of the greatest revolutions in architecture: columns and the use of stone (in place of mud bricks). At least, that's what legend tells us. It was later discovered that stone had already been used long before Imhotep was even born. Nevertheless, Imhotep's name was preserved by history, to the point where he was deified: in certain regions, he was considered the son of Ptah himself (one of the Egyptian demiurges), and he was often confused with

1. Step pyramid: a stack of several mastabas, from the largest (at the bottom) to the smallest (at the top), forming a pyramid with faces in the shape of giant steps.
2. Mastaba: a trapezoidal burial monument from the Old Kingdom of Egypt.
3. Flat-faced pyramid: the step-shaped sides were abandoned in favor of a perfect geometric form symbolizing the rays of the sun. The most well-known pyramids, the pyramids of Giza, are flat-faced pyramids.

Thoth, the god of knowledge. I could go on talking about the history of architecture, a fascinating subject, and could mention notable figures such as Ictinus in Greece or Agrippa and Vitruvius in Rome. However, I'm not sure that you bought this book for that reason, and perhaps you don't see how architecture is relevant to *Kingdom Hearts*.

Though you should.

Five thousand years after the first architect, it's fascinating to see how nothing has changed. The architect is still:

— Backed by a project owner (or owners).

— The person who designs, implements, and supervises work.

— Given mythical, almost godlike, status.

— Someone who transforms the old while looking toward the future.

— At the heart of it all; we tend to forget that they are not alone in creating an architectural work.

If you still don't see how this relates to video games, then it's a good thing you bought this book. If, on the contrary, you do see the connection, then it's a good thing you bought this book. Whatever the case may be, it proves that you are a smart person. As such, we'll get along well, you and me. Let's start by dispelling three misconceptions about *Kingdom Hearts* that have been swirling around since 2002 when the game was first released.

— No, the creator of *Final Fantasy*, Hironobu Sakaguchi, was never the originator of the project. He was, however, important from a philosophical standpoint and contributed at two key points during development (of the first game).

— No, the game was not conceived during a conversation in an elevator between Shinji Hashimoto—the game's real project owner— and a Disney executive; it was conceived long before that.

— No, Tetsuya Nomura was not solely responsible for laboring to make *Kingdom Hearts* the "third pillar" of Square Enix—although he was the series' architect and guru.

I'm here to offer the truth. Pure and simple. To explain what the history behind the development of the game's many iterations reveals about the series, its publisher, and the architect himself. How his

personal history and the trajectory of his career inform *Kingdom Hearts*. How his hardheadedness won out over the world's greatest creative empire. I'll explain who the other contributors to its success are and how they've participated. I will talk about Nintendo, *Cowboy Bebop*, *Harry Potter*, *Doctor Who*, and pop culture in general. Religion too. And symbolism, in all its forms. Childhood will be our most important point of reference throughout this book, in the hopes that it will inform and guide our analysis of the different subjects covered.

At least, that is how I originally planned this book. Alas, I have loads of things to tell you about the history of the series' development. Fifteen years of work is a lot. Eighteen iterations, even more. "What do you mean? There were only two installments!"[4] From your point of view, perhaps. But, the reality is quite different. With just two exceptions, not a year has gone by since 2002 without the release of a game under the *Kingdom Hearts* banner. Are you surprised? I'll be perfectly honest with you: originally, my plan was that the whole book (with six or seven chapters) would be about 300 pages long; what was supposed to be just the first chapter ended up turning into this first volume. So, I missed that mark by a bit. As such, you can see that the previous paragraph, when it was written a few months ago, was just an optimistic vision from an author full of energy and enthusiasm. My passion remains, but it will be spread across two volumes instead of just one. Unless, of course, I'm mistaken again…

Just because chapter one has become volume one, that doesn't mean that there's no chapter one. And of course, this first chapter of volume one is dedicated to the Architect: Tetsuya Nomura, his work, and his life. What does his extraordinary career tell us about him and, above all, about *Kingdom Hearts*?

Never doubt it, the Architect IS the edifice. *Ergo*, Tetsuya Nomura IS…

---

4. Editor's note: the book was written and initially published (in France) before the release of *Kingdom Hearts III*.

THE LEGEND OF KINGDOM HEARTS

MAYBE I'M A LION

Tetsuya Nomura was born on October 8, 1970. He lived in Kôchi, in the south of the Japanese island of Shikoku. It's a city located in the delta of the Kagami River with a 17th-century castle perched above it. With its forests filled with centuries-old trees, its fine sandy beaches like Katsurahama beach, its botanical garden, Ryugado Cave (one of the largest and oldest limestone caves in Japan, famous for its stalactites), its many rice paddy fields, and, of course, its various capes jutting out into the Pacific, Kôchi is heaven on earth.

It's in this setting that Nomura grew up. He was a normal kid. He played baseball, built "forts" and "huts" in the rice paddies, and swam and fished in the river and the ocean. He spent most of his time outside and nature was very important to him. However, he also had a passion for drawing. In fact, his earliest memory is of drawing a lion on the lid of a box on his third birthday. When he came home from school, he would draw or play *sugoroku*[5] using his father's sets, with specific rules, then with his own sets (starting in elementary school) that he created himself and shared with his friends.

His father was very important to him, teaching him the basics of drawing, as well as the philosophy of creation. In middle school, his father bought him his first computer because "it was the age [of computers]," the new standard for moving ahead in the world. Young Nomura learned the BASIC coding language and programmed little games, while he also continued to draw. Around the same time, he discovered video games with his Color TV-Game 6[6].

In addition, he can remember spending countless hours playing *Star Arthur Densetsu 1: Wakusei Mephius* (*Star Arthur Legend: Planet Mephius*), a revolutionary game[7] at the time made by T&E Soft. He

5. *Sugoroku*: a Japanese board game similar to backgammon, played with a die.
6. Color TV-Game 6: one of the first Nintendo consoles, developed with Mitsubishi and released in June 1977. The version that Nomura had was the very first. It offered six variations of *Pong* (including *Tennis*, *Hockey*, and *Volleyball*).
7. *Star Arthur Densetsu* (1983) was revolutionary in that it was the first episodic adventure game to offer a point-and-click interface (a cursor that interacts with objects on the screen) that could be played with a mouse, and that had entirely spoken dialog. The MSX version (1985) went even further, introducing full-motion video backgrounds and cutscenes. A first for an adventure game.

didn't buy a Famicom[8] right away, instead waiting until high school to get one. With the Famicom, he discovered his first life-changing game (and to this day, probably his favorite): *Dragon Quest*. It was a revelation for him, but did nothing to draw him away from his dream of becoming a manga artist. That dream led him to pursue art classes at a high school called Tachioka Toyokata, located an hour's bus ride from his home. At school, he spent his time coming up with stories and drawing. For that matter, he holds a record at his high school as the person who participated the most in Manga Koshien, a school-sponsored event related to manga, doing so 11 times. Tateki Sofue, his art teacher and first mentor, introduced him to many artists, including a certain Yoshitaka Amano. This was another revelation for the young Nomura, who was immediately taken by the charm of "this style somewhere between fiction and reality," between "the impossible and the possible." These impressions would stick with him for the rest of his life. Like most young Japanese teenagers, he abandoned his dream once he finished high school and pursued a career in advertising, enrolling in a *senmon gakkô*[9] in hopes of finding a job. While perusing want ads[10] one day, his attention was drawn to a somewhat unusual job ad with an illustration by Yoshitaka Amano. He decided to apply, without a clear goal in mind. He just wanted a job that would let him keep drawing.

Young Nomura's first day at Square was April 16, 1991. As always, it was a busy day. No one had time for the new guy. When he asked if he could help, someone (probably Takashi Tokita[11]) told him to just join the other "kids" in doing one of the most important, but also most thankless, tasks in video game design (the typical hazing for newcomers at Square): debugging[12]. Nomura got to work without a word. Still wearing his suit.

---

8. Famicom: abbreviation of Family Computer, also known as NES or simply Nintendo, a home video game console released in 1983. Over 61 million units were sold worldwide.
9. *Senmon gakkō*: what's known in certain countries as a "vocational school," a school with training for a specific job. In Japan, this type of school is part of higher education. Training there lasts two years after high school.
10. Want ads were a very popular way to recruit in the 1980s, especially for video game publishers. Quite a few major creators were recruited this way.
11. Takashi Tokita: director of *Chrono Trigger* and *Parasite Eve*, and the real lead designer for *Final Fantasy IV*. On a side note, he decided to use barely a quarter of the script, which he wrote himself, in addition to managing game design.
12. *Debugging*: work that involves playing a video game in order to provoke and reproduce logical defects (bugs) so that they can be corrected.

FOUR HEARTS

A few weeks after the release of *Final Fantasy IV* (on July 19, 1991), the founder and president of Square, Masafumi Miyamoto, was on his way out. He appointed Hironobu Sakaguchi as executive vice president of the company, a logical choice[13]. This gave Sakaguchi a management role that required much delegation. Moreover, he could impose new ways of working. The first thing on his agenda was to hold a "global" meeting to share his philosophy, the goal of which was to fairly distribute personnel according to the needs of each project. This was a change from the dusty old model in which employees had to "prove themselves" to their co-workers. I want to warn you, what happened next will seem unreal to you. Sakaguchi was in the meeting room facing the 50-odd Square employees. Next to him, there was a large whiteboard with three columns, each with a title at the top: *Romancing SaGa*, *Seiken Densetsu* (*II*) and *Final Fantasy* (*V*). Three major series in the making and also three developments intended for the Super Famicom[14].

One by one, the employees saw their names added to one of the columns; Nomura was put under *Final Fantasy*. It was fate… or something like that. In any case, this was a defining moment for him: the day that Tetsuya Nomura joined the *Final Fantasy V* team.

INTERLUDE – MENTORS

From the outset of *Final Fantasy V*, and mirroring its main concept (the Warriors of Light), the *Final Fantasy* myth essentially relied on a foursome. They were the cornerstones of the series, but also mentors to Tetsuya Nomura, the only real "child" of the series. Their heir, custodian of their tradition and methods. Guardian of a certain "punk" philosophy of video game creation according to which the work and the player are given priority over the interests of the company.

---

13. Tetsuo Mizuno arrived in 1992 and replaced Miyamoto as president of Square until 1998. He was the only person above Sakaguchi during the "golden age."
14. *Final Fantasy V* was the first game under the Squaresoft "brand." On a side note, at the time, everyone used this name to refer to the company (especially in the late 90s), which was incorrect because it was actually just the name of a collection.

HIRONOBU SAKAGUCHI: THE FATHER

The greatest figure in the history of Square. One of its first employees and the father of the *Final Fantasy* series. This primordial role led him, in 1991, to take on managerial roles that required him to take a step back from "pure" development. *Final Fantasy V* was, incidentally, the last installment he directed. From there, he became one of the best producers in video game history before committing the irredeemable act of trying his hand at show business (the animated film *Final Fantasy: The Spirits Within*), plunging Square into the worst crisis in its history. He then founded his own studio—Mistwalker—but has never since achieved (as much) success. In spite of the fact that he departed the company in 2001, his spirit lives on at Square. He was a father-figure, almost godlike, to Nomura, who has tried, even to this day, to walk in his footsteps.

TETSUYA TAKAHASHI: THE ARTIST

Before beginning his life's work (the *Xeno* series, which he still continues to work on for Nintendo today), he was the graphic director for the *Final Fantasy* games for Super Famicom, then for *Chrono Trigger*. He also collaborated on the backgrounds for *SaGa*, *Seiken Densetsu*, and *Front Mission*. One of Nomura's mentors and closest friends.

HIROYUKI ITÔ: THE DESIGNER

Responsible for the game systems in *Final Fantasy*, then the "signature" combat system of the series starting with *IV*, the *Active Time Battle* (collaboration with Akihiko Matsui and Kazuhiko Aoki). He was also co-director of *Final Fantasy VI*, *Final Fantasy IX* and *Final Fantasy XII*. And, "among other things," game designer for *Final Fantasy Tactics*.

YOSHINORI KITASE: THE WRITER-DIRECTOR

While Sakaguchi is the creator of the series, *"Kitase is Final Fantasy,"* as Nomura puts it. Heir to the throne. After writing *Seiken Densetsu*, he wrote and co-directed (unofficially) *Final Fantasy V*; he then became co-director (officially this time) of *Final Fantasy VI* and *Chrono Trigger*. After that, he directed *Final Fantasy VII* and *VIII* and produced *Final Fantasy X* and *XIII*, leaving the "hard work" to his protégé, Motomu Toriyama.

Nomura was assigned to work on battle graphics and monster design, reporting to the graphic director, Tetsuya Takahashi. He also became a student to Hiroyuki Itô. Square's demure genius taught him the science of game design and the subtle balance between gameplay and plot, to which he held the key. In spite of his very busy schedule, Sakaguchi held onto his role as director for *Final Fantasy V*, trying to multi-task. During development, he realized that it was impossible and found in writer Yoshinori Kitase, the perfect right-hand man. In addition, he started a new method of production: regular meetings were held, led by himself and Kitase, where all could speak freely and make suggestions. The members of the team developed the habit of coming to the meetings with ideas written on notepads or written ahead of time (on a computer) and printed out.

Nomura developed his own unique technique, somewhat of a vestige of his advertising studies: he would make drawings with hand-written annotations. This original technique got the attention of Sakaguchi and Kitase. At every meeting, they wanted to see Tetsu's infamous notebook.

[On a side note, it was during these meetings that Nomura proposed—among other things—two new characters: a ninja accompanied by a dog and a gambler who fights with cards and dice. As everyone knows, these ideas were then "set aside" and used later.]

This way of working suited Nomura well. He gained confidence in himself. He would also regularly visit Kitase's office—outside of meeting times—to suggest adjustments, as well as new concepts. Today, he recognizes that his boss was very patient with him and that he probably drove him crazy with totally inadequate and uninteresting ideas. But he has no idea how many. It's an instinctive impulse. Like when he changed the tradition of the final boss.

To fully understand the role and importance of Nomura, you have to put things in context and explain how design worked before him. Yoshitaka Amano, the historical image designer and character/monster designer for the series, was tasked with bringing the development team's ideas to life. Whether it was from Hironobu Sakaguchi or, more often than not, Koichi Ishii, the true creator of the *Final Fantasy* universe, he would receive keywords that he would use to "characterize" the characters and monsters using illustrations, including on canvas. Then, Kazuko Shibuya would "translate" Amano's art using pixels, sometimes having to add color herself (this was the case for the first two installments, for which Amano only produced illustrations in black and white). Thus, as a technician, she always tried to *reproduce his work* as best she could without attempting to *recreate*. Indeed, the "many forms" of the final bosses of the series were always "simple graphical evolutions" as Amano saw them.

As monster designer for *Final Fantasy V*, Tetsuya Nomura got to work creating new monsters while sticking—as best he could—to Amano's style. Notably, this was the case when he created Gilgamesh. However, for Neo Exdeath, he drew a "monstrous composition" inspired by Romantic paintings. The result was a grotesque being composed of multiple forms and creatures, a "mutation" that was both visual and symbolic. This revolution, though minor, was important because this "concept" became the new standard for *Final Fantasy*, as well as a new way of understanding narration as a visual representation—the story of the bad guy is told through its monstrous form—in all of the games that he contributed to.

To summarize, in less than a year, he became the student of Tetsuya Takahashi and Hiroyuki Itô and was able to make himself stand out in the eyes of his two bosses, Hironobu Sakaguchi and Yoshinori Kitase.

Additionally, he succeeded in "copying" Amano's style, making himself totally invisible and allowing the game to keep its peculiar artistic touch. Not bad for a 21- or 22-year-old kid.

Troops March On

What followed was a natural progression. Acclaimed by his peers, he continued his journey by joining the development team for *Final Fantasy VI*. Better yet, he was promoted to graphic director[15], working alongside Tetsuya Takahashi, Hideo Minaba, and Kazuko Shibuya. Naturally drawing inspiration from the prep work done by Yoshitaka Amano, this fantastic foursome created the "face" of *Final Fantasy VI*.

To be more efficient, they divided up the work:
— The world map and external environments went to Tetsuya Takahashi.
— The "overall" architecture of the world and the interiors were handled by Hideo Minaba[16].
— Kazuko Shibuya[17] handled design of ALL of the sprites.
— Lastly, Tetsuya Nomura concentrated on the battle graphics and everything related to it, including monster design, the difference being that this time, he was no longer working under Takahashi, instead becoming his "equal."

Nomura took the opportunity to do what he does best: create. Indeed, he created, for example, the Warring Triad (Sophia, Sefirot, and Zurvan... shamefully renamed *Goddess, Fiend and Demon*" in the American version) and the entire final battle against Kefka, including the "very graphic" animation of his ascension to his angelic/demonic

15. *See the special section "Graphic director".*
16. Hideo Minaba: another major figure from Square, who was art director for *Final Fantasy Tactics*, *Final Fantasy IX*, then later for *Final Fantasy XII*. After that, he launched his own company, Designation, and, not long after, was asked by Sakaguchi to work on games for Mistwalker.
17. Kazuko Shibuya: The "pixel craftswoman." A little-known legendary figure from Square who, for years, was in charge of "translating" the work of illustrators (Yoshitaka Amano for *Final Fantasy*, Tomomi Kobayashi for *SaGa*) into sprites.

form. This time, he mainly blended two styles of painting—Romanticism and High Renaissance—drawing inspiration largely from Michelangelo, going so far as to blend pieces of the *Pietà*, *The Creation of Adam*, and *The Last Judgment* with monstrous industrial piping (that Katsuhiro Otomo[18] would've been proud of) evoking the Kafkaesque concept (indeed, leading to the transformation of the Japanese name Cefca to Kefka in the American version) of *The Metamorphosis* as seen by Nabokov[19], but also the Kabbalah's Tree of Sephiroth[20], all while carefully adhering to Amano's visual style.

This was probably Nomura's first real masterpiece, which says a lot about him and his incredible Frankenstein-esque talent for appropriating things, incorporating them, transforming them, enhancing them, etc., while making their basic meanings accessible without misrepresenting them and telling his own story. In a way, the "Ascension of Kefka Palazzo" was the first real "ideological" demonstration of the future *Kingdom Hearts*.

INTERLUDE – GRAPHIC DIRECTOR

So as not to clog up the main text with too many references, I've decided to dedicate a full passage to the famous foursome of graphic directors.

In the 1980s, corporate vocabulary, specifically in the video game world, was quite limited. Given the small size of teams (each with no more than a dozen people), there was no need to establish roles. Everyone was considered a designer or a planner. This same idea applied to the organization of work. With the exception of managers, no one was "limited" to a particular skill set. That's why in one game, a designer would be in charge of the game system while in another, they

---

18. A legend of Japanese comics whose most emblematic work is undoubtedly *Akira*.
19. The author of *Lolita* wrote many commentaries on various authors, including Franz Kafka, who wrote *The Metamorphosis*. In his commentary, Nabokov depicts Gregor, the hero who transforms into an insect, as an icon of nihilism. His mutation is the result of his genius. It's everyone else who are the "cockroaches."
20. A depiction of the tree of life in mystical Judaism. We will cover this in detail in another book (*teasing*).

would design the backgrounds. They were all "jacks of all trades." The idea of an "art director" was even more difficult to evaluate, probably because of how "basic" the backgrounds and characters were.

In the 1990s, companies realized that video games were an industry, not just a group of friends making something together. The teams grew and required specific skills (particularly technical skills). Roles were defined, but the notion of art direction still remained hazy. However, team members were given responsibilities regarding graphic design. Naturally, the position was called graphic director, while in reality, the proper term should have been "art director." I felt this side note was needed to put things in context.

So, *Final Fantasy VI* had four of these graphic directors: Tetsuya Takahashi and Tetsuya Nomura, already covered in detail on previous pages, in addition to Hideo Minaba and Kazuko Shibuya.

Incidentally, Tetsuya Takahashi, besides handling the world map and the exteriors, was also responsible for the Magitek armor you see in the *Final Fantasy VI* opening. Knowing that he went on to work on *Front Mission* and *Chrono Trigger* at the same time, as well as knowing his future (*Xenogears*), you can't help but smile.

However, Nomura's work was not limited to "graphic design." To a certain extent, he also contributed to the writing, with the result that he definitely entered the series' core team. Exhausted by his concurrent positions, Sakaguchi decided to give up his central role in the development of *Final Fantasy VI* in order to better concentrate on production matters (and his managerial role at Square). It was a pragmatic move. As such, he delegated out his director position, splitting it between Itô and Kitase: "Given that the two essential elements of *Final Fantasy* are combat and drama, Hiroyuki Itô took charge of combat while I supervised the dramatization and script," says Kitase. Starting with a basic scenario established by Sakaguchi (a conflict with an empire), they came up with a brand-new concept[21]: each character is a protagonist.

---

21. The idea came from Akitoshi Kawazu and his *Romancing SaGa*. You might even say that this "multi-protagonist" concept became a trend at Square, as Takashi Tokita used the same idea for *Live A Live*, which was produced at the same time as *Final Fantasy VI*.

To get different viewpoints and thus achieve his goal ("make them all memorable"), Kitase got the team involved using The King's[22] methods to first determine which characters would be playable. A list of jobs was created (Magitek soldier, thief, machinist, etc.). Given that the number of people working on the project had doubled (about sixty people for this installment), it was impossible to have everyone on the same level. Kitase instead decided to focus on a core group.

"You can't say that I wrote all of *Final Fantasy VI*. Everyone contributed. And we divided up the main characters." That's true, but it downplays Kitase's role. Kitase was responsible for the overall story and the major moments, like the opera and the destruction of the world. He even admits that he let himself get carried away with "his" characters, Kefka and Celes. Meanwhile, Sakaguchi influenced the "central" characters, Terra and Locke, and Itô influenced Cyan.

Kaori Tanaka[23] was in charge of the Figaro brothers and, actually, the "kings of sand." Lastly, Nomura brought back his shelved proposals from *Final Fantasy V*: a ninja accompanied by a dog and a gambler. These became Shadow and Setzer, respectively. They are two very interesting protagonists because they establish plot devices that Nomura, the writer, loves to use: solitude, tragedy, depression, individualism, freedom, escape, and blurred the lines between good and evil. Fundamentally, they are the most tortured characters in *Final Fantasy VI*, each fulfilling the same archetype in their own way: the troubled outlaw. The "Han Solo" characters of the game. Shadow appears "invisible" and elusive. He's the one who intervenes the most to help the team, but then also disappears the most. Setzer is the pirate. Godless and lawless, he loves his freedom. A show-off, a compulsive gambler, and a fan of forward falls. Both characters are hiding from reality (and a tragic past) and are marked by the theme of memory, which factored heavily into the considerations of Nomura and his associates for *Kingdom Hearts*, Kazushige Nojima and Daisuke Watanabe. There's also the presence of dreams/nightmares, once again, a favorite subject for Nomura. Besides designing these characters, he

---

22. The King: nickname given to Sakaguchi by his team.
23. Kaori Tanaka: known by her pseudonym Soraya Saga. She joined Square in the early 90s. Tanaka made her career in graphic design and she loves philosophical, psychological, and theological subjects. She also writes. Besides co-writing the scripts for *Xenogears* and *Xenosaga*, she came up with the basic concept.

wrote their stories and made sure that they were properly incorporated into the rest of the plot. Carrying out these dual roles (designer and writer) would become his calling card.

Final Fantasy VI was released in April 1994. At the same time, with the exception of the programmers (who work on almost all games at the same time), the core team and the other designers were left with nothing to do. As such, Sakaguchi decided to launch pre-production of a new installment, which would be the last for Super Famicom: *Final Fantasy VII*. In doing so, he relied on a smaller team of around 20 people, including Yoshinori Kitase, Tetsuya Takahashi, Hiroyuki Itô, Kaori Tanaka, and Tetsuya Nomura.

A small group that really didn't have a choice in the matter. All the other projects had already started and most were much too far along. There was no way these designers could jump in halfway. Takashi Tokita came in just as *Live A Live* was wrapping up. Toshiro Tsuchida[24] had been working for about a year on the first *Front Mission*. Akitoshi Kawazu[25] had already gone back to work on *Romancing SaGa 3*. Koichi Ishii[26] had been working for a few months on developing *Seiken Densetsu 3*. Akihiko Matsui[27] was deep into working on *Chrono Trigger*.

THE PRELUDE

In this way, Sakaguchi got the ball rolling on the planned *Final Fantasy VII*. The installment was supposed to take place in New York in 1999. It was to follow the journey of a group of activists trying to

---

24. Toshiro Tsuchida: he began his career at Masaya producing, notably, the games *Ranma ½* and the first *Langrisser*. He then founded the company G-Craft, which created *Front Mission* for Square and *Arc the Lad* for Sony. Later, under contract, he designed the combat system for and co-directed *Final Fantasy X* and worked again with Motomu Toriyama on *Final Fantasy XIII*, for which he also created the combat system.
25. Akitoshi Kawazu: game designer for *Final Fantasy* and *Final Fantasy II*. He was then director of the first *SaGa*, for which he was the strong man, and also produced an incalculable number of games, including *Final Fantasy XII* and *The Last Remnant* (for which he also wrote the script).
26. Koichi Ishii: "Mister *Seiken Densetsu*." Creator of the main elements of the *Final Fantasy* universe: the crystals, the chocobos, the moogles, the view during combat, etc.
27. Akihiko Matsui: one of the creators of the Active Time Battle system for the *Final Fantasy* series. (Original) director of *Chrono Trigger* and game designer for *Legend of Mana*. He also worked on the *Final Fantasy XI* combat system, became its director in 2010, then took over from Hiromichi Tanaka as producer after he left in 2012.

destroy energy reactors. They were tracked by a detective named Joe. For about two or three months (according to Kitase), the small group worked on a first draft. Takahashi designed the city, while Nomura worked on creating potential characters. He decided to start by brainstorming about one of the "activists," who he saw as being more like terrorists. "The starting point was the character named Cloud," Nomura later confirmed. But, not in terms of the design, since the original Cloud had semi-long, straight brown hair that was pulled back, a far cry from the final version, I'm sure you'll agree. He also sketched a witch character[28].

As Sakaguchi made progress with writing the story, Nomura and Takahashi produced concept art and annotated each piece to help get production started. However, production wouldn't start until much later, and for good reason: a disaster was looming for *Chrono Trigger*. In spite of their best efforts to keep the ship afloat, Akihiko Matsui and Kazuhiko Aoki[29] were overwhelmed and starting to drown. Takashi Tokita, who had just finished *Live A Live*, immediately came to the rescue, but the situation was worse than they thought. During an emergency meeting, it was determined that the new priority for the *Final Fantasy* team was *Chrono Trigger*. Yoshinori Kitase became co-director (alongside Akihiko Matsui and Takashi Tokita) and Itô joined the events team. Takahashi and Nomura worked together on *Chrono Trigger* and *Front Mission*, mainly creating the backgrounds. Nomura also at this time wrote the concept for a game for the future Nintendo Satellaview: *Dynami Tracer*[30]. Thanks to the team's response, *Chrono Trigger* got back on track and was released in March 1995, with a big sigh of relief.

Finished with *Chrono Trigger* a few months before its release[31], the *Final Fantasy VII* core team picked up where they had left off. Which

28. The witch in question would later be used in *Final Fantasy VIII* for Edea, but was also a first draft for Eve in *Parasite Eve*.
29. Kazuhiko Aoki: director of *Hanjuku Eiyū*. He was also one of the three creators of the Active Time Battle (ATB) system, producer of *Chrono Trigger*, and director of *Final Fantasy Crystal Chronicles*.
30. *BS Dynami Tracer*: although the idea came from Nomura, this game for Satellaview (a Super Famicom extension with a satellite connection service) achieved the same level of popularity as its console extension: it was a total failure. Well, not total, because it laid the foundations for a concept that would be used for the map in *Kingdom Hearts*: an open-ended journey with several planets in outer space, each its own distinct world.
31. A team is never involved from end-to-end in a game's development, especially if that team is just lending a hand to support the main project team. The creative team's work gradually winds down and, even before the game is finished, they can start thinking about their next project.

is to say, still at square one. Takahashi submitted a plot concept[32] in which there was a young soldier with dissociative identity disorder capable of riding *Genjū*[33] (the famous "Summons," a staple of the series since the third installment). While the idea was rejected for a *Final Fantasy* game because it was considered "too dark," "too complex," and "too science-fiction," it was such a genius concept that Takahashi was strongly encouraged to pursue it through a different game.

At that time, the project had no name, but the idea quickly gained traction. As he was no longer constrained by the *"FF* protocol[34]*"* and he was a fan of robots, he decided to replace the summoned monsters with mechas. And the rest is history. However, what you might not know is that Nomura, at that time, joined Takahashi's project team.

THE BEGINNING AND THE END

In late spring 1995, Takahashi and Nomura were working together[35] on *Final Fantasy VII* and *Chrono Trigger 2*. In fact, this was not *Chrono Cross*, it was just a code name[36] for what would later become *Xenogears*. A side note for the aficionados out there: at the time, the script was a draft for volume *IV* (i.e. the volume preceding the adventures of Fei and focusing, among other things, on Joshua Blanche's Elements) for which Nomura actually suggested an Asian character, a scientist and tactician who wears glasses. Takahashi liked this idea and used it for Shitan Uzuki; the idea also grew on Nomura who used it for all of

32. While the first script for *Final Fantasy VII* was indeed proposed by Tetsuya Takahashi, it was actually written based on a concept from Kaori Tanaka, who, incidentally, he married in 1995. It wasn't until after Tanaka's concept was rejected that she came up with the story involving a female AI-based being establishing a new human race on an unexplored planet.
33. *Genjū* is a Japanese term for "spectral beasts." Another term used is *"Shōkanjū,"* which means something more like "summoned beasts."
34. The idea was rejected because, like all great video game series, *Final Fantasy* has a "protocol" with rules to be followed. Developers can't do whatever they want, however they want, with whoever they want, though it seems that more recently these rules have been forgotten...
35. At that time, the trio of Takahashi, Tanaka, and Nomura spent a lot of time together. Both during and after work hours. They were motivated by the idea of working together on their exciting new project. As such, you can imagine that there was an intertwining of the stories for *Final Fantasy VII* and *Xenogears*. That's probably why *Xenogears* was for a long time referred to as *"Ura FFVII"* (basically, "the dark side of *FFVII"*) in Japan.
36. This was the second time the code name *Chrono Trigger* was used, the first time being for a game unrelated to *Final Fantasy*. It was actually *Seiken Densetsu II*. If you understand French, I invite you to check out *Level Up Niveau 3*, published by Third Éditions, for more on the subject. It has a section by yours truly.

"his" scientist characters (Hojo in *VII*, Maeda in *Parasite Eve*, Fuhito in *Before Crisis*, and more recently Ignis in *XV*). A few months later, Takahashi established the final code name, Project NOAH: an epic saga in six installments, divided into three major stages. The project at that time brought together installments *IV* and *V*. We already know what happened next: development of *IV* was incorporated into the background for *V*, which would be truncated and become the game released in February 1998. The title—*Xenogears*—would not be chosen until later, probably sometime in 1996. In any case, at the end of 1995, Takahashi realized that he couldn't keep working on both games at once. He expressed to the teams his need to be 100 percent focused on his project and they agreed. He thus left the *Final Fantasy VII* team.

When production of *Chrono Trigger 2* was announced, Kitase, who was then the sole captain of the *Final Fantasy VII* ship, offered the position of art director to Yusuke Naora[37], a graphic artist who had really proven his talent with *Final Fantasy VI*, particularly in his unique work on the village of Zozo. The question of how to use Nomura's talents quickly became an issue and led to arguments between Takahashi and Kitase: both wanted him to work exclusively on their respective projects. Sakaguchi was the decider and assigned the young designer to focus solely on *Final Fantasy VII*. It was a wise decision. As time went on, Nomura increasingly became a key team member. He ultimately:

— Co-wrote the basic story, later scripted by Kazushige Nojima[38] and Yoshinori Kitase.

— Replaced Yoshitaka Amano in the position of character designer as Amano rapidly rose to international prominence (his speech at the Biennale d'Orléans in France in late January-early February 1995 was just the first in a long series of appearances, notably in New York where the *Think Like Amano* exhibition was held in 1997; he also had a number of new projects, including his own series called *Hero*: in

37. Yusuke Naora: the art director for *Final Fantasy VII, VIII, X*, and *Type–0*; also worked on *Advent Children* and more recently on *XV*, during which he unexpectedly left Square Enix. He also served as character designer a number of times (*The Last Remnant* and *Chaos Rings*) and even had his own series, *Code Age*.
38. Kazushige Nojima: now an old "war buddy" to Nomura and a legendary scriptwriter. He has worked on *FFVII, VIII, X, XIII, Kingdom Hearts, Kingdom Hearts II, Final Fantasy Versus XIII* and more. We'll talk more about his role later on.

short, he could no longer be as involved in developing the game as he was before).

Before the end of 1995, some decisions had to be made. The "New York 1999" idea was finally abandoned. However, the idea of setting the action in an anxiety-inducing megalopolis was kept, as was the activist organization. Kitase, tired of the typical bad guys, suggested that the activists face off against a corporation[39].

However, Nomura didn't think that would be enough, so he added a nemesis[40] to give the hero extra motivation. According to his plan, the hero would be an amnesiac former soldier for the corporation (probably inspired by Kaori Tanaka's initial concept) searching for his identity.

These two ideas established the premise for *VII*: an amnesiac former soldier, searching for his identity, who has become an activist and enters a fight against his former employers, an evil corporation and a mysterious sworn enemy that the hero pursues throughout the entire game. Pretty much, Jason Bourne. Jokes aside, shortly after the plot was established, it was decided that a character would die.

OPEN YOUR HEART

Nomura began fleshing out the game by sketching. The hero was the first character he designed, that's why the story revolves entirely around him. Besides designing his physical appearance and his backstory, he added an extra dose of symbolism by giving him a name with real importance: Cloud Strife, perfectly consistent with who the character *is*. This set a new standard for Kitase's *Final Fantasy* games: through their designs, costumes, and names, the characters become vectors for concepts (Squall: a gust of wind; Tidus: from the Okinawan word for sun; Lightning; etc.). He then got to work on Aerith (from the Latin word *aero*, "air"), who for a long time was the only female character,

39. Shin-Ra: an electric company (that represents the United States). The company has its own army and an in-house "FBI" called the Turks. Incidentally, in 1983, when Masafumi Miyamoto founded Square, his father was the head of Den-Yu-Sha... an electric company.
40. Nemesis: the goddess of vengeance in Greek mythology. She has come to represent the sworn enemy, recurring confrontation, and pursuit. Above all, the concept of a nemesis evokes an inseparable bond. For example, Moriarty is the nemesis of Sherlock Holmes, and vice versa. Same for The Joker and Batman. Neither can exist without the other.

and Barret, in order to create the trio—and yes, *Final Fantasy VII*, at the beginning of its production, only had three characters in total. Nomura thus played a very important role, proposing the game's other characters. Since they don't like to repeat concepts, in defiance of logic[41], he proposed a lion called Red XIII. After some feeble attempts at a mane, Nomura finally let go and conjured up his spirit animal.

At this point in development, they still didn't know what mode of animation (2D, 3D, or other) they would opt for, nor which console they would choose. Kitase thus decided to start a second[42] technical demo. This was a "secret" operation, even within Square. Naturally, Nomura took part. With the basic casting set, it was time to work on the bad guy: Sephiroth[43]. Initially, he was the brother of Aerith (which explains the similarity in their bangs), then he was her first love. Finally, Kitase came up with an ingenious idea: Sephiroth would never be physically present; instead, he would haunt the hero, adding an extra layer of ambiguity. Is he just as figment of the hero's imagination? A memory? Is he a real person? A second personality? It's a mystery that has still never been completely resolved. Maybe in the remake?

The team was completely engrossed in this project. Their discussions continued wherever they went: the break rooms, when they went for a smoke break, even over the phone from home. For example, one Sunday night, Nomura called Kitase to suggest that they kill Aerith. After a long discussion, the director went with it and incorporated one of video gaming history's most iconic scenes to the script. Besides being an amazing plot twist and an emotional shock, this fantastic idea also led to the introduction of a new female character: Tifa, who would go on to play a significant (and welcome) role in the script. This was once again thanks to Nomura, who had the brilliant idea to include her in a love triangle involving Cloud, Aerith, and Tifa (in

---

40. He didn't consider whether or not an animal would cause problems for programming or animation. However, Sakaguchi was won over by the idea and approved the proposal.

41. In 1994, Square produced a demo with Onyx visualization systems (from Silicon Graphics) entitled *Final Fantasy VI: The Interactive CG Game*. It was presented at SIGGRAPH '95. At the time, it was considered an alpha for the Ultra 64 (the former name of the Nintendo 64), which was incorrect. In reality, it was just "a 3D test."

42. The name Sephiroth was not chosen randomly. As the perfect warrior, created from a god, he is the link between science and religion and thus symbolizes absolution. Nomura was bothered by this idea, which he had already developed for Sefirot (Fiend in the American version, one of the members of the Warring Triad in *FFVI*) and also developed, in particular, for the scene showing the transfiguration of Kefka into the final boss.

addition to the "central" triangle that essentially pits Cloud against Sephiroth for the heart of Aerith).

And then there's her name: Tifa Lockhart. Lockhart.

March 1996. After finishing *Bahamut Lagoon*, for which he was director, Kazushige Nojima joined the *Final Fantasy VII* team. As such, he was late to the game (as a reminder, the game was released on January 31, 1997, only about 10 months later). Nevertheless, he wrote dialog, gave new ideas, and strengthened the backstory, in particular everything that takes place in the past in Nibelheim, including the "Vincent segment." He also managed to work in his own obsession—memory—by introducing *"at the last minute[44]"* the character Zack. This character plays a crucial, dual role: he undergoes a personality transfer (with Cloud) and is also Aerith's ex-boyfriend; this freed up the character of Sephiroth to have a less stereotypical confrontation with Cloud.

So, let's sum up Nomura's work on *Final Fantasy VII*. He played a decisive role with regard to both the script and the visual design. Besides creating the characters and their backstories, he also designed all of the Summons and suggested creating animations for their "arrival" during combat. The series' entry into the world of 3D also helped him learn how to direct: for example, he suggested certain camera movements during battles to make them more "dramatic." In addition to the new entry for the *Shôkanjū* involving fancy animations, he also suggested very impressive special moves for the heroes. However, unlike *Final Fantasy VI* and its concept of "desperate moves" (basically special moves that can only be used when the hero is knocking at death's door), he wanted these new special moves to be tied to the characters' anger. Hence their name, *"Limit Break."* These ideas went on to become standards in the series that players have loved. *Final Fantasy VII* is the quintessential RPG for combat. Its battles are the most impressive, the most beautiful, the best directed, and the most enjoyable. And all of that is, of course, thanks to the "combat team," which included Takatsugu Nakazawa and Goro Ohashi, with

44. Zack was added to production so late that Nomura didn't even have the time to color his artwork. Audiences had to wait for the international version to see the flashbacks for him.

help from the extraordinary instincts of the core team, including Tetsuya Nomura.

A NEW LEGEND

After the worldwide success of *Final Fantasy VII*[45], Square took off and—finally—gained international recognition. Overnight, Nomura became a star in the eyes of players (unaware of his real involvement and his less successful work). Additionally, at Square he became a "firefighter," working on most of Sakaguchi's productions in 1997-98 (*Parasite Eve*, *Brave Fencer Musashi*, and finally *Ehrgeiz*). However, for these games, his role was limited to design only.

— The "New York 1999" plot, the first true version of *Final Fantasy VII*, intended for the Super Famicom, progressed in Sakaguchi's imagination and eventually became *Parasite Eve*. It was an adaptation of a novel by Hideaki Sena, written and directed by Takashi Tokita. Contrary to popular belief, the protagonist, Aya Brea, was not "purely" created by Nomura, but rather by Sakaguchi. Because Sakaguchi was unhappy with the designer at the time (we'll never know who), he brought Nomura on board. Fun fact: Tokita asked a certain Yoko Shimomura to create the music.

The case of *Brave Fencer Musashi* is interesting for a few reasons:

— The idea came from Sakaguchi (basically, to use the historical figure of Musashi in another dimension), who asked Nomura to create the characters.

— As the game wasn't considered very important, it was handed off to Division 5, the team responsible for *Einhänder* (which came out the same year as *FFVII*), led by Yusuke Hirata, a former advertising specialist from Tokyo sent to Osaka to manage this subsidiary composed mainly of former Konami team members, including the very influential Yoichi Yoshimoto[46].

---

45. Over 10 million copies sold, the second-best selling game for the PlayStation after *Gran Turismo*.
46. Yoichi Yoshimoto began his career at Konami as a character designer (*Green Beret, Salamander, Top Gun, Akumajō Special: Boku Dracula-kun*). He was then promoted and directed *Batman Returns* and the excellent game *The Adventures of Batman & Robin*. When he arrived at Square, along with his team, he was thrown into the deep end as director of *Musashi*.

— *Musashi* was the first action-RPG by Square since the series *Seiken Densetsu*.

— It marked Nomura's first experience with the "tough guys" from Osaka.

Given that *Ehrgeiz*[47] was a game produced by a contractor (Dream-Factory), at the beginning, Nomura was simply tasked with supervising the usage of characters from *Final Fantasy VII*. Eventually, he went on to design the other characters. All of these projects kept Nomura busy for part of 1997 and 1998. On the side, while he was working on *Parasite Eve*, he started exchanging emails with Kitase about *Final Fantasy VIII*. While the seventh volume had given his career a good jump start, it really took off with volume eight. Without a doubt, he was one of the most influential team members for its direction.

Final Fantasy VI tells the story of the rise of a deranged, sadistic, dramatic, bloodthirsty clown who tries to destroy the world; that is, after he has poisoned a town's water, shown off his pyromania skills, etc.

Final Fantasy VII tells the story of a mercenary with amnesia searching for a phantom from his past created by a fascist corporation that harshly cracks down on anyone who challenges its power. Secondarily, it's an apocalyptic story that is resolved with the defeat of the monsters known as Weapons. In short, at the time, the last two chapters were not a barrel of laughs. They were dark. They were tragedies filled with betrayal, despair, and genocide. These themes are communicated in the games' scripts, but also, and particularly, in their images. For example, in the case of *Final Fantasy VII*, the setting is oppressive. From the quasi-eternal night over Midgar to the heavy ambiance of the apocalypse in the last third of the game, represented by the blood-red meteor, serving as a terrifying, inescapable countdown to the end of the world.

For over five years, the development team "lived" in this depressing atmosphere day in and day out. For that reason, Kitase wanted a breather. For *Final Fantasy VIII*, he wanted sunshine, bright colors, and a lighter setting. A less serious plot.

After darkness, they hoped for light.

---

47. *Ehrgeiz* was created by Seichi Ishii, a video game legend. He was game designer for *Virtua Racing* and *Virtua Fighter*, then director and game designer for *Tekken* (1 and 2), and director for *Tobal* (1 and 2). Nomura has worked with him several times and, naturally, learned a lot from him.

DON'T BE AFRAID

At the same time, Nomura was working on *Parasite Eve*. Given that the game was no lighthearted romp, with victims of spontaneous human combustion and a bacterium that mutates cells, Nomura also needed a breath of fresh air. He also needed to get out of the nocturnal setting. While in Los Angeles, Nomura received an email from Kitase, who told him about his need for a change and asked him if he had any ideas. Nomura then suggested something very different[48], a school-based concept with young teenage students who have to follow their destiny. He also proposed that they refocus the project on the "fantasy" side of *Final Fantasy*, with a story involving knights and sorceresses. Kitase loved the idea. He especially liked that it fit perfectly with Nojima's idea to have characters of the same age.

Nomura began to come up with the hero of the story, Squall Leonhart. Leonhart[49].

Before starting to design the character, he asked Kitase to abandon the **SD** (*super deformed*) animation in favor of something more realistic; he did so with support and good arguments from Yusuke Naora (serving once again as art director). He could finally use his "true style."

The first version of the hero was not to his boss' liking. Squall had long hair and looked too effeminate. As Kitase put it: "The issue with Tetsu is that his characters are much too pretty." Nomura revised his draft and fleshed it out more, giving the character a more conservative hair style and also adding a nasty scar and a pendant shaped like a lion's head (of course). Finally, he came up with a "signature" weapon that was totally over-the-top: the gunblade[50] with a keychain on the end of its handle. From the outset of the game's development, Nojima had planned for two heroes, with no further details. For the second

---

48. The pre-production phase of *Final Fantasy VIII* began in 1997. At the time, a certain book was making waves all around the world. It was the story of a young "chosen one" with a scar on his forehead who had to fight the most evil wizard the world had ever known, all of this in the setting of… a school. I'll let you do the math. We'll come back to this in Volume II.
49. Beside its symbolism, Squall's last name, Leonhart, makes reference to one of the four heroes in *Final Fantasy II*.
50. The gunblade: a type of knife composed of a handle and a blade whose guard is replaced by the mechanical portion of a pistol (hammer, cylinder, trigger guard, and trigger). There are several types of them in the *Final Fantasy VIII* universe. Squall's gunblade is modeled off of a revolver.

hero, Nomura came up with a character, Laguna, who was to be the opposite of Squall. While focusing on creating Laguna, they finished developing the concept together.

Final Fantasy VIII would be a double game, with two different teams in two different eras:

— The high schoolers, led by a secretive, introverted, shy, tortured hero who comes into his own thanks to friendship and, most importantly, love, thus offering a coming-of-age story.

— A group of young adults faced with war, led by a jovial, extroverted, slightly clumsy hero, with an irresponsible attitude who gets strength from his two companions and whose fate is turned on its head by a romance.

Naturally, love became the central theme of the game. Next came the hard part for Nomura, creating his main female character: Rinoa Heartilly. Heartilly.

As we know, this is truly his specialty. His simple style and interest in fashion help him get it right every time. However, this time, he wanted to stretch his own limits. His goal was for the player to "really" fall in love with Rinoa because of who she is. Her personality. Her quirks. Her sweet side, but also her irritating side.

FRAGMENT OF MEMORIES

As Nomura would later confirm, he really gave his all in creating the characters for *Final Fantasy VIII* and Rinoa was the character who posed the greatest challenge for him. He couldn't find the perfect balance. After multiple versions, he decided to reach back into his own personal history and give the female character the traits of a woman he had known. He was even more careful than usual in adding this extra touch. You should know that, according to Nomura, creating a character means not only giving them a face, a name, a backstory, and a personality. In this specific case, he also added instructions for the developers about her body language, including gestures and facial expressions, to give Rinoa a unique way of looking, hearing, laughing, and charming. Nomura brought her to life. And Kitase got it completely. Seeing the energy that Nomura poured into his work and

the incredible result, Kitase understood that Squall and Rinoa would be his celebrity couple. He then asked Nojima to make changes to the script to give Rinoa a much more important role. That's when Kitase got the idea for THE scene of *Final Fantasy VIII*: the famous sequence where Squall goes looking for Rinoa in outer space. Killing two birds with one stone. He used the opportunity to pay homage to one of his favorite films, *2001: A Space Odyssey*. Nojima decided to emphasize the complexity of human relationships by using more "inspired"[51] dialog. He regularly consulted with Nomura to make sure that he was being faithful to his characters and the two creators occasionally had brainstorming sessions together. For example, that's how they worked together to come up with a special moment when Squall meets Rinoa during a school dance. Nomura continued creating characters as development progressed. He remained faithful to his convictions. His hero needed a nemesis. However, this time, he wanted a true rival, a mirror image. Seifer Almasy was born.

The two characters are similar in many ways: they have the same dreams, use the same weapon, each has his own crew, they both try to win the heart of the same girl (creating a love triangle), and each has a scar in the same place inflicted by the other. However, when you look closer, they are also perfect opposites. Squall has brown, tousled hair and wears dark-colored clothing. He's sophisticated and has lots of accessories. He declares allegiance only to himself (the lion symbol is all over him: his pendant, his weapon, his ring). Seifer has short, blond hair and wears clothing that reveals his belief in divine justice (his many crosses). Also, his manner of dressing is quite conservative and he wears no accessories other than a silver ID necklace. Whereas Squall is introverted, not very talkative, and doesn't care about anyone or anything, Seifer is extroverted, is constantly asserting his personality, and judges others like a modern-day Spanish Inquisition.

In short, they're two sides of the same coin, two brothers who grew up both mutually hating and respecting each other. They're indivisible. They clash from the very beginning (starting in the introduction)

---

51. When asked about his work, Nojima recognizes that the dialog in *Final Fantasy VII* was simply awful. He was young.

through to the very end of the game. Naturally, each is determined to prove that he's better than the other. What's interesting is that *Final Fantasy VIII* is centered on the concept of dualism. In addition to its two heroes (Squall and Laguna), its narrative structure constantly relies on doubled characters, of which the rivals Squall and Seifer are a perfect example[52]. Nomura created his main antagonist, but, as we all know, he's just a red herring. The real challenge is the sorceress(es). In creating the sorceress(es), he started with his sketch that, as you'll remember, he created for the first version of *Final Fantasy VII*. From there, he made a compilation of his "femmes fatales" designed in the spirit of Amano's work (including Melusine from *Final Fantasy V* and the "goddess" Sophia from *Final Fantasy VI*) to create the ultimate antagonist: Ultimecia.

FORCE YOUR WAY

In addition to the other characters[53], Nomura indulged in a few eccentricities, including trying to create a new creature (along the same lines as the chocobo, moogle, pampa, and tomberry): the mumba, as a sort of lion, as it were.

However, his role didn't stop there. The aspects he initiated in *Final Fantasy VII*—the Limit Breaks and animations for the arrival of the Summons—come completely under his control. He was no longer content with just suggesting; he wanted to do it himself. He was entirely responsible for directing combat scenes. As such, in addition to imagining, conceptualizing, and storyboarding each of the "furies," he did the same for the elaborate animations of the Summons (renamed the "Guardian Forces.") In fact, he redesigned all of them so that they would fit with the "realistic" style of the game, consistent with the brand-new junction system developed by Hiroyuki Itô: this system

---

52. To a certain extent, Raijin and Fujin, as well as Kiros and Ward, correspond to Zell and Selphie. Rinoa to Edea. Ellone to Ultimecia. Raine to Julia.

53. The point of this is to just skim over Nomura's work so that you understand his way of thinking and how that applies to *Kingdom Hearts*. As such, I won't detail all of his work on *Final Fantasy VIII*, even though the story of each of his characters is fascinating. Particularly Zell and his tattoo. I encourage you to get the book on *Final Fantasy VIII*, brought out by the same publisher and in the same collection.

"junctions" the *Shôkanjû* to make the characters evolve, underpinned by a concept of "evolving relationships." However, Nomura saw it more as a concept of rearing animals (thus similar to one of the main pieces of symbolism in the game: school campuses are "Gardens" and the alumni are "SeeDs"). In fact, he decided that the "guardians" would all be non-human creatures. That's why Ramuh, for example, is replaced by Quetzalcoatl and the indispensable figures, Siren and Shiva, are nude (or almost nude), as clothing is synonymous with "civilization." Yep, the concept went pretty far.

In the end, Nomura also influenced certain full-motion video (FMV) scenes, also called "cinematics." Not only was he involved with the editing by choosing camera angles and cuts, but he also provided the idea for a grand introductory sequence. He wrote and storyboarded it, in addition to giving editing instructions. Yes, the famous introduction, accompanied by a fantastic musical piece by Nobuo Uematsu, *Liberi Fatali* (*Fated Children*). You know, it's the introduction that starts with a view of an ocean that transforms into an arid desert and foreshadows the duality of the knights (Squall and Seifer) and the sorceresses (Rinoa and Edea). Yes, that incredible introduction—good enough to be used on its own as a trailer—that we've all rewatched hundreds of times because it was so emblematic of Square and *Final Fantasy* at that time. It was as impressive as it was symbolic. It was a real surprise that has become another hallmark of the series. On a side note, the reason the introduction was so technically advanced was because Nomura refused to back down on anything, deliberately giving challenges to Motonori Sakakibara's team[54]. Nomura tried things out, unafraid of attempting the impossible. He never limits himself. It may not be a very pragmatic approach, but it's one that pays dividends. From the fur on Squall's coat, to his pendant, to the many feathers, the angel's wings, and animations of flowing hair. Though they may look ridiculous today, it was not the case in 1998.

A final notable thing about *Final Fantasy VIII*: after being in charge of promoting *VII*, Shinji Hashimoto crossed over to the other side

---

54. Motonori Sakakibara: director of the cinematics for *Final Fantasy VII* and *VIII*, and co-director of the film *Final Fantasy: The Spirits Within*. After the failure of the film, he left the video game industry. Recently, he co-directed *Rudolph, The Black Cat*, an animated film.

and became producer of the series, "replacing" Sakaguchi. The series creator had to support the war effort behind *Final Fantasy: The Spirits Within*.

In February 1999, *Final Fantasy VIII* hit the shelves. While it didn't match the records set by *VII*, it is still to this day the second-best selling game in the series (just under 8 million copies sold). Some would argue that this success was thanks to previous games, but that would be too reductive. One thing is certain: the new leading foursome—Kitase, Nojima, Nomura, and Naora—outperformed expectations.

Square then offered Nomura a "little break." They sent him to France to work with a small team for a few weeks. While this incredible adventure has nothing to do with *Kingdom Hearts* (let's be honest), it still merits a little detour. It'll be good for your video game knowledge.

INTERLUDE — *DARK ELEMENT*

[Shortly after *Dark Earth* came out (October 23, 1997), Nicolas Gaume, founder and head of Kalisto[55], started work on a sequel for the PlayStation. A few weeks later, he traveled to Japan for the Japanese release of *Nightmare Creatures*, but also to find a distributor for *Dark Earth*. During his business "tour," organized by François Hermelin (one of the first French video game media correspondents in Japan—first for *Consoles+*, then for *Joypad*—also known by his pseudonym Banana San), he met with people from Enix. He presented the first samples from *Dark Earth 2*, but nothing really came of it. When he returned to Japan in April 1998, he was invited to meet with Square, as the company was quite interested[56]. The meeting went well, but Square imposed a condition before signing the deal: Nomura had to be involved in creating the characters. A few weeks later, there was a second meeting (just before summer 1998). This time in Bordeaux. Hashimoto, accompanied by Junichi Yanagihara (business development), came to visit the studios to make sure, without a doubt, that

---

55. Kalisto: a Bordeaux-based development studio founded in the early 1990s, responsible for, notably, the hit game *Dark Earth* (2 million copies sold) and *Nightmare Creatures*.
56. There are always squabbles between Square and Enix.

production was going well. They only stayed a few days, but before they left, they visited the medieval town of Saint-Émilion.

It was a confluence of circumstances. Since the beginning of that year, a certain Yasumi Matsuno[57] had been working on developing his next game (with a team of about 20 people). After turning down the idea for a *Final Fantasy Tactics 2*, he wanted a "realistic" game in a "medieval" setting. As it happened, he had been stuck on the setting for several weeks. And then Fate came knocking at his door. His colleagues returned from France. While in video games they enjoyed destroying the world many times over, they remain nonetheless steadfastly Japanese, and thus accorded it a great deal of respect and awe. As such, they came home bearing hundreds of photos. When Matsuno saw their photos of Saint-Émilion, he literally fell under the spell of the architecture of the small medieval town. He then started collecting material on the region. In September 1998, Matsuno made his own trip to France with four important members of his team, most likely including (because it hasn't been confirmed) Hiroshi Minagawa, Akihiko Yoshida, and Kazutoyo Mehiro. This unlikely sequence of events gave rise in January 2000 to *Vagrant Story*, an extraordinary game.

Going back to February 1999, Nomura (accompanied by production manager Koji Nonoyama, who went on to have an impressive career at Rockstar) was at Kalisto. Before long, issues arose due to both the language barrier and differences in method. While Kalisto was focused on technical aspects, Nomura worked off of imagery. And, as usual, he designed a superb character without worrying about how it would affect development. He didn't stay there long, but it was long enough that Sakaguchi came to join him and even brought up the possibility of Square buying out Kalisto. Good old Saka. In any case, after two years of development, in late 1999, *Edge of Chaos*, finally renamed *Silent Chaos*, was completed. However, due to financial difficulties brought on by the production of *Final Fantasy: The Spirits Within*, Square put

---

57. Yasumi Matsuno: the legendary T-RPG figure who began his career at Quest (licensed by Enix) where he created *Ogre Battle*, then *Tactics Ogre*. Sakaguchi took notice of him and proposed that he make a similar game at Square using the *Final Fantasy* license. This gave rise to *Final Fantasy Tactics*. After that, Matsuno was given the freedom to create *Vagrant Story*. He later went on to direct *Final Fantasy XII*, but couldn't finish it for "medical reasons."

on the brakes and, after months of radio silence, ended up canceling the game (that they had fully produced).

End parenthesis.]

RUN!

1999. Things were taking off. For Square, but also, and especially, for Nomura. Besides working on promoting *Final Fantasy VIII* and developping *Silent Chaos*, Nomura was called in to help save *Parasite Eve II*. When he was contacted, there were only 10 months until the game's release, which was already planned for December 1999. The first designer had thrown in the towel. As such, Nomura had to come in to handle character development while applying changes made to the story. Thankfully, from a visual standpoint, Aya had remained consistent because the original designer simply followed the notes from many concepts created for the first chapter, written by none other than Nomura. A stroke of luck. On a side note, the game was created by the Osaka team and Kenichi Iwao, the scriptwriter for *Biohazard 1* (*Resident Evil 1* in English) for Capcom. It's a small world. Nomura had no time for a break: he had already been asked by Hashimoto a few weeks earlier to work on a very important game for Square, one of the games to be launched with the PlayStation 2[58], *The Bouncer*. It was an action-RPG that marked the first collaboration between Seichi Ishii (and his studio DreamFactory, which has created *Tobal* and *Ehrgeiz*) and Takashi Tokita. Nomura was probably asked to help out so that it wouldn't just be a fighting game. Nomura was under pressure because he had to deliver enough "assets" to create a promotional clip for the PlayStation 2 before the end of March 1999! In other words, he had a month. In the clip, you can see a few seconds of an unidentified game that the media at the time suspected was *Ehrgeiz 2*.

In the end, it was a complicated job that he spent a lot of time on (too much, in fact). This included numerous visits to DreamFactory

---

58. Originally, *The Bouncer* was supposed to come out at the same time as the PlayStation 2, on March 4, 2000. However, the infamous programming problems forced the game's release to be pushed back by several months, until December 23.

over almost a year. Nevertheless, he still has good memories from this time, particularly thanks to the character Dauragon, who he is quite proud of.

After the promotional phase for *Final Fantasy VIII*, Kitase took a few weeks off, but soon thereafter, he had to start work on the difficult localization phase so that the game could be released "for Christmas" in the United States and Europe—an imperative. However, he already had a sequel on his mind and began to plan the next chapter. It would be the tenth, since Sakaguchi had been working since July 1998 with another team (notably including Hiroyuki Itô, Hideo Minaba, Kazuhiko Aoki, and Toshiyuki Itahana) at his new studio in Honolulu on the ninth installment, which was a return to the series' roots to mark the end of an era, symbolized by its number[59] and the choice of console, PlayStation, at the end of its life. As such, Kitase had to take this into account and look toward the future, i.e. PlayStation 2. He was also very attuned to negative opinions (and numerous petitions—the Internet was already starting to bring mischief) from players saying there was not enough "fantasy" in the settings of *Final Fantasy VII* and *VIII*. Apparently, the dumbing-down of games had already started because, in spite of *appearances*, it doesn't get more "fantasy" than *Final Fantasy VIII*, whether you're looking at its themes, its structure, its story, or its characters. No matter, because Kitase wanted to offer a "new vision" of what is "fantasy." He wanted to convince players that "fantasy" did not only include what they imagined, i.e. a medieval universe with dragons. But to do this, he needed strong support. This time, the idea came from Nojima: an Asian setting. The union between a *Final Fantasy* universe—one that contrasts technology and tradition—and an authentic ancestral culture. It was unprecedented for the series and would feel completely foreign for international audiences. It was a lucky bet.

Kitase compiled his team with more care than usual. This was because he was assuming the role of producer instead of director. For several

---

59. The number 9 makes it the last single-digit chapter, marking the end of a cycle; indeed, this is perfectly represented in the way 9 is written. Then again, given the change of consoles and the technical challenges to be overcome for future iterations, it would be inconceivable to go back. As such, it was the only opportunity to do another old-style *Final Fantasy* one last time. And to top it all off, ironically, it ended up being the last story led by Sakaguchi.

reasons. Taking a step back allows you to better manage a project. For many years, he had ended every project exhausted. He had earned the right to let others do the heavy lifting. He also rolled out the red carpet for his protégé Motomu Toriyama, whose potential he wanted to test (before entrusting to him *Final Fantasy X-2* and then *XIII*). Another big production (*Kingdom Hearts*) was also beginning to take shape behind the scenes. To remain perfectly concentrated, he needed to remove himself from the epicenter of developing such a challenging game to put together like *Final Fantasy*. But also, it was just a natural progression. By that time, he was considered a company veteran and thus a point of reference. It was time for him to pass on knowledge... and to prepare to take over from Sakaguchi. Once again, he couldn't imagine making this *Final Fantasy X* without Nomura; however, the young designer could no longer be as involved as he had been in the past. He remained valuable for his unique style, contributing ideas and bringing the characters written by Nojima to life. In turn, Nojima followed the concepts developed by Nomura in previous installments, particularly by giving meaningful names to characters. For example, Tidus means "sun" in the Okinawan dialect, Yuna means "moon," and Wakka means "water." In addition, he paid homage to Nomura in a certain way by including a lion in the cast: Kimahri. No need to explain further. I could tell you lots of fun facts about Nomura's design choices (like the 40 belts that make up Lulu's dress or the two different colors of Yuna's eyes), but most of those things have already been covered more or less in the *Final Fantasy* book from this same publisher, which once again I recommend that you read.

So now, I'll give you a little summary. In that last year before the start of the new millennium, Nomura was collaborating on the creation of characters and other visuals for four projects at the same time, and they weren't small. What you don't know is that, in addition (and in total secrecy) he was particularly busy brainstorming and developing, on his own, what would become his masterpiece. Which puts some of the criticisms leveled against him into perspective. He was accused of always drawing the same characters. For example, people said Sion (the hero in *The Bouncer*) is a copy of Squall. In total, Nomura designed dozens

of characters in 1999[60] and he had to make sure the "main casting" was successful and memorable. On top of that, he was working on his own game.

Let's pause there for a moment to think about that. After all, we are just tourists in the history of Square, seen through the lens of Nomura. But this book isn't really about him or about *Final Fantasy*. Still, understanding *Kingdom Hearts* means, above all, examining its architect, as he was so critical in making the game.

LORD OF THE CASTLE

Now that you know more about his life and career, we'll take a closer look at the man and his philosophy. Who are you, Architect? Why are you so often maligned? Why do you take sick pleasure in surprising your audience, or even being unfaithful to your world? Why do you have such an odd approach to communication? You can consider this section a way of introducing the architect before really getting to know him in the remaining 363 pages to be read.

THE (NON-)COMMUNICATOR

He considers himself a video game creator, and that's all. He has no interest in politics, business, media, celebrity, or marketing. For example, he doesn't understand when people start talking about "targets." He doesn't like Twitter and only uses it when he has to. All he wants is to be at home getting ideas while watching movies or playing games, to write and design the basis for his next project, to reflect on how to surprise and amuse his audiences, and then to "grow" his ideas by working with his team. All the rest comes from there, but is almost secondary, when it comes down to it. The phrase that best sums him up is perhaps: "The only thing that I'm sure of is that if you make good games, people will play them."

---

60. A dozen main characters and the enemies for *The Bouncer*, as well as around 50 characters for *Final Fantasy X* and *Parasite Eve II*, not to mention all of the weapons used. The rest (the non-playable characters, or NPCs, and secondary characters) were, as always, handled by his assistant, Fumi Nakashima.

THE WHIP-CRACKER AT WORK

He's what you might call a "workaholic." He works all the time and doesn't sleep much.

He has no concept of time, to the point where he only realized a few days AFTER the fact that he had missed his twenty-fifth work anniversary. Disney team members have also said that when they come to Tokyo, they have dinner around 11:00 pm, which is very unusual for them. For him, it's normal. He doesn't hesitate to call his co-workers in the middle of the night if he needs to, or if he has the idea of the century and wants to share it right away. This fact has been confirmed by Nozue, Nojima, Kando, Hazama, etc. That is, when they're not in the office themselves until the wee hours of the morning.

At the same time, he believes in the philosophy of work hard, play hard and is never against going out for a drink or having a good time at a restaurant. This is also very typical of Osaka, and it's probably one of the things that explains why the team gets along so well and is so successful.

THE PERFECTIONIST

He is his own greatest enemy. He puts enormous pressure on himself, which pushes him to meticulously check every detail. He never leaves anything up to chance. Everything must have meaning. "Be connected," as he puts it. Worse yet, everything must be explained. He feels the need to justify his own ideas to himself. He sometimes places unnecessary restrictions on himself. He is a perfectionist to an almost pathological level, to the point of giving importance to the smallest of details. Either the ideas come from him or he approves them; but everything must go through him. From the story to the script, from the game systems to the smallest icons, from the descriptions of objects to casting, from the music to directing. He even handles promotion (game titles, slogans, posters, *kakemono*, etc.) and supervises, or even creates by himself, trailers for all of his games, including those for which he serves as creative producer. As he puts it: "I only put out information or a game when I'm completely satisfied with it." This explains why his communications are so... scant.

This neurosis places him on an emotional roller coaster. He handles failure very poorly and is even worse with mourning. He isolates himself when he's suffering and completely disappears from "public life" while he puts the pieces back together. When he feels something is unfair or he has been betrayed, he tries to forget about it by plunging himself deep into his work.

The enigma

One of the main facets of his personality. His goal in life is to surprise people. When he designs a system or writes a plot, he first considers what the player might expect in order to then catch them off-guard. He takes sick pleasure in torturing players by raising new questions, setting traps, or laying false clues to leave players disconcerted. In particular, he likes endings and the idea of a revelation. However, he also likes challenging players, giving them a little push with an unexpected event, and making them face their responsibilities. He does this with one of the mainstays of the *Final Fantasy* series: secret videos. They're accessible only to those who go above and beyond to get them. Ultimately, the idea is that the player will suffer while also enjoying themselves, eventually reaching an emotional climax that ends in tremendous frustration.

Calm yet nervous

No stress. Ever. He never questions himself and doesn't care about what others think of him. He has no concern for hierarchy. He feels close enough to Shinji Hashimoto, for whom he is truly the right-hand man, and Yoshinori Kitase, for whom he has great respect, that their higher ranking in the company doesn't faze him. He has his own priorities: the highest quality down to the smallest detail. No matter how long it takes.

Paradoxically, he lacks confidence in his work and rethinks his decisions. Did I do the right thing? Will people understand? Will neophytes get it? Is this scene impactful enough? Is the ending "shocking" enough?

He hates public speaking because, simply put, he's shy. He has to really force himself to address an audience; it distresses him. That's why he rarely attends conferences, or if he does, he chooses to stay backstage. When he makes the special effort for a public appearance, he gives a great performance and it's always way of connecting with fans, notably at the D23 Expo. He chooses the right place, time, and people. At heart, he is not a producer, at ease in all situations; he is a creator. And he expects that people respect his particular form of self-expression: video games. In addition, on multiple occasions, he has expressed the desire to promote other members of his team who would be more affable with people. For example, on his recommendation, starting in early 2013, Tabata was put on stage to talk about *Final Fantasy versus XIII*.

THE CREATOR

He is a sensitive creative-type. He "sees" things. His mind is constantly at work, teeming with ideas. He has a lot of them and they come to him naturally. They're not forced. Everything is material for potential concepts, often tied to combat, which remains his number-one obsession. Nomura takes in anything and everything. Film is one of his top sources of inspiration. He watches two to three movies per night. They inspire him. The same is true for music videos on TV and fashion magazines. Even walking in the streets[61].

Above all, he's a person who, while working on several projects at once, influences himself and draws from all different sources to make others better. He's a champion of combining references. His two greatest examples are *Final Fantasy V*, for its game systems, and *Final Fantasy VII*, for the story and directing. For example, by the end of development for *Kingdom Hearts*, he had created a modern, dark megalopolis (The World That Never Was) with little regard for the fact that it might change the tone of his own nascent series. If you look at the dates, this also helps explain his work on *Before Crisis: Final Fantasy VII*, and, of course, *Advent Children*. It marked a definite

---

61. See page 316.

new stage for him that would strongly influence him and shape a good portion of his career (still to this day). First and foremost, this influence is seen in *Kingdom Hearts II* and, given that the series lives *within* him, his influence spread to the rest of his team. For example, this led Kando, Hasegawa, and Arakawa to choose a distinctly modern setting, Shibuya, for *their* game. This gave Nomura a new idea: why not just look out the window? Laid out in front of him was Shinjuku. The neighborhood is a hub for nightlife in Tokyo, as well as a seat of government filled with skyscrapers, including the Tokyo Tocho, also known as the Metropolitan Government Building. An inspiration for Insomnia, the realm of Noctis' power. This plan was eventually scrapped, but its "spirit" can be found in the upcoming *Final Fantasy VII Remake*, of which the first volume will largely take place in the modern, stressful megalopolis of Midgar, which inspired... The World That Never Was. And thus it comes full circle. There are many cases like this throughout his career and you will find a modest recounting of them in the coming pages. One last thing: he doesn't give a crap about trophies in games and has already suggested a number of times that he wants to avoid using downloadable content (DLC) at all costs unless it's offered for free.

THE HEIR

"You must keep Square's creative culture alive," Koichi Ishii told him when he left Square Enix in 2007. A very meaningful sentence coming from the creator of the *Final Fantasy* universe and the *Seiken Densetsu* series. He understood the direction in which the Square Enix ship was sailing. He knew that Nomura was the company's "last hope for creativity," the last guardian of a certain philosophy he was taught by his elders. First and foremost, there was Hironobu Sakaguchi, who, upon his departure, asked Nomura to remain and perpetuate the things he taught him. Hiroyuki Itô who taught him game design and gave him an appreciation for "creating combat." And finally, Tetsuya Takahashi, a dear friend and, in particular, a valuable mentor, who very early on helped reveal his enormous potential.

A heavy legacy to bear on his shoulders. Nomura says it himself: he doesn't like to disappoint, but he doesn't always feel like he's on the same level with his peers. Nevertheless, he pushes himself to do right by their legacy and never depart from the precepts taught to him. In particular, he avoids drama, as taught to him by one of his gurus, the wise and kindly Tadashi Nomura, his head of advertising for the first *KH* (and producer of the series *Baten Kaitos*[62] and *Xenoblade*, among others).

His relationship with the media

Very complicated. Besides the "historic" Japanese magazines, which he inundates with very carefully controlled information (often delivered by email), it is difficult to get him to grant an interview. Though he will do so mainly for foreign outlets. Of course, he has good reasons: he has gotten nasty surprises from interviews on many occasions. For one thing, Westerners are very expressive. Which is great, but out of the ordinary for a Japanese person. Some Japanese are even sometimes terrified by this gushing enthusiasm. It's a major cultural difference: when you're used to silent customs like exchanging business cards, responding to overexcited people who always want autographs can indeed be frightening. In addition, on a number of occasions, he has been the victim of translation errors that led to serious repercussions at work. He has learned to be wary of these rabble who will write complete BS to get people to buy their publication, or worse, and more recently, just to get page views. And he's not shy about calling them out. Which gets on people's nerves. In fact, some of these people have taken a dislike to him and have taken petty revenge against him, even acting in bad faith and using quotes out of context to take shots at him. This was the case for a very well-known British magazine that recently published lies about Nomura. Another such example, for a time Nomura was upset by ignorant, ethnocentric people who often scorned his artistic style. He had to constantly explain his choices. And

---

62. I invite you to read a summary of this extraordinary series (I weigh my words carefully) by yours truly in *Level Up Niveau 1* by this same publisher.

he got fed up with that. Over time, this led him to become disagreeable, or even aggressive, especially when things got difficult for him. It's hard to hold back when you're harassed 20 times in a single day for "supposed delays" or "the androgynous has-been appearance of your characters." Long story short, he's not very fond of the media. When being interviewed, he gives the impression that he does not want to be there. Often, he is even purposely terse to keep things short, or he's totally cynical, toying with ill-prepared journalists. He also doesn't give out any "tasty tidbits," i.e. dirt on other people, his company, his bosses, competitors, or other games… which the media has a field day with when they can get it. You have to know him and learn how to negotiate with him for him to become a good interviewee. As a result, the media, often full of hot air, get offended and call him autistic, "in his own little world," or they claim he acts like a "diva." However, the worst is when articles openly mock him, one notable occasion being when he enthusiastically expressed to a journalist that he admires the work of Baz Luhrmann (*Romeo + Juliette*, *Moulin Rouge*), explaining that Luhrmann's aesthetics and directing greatly inspire him. Or the infamous *Les Misérables* incident: Nomura liked it so much that the day after seeing it, at the office, he declared, "I want to do that for *FFXV*." His words were taken literally, which led to: "Nomura wants to turn *Final Fantasy XV* into a musical." The damage was done. Fans revolted. Tired of years of waiting, they shared the false information, throwing out insults, arguing over details, and shaking their little fists at Nomura. In short, none of this has given Nomura any confidence in the media. However, on a good day, he can be charming and very affable if he sees that someone is truly interested in his game (I'm saying this from experience).

His relationship with his team

This relationship is based on something close to childlike innocence. He sees his closest coworkers as family and says that he would find it much harder to stay motivated at work if they were no longer there one day. When it comes to management, he trusts the people who work with him, perhaps too much. As he sees it, this is necessary. He has to be able to count on others and they can always count on him. He has a very particular way of managing his troops by being as captivating as he is elusive. His beloved concept of duality even shows up in his behavior. Hard, but fair; jovial, but unbending. He doesn't take it easy, so he doesn't see why it should be any different for his team, which he nevertheless tries to protect. He cherishes his relationships with his team more than anything and it's clear that in Tai Yasue, he has found the ideal work partner. Yasue is just as creative as Nomura, but he is also incredibly good-natured. This helps Nomura "heal." Yasue heaps praise on Nomura and appreciates every day the honor and luck he has to work alongside him. All of his coworkers agree, including Roberto Ferrari, who says that, "he's the first person that I've met in Japan who respects artists." He has also served as a mentor to a number of young people to whom he gives opportunities, agreeing to do more to help them in their "growth," as Nomura puts it. Lastly, he is loyal and is even willing to put himself in a tight spot to help out a friend (recently, Tetsuya Takahashi when he asked Nomura to design the team of "bad guys" for *Xenoblade Chronicles II*). Conversely, he hates people who disrespect video games as an art and see them, above all, as a commercial product intended to make money. He also holds quite a grudge against anyone who betrays him. For example, the design for the cover of *Kingdom Hearts HD II.8 Final Chapter Prologue* is a marvel of subtle revenge.

"Nothing is impossible"

"The designers don't need to be familiar with the technology. If they are, they'll immediately say that it's impossible before they even try, which is not a good thing," said the late Gunpei Yokoi[63]. Nomura shares this same philosophy. While he takes an interest in all different subjects, technical subjects are not his forte. In fact, he kind of doesn't care. As such, he sets no limits on himself and regularly pushes his

---

63. Gunpei Yokoi was one of the stars of Nintendo up until the mid-1990s. He was one of the first game designers ever, a toy designer, creator of ROB (the robot for the Famicom) and of the Game Boy, mentor to Shigeru Miyamoto, and producer for all of Nintendo's biggest games in the 1980s. In short, he was an unparalleled legend (along with Genya Takeda, the creator of *Punch-Out!* and longtime head of R&D at Nintendo).

teams to take on serious challenges. "Nothing is impossible" is more than a saying to him; it's both his philosophy and his calling in life. For example, he followed this creed when he suggested using Limit Breaks and more theatrics in combat scenes in *Final Fantasy VII*, when he doubled down on this idea and raised numerous technical challenges in the introduction to *Final Fantasy VIII*, and when he came up with the improbable collaboration between Square and Disney and got Japan's biggest pop star to write and perform the game's theme song. He never backs down from a challenge, ever.

This (admittedly) has been a long introduction, but it helps you understand many things:

— Considering Nomura to be "just" a designer is, at best, reductive and, at worst, insulting.

— Why Kitase put him in charge of everything to do with *Final Fantasy VII*, including giving him the keys to the remake currently in production.

— To what extent *Kingdom Hearts*, beyond the history of its actual development, has always been *within* Nomura.

— I've been lying to you since the beginning because this is, in fact, a book about Nomura seen through the lens of *Kingdom Hearts*—unless it's the opposite, I don't really know anymore…

BEFORE WE MOVE ON

We're going to play a little game. I don't know if you've noticed yet, but a number of terms have been highlighted. I've been doing so since the beginning of this first chapter. There is, of course, a reason for this. These are keywords. Because I'm a sadist, I will now ask you to go back, find the highlighted words or phrases in the text, and write them down on a piece of paper. There should be 106 instances; don't miss any or the game won't be as fun. Once you've finished, come back to this page, close your eyes for a solid 10 seconds, count aloud to 15, then turn the page. I'll be waiting for you on the other side.

THE LEGEND OF
KINGDOM HEARTS

VOLUME 1: CREATION

Genesis of Hearts

CHAPTER II — THE KINGDOM

Turning the Key

I'm not as sadistic as you think I am. At worst, I'm toying with you. The task I gave you on the last page of the first chapter was certainly outrageous given that it's difficult to complete. So, I've done the work for you. As I said before, there are 106 key words/expressions/sentences "hiding" (in reality, you just have to look for the highlighted words) in the first chapter. To be perfectly honest with you, that's really the only purpose of the highlighting—to pull out keywords. Your task now (if you haven't completed the last task already) is to copy the list onto a scrap of paper, or photocopy/scan the next page, or to visit the Third Éditions website to download the list in PDF format. It's a guide just for you. A user guide, if you will, that you can use as you read this book. It will prove two things to you: the creator or architect has creative mannerisms that correspond, above all, to their way of seeing things and/or the world. *Kingdom Hearts* has always been *within* Nomura and his previous work just served as unconscious prototypes for his development both as a professional and as a man.

Turn the page for the list. →

Island of Shikoku — Fine sandy beaches — Limestone caves — Heaven on earth — It's in this setting that Nomura grew up — He spent most of his time outside — Passion for drawing — A lion — *Star Arthur Densetsu 1: Wakusei Mephius* — *Dragon Quest* — Coming up with stories — Drawing — Fiction and reality — The impossible and the possible — Heir — In his [Sakaguchi's] footsteps — New concepts — Impulse — A grotesque being — Mutation — Told through its monstrous form — Blended — Frankenstein-esque talent — A core group — Plot devices — Solitude, tragedy, depression, individualism, freedom, escape, and blurring the lines between good and evil — *Shadow* — Memory — Dreams/nightmares — Core team — An open-ended journey with several planets in outer space, each its own distinct world — Riding *Genjū* — Kazushige Nojima — Anxiety-inducing megalopolis — A nemesis — Searching for his identity — A name with real importance — Vectors for concepts — The trio — Red — XIII — His spirit animal — Plot twist — Emotional shock — Love triangle — Lockhart — Transfiguration — Transfer — Camera movements — Fancy animations — The characters' anger — Yoko Shimomura — Yoichi Yoshimoto — Action-RPG — Tough guys — Osaka — From the quasi-eternal night — Darkness — They hoped for light — Nocturnal setting — Leonhart — The first version of the hero — Pendant — "Signature" weapon — Gunblade — Chain — Two heroes — Double — A secretive, introverted, shy, tortured hero — A jovial, extroverted, slightly clumsy hero — Heartilly — Fashion — Her personality [referring to Rinoa] — Balance — Reach back into his own personal history — Instructions for the developers —Nomura brought her to life [referring to Rinoa] — His convictions — True rival — Mirror image — The same dreams — The same weapon — Dualism — Doubled characters — Storyboarding — Junction system — A concept of animal rearing — Grand introductory sequence — Fated Children — View of an ocean — Arid desert — Knights — As impressive as it was symbolic — Shinji Hashimoto — Producer — Notes from many concepts — Asked by Hashimoto — In spite of appearances — Technology and tradition — Unique style — Four projects at the same time — Developing, on his own — Fumi Nakashima — Guardian

TRAVERSE TOWN

To really understand who does what, you first have to understand what goes into a video game. When people use words like "father," "creator," or "architect," they're only referring to <u>the creative side of things</u>. People emphasize what's most important for the public, and particularly for players. However, a video game can be viewed through different lenses according to the person working on it:

— A consumer good, in actuality.

— A piece of IP (intellectual property) or a license, from a legal perspective.

— A product or brand, from a marketing perspective.

— A work of art, from an artistic perspective.

— A production, while it's in development.

— A project, while creative staff are working on it.

— Lastly, an idea coming from a company or a person (a representative of the company, an employee, or an external third party that proposes the idea in the hopes of launching production; recently, this was the case for *NieR: Automata*, for example). In such a case, we say that the game is "pitched."

With this said, it's important to put things in context. The video game under the *Kingdom Hearts* license belongs to The Walt Disney Company. It is a co-production of Square Enix and Disney Interactive Media Group. It was developed and published by Square Enix, but distributed by Disney Interactive. The game is the culmination of a joint project that came from a request from Disney. On the other hand, it is also the work of director Tetsuya Nomura and his team—mainly employees of Square Enix—under the supervision of several producers from Square Enix. As such, if Tetsuya Nomura (director), Shinji Hashimoto (executive producer), or the leaders of Square Enix (Yosuke Matsuda and Keiji Honda, current general producers) were to leave Square Enix, the series would be able to continue under the control of other people; and/or if Disney wanted to use the game's heroes in a movie (or some other medium), they can do so without having to ask for permission from anyone. Let's cross our fingers and hope that never happens, but you need to face reality: as long as *Kingdom Hearts* is making money, Disney will have no reason to get rid of it.

While we have to recognize all of this, the only thing that really matters is, of course, the creative side. And once again, everything is extremely standardized and hierarchical.

PRODUCTION EXECUTIVES[1]: HISASHI SUZUKI AND YOICHI WADA

From 1995 to 2001, Hisashi Suzuki was Chairman and CEO (Chief Executive Officer) of Square. He resigned following the company's financial collapse brought about by production of the film *Final Fantasy: The Spirits Within*. Given that *Kingdom Hearts* was mainly created under his authority, even though he was no longer physically at Square at the time of the game's release, it is completely legitimate to give him credit.

Yoichi Wada replaced Suzuki starting in 2001; up to that point, Wada was COO (Chief Operations Officer, largely focused on financial aspects). He significantly restructured the company, acquired several other companies (including Eidos Interactive and Taito), and despite the merger with Enix in 2003, he kept his position as CEO until 2013, at which point he handed over the reins to Yosuke Matsuda.

EXECUTIVE PRODUCER: HIRONOBU SAKAGUCHI

Appointed by the general producer(s) (i.e. the company, in this case), the executive producer is, essentially, the management's "representative." Their political interface, if you will. The executive producer is in charge of supervising production and making sure that guidelines set by those higher up are followed. Their job is to step in if a producer is having trouble. As such, they are the "supreme" authority over game development, even if they're not involved at the creative level.

---

1. This term doesn't really fit because they're really more like "general producers." Long story short, they're the highest authority.

PRODUCER: SHINJI HASHIMOTO
CO-PRODUCER: YOSHINORI KITASE

The role of producers and/or co-producers (just a distinction of involvement, that's all) is to supervise development and answer for the final quality, in accordance with the expectations of their superiors. They are the buffer between the development team and management. Their work is essentially administrative: they have to keep costs under control and manage deadlines and exchanges with external partners, such as various service providers. The producer has no decision-making power from a creative standpoint. If they are in charge of producing something that gets too technical, they can designate an associate producer who has specific skills to assist the producer.

Lastly, there can also be a creative producer. A creative producer has a budget and can make "their own orders" without being a messenger for management. This type of producer gets involved at the start of the process to launch a project, then hands it off to a producer who must then report to the creative producer. The creative producer has all decision-making powers, even (and particularly) for creative aspects. Nomura has served in this role for a number of games, which we will talk about later.

DIRECTOR & CONCEPT DESIGNER: TETSUYA NOMURA

The director in the cinematic sense of the word. Not "director" like that of an organization. The director puts together and leads a team. They are paid to provide a creative vision to a game while adhering to limits (time, money, editorial policy, licenses, quality control, and sometimes personnel assignments) set by one or more producers. Besides directing, Nomura was behind everything: the outline of the story, the universe, and even gameplay ideas (credited as concept designer). For this reason, we say that *Kingdom Hearts* is "his" series and I've referred to him as the "architect" since the beginning of this book. In reality, he's more of a creative director[2]

2. *Creative director:* the person who designs the game overall (from its universe to its gameplay). They are involved in artistic direction, writing, the universe, and game systems. However, they do not handle technical aspects or day-to-day work. They have "the vision" for a project and have authority over creative aspects.

who relies on a lead designer[3] (who reports to him) for day-to-day work. Nomura doesn't fail to recognize the work and importance of his lead designer(s), going so far as to credit them as "co-director(s)." He's a good sport. For example, this is currently the case for Tai Yasue, who's working on the *Kingdom Hearts* series. Nomura imagines, designs, gives direction, supervises, and approves. Yasue supervises the team (from Osaka) and makes sure things progress. He is Nomura's "right-hand man."

While Nomura may be the architect, the edifice that is *Kingdom Hearts* required the involvement of around 150 people over two years, organized into several departments led by different managers, collectively known as the "core team." It is time to shed some light on them, especially because most of them are former colleagues from the PlayStation editions of *Final Fantasy*. It is important to note that the core team has, of course, evolved over time and some of the names given only apply to the first and second installments. I will mention the others when telling the story of the game's development.

MAIN PROGRAMMERS: HIROSHI HARATA AND KENTAROU YASUI

The craftsmen. As their title indicates, they were in charge of the main programming tasks, often related to the most complex game systems and, notably, everything related to battles. In addition, they are the points of reference for the other programmers, who they must sometimes help with correcting code, among other things.

Harata and Yasui were in charge of programming combat scenes for *Final Fantasy VII* and *VIII*, for which Nomura provided directing and design for visuals. As such, it's no surprise that they were chosen as main programmers for *Kingdom Hearts*.

---

3. *Lead designer*: they are the manager for the designers. They make decisions about development itself. They are also the "representative" of the development team who communicates with the director (or creative director).

TECHNICAL ART DIRECTOR: AKIRA FUJII

The guardian. He has a flexible profile—half artist, half programmer. His role was to use his technical skills to determine which software to use and how. He also had to troubleshoot the development team's technical issues and find solutions. For example, by improving the software used.

Akira Fujii was responsible for technical aspects of the *Final Fantasy* games in the PlayStation era. He was battle stage director for *Final Fantasy VII*, then real-time polygon director for *Final Fantasy VIII* and *IX*.

ART DIRECTOR: TAKAYUKI ODACHI

The title says it all. He gave direction with regard to the operations of the art department, which in this specific case included adhering to guidelines from Disney. He was also responsible for most of the concept art, notably the backgrounds.

Takayuki Odachi is a video game veteran who met Nomura while working on *Chrono Trigger*. They designed the backgrounds together. His talent caught the attention of those higher up and he was appointed concept artist for *Final Fantasy VII*, then asked to work on design for *Legend of Mana*. He's a beast.

MAP/EVENT/BATTLE PLANNING DIRECTORS:
TAKESHI ENDO, JUN AKIYAMA, YUUICHI KANEMORI

The planning directors, not to be confused with the *planners* (see page 77). Basically, they are the assistants for the three key positions, which are level design[4], cutscenes, and battles. In subsequent chapters in the series, the distinction of "planning" was eliminated and they were designated as directors, then supervisors.

---

4. *Level design* refers to the design of the different levels the player goes through using the established gameplay.

Before joining the *Kingdom Hearts* team, Takeshi Endo handled level design for *Final Fantasy VII* and *VIII*, Jun Akiyama directed the cutscenes for *Vagrant Story*, and Yuuichi Kanemori was battle director for *Parasite Eve II*.

CHARACTER MODELING DIRECTOR: TOMOHIRO KAYANO

His role was to develop the *rigging* to be used by animators: the physical aspects of the bodies of characters determining the visual reaction of the different parts of the body in relation to movements. For example, a smile causes a contraction of the mouth which reshapes the skin and softens the character's expression. This is part of his work.

Tomohiro Kayano has been the in-house specialist for character modeling since Square started working with 3D. Notably, he served in this same role for *Final Fantasy VII* and *VIII*. Since then, he's had an impressive career (*Dirge of Cerberus*, *Crisis Core*, *The World Ends with You*, *Final Fantasy XIII*, *World of Final Fantasy*).

BACKGROUND MODELING DIRECTOR: MASAHIDE TANAKA

Without going into too much detail, he gives the backgrounds their "physical" properties. For example, so that characters don't collide with animated elements. It's a technical job

Masahide Tanaka has also worked with Nomura since *Final Fantasy VII*, for which he worked in the battle stage team. After this, he worked on the maps for *Final Fantasy VIII* and *IX*.

ANIMATION DIRECTOR: TATSUYA KANDO

The magician. In short, he was responsible for the extraordinary animation in *Kingdom Hearts* and, particularly, the preciseness of the movements of the Disney characters. Both during the game and in cutscenes. It was a huge job, even though he, of course, had a team to rely on.

Tatsuya Kando is another person who's been in the trenches with Nomura since *Final Fantasy VII*. At that time, he was just an animator (working under Hidetoshi Omori). He then modeled enemies for *Parasite Eve* before becoming animation director for *Final Fantasy VIII*. After a push from Nomura, he launched his own game, *Subarashiki Kono Sekai* (*The World Ends with You*).

MENU DIRECTOR & VFX SUPERVISOR: TOMOHIRO ISHII

Once again, the title says it all. He handled the design of the menus and also supervised special effects.

Tomohiro Ishii came out of DreamFactory and worked on *Tobal No. 1* and *2* before meeting Nomura while working on *Ehrgeiz*. They then worked together on *The Bouncer* before Nomura hired him for *Kingdom Hearts*.

TEXTURE DIRECTOR: TAKESHI ARAKAWA

In 3D, once you've finalized the design of a character or a background and then modeled it with a wire frame, you then have to "dress" the frame with a texture, a sort of "wallpaper." He was in charge of choosing these, or even designing them himself.

Takeshi Arakawa is originally a designer who worked in the texture department for *Final Fantasy VIII*, *IX*, and *X* before being promoted for *Kingdom Hearts*. With support from Tetsuya Nomura, he tried his hand at directing for *Dissidia: Final Fantasy*, then co-produced *Dissidia 012 [duodecim]*.

CHARACTER DESIGNER: TETSUYA NOMURA
LEAD CHARACTER DESIGN: FUMI NAKASHIMA

The character designer is the creator of the characters—all of them. The main characters, secondary characters, and also NPCs. In addition, the character designer may also create monsters, weapons, vehicles, objects, accessories, and even logos. In the case of *Kingdom Hearts*, Tetsuya Nomura was, of course, at the helm. Not only did he create the main characters, including redesigns of characters from *Final Fantasy*, he also designed many of the weapons and objects and all of the symbols used in the game. For the Disney characters, Nomura provided sketches to the Disney Interactive teams, who made corrections and then sent them back. They were then completely redesigned, taking the corrections into account. Only the special costumes—specifically those for Halloween—were originals and thus required no approval from Disney. For the rest, Nomura relied on his assistant, who managed all of the designers.

Fumi Nakashima is Tetsuya Nomura's shadow. They first met while working on *Chrono Trigger*, for which she was part of the character design team, a group whose job was to "translate" Akira Toriyama's designs into pixels. From there, she became Nomura's assistant on *Final Fantasy VII* and *VIII*, working on the design of secondary/ancillary characters. She also did so for *The Bouncer* and *Final Fantasy X*.

VFX DIRECTOR: SYUUICHI SATO

The pyrotechnician. He was in charge of special effects. He determined what to use and how. He created the most important effects.

Syuuichi Sato was an "ordinary" artist for *Final Fantasy X* when Nomura met him and asked him to join the adventure. After supervising the special effects for the *Kingdom Hearts* series, he was one of Nomura's many great co-workers "stolen" by Naoki Yoshida to work on *Final Fantasy XIV Online: A Realm Reborn*.

MOVIE DIRECTOR: TAKESHI NOZUE
STUDIOS: VISUAL WORKS AND DIGITAL MEDIA LAB

The director of the movie scenes using computer graphics (CG). He set the scenes (camera angles, cutaways, editing) for the previously-written script while referring to storyboards.

Takeshi Nozue started his career as CG designer for *Final Fantasy IX* before meeting Nomura while working on *Final Fantasy X*, for which he supervised animation. Nomura was the one who brought his talent to light. He first did so by asking Nozue to be director for the movies in *Kingdom Hearts*, then by having him as co-director for *Final Fantasy VII: Advent Children*, the first animated feature-length film proposed by the Visual Works team (we'll come back to this later). Nozue followed Nomura to work on most of his projects until *Final Fantasy versus XIII*, which marked their divorce for reasons I'll explain later (or maybe I won't). His most recent notable work has been the cinematic scenes in *Final Fantasy XV* and the related feature-length film *Kingsglaive*.

While he was the director, the quality of the images was thanks to the incredible talent of two studios that have long remained unparalleled, even in the West (with the exception of Pixar):

— Visual Works, a computer-generated imaging film production company founded in 1997 by Square to meet the needs of *Final Fantasy VII*. Visual Works does not simply do the bidding of Square; most of the time, it has true creative freedom. When they work with *"Final Fantasy* people," they're so in tune with their parent company that they no longer even receive instructions. And they have the following impressive list of accomplishments: *Final Fantasy VII, Xenogears, Parasite Eve, Final Fantasy VIII, Chrono Cross, Parasite Eve 2, Vagrant Story, Final Fantasy IX, The Bouncer, Final Fantasy X*, and they recently worked on *Rise of the Tomb Raider, Deus Ex: Mankind Divided, Final Fantasy XV*, and the movie *Kingsglaive*. For *Kingdom Hearts*, one of Visual Works' talented directors—Hiroshi Kuwabara—provided support to Nozue. On a side note, before joining Visual Works, he directed the extraordinary introductions for *Soul Edge* and *Tekken 3*.

— Digital Media Lab, which specializes in creating advertisements and churns out videos for many different media, including video games (but also for TV, exhibitions, corporate videos, etc.).

Now that we've given an overview of the technical and artistic areas... No, wait, we're missing one of the most important: the sound department.

MUSIC: YOKO SHIMOMURA

As was written in the first worldwide magazine devoted entirely to the RPG genre almost 17 years ago (time flies when you're having fun): "Music is half of the attraction of a game, and it is probably even more important in an RPG."

As the composer for *Street Fighter II*, *Super Mario RPG*, and *Parasite Eve*, Yoko Shimomura is a virtuoso. She made a huge contribution to depicting the soul of *Kingdom Hearts* thanks to her extraordinary soundtrack.

THEME: HIKARU UTADA

A song specially composed by an artist or group for a film (played during the opening and/or final scene) is no surprise to anyone. In video games, however, this was uncommon for a long time. Nevertheless, the Japanese have never had a problem inviting popular musical groups or idols to participate. Starting with *Final Fantasy VIII*, Square popularized the idea on the international scene with *Eyes on Me* and continued with *Melodies of Life* in *Final Fantasy IX*, then *Suteki Da Ne* in *Final Fantasy X*. A tradition was born. As such, it was only natural that Nomura would want to do the same thing for *Kingdom Hearts*, the "twin" to *Final Fantasy*.

But, he went further: he had the audacity to get the best-selling artist of all time in Japan, Hikaru Utada, to participate. She was THE pop superstar, with 14 gold records. Contrary to what you might think, she was key to the success of *Kingdom Hearts*.

SOUND PROGRAMMER: HITOSHI OHORI

His job was to create the sound effects (SFX) for the game. Today, he would have the title of sound designer. He was responsible for the sounds of footsteps, interactions with surfaces, hits, magic, and much more.

Hitoshi Ohori served in the same role for *Virtua Fighter 2*, then later for *DewPrism*. He met Nomura while working on *The Bouncer*.

SOUND EDITOR: RYO INAKURA
DIALOGUE EDITOR: ASAKO SUGA

Editor does not mean the same thing here as it does in the print industry. "Editor" here is more similar to the role in the film or recording industry. In the case of sound editing, this involves mixing: creating a balance between the different sources of sound (in terms of volume, but also effects) and recorded voices. The artist who performs this work is a sound engineer.

Ryo Inakura had previously performed the same job for *Final Fantasy VIII* and *IX*. After doing SFX for *DewPrism* and sound mixing for *The Bouncer*, Asako Suga developed a specialty in voices thanks to *Kingdom Hearts* and became the expert in this area at Square (still to this day). His latest work has been for *World of Final Fantasy* and *Final Fantasy XV*.

INTERLUDE — PLANNERS

If you look closely at the credits for a Japanese game, you'll find a huge number of "planners." This is also the case for *Kingdom Hearts*. If I'm being honest, this is just an aside, but it is nevertheless a subject of some importance: it reveals the hidden side of the Japanese development style and thus helps you better understand the "why" of just about everything.

"Planner" is one of the most cryptic, yet key, roles in the Japanese video game industry. The term exists nowhere else and does not necessarily mean what you might think it would. The exact role is difficult to define because it can refer to anything and everything. Above all, it comes from a reality of Japanese society: when young Japanese people finish their studies, they're willing to take any job, no matter what's offered to them. And Japanese companies are very aware of this. The basic idea is quite attractive for corporations: motivated young people who will work for little money, but who have few qualifications. But, it doesn't really matter what they know how to do, they'll be trained in-house. The idea is that it's a win-win for both young employees and their employers. However, in reality, that's a sham because the

young people are quickly considered to be a burden; no one supports them, helps them, or trains them. Since they have no skills and know nothing about the creative process or the tools used, they are relegated to a corner of the office to write ideas in a word processor or to draw if they know how to do that. For some games, they make up as much as 50 percent of the development team. This should now give you a bit of perspective when you learn that a game was made by a hundred people, while only about 30 of them were actually qualified.

Of course, this means that production suffers. While the Japanese could get away with this in the era of 2D (reproducing a design or making a background with pixel art was "easy"), advancements in technology quickly backed them into a corner. With each generational change, every new version of an engine—basically, every technical advancement—there has been growing pains. And this is far from a new phenomenon. The trouble started to show in the transition period from 16-bit to 32-bit graphics[5]. Conversely, Western game creators have constantly professionalized the video game industry and recruited more and more highly-qualified people. That's why the tables turned on Nintendo's glory days and American video games have had an unprecedented boom in the last decade; of course, they've also benefited from profligate spending, particularly when it comes to marketing.

The Japanese took a long time to understand the (gravity of the) situation, and just as long to react. Their system was incredibly slow, completely out of tune with the times. It was a system the Ents would've been proud of[6]. What's worse, for a long time (the Xbox/PS3 generation) they tried to go head-to-head (in spite off their technical deficits and their *planners*) with Westerners while looking down on *gaijin*[7], who could have provided them with what they needed most: technical support.

---

5. In the video game industry, this is also called the fourth generation of consoles, which includes the Super Famicom and the Sega Genesis (Mega Drive), but also the TurboGrafx-16 (PC Engine), the Neo Geo, etc. The next generation (the fifth, i.e. with 32-bit graphics) included the Sega Saturn and the PlayStation, as well as the Atari Jaguar and the 3DO.
6. Ents: the guardians of the forests in Middle Earth, the universe invented by J.R.R. Tolkien (*The Hobbit*, *The Lord of the Rings*). Ents are know for their slowness.
7. A pejorative term for a foreigner in Japan. However, this is not the case everywhere.

Let's take the example of Square and its two-pronged response:

— Develop their own engines (Crystal Tools and Luminous Engine), which ended up being very expensive and made their technical deficits even more pronounced.

— Invest in studios outside Japan, a pseudo-success that was more thanks to the willingness of the Westerners than of the Japanese; their reaction included disinterest for Eidos and a total lack of confidence in its contractors, a situation that inevitably ends in tears[8]... In spite of the strife, in the end, Square took Eidos' technical director, Julien Merceron, and continued his policies by putting another Frenchman, Rémi Driancourt, in charge of the Advanced Technology department.

Paradoxically, while the Japanese came to understand that they were falling behind in technical areas, they remained bogged down in their old mindset with the infamous *"planners."* The only difference was that they started referring to "mid-workers," those who never moved up. Social pressure is so stifling in Japan that some employees, with no ambition or on the verge of *hikikomori*[9], have no desire to move (either up in the company or physically). Moreover, losing your job is perceived as being extremely bad form, to the point where a person's family and/or that of their spouse will remind them, at home or every Sunday, what a failure they are. Consequently, you can understand why people who join a company will not do anything to rock the boat. That being said, the real question is why companies themselves continue with this policy. For one logical reason: brain drain is such that companies are forced to hold onto their unskilled workers.

With the rise of smartphones, the "big names" all made a break for it and went freelance or opened small studios with 20 or 30 hand-picked professionals who enjoyed working together. On small-time games.

---

8. The damage was shocking and included, among others, the sacrifice of *Fabula Nova Crystallis*, ten years of development for *Final Fantasy versus XIII/XV*, the failure of *Final Fantasy XIV Online*, the downfall of GRIN (a contractor on *Fortress*, a canceled sequel to *Final Fantasy XII*), the likely definitive end to the *Deus Ex* license, and the slow agony of the Taito games.

9. *Hikikomori*: this generally refers to a condition affecting people in their thirties (but also adolescents) in which they are so overwhelmed by society that they curl up at home and cut themselves off from the world for weeks or even months, refusing to communicate with the outside world. It's a social phenomenon in Japan of which there were around 700,000 cases in 2010, with 1.55 million more people on the verge of being affected. It is the greatest social disorder in Japan, to the point of being labeled the *2030 problem* (or "what's going to happen with all the *hikikomori*?").

Without any real pressure. Without the inconveniences of big productions, the pressure from their company, and all that; and also with minimal usage of *planners*, or, in their stead, well-supported interns. Rediscovering the joys of yesteryear. Taking pleasure in your work, like back in the 1990s. This brain drain was a real problem for the big companies, who lost their veterans. Unable to adequately train their workers, a number of projects were handed off to any random person, often average people without any real skill, particularly at the managerial level, who didn't know how to take the pressure and would often crack while in the thick of it (the infamous phenomenon of burn-out).

Of course, we can't blame the *planners* for all of the studios' problems and there were certain exceptions that proved the rule. Especially in the 1990s. Producers or directors discovered some real diamonds in the rough who, although they were planners, suggested ideas that were both totally crazy and doable.

From the start, Nomura, who saw his peers suffering in this situation, did what he could to end the usage of planners. However, despite his best efforts, he couldn't do away with the position completely, particularly for the portable versions. It's no surprise that they would go on to drop the ball on *Final Fantasy versus XIII*, but we'll talk more about that later (or maybe not).

Great, how nice, this dude's giving us several pages about planners, but not once has he talked about the script. Indeed, the most observant of you will have noticed that there's no mention of Kazushige Nojima or Daisuke Watanabe. This is not an oversight. That department is so crucial and tied to the story of development that, of course, we will take a good, long look at it. While we're on the subject, I would like to offer a sincere apology for these many pages of names and job titles. I'm sure you've learned things, but still. Also, sorry to the hundred or so people who worked on *Kingdom Hearts* and were not mentioned, as a significant percentage of them were planners. Nonetheless, they deserve some respect for having participated in the efforts.

Now, be nice: give all these people a round of applause for the hours of joy they've brought you to this point, and then turn the page. We will FINALLY move on to serious business.

BEFORE WE MOVE ON

I'm sure you've already noticed, (almost) all of the subheadings are more or less explicit references to musical tracks from various original soundtracks (OSTs). This was not a trivial choice. It goes without saying that I will follow the same pattern for the rest of the book and you will find the complete list, along with the sources of these song titles, at the end.

THE LEGEND OF
KINGDOM HEARTS

VOLUME 1: CREATION

Genesis of Hearts

CHAPTER III — THE TWIN

NIGHT OF FATE

Summer 1996. Somewhere in Japan. A player sits in awe in front of his TV: he's just finished a game. No. Not a game. An avant-garde masterpiece from Shigeru Miyamoto[1].

What's more, this player happens to be a video game industry professional who has himself contributed to two major games and who is currently very busy working on a third, one of the greatest works in video game history.

But, in this moment, he's just a humble player, grateful for the joys of playing the game. When he gets back to the office, he shares his enthusiasm for the game with his colleagues and explains what an awesome experience it was. He had never seen anything like it: a game entirely in 3D, allowing an unprecedented level of freedom of movement. He then throws this out there: "I want to make a game like that." His colleagues hold back their smiles. Everyone knows that it would be crazy to try to compete with the world's greatest video game icon. The discussions continue and a pragmatic colleague says, "No, seriously Tetsu, nobody can compete with *Mario*;" he then adds: "Except perhaps Disney characters." This very common-sense sentence[2] would stick with Tetsuya Nomura.

Time passed.

---

1. I won't insult your intelligence by giving a portrait of the undisputed video game master (the creator of *Mario*, *Zelda*, *Donkey Kong*, *Star Fox*, *Pikmin*, etc.). Instead, I'd like to note that, for this game—*Super Mario 64*, not even mentioned before (out of decency)—he received major assistance from Takashi Tezuka (his faithful companion) and Yoshiaki Koizumi, a.k.a. The Man Behind The Switch (and also the co-director of *The Legend of Zelda: Ocarina of Time* and *Majora's Mask*). Just to give you some background.
2. Mario and Nintendo are to video games like what Mickey and Disney are to animation. The ecosystems, products, communication, ways of working, and even the philosophies of the two companies are very similar. You could even say that one company was highly inspired by the other, to the point of planning its own theme parks… The latest crackpot scheme from the company founded on a "plumber."

[A small side note. To be completely honest with you, it was very difficult to establish an exact recounting of this inception. Today, none of the people involved remember the facts precisely. The story was also told to me a dozen times and changed with each new version, depending on the story teller. The sources even contradict themselves from year to year. An interview published in the *Kingdom Hearts* Ultimania[3] (in 2002) says one thing, contradicted by a sponsored article on the creation of the game published the next year. An interview with Satoru Iwata[4] in 2012 tells yet another version; a more recent one gives a slight variation. And the same goes for all 15 or so sources. After cross-referencing and analyzing the different versions, I've arrived at a conclusion that still can't be 100 percent guaranteed. We can just agree that it's the version that gets closest to reality. To be absolutely certain, we would have to have a time machine... Once again, the resemblance between architecture and video games is uncanny.]

In a 2003 interview, Dan Winters, the Disney Interactive vice president in charge of console games, declared: *"Kingdom Hearts* was born in an elevator, you know." A myth. An "alternative fact," one might say. It's what we call "storytelling," a communications strategy in which ordinary reality is transformed into urban legend. It's a very American phenomenon. In this way, we go from, "Square and Disney had their offices in the same building (the Arco Tower in the Meguro neighborhood of Tokyo) and naturally crossed paths, ultimately leading to collaboration," to *"Kingdom Hearts* was born in an elevator, out of a discussion between Shinji Hashimoto and a Disney executive."

When it comes down to it, the elevator story may not be false, per se, but the facts are much more... ordinary. It's now 1998, just a few months after the smashing success of *Final Fantasy VII*. People of all ages are crazy about video games, and particularly Sony's system, the PlayStation. This means a (huge) new market for Disney. However,

---

3. Ultimania: since 1998, a collection of books about Square's games. As a combination of art book and encyclopedia, Ultimania books contain a load of information, interviews, and lots of annotated visuals. The "ultimate" guide for fans of both the games and the Japanese language.
4. Satoru Iwata: former president of Nintendo. Responsible for, among other things, the DS and Wii consoles, as well as several communications initiatives, including *Iwata Asks*, a series of interviews from 2006 to 2015, and the now-famous *Nintendo Direct*. He passed away in 2015 due to complications from a chronic illness.

while the company has tried to connect with its audiences through some crappy movie adaptations, it has yet to create a real hit. That is to say, since the twin *Aladdin* games (the one by David Perry[5] and the one by Shinji Mikami[6]; it's always good to remind people) for the Sega Genesis and the Super Nintendo. Disney's Japanese division, or more specifically Emiko Yamamoto[7], then has a stroke of genius: "What if we asked the creators of *Final Fantasy VII* [*THE* game at that time] to make us a game along the lines of *Super Mario RPG*[8]? Oh, and what do you know? This is perfect, we're in the same building." That's the simple truth.

Tetsuya Nomura was called to Sakaguchi's office (probably for something related to *Final Fantasy VIII*, given the time period). When he got there, his boss was deep in discussion with Hashimoto. Nomura heard, "That would be great, but we don't have the rights to Mickey!" What were they talking about at that exact moment? One could reasonably deduce that, having crossed paths in the elevator, Yamamoto and Hashimoto had started a dialog and Hashimoto had come to tell Sakaguchi about it.

Nomura was just an employee, and while he played an important role in production, he knew nothing about management matters. However, the word "Mickey" struck a chord with him. He raised his hand and said, "I don't know what you're talking about, but please,

---

5. David Perry is the legendary founder and president of Shiny Entertainment. He was responsible for games with a cult following in the early 90s such as *Cool Spot*, *Earthworm Jim*, and *Aladdin* (Sega Genesis).
6. Shinji Mikami, the world-famous creator of *Biohazard* (*Resident Evil*). He started his career at Capcom working on Disney-branded games. He was responsible for *Aladdin* (Super Nintendo) and *Goof Troop*. It's also interesting that his career took off in much the same way as Nomura's: Mikami worked alone for a year on developing *Biohazard* with a change in direction midway. And the rest is history.
7. Emiko Yamamoto is a living legend of the video game industry. She has served as game designer (and director, even though the term wasn't in use at the time) for *Castle of Illusion*, as well as for *QuackShot* and the extraordinary game *World of Illusion Starring Mickey Mouse and Donald Duck*. She was also, more importantly, executive producer (for Disney) on *Kingdom Hearts*. She was the famous Disney executive in the elevator. In any case, without her, there would be no *Kingdom Hearts* and, if for no other reason, she deserves our lifelong respect and gratitude.
8. *Super Mario RPG* is an RPG developed by Square, produced and financed by Nintendo, that came out on March 9, 1996, in Japan and two months later in the United States with the subtitle *Legend of the Seven Stars*. On a side note, it was co-directed by Yoshihiko Maekawa and Chihiro Fujioka. Maekawa ended up leaving Square to head up the *Mario & Luigi* license. Fujioka happens to be one of the members of the musical group Earthbound Papas (led by Nobuo Uematsu) which, just so you know, is in no way connected to the game *Mother 2* (whose US name is, coincidentally, *EarthBound*). The group's name is actually a nod to a legendary live album by the British group King Crimson.

I want to be a part of it. I have some ideas." Sakaguchi asked him to continue. "If I were to work on a Disney game, I would make an action-RPG with stylized characters." Sakaguchi weighed Nomura's words, conferred with Hashimoto in hushed tones, then said, "Alright, we'll let you give it a try."

The young designer had been so caught up in the moment that this response caught him a little off guard. That being said, he had already considered the idea extensively since the world-famous discussion after playing *Super Mario 64*. Indeed, there in Sakaguchi's office, he already had the beginnings of an idea in his head for the characters, the game systems, and the visual styling. Nomura is a creative type and, as such, had already started imagining everything in the game. Without any real purpose to start. But, since the opportunity presented itself...

However, at the same time, he was hesitant about heading up such a project: "A director's work is difficult, especially in this configuration." But he soon reasoned with himself that it was an unexpected opportunity. It was probably the work of fate, in which he is a believer. He pushed his doubts aside. It didn't matter that he was overworked, that he would have to pull all-nighters, or the fact that he had no team in place: he had to do it.

As a dutiful employee, he waited until development of *Final Fantasy VIII* was finished before tackling his new project. He's the kind of person who needs to have a clear head. In spite of his busy schedule and his many character creations in progress, he decided to dedicate his free time to the new Disney collaboration.

Almost from the very beginning, he got the idea of traveling through the Disney universe (like Mario in *Super Mario 64*, who jumps into paintings to visit different worlds) and of using combat systems based on *Final Fantasy*, but with more action. He saw the idea coming together before his eyes. No need for virtual reality: his brain generated the future *Kingdom Hearts* right there in front of him. Indeed, Nomura could "see" it all, but he was acutely aware that this was not the case for everyone and that he would have to do some convincing, especially given that recent discussions at the time suggested that Square wanted a game based on Mickey Mouse and Disney wanted one based on Donald Duck. And, of course, the big multinational expected its ideas to win out. It was force of habit.

OLYMPUS COLISEUM

Nomura went to the United States to officially meet with Disney for the first time. The purpose of the trip was just to talk with them. He didn't know exactly what to expect, but he was no fool: he knew he would have to negotiate with people who eat this type of contract for breakfast, people who were pros at this kind of exercise and who would, quite likely, try to get the upper hand.

When he took his seat in the meeting room, he looked around him and felt very alone for a moment. There were several people facing him. He let them speak. Each gave their spiel. While Nomura only half listened. He quickly understood what was going on: "They must think that I'm just a simple underling." However, he let them go on. Each Disney person went on with their concepts, brimming with both enthusiasm and authority. Like a motivated client talking to their contractor: "We want this and that. This idea—awesome, right?—would go well here." Time passed. Nomura had trouble staying focused. He didn't understand what the Americans were telling him. Literally: he doesn't speak English (well). He had come with a specific idea in mind, not to do Disney's bidding. So, he decided to interrupt the umpteenth speaker: "I don't want to do that."

This was met with consternation. An awkward silence. Then, confident and serene, he presented his idea: "I'm going to create new characters and they will travel through the Disney universe." He then showed them the initial sketch of the hero he had in mind. The Americans were wary. They knew that the Japanese are known for their audacity, but they weren't expecting this.

A half-human, half-animal character—a humanoid lion with a "cool-kid" getup: a jacket, shorts, and high-top shoes. His pose—in profile—showed off his feline tail and a crown-shaped pendant; the same crown appeared on top of his head and as an insignia on his jacket. His face was similar to Cloud's, but more cartoonish. He had an unusual hairstyle: almost shaved in back and a wild lock in front. Instead of hands he had paws—in wraps[9]—with clawed fingers. On the

---

9. *Wraps*: protective strips that wrap around the hands without covering the fingers. Worn underneath gloves when boxing. To imagine it, just think of a stereotypical boxer with those white bandages around their hands.

right, he held a weapon on his shoulder that looked like a combination of sword and chainsaw, equipped with a keychain shaped like a lion's head.

One of the Disney people pointed to the weapon in the drawing: "What is that?"

"A chainsaw."

Deadly silence in the room. The Americans who had been so talkative were left speechless. A few comments were made in English, but Nomura didn't understand them. It seems they were – well – shocked. He observed their reactions: "I guess you don't like it." The Americans regained their composure and explained to him that the chainsaw was not possible in a Disney game. If only for legal reasons; though, more mundanely, also for reasons of corporate image. It's likely that when they saw this weapon, they started imagining a game that would be violent or gory or both. Of course, in Nomura's head, the weapon meant something completely different[10].

They weren't on the same wavelength. It was most likely a question of culture clash. However, Nomura understood their apprehension and reworked his sketch. His second iteration was less animal, but kept the lion's ears and tail. His clothing evolved a bit. His shorts became baggy pants held up by suspenders. His jacket was more detailed and looked a little more like a zippered vest. The insignias changed too. The crown only appeared on the pendant. The biggest change was, of course, to the weapon. In the new version, it became a giant key with a keychain shaped like Mickey's head. An almost-ideal version that was nevertheless abandoned because Nomura realized that this hero looked too much like Zidane (from *Final Fantasy IX*). He decided to spend an entire night reworking the character. He was then suddenly struck with inspiration.

He gave the hero a more cartoonish appearance, inspired by Mickey Mouse, particularly in the color scheme: the baggy pants were red and the shoes were yellow. In addition, he purposely exaggerated the size of the shoes to accentuate the resemblance to Mickey. Then, he redid

---

10. The chainsaw was not on a trial run at the time as it had already appeared among Edgar's tools (*Final Fantasy VI*) and Barret's weapons (*Final Fantasy VII*). What's more, the weapon rejected by Disney would—gradually—lead Nomura to create Noctis' Engine Blade (*Final Fantasy XV*). In which case, there wasn't much to worry about.

the last animal features, finished off the hairstyle and the accessories, including giving him a belt. He kept the giant key, which became the Keyblade[11].

Thus, Sora was born, and with him, a defining feature of *Kingdom Hearts*, even though at that point the project had a different title...[12] This version was very well received by Disney.

DESTINY'S FORCE

Nomura may have convinced Disney to trust him, but he still had to face an army of decision makers, IP right holders, and marketing professionals on his own. He was in over his head. Still, he held steady: "There was never a moment where I said to myself, 'it's impossible so I'm giving up on this idea.' Instead, it was, 'let's try to make this happen and if it really won't work, then I'll try something else.' Even when they imposed restrictions or turned down my ideas, I told myself that my plan was solid and that it was always possible to convince them."

Would the Disney Goliath lay down its arms before the determination of this young Japanese David? Would the entertainment conglomerate give in and decide to let him work however he wanted to, reasoning that their creator had a strong personality and all they wanted was a strong hero for their game? In reality, it was a bit more complex. The real question is, why did Disney turn to Square to make a game in the first place? What exactly were they aiming for? Disney was struggling to establish itself in the East, particularly in Japan.

The Land of the Rising Sun was simply resisting:

— Animation is popular in Japan, but it considers cartoons to be the direct legacy of *its* comics. Everyone, from children to "salarymen"[13], reads manga and watches *anime*. With no shame.

---

11. Keyblade: Nomura has never been wildly original with the names for his weapons. It means exactly what it sounds like: a key and a blade; like his Gunblade in *Final Fantasy VIII*.
12. See Volume II.
13. *Salaryman*: a Japanese employee easily recognized by their suit, their briefcase, and their habit of finishing the evening in a karaoke bar before going back to their capsule hotel. It's not just a stereotype: it's a reality.

— Many young Japanese dream of becoming manga artists because of Japanese creations[14], not American ones.

— Prime-time TV shows often include the latest popular *anime* programs, or even live broadcasts of launch events for animated films or video games.

— Japan is a, shall we say, unique country. Humiliation is part of daily life and easily attracts an audience (the infamous prank shows that they love so much). Exaggeration (with noise, movement, tone, eccentricity) is normal. They're over the top. That being said, Japan is also an extremely modest country, and one way for people to express themselves is through silent art, i.e. comic strips.

— Japan is a land of contrasts where the present is non-existent. This is both its greatest strength (leaving foreigners in awe of the country's culture) and its greatest weakness. Japan's clash between the past and the future, between tradition and change, is probably the greatest manifestation of the country's angst. Like an eternal teenager struggling to become independent, but also scarred by war and castrated by extremely rigid social codes.

— Image comes before absolutely everything else in Japan. This often leads the Japanese to be extremely creative and surprising; at least, they're certainly less formulaic than Westerners. Blending references, colors, textures sounds... They have a different artistic vision of the world.

— The specter of the atomic bombs dropped on Nagasaki and Hiroshima still hangs over the country[15].

For all of these reasons, Disney had at this point never succeeded in gaining a foothold in Japan. At best, they were shadowy figures in the

14. Certain creators are considered real live demigods. For example, Akira Toriyama (*Dragon Ball*, *Dragon Quest*), Eiichiro Oda (*One Piece*), and Masashi Kishimoto (*Naruto*), as well as the masters Katsuhiro Otomo (*Akira*) and Hayao Miyazaki (I refuse to insult your intelligence by listing his accomplishments). The same is true for a new generation, successors to the old guard of demigods, like Hajime Isayama (*Shingeki no Kyojin*), ONE (*One-Punch Man*, *Mob Psycho 100*) and Makoto Shinkai, who was recently behind *Kimi no na wa (Your Name)*, which broke all records in 2016.
15. Hiroshima on August 6, 1945, then Nagasaki on August 9, 1945. There were 250,000 deaths and innumerable illnesses caused by radioactive fallout that continue to claim victims to this day. A crime against humanity masquerading as a warning shot to the Soviets. For the proud Japanese, beyond the trauma it caused, it was also, above all, a terrible humiliation.

background. Of little interest to children, who enjoy *kawaii*[16] culture and/or to teenagers, who are more accustomed to reading/watching portrayals of their society or dreaming of superheros with magical powers. Basically, Disney was struggling in Japan. Which was unimaginable for Americans.

Disney saw the problem and decided to take action. The plan for Japan was simple: create a Japanese video game to connect with Japanese audiences, but also the rest of the world (video games being Japan's greatest cultural ambassadors in the early 2000s, especially since the release of none other than *Final Fantasy VII*). The second part of the plan was to create an amusement park based on travelling, which in Japan is considered an intellectual exploit that comes with a certain social status. And they chose Square—other than for the obvious reason of proximity—because, most importantly, Square had become the leading game studio among Japanese youth thanks to the *Final Fantasy* series. And the series' success was thanks to, among other things, the very unique style of its designer, Tetsuya Nomura. The president of Disney Interactive, Jan Smith, alluded to this in the announcement of her company's collaboration with Square: they chose Square for two reasons—*Final Fantasy VII* and Tetsuya Nomura. Of course, once again you can see some storytelling going on here given the context. However, if you analyze the situation a bit, the coincidence of Nomura's arrival in Sakaguchi's office and his near-immediate assignment to the game remain two, shall we say, intriguing bits of information, if not suspicious ones. You can choose the explanation for yourself: Japanese humility, which operates by omission, or American storytelling, the art of "alternative facts." The truth lies somewhere in the middle. But one fact suggests we should lean toward the American version of the events: behind the scenes, a man appeared at just the right moment to help the Japanese make their case. A heavyweight ally. A certain Robert Iger.

Probably one of the most successful men in America, he joined the TV network ABC as a weatherman in the 1970s. He slowly climbed the corporate ladder, becoming president of the company 20 years later. In 1996, ABC was bought out by The Walt Disney Company. Iger stayed

16. *Kawaii:* the culture of "cute," or more specifically, of things designed for small children.

on as head of ABC for three years. Then, in February 1999, he was asked by Michael Eisner, the head of Disney at the time, to supervise the development of Disney's international operations, including two major projects in Japan: the opening of a new theme park, DisneySea[17], and the development of a game by the creators of *Final Fantasy*.

Iger was appointed as Disney's number two in January 2000 by Eisner, who was himself grooming Iger to succeed him as CEO. Indeed, in 2005, Iger took the helm of The Walt Disney Company. Shortly thereafter, he proved to be an incredible visionary by acquiring Pixar in 2006, Marvel in 2009, and then Lucasfilm in 2012. Today, besides leading an unstoppable empire, he also serves on the board of Apple, where he replaced Steve Jobs. His contract with Disney is set to end in summer 2018; he will probably stay in his position, unless he decides to enter the political arena, as increasingly persistent rumors have suggested: some think he will be the Democrat's candidate in a future presidential election.

Nomura has said of Iger: "Even when people around him were reluctant or turned down our ideas, he always supported us and helped resolve issues. We have met with him a number of times and he has always been understanding and generous."

Undoubtedly, the *Kingdom Hearts* project was much more important from a political point of view for "Disney in Japan" than it might seem. As such, everything was done in this manner because everything had been decided upstream by Disney, under the supervision of the future head honcho himself. Whatever the case may be, there's something sensational about the story: the man who helped facilitate *Kingdom Hearts* is also the man who transformed Disney with the acquisitions of Pixar, Marvel, and Lucasfilm, and who may also be a potential presidential contender. That just goes to show how unique the series *Kingdom Hearts* really is. I think the song *When You Wish Upon A Star* (Disney's anthem and the theme song from 1940s *Pinocchio*) applies perfectly to the situation:

---

17. Tokyo DisneySea opened on September 4, 2001. A very important place, both for *Kingdom Hearts* and for… *Final Fantasy XV*. Well, we'll come back to that in Volume II.

When you wish upon a star
Makes no difference who you are
Anything your heart desires
Will come to you
If your heart is in your dream
No request is too extreme
When you wish upon a star
As dreamers do
Fate is kind
She brings to those who love
The sweet fulfillment of
Their secret longing
Like a bolt out of the blue
Fate steps in and sees you through
When you wish upon a star
Your dreams come true

With a lucky star named Bob Iger, the impossible became possible. That's the magic of Disney.

IT BEGAN WITH A LETTER

Tetsuya Nomura threw his heart and soul into the project. For a year, he worked alone and developed the plan down to its smallest details: the artistic style, the characters, the general concept, as well as the game systems, the story, and even a first draft of the script. He drew, annotated, and prepared.

He was obsessed with the question, "what will make this game interesting?" He wanted to provide instant pleasure. He also wanted to do justice to the visual quality that would become possible with the PlayStation 2, whose arrival was imminent.

He considered the different Disney worlds to explore and "pre-selected" around 20 of them[18]—based on their popularity[19], but also based on

18. We will never know what was on that initial list created when Nomura was working alone. For one thing, Nomura likes to keep secrets and he has suggested that his initial selections might be used in the future. For that reason, it would be a shame to reveal them and ruin the surprise in *Kingdom Hearts III*. Clever.
19. The Walt Disney Company has created a ranking of its most popular animated films and, of course, its greatest successes at the box office.

what he could get out of them in terms of game design. Although a movie may be popular, can its world be used in the context of a game? What ideas can you bring into it to make it interesting and fun? Which Disney character could be interesting in an RPG team? Which one would I want on my team?

Additionally, since it was an original game with its own universe and brand-new characters, he created several "in-house" worlds outside of the Disney ecosystem. In thinking about the inhabitants of these worlds that his hero would come across, he considered their purposes (in terms of both narrative and game systems). For example, he needed a mentor for Sora in Traverse Town. A swordsman who would teach Sora more about the Keyblade. Perusing the Disney catalog, no one popped out at him. So, he initially thought of creating a new character. However, he decided quite early on that the nature of Traverse Town meant that the player would come across Disney characters and, as such, the mentor would be drowned out in all that noise, in other words, the player wouldn't be able to notice him. Trying to come up with a solution, he said to himself, "I need someone like Squall." And there he had the solution: use his own stock of characters from *Final Fantasy*. Thus, as Nomura has said, essentially: "The idea to incorporate characters from *Final Fantasy* came only to fill certain roles." Thus, Squall is the mentor, Cid is the mechanic, and Cloud is the formidable foe in the tournament, the trio led by Tidus serve as tutors, etc.

Of course, he redesigned them, rewrote them, redrew them, so that they would fit perfectly into the *Kingdom Hearts* universe. Finally, Traverse Town became the game's emblematic city, a crossroads—both literally and figuratively—connecting Disney and *Final Fantasy*, in a totally new environment.

When he got the green light from Square to officially start development, he started by deciding on who his partners would be. As Nomura put it, "I knew from the very beginning that I couldn't do everything myself, especially if I was designing at the same time. As such, I had to find some excellent leaders. I think that relying on people that you trust means that you don't waste time constantly re-explaining what you want, especially for the smallest details. They just get it and they anticipate your wishes."

There were two main criteria: his team[20] had to be efficient and had to be familiar with Disney. He started by asking people in whom he had already seen potential. They were mostly former colleagues from *Final Fantasy VII* or *VIII* who were available, as well as a few defectors from DreamFactory. A few even came to him to apply for jobs, like Jun Akiyama. After finishing his work for *Vagrant Story* (as event director), he went to see *Tarzan* (released in November 1999 in Japan) at the movie theater and loved it. Aware that Nomura planned on having a world based on the film in his script, Akiyama simply asked if he could work for him.

On a side note, this is also what pushed Eri Morimoto to assist Koji Nonoyama on production management[21]. Morimoto was probably the biggest Disney fan at Square. According to several developers, including Akiyama, he intervened during development by telling Nomura, "no, you can't do that." He was one of the protectors of "Disney's integrity" for *Kingdom Hearts*.

By the end of 1999, the team had taken shape. Production began in earnest in February 2000.

ONCE UPON A TIME

Development was based around several guiding ideas:
— An action-RPG with stylized characters.
— It should be as beautiful to look at as it is fun to play.
— Instant pleasure.
— Incorporate *Final Fantasy* characters into a mostly-Disney universe.
— A comfortable longevity, with the idea that a person can play the game for a long time (and come back to it).
— A simple story.

Nomura reasoned that the target audience was <u>children</u>. As such, the game had to be easy to follow, with a basic narrative structure. As a true student of the Square philosophy, he first came up with a theme:

20. For more details, review previous pages.
21. A producer who is part of management.

connection [of hearts][22]. "In writing *Kingdom Hearts*, I want to prove that connections are made between beings through their hearts. Even when separated, that connection remains," Nomura has said.

Based on this idea, he wrote a first draft of a synopsis. The princesses of the Disney worlds were captured and locked away in the Hollow Bastion, a new location, by the witch Maleficent. Her goal: to steal their pure hearts. In response to this threat, a hero from an island travels through the Disney worlds in order to unite the princes from the different stories and come to the rescue of the young ladies.

So, a purely Disney game? Not really. Nomura wanted real dramatic stakes in order to embrace the typical contrast found in fairy tales[23].

To illustrate this, from the beginning, he asked Yoko Shimomura to write music that would be "classical, epic, and with a strong religious tone, in the spirit of Verdi's *Requiem;*" this would, of course, become the emblematic track *Dive into the Heart — Destati.*

While the script remained simple, is was a bit more, shall we say, profound than expected. The protagonist had to fight creatures of the Darkness—the Heartless—born from the dark side of people's hearts. However, he also had to fight his best friend, who was manipulated by the evil witch. The two friends are also rivals who compete to win the heart of a girl. A love triangle.

Initially, the game was supposed to end in the Hollow Bastion, where Sora was to bring down Maleficent, transformed into a dragon. A Disney game with a Disney final boss.

The writing took shape: Nomura wrote the plot and Akiyama focused on everything taking place in the Disney worlds; on top of working as the event planning director, he also unofficially served as lead scena -rio writer.

A few months after development started, Nomura had doubts. He wanted the approval of his *sensei*[24], Sakaguchi: "If you don't bring it

---

22. This purposely obscure way of referring to the concept simply means "friendship," according to Myu Irino, the voice artist for Sora in the Japanese version.
23. The "marvelous" is a literary sub-genre, specifically intended for children. As such, the stories in this sub-genre are often either abominable, covered by enchantment, or are totally symbolic. More on this in Volume II.
24. *Sensei*: a Chinese word (originally) that refers to a person who holds experience in a technique or an art. An instructor. A master. For example, Master Eraqus is Terra's *sensei*. No, that's not a trivial example… what did you think?

up to the level of *Final Fantasy*, the project will be a failure." Nomura confirms, "I knew it even before he said it." He decided to definitively force himself to adhere to his own self-imposed restrictions and reworked the script: "The heart of the game, the playable part, didn't change; however, the story evolved significantly."

He needed to add something more… something *Final Fantasy*-esque. As such, he called on Kazushige Nojima and Daisuke Watanabe, in spite of the fact that they were in the middle of producing *Final Fantasy X* (and were rather heavily involved). He framed it as a sort of quid pro quo: since he was making the effort to give them fabulous characters for *FFX*, he wanted them to give him a hand on the script for *KH*.

Watanabe took the idea of the captured princesses as the script's main plot line; however, he largely reworked this part of the story (throwing out the princes along the way). Akiyama adapted the scenes and dialog[25]. Nojima broadened the spectrum by considering what would come after the Hollow Bastion. He came up with a true bad guy—Ansem—and a final level typical of *Final Fantasy*: the End of the World. Nomura immediately bounced back and introduced one of the series' most important concepts: the Dark Seeker. We don't know if Xehanort was created at this same time, but it's very likely; the vast majority of *Kingdom Hearts* was set with this rewrite. Additionally, it was at this same time that Nomura "saw" the next chapter: "The story of *Kingdom Hearts II*[26] was already there when we were working on *Kingdom Hearts* [I]." As such, it's no surprise that he later made this official with a video[27].

To make sure that the works used in the game were respected, that a balance was struck between the basic plot line (developed by Nomura, Nojima, and Watanabe) and the sub-plots in the different Disney worlds (Akiyama), and above all, that the same rhythm was maintained from

25. Not many people know this, but Akiyama provided comic relief for *Kingdom Hearts*. He was responsible for numerous "jokes" and classic cartoon gags, notably those involving Donald Duck. He also directed the extraordinary prologue for *Vagrant Story*.
26. This statement requires some context. The story for *Kingdom Hearts II* was not yet created. Rather, they had elements that could be used to create the story: a more adult tone, a dark megalopolis (that would become The World That Never Was), the fact that it would take place a year later, etc. In addition, they had already come up with the Nobodies, including Roxas.
27. Reference to *Another Story, Another Dive…*, the secret video found in the Western versions of *Kingdom Hearts* and *Final Mix*.

beginning to end, Nomura decided to entrust supervision of the writing to Keiko Nobumoto. It was a smart choice:

— Because of its concept of visiting different worlds, *Kingdom Hearts* was to be written "like a series[28]," which was perfect because she had a background in this type of work and even wrote the best of all time, *Cowboy Bebop*.

— She's a tightrope walker, specializing in developing characters following an underlying theme[29], and also maintaining a high quality of writing for each episode.

— She had already reworked a movie script to turn it into four OAVs[30] without losing anything. So, she knows how to play around with duration and rhythm.

On a side note, in addition to her work with Satoshi Kon (*Tokyo Godfathers*) and Shin'ichirô Watanabe (*Cowboy Bebop*, *Space Dandy*), while she was working on *Kingdom Hearts*, she created her own series: *Wolf's Rain*. With such a great writing team (Nomura, Akiyama, Nojima, Watanabe, and Nobumoto), it was hard to mess it up. This being said, while the story and script are crucial, they are far from being the director's top concern.

HAVING A WILD TIME

Nomura quickly realized that recruiting his team solely based on talent and familiarity with Disney was not sufficient. He had never thought about the fact that (the majority of) his team had, to that point, only worked on RPGs, never on action games. And this is no small matter. As Nomura explained, "The team was often anxious, or even in panic mode, wondering if it was fun enough or not."

---

28. We will look at the serial nature of *Kingdom Hearts* in greater detail in Volume II, including an analysis of the contributions of Nobumoto.
29. This type of underlying theme is a typical story arc in TV series. Generally related to a character or a situation, plot points are gradually revealed throughout a season, in addition to the individual story lines for each episode. The underlying theme in *Cowboy Bebop*, for example, is centered on the fate of its hero, Spike. Clues are occasionally revealed and there are even several climaxes (the meetings between Julia and Vicious) before the everything is resolved in the last episode, bringing an end to the overarching story of the series.
30. OAV: *Original Animation Video*. In this case, I'm referring to *Macross Plus*. Originally written for a film that would not be made until after having been rewritten for a series of four OAVs of 35 minutes each.

What's more, from a technical point of view, level design had to be developed in a completely different way: "In terms of programming, there is no demarcation between movement and combat. In concrete terms, this means you can do anything, anywhere," explains Hiroshi Hirata (main programmer). Yes, it seems simple, but that changes everything. Planning backgrounds capable of working with three functions—exploration, scenes, and combat—is nothing like the typical maps in a *Final Fantasy* game. This is also why *Kingdom Hearts* offers a series of enclosed arenas (that are perfectly disguised)[31] with relatively limited interactions between them, at least in the first installment.

This openness also had repercussions for how the sound team worked: "It was a space problem. For *Final Fantasy*, there was no issue. The fields and the battles are clearly separated, so the people working on each have their own specific sets of sounds. But in this case, since there was no separation, we had to distribute the two sets of sounds across the same space. And since it was an action game, you couldn't tell what partners might do. We thus had to add the reactions and potential sounds on top of the rest," explains Chiharu Minekawa, one of the sound engineers.

Masahide Tanaka (background modeling director) explains that skills themselves may have consequences, particularly for the camera: "When you make an action game where the character gets around on foot, you tend to forget that that can and will change. Naturally, this can lead to more bugs, like the camera getting stuck in new, unexpected zones. You start to panic, thinking that you'll have to redo all of the backgrounds accordingly. When I discovered the glide, which really lets you go anywhere [within a fixed space[32]], I wanted to cry."

Beyond the purely technical challenges, the design and technical aspects don't always line up: many ideas turn out to be impracticable. Either because of a lack of time or experience, or simply because they don't fit together. For example, in addition to looking around (with the SELECT button), it was also originally possible to fight in a first-person view. After bending over backward to incorporate this option,

31. Everything related to the game systems and construction will be covered in Volume II.
32. In concrete terms, the 3D engines generate full volumes into which the level designers "dig."

the team realized that it was impossible because the result was difficult to follow and thus unplayable; what's more, the skills—like glide—made it even more ridiculous. Thus, the idea was abandoned.

Nomura insisted from the beginning that there be a world based on *The Lion King* where Sora would himself transform into a lion cub. No doubt, for Nomura, this was a way to get back to the roots of his hero (and his own spirit animal). When the developers looked into it, they realized the differences between animating a biped and a quadruped, which were complicated by the fact that he would also be fighting. They arrived at the conclusion that they couldn't do it without a special program. It would take too much time and the development team was much too busy to get involved in that kind of mess. Logically, the idea was thrown out, but it was reused in *Kingdom Hearts II*. Following this disappointment, Nomura added the summoning of Simba, which he supervised himself (particularly the storyboard for his arrival).

On a side note, for a long time, the worlds of *Tarzan* and *The Jungle Book* were in competition with one another. It was based on the advice of his team that Nomura opted for the former. Similarly, he planned on a world taken from *Toy Story*[33], but Pixar did not become part of Disney until 2000. As such, it was too complicated to get the rights and he gave up on the idea. Perhaps so that he could later use it in *Kingdom Hearts III*[34]?

GUARDANDO NEL BUIO

Finally, the biggest problem for *Kingdom Hearts* was the project itself: creating an ambitious game using the Disney universe. The guiding principle for all departments was to "be as faithful as possible." Even if that became a real challenge to stick to. Actually, development could have been much simpler, but everyone was determined to do their best work possible. The team outdid themselves, willing to sacrifice their own well-being for their work. As Nomura put it: "If you ask

33. Models of the characters Woody and Buzz can be found in the game's files.
34. A fact confirmed on July 15, 2017, at the D23 Expo, a Disney annual conference.

any member of the team, they'll tell you: this project was something special for all of us (…) What's more, the team was waiting impatiently for it [*Kingdom Hearts*] to come out so that they could play it as soon as possible, which is unprecedented for the games that I've worked on up to this point."

Before you can get started, you have to understand what you're working with. Before they even began anything, they started by studying their subject: "We had several meetings with Disney people and we all rewatched their films numerous times. By the time we started development, we were steeped in it [Disney culture]." That's where the problems began.

Let's not forget that at that time, Disney characters were in 2D[35]. It was already difficult enough to imagine the 3D technique in an animated film[36], so for a game with cartoon rendering…

An initial, fundamental question was bugging the team: how could they successfully translate such distinct 2D characters with their own style—considered to have "soft" textures—into 3D without distorting anything? This is one of the greatest strengths of *Kingdom Hearts*: you forget that the Disney characters are modeled, when in fact they are! So, how the hell did they do it? One answer comes from Takeyuki Arakawa (texture director): "We spent a long time trying to strike the right balance because when we would illuminate the polygons, that caused problems on the smooth surfaces: the shadows were the same color as the light. In particular, we had skins that were too shiny and we lost the "softness" that's typical of Disney. So, we simply decided to stop lighting them and give extra effort to the textures and, especially, the colors, with more shades to simulate light." Basically, it was the work of a true artisan. A similar process occurred for the 8,000-something movements. Everything was animated by hand. Read that last sentence again. Tatsuya Kando (animation director) grudgingly laughs: "It goes without saying that the animations would have been much easier with motion capture, but they would have been

---

35. Using an ingenious technique that I will explain in Volume II.
36. In 2000-2001 (the period in which the game was developed), 3D was still not a frequently used technique because it was too expensive and required serious specialists. The only real exception was the *Toy Story* series by Pixar (which was not yet part of Disney). To put things in context, *Final Fantasy: The Spirits Within* and *Monsters, Inc.* came out in 2002, the same year as *Kingdom Hearts*.

much too realistic and totally out of sync with Disney's very specific style of animation."

And Tomohiro Kayano (character modeling director), content yet slightly bitter, concludes: "It's very difficult to animate a 2D base model in 3D. Much harder than you might think."

For the sound team, things were no better. "The priority was to design the sounds with Disney style. That meant that hits to the Heartless had to be accompanied by cute sounds that wouldn't be too violent." This same line of thinking extended to the entire inventory of sounds, leading to the creation of over 15,000 different sound effects. Which is a number much higher than average, as even the smallest object had to have its own "personality." The team was even sometimes quite (too) overwhelmed by this daunting task. This was the case for Yoko Shimomura, who remembers struggling with her own choices: "My priority was to create music that would flow with the action. However, I was very concerned about the idea of not adhering to Disney's rules." Undoubtedly, Nomura's instructions, particularly for the creation of a piece like *Dive into the Heart*, reassured her.

I'm sure you've gotten the idea: the development team got all worked up with their challenges. But what about Disney? Was their collaboration always ideal? According to Nomura, yes. Most of the time. However, that hasn't stopped him from mentioning multiple times: "The biggest problem for development was getting approval [from Disney]. We lost about a year " [implying because of them].

According to Nomura, the only real restriction set by Disney was in regards to "the established roles of their characters, as well as the types of dialog permitted." He's also said, "we really had to make sure to color inside the lines." For example, Disney vetoed the usage of Mickey, even putting it in a contract: "We had permission to use him as an agitator in a crowd." In other words, he could only be used in such an emblematic way that he would outshine everything else. Again, nothing was said in definite terms, but it's a safe bet that Disney didn't want to see its crown jewel pushed into the background. To give Mickey the representation expected, Nomura proposed a bold idea: "We should show him just once so that he makes a huge impact. There was only one place where we could use him."

Nomura and his team may have made smart choices for the worlds, but nonetheless, Disney had to give its two cents... for absolutely everything. Let's not forget that they own the license, and also the characters created by Nomura. Everyone (the people from both Disney and Square) still remains mum about Disney's "real" influence. Disney probably refused certain plot lines using their business calendar as an excuse. This has never been said directly in any interview, but on several occasions, you can feel Nomura's frustration, expressed tacitly; this is particularly the case in an interview about *Kingdom Hearts II* where he said clearly that he had to deal with rejections.

All this being said, let's not forget that the "worlds" in question don't really belong to Disney. We tend to forget that *Alice In Wonderland* is a book by Lewis Carroll, that *Den Lille Havfrue* (*The Little Mermaid*) is a story by Hans Christian Andersen, that *Aladdin* is taken from کی و رازه بش (*The Thousand and One Nights*), or finally that *Tarzan of the Apes* is a novel by Edgar Rice Burroughs.

For example, I'm sure you noticed, that last one is the only line of copyright (besides for Disney and Square) that appears on the title screen. And there's a good reason for that: using Tarzan means working with Burroughs' powerful heirs and the very specific rules that apply to using the character. Here are three examples: "His image must appear strong, energetic, clean-shaven, and in superb physical condition," "under no circumstances shall TARZAN be portrayed as losing life or limb or as suffering any permanent physical or mental disability," and he must not be shown "as being insensitive to the sanctity of marriage, religion, or the home." In other words, rules that absolutely must be followed. Thus, Tarzan must be a son of British aristocrats raised by monkeys, but well groomed, shaven, more intelligent than average, polite, and a man of faith. When Disney was making its Tarzan movie, it had to scrupulously adhere to the provisions mentioned above (as well as many others). And Burroughs' heirs don't joke around. In the past, they have filed various lawsuits pushing a number of directors (for example) to change the names of their movies in order to slip through the cracks. But we'll come back later to this hidden side of intellectual property rights and hazy legal matters, particularly when we talk about *Peter Pan*[37].

Getting back to *Kingdom Hearts*, with this in mind, you can imagine the triple pressures of working on a world like the Deep Jungle with Burroughs' heirs imposing conditions, Disney having to approve everything, and, of course, the team itself stressed out about the idea of handling any little thing, like having to recreate the hut from the movie because "the location was too confined to have a battle inside. As such, we had to increase the scale compared to the hut in the movie. However, we made it a bit deceptive by keeping the objects at their normal scale," explains Masahide Tanaka (background modeling director), with beads of sweat on his forehead. Nothing is ever simple for the loyal subjects of Kingdom Hearts.

HIKARI

"Let it go, she's going to say no." For months, Tetsuya Nomura heard this sentence. He had his heart set on a (supposedly) impossible goal: having Hikaru Utada sing the game's theme song. In spite of the naysayers, he trusted his instincts and told himself that you don't know until you try. He says that the hardest part was convincing his own team that he would succeed. No one could even imagine it. No one, except Nomura: "I wanted Utada, no matter what, from the very beginning." As such, he spent months fighting to get what he wanted: "I contacted her people and I got a reply. That alone was a small victory." He continues, "Their response was even rather encouraging. They told me, 'She likes games and Disney,' so why not?" It took some time, but while the star was on a visit to Japan, Nomura managed to get a meeting with her and made his offer. "She then asked me if she could see it [the game]. I quickly sent her a demo video. A day or two later, she called me back to say 'I'll do it.' She also said that she was taking this seriously. I was over the moon."

---

37. Chapter IV of Volume II is completely dedicated to understanding *Kingdom Hearts* as a (pop) cultural agitator. Sounds great, doesn't it? See Volume II.

It just goes to show that nothing is impossible. But really, who is Utada? Why all the hype about her? While she's not well known in the West, she is THE Japanese superstar. A well-rounded international artist (singer, songwriter, arranger, and producer) who draws a sharp contrast with the "idols"[38] who abound in the Japanese market. She has had an exceptional career. She came out with her first album, in English, at the age of 13, then pivoted to respond to demand in the Japanese market, in 1998, with two singles that sold over 2 million copies. Her first Japanese album, *First Love*, to this day holds the all-time record for most albums sold in Japan, with around 8 million copies sold. She was just 15 at the time. Each of her singles and albums has set records in the country. *Addicted to You*, for example, sold 1.5 million copies in less than 24 hours. She has also won numerous awards: 10 times number one on the Oricon[39] charts, 14 golden singles, including five that broke the barrier of a million sales, four gold records for albums, including three ranked in the top 10 most sold of all time. This being said, agreeing to participate in *Kingdom Hearts* was beneficial for her: the game gave her career a boost in America, where she was struggling to get attention, and (finally) got her into the European market.

The question is, why did Nomura set his sights on her (while she was still a minor figure)? Firstly, plain and simple, he's a fan. He likes her music and admires her as a person. With her carefree attitude, she symbolizes *Kingdom Hearts* better than anyone, being a multicultural (Japanese-American) artist, still quite young, and a lover of video games and Disney. Finally, she probably influenced Nomura's choices in a number of cases.

Just 17 years old when she collaborated on *Kingdom Hearts*, Utada didn't just belt out the theme song: she composed the music and wrote the lyrics. Yoko Shimomura says that she was nervous when Utada was just an idea in Nomura's head, but she was completely reassured once she heard her song, *Hikari* (which means "light" in Japanese). Contrary

---

38. "Idols" are products of marketing, created by music production studios. They are groups of girls or guys with a very formulaic style, targeting teenage audiences and sometimes using manga imagery.
39. Oricon: annual and weekly musical rankings in Japan created by a company of the same name.

to what you may think, Shimomura didn't just compose the music for *Kingdom Hearts*, she also supervised the entire sound department, deciding on, for example, the timing of sounds in cutscenes and the usage of sound effects. To help her in this, she had a team with solid experience and versatile sound engineers, capable of creating a dozen different sounds for footsteps according to different surfaces, of offering four voice tracks at the same time (while games at the time only offered two), and of immediately stopping a track when a character finished a sentence. And then there were the team's strokes of genius.

For example, the track *Dive into the Heart* evolves as it goes and is actually composed of nine musical phrases in a loop. Thus, from a sound editing point of view, there's not just one track, but nine, with as many distinct phrases or melodies. In the game, *Dive into the Heart* starts at the very beginning of the adventure. Each of the musical phrases corresponds to a (symbolic) stage in the player's journey, experienced as an actual stage on the screen. Thus, the first phrase symbolizes the player's first steps; the second, the first stage; the third, the choice; the fourth, the confrontation, etc.

This musical direction, introduced by Hitoshi Ohori (sound programmer) and reused since in many different games (including *NieR*), will be discussed later in more detail because, in reality, it represents narration in its purest form. During exploration, the addition of a few notes (or entire musical phrases) signals a new discovery and, during combat, the intensity is constantly reinforced by a combination of the visual and auditory action. It's all beautifully done, especially given that, because of the nature of action games, it's impossible for the creators to really predetermine what will happen. Shimomura, as head of the sound department, made good use of this fact by composing 20 or so phrases that are not, strictly speaking, themes (and are thus absent from the OST), each one communicating an idea (passion, memory, dreaming, etc.) and coming into play to fulfill an emotional need. Once again, the music reinforces the narration, which remains, of course, completely hidden.

PRECIOUS STARS IN THE SKY

In 2001, Nomura visited Los Angeles for the recording of the voices[40] for *Final Fantasy X International*. Just before leaving, he went to see Shimomura and warned her, "Actually, there will be voices in *Kingdom Hearts*." Crazy, right? Not so much:

— Square had just taken the plunge with *Final Fantasy X*[41]. As usual with Square, once the test was successful, they quickly made it standard.

— It seems unthinkable to make a Disney game with cutscenes without going through casting.

— This was probably the greatest contribution from Disney (besides the budget). For them, voice artist casting is totally routine and they do a great job of it. As such, they took care of this entire chunk of work.

— Disney has many highly skilled talents (among the best in the world) that they regularly work with.

— Voices are so essential in a Disney cartoon that, inevitably, they become a priority and thus the exclusive domain of the director. As confirmed by Teruaki Sugawara (supervising dialogue editor, basically the person in charge of balancing the voices), beyond the technical aspects (mixing, balancing, digitizing), the sound team didn't have to do much for the voices because Nomura did everything—the where, when, who, how, and why.

Let's stop here for a few seconds to marvel at how the casting for *Kingdom Hearts* shall for now and forever be totally unique in the history of video games, or possibly of any media.

The Disney universe comes with a whole host of voice acting stars (including a few big names from Hollywood), the kind of casting rarely seen elsewhere. Few studios can lay claim to such an incredible talent pool. For *Kingdom Hearts*, a game dedicated to Disney, it seems obvious that they would want to use the original voices and with very few exceptions (essentially due to the passing of the actors), they did. These included official Disney voices like Wayne Allwine (Mickey),

40. Indeed, because Tetsuya Nomura was in charge of more than designing the characters, he had to make sure that the voices were right.
41. *Final Fantasy X* was the first Square game to use voices for the main dialog sequences.

Russi Taylor (Minnie), Tony Anselmo (Donald), Bill Farmer (Goofy), and Jim Cummings (Winnie the Pooh and Tigger), along with prolific voice talents like Corey Burton, Jeff Bennett, and Tress MacNeille who have filled many different roles (both in the game and in various films). Also, let's not forget the roles filled by Hollywood stars like Kathryn Beaumont (Alice, the same voice as from the 1951 film!), Eddie Carroll (Jiminy Cricket), Sean Astin (Hercules), James Woods (Hades), Tony Goldwyn (Tarzan), Brian Blessed (Clayton), Scott Weinger (Aladdin), Jonathan Freeman (Jafar), Jodi Benson (Ariel), Pat Carroll (Ursula), Chris Sarandon (Jack Skellington), Ken Page (Oogie Boogie), Robby Benson (The Beast), and more.

The main roles (original and non-Disney characters) received the same level of attention, garnering a few big names (probably so that they could pass muster): Haley Joel Osment (Sora), David Gallagher (Riku), Hayden Panettiere (Kairi), David Boreanaz (Squall), Mandy Moore (Aerith), Steve Burton (Cloud), and finally Billy Zane playing Ansem.

Generally speaking, this cast of voices was one of the best in history, carefully crafted in every version, all using the official voices of the Disney characters for each language. In Japan, the main characters were voiced by mostly veteran *seiyū*[42], including some who have worked with Hayao Miyazaki[43], Mamoru Oshii[44], or Makoto Tezuka[45] (son of Osamu Tezuka[46]), or even starred in Disney movies. That's no surprise given that Japan is, in a way, the other big voice talent country. There I go, name dropping left and right. If you don't like it, put the book down now because there's a lot more where that came from.

---

42. *Seiyū*: actors that specialize in voice acting. They are real stars in Japan. Because of its culture of imagery, Japan is the biggest consumer of *anime* (animated TV series and films), even preferring animation over live-action movies. In the case of *Kingdom Hearts*, Miyu Irino (Sora), Mamoru Miyano (Riku), Risa Uchida (Kairi), the incredible Akio Otsuka (Ansem), and Māya Sakamoto (Aerith) contributed.

43. Hayao Miyazaki is probably the most well-known director in Japanese history. He was the creator of numerous animated masterpieces, including *Kaze no Tani no Naushika* (*Nausicaä of the Valley of the Wind*), *Tonari no Totoro* (*My Neighbor Totoro*), *Mononoke Hime* (*Princess Mononoke*), and *Sen to Chihiro no kamikakushi* (*Spirited Away*).

44. Mamoru Oshii is a Japanese director, responsible for the screen adaptation of the manga *Koukaku Kidoutai* (*Ghost in the Shell*), as well as the movies *Avalon* and *Blood: The Last Vampire*. Among others.

45. Finally, Makoto Tezuka is the director of a number of films, OAVs, and animes based on the character created by his father, *Black Jack*.

46. Osamu, Makoto's father, was one of the greatest *mangakas* in history, responsible for works including *Mighty Atom* (*Astro Boy*), *Jungle Taitei* (*Kimba the White Lion*), *Buddha*, *Hi no tori* (*Phoenix*), *Metropolis*, *Ludwig B*, *Boku no Son Goku*... You get the idea.

The voices were recorded quite late in development (not until late 2001) and while that wasn't much of an issue for the sound team, it was a real challenge for the animators. Sugawara remembers: "The animators in charge of getting the mouth movements to match the voices [lip-synching] gave it their best in spite of the very short time they had." Barely two months. A gargantuan task, especially when you take into account that the first *Kingdom Hearts* included around three and a half hours of cutscenes.

(RE)CONNECT

You'll find this section at the end of each game's development discussion so that you can see things from a communications perspective. Now that you've seen how things played out internally, you'll see how Square presented the game to the outside world.

January 25, 2000, Tokyo. During its Square Millennium event, Square makes waves around the world by unveiling not one, not two, but three *Final Fantasy* games, all with planned release dates: *Final Fantasy IX*, *X*, and *XI*, with the last two intended for the PlayStation 2. A sensational announcement remembered the world over to this day.

February 17, 2000, Tokyo, PlayStation Festival. Jan Smith, president of Disney Interactive, and Tomoyuki Takechi, president of Square, announce their collaboration on a game for PlayStation 2, planned for late 2001. Shinji Hashimoto and Tetsuya Nomura are both present. Smith kicks off the press conference by speaking of an "unsurpassed gaming experience" and of a unique game "revolutionary in game design, content, and gameplay, for a worldwide mass-market audience." She then explains that her company chose Square for two reasons: the critical acclaim for *Final Fantasy* and Tetsuya Nomura. The presidents of the two companies take turns explaining how this type of collaboration can be beneficial for each one. A looped demo shows Goofy walking, running, and bouncing a ball against a wall. Disney trumpets the first foray of their characters into the realm of 3D, then mentions their usage of the network capabilities of the PlayStation 2, similar to *Final Fantasy X*. The presentation ends with the appearance of Donald, Daisy, Mickey, and Minnie, who start to dance.

Not saying much, as is his habit, Nomura nonetheless mentions that it's a hybrid adventure/action-RPG starring a character that he created in the Disney universe. No more details than that.

At this moment in time, nothing concrete exists. The team has just barely started the first draft of the script. Also, the project has no name. In the following weeks, it becomes *KINGDOM*, a title chosen by Nomura for three reasons:

— The word "sounds Disney," as in Magic Kingdom[47] or Animal Kingdom.

— It has weight to it, "so it won't be taken lightly."

— The project started from zero and the team was created specifically for it. As such, symbolically, it is "in a way, the creation of our own space."

Of course, this name is too generic to be trademarked, but Nomura gets attached to the word. After consulting with his team, he decides to add "of hearts," because the heart is central to the game; this later becomes *Kingdom Hearts*. The KINGDOM HEARTS trademark is registered on January 11, 2001, with WIPO[48] by Square; it is then abandoned exactly one month later to allow Disney to register it. Incidentally, Disney's filing is made for the video game in Sydney, Australia, and for the other trademark classes[49] in Wellington, New Zealand.

May 19, 2001, Los Angeles, E3. The media hasn't had any news since the big announcement. Finally, the notorious "Disney RPG" is unveiled during the world's biggest video game expo. And what an unveiling it is. A trailer over two and a half minutes long entitled *Destati Drammatica*. Writing and editing of the trailer were supervised by Nomura himself (incidentally, a habit that he will keep for all of the series' installments). For the first time, the world can see the game

---

47. Magic Kingdom refers to the name of the Disney World park in Florida, of which Disneyland Paris was supposed to be a European replica. Disney World is similarly composed of several "regions" (Adventureland, Frontierland, etc.). Animal Kingdom is Disney's biggest theme park, dedicated to animals as the name suggests. It is also located in Florida.
48. WIPO: *World Intellectual Property Organization*, a United Nations body. It is the institution that protects trademarks and patents on a global scale.
49. Classes refer to the types of products or services for which a trademark will be used.

in motion; the trio of Sora, Riku, and Kairi; as well as Donald and Goofy. Some battle samples show certain forms of magic (and the summoning of Dumbo) and demonstrate the freedom of movement. And, of course, a giant Heartless that the hero can climb is unveiled. The images are accompanied by an orchestral version of *Destati* and have no SFX (no sounds or voices, which is actually perfectly normal since the recording of voices won't start until the end of 2001). This trailer, based on a beta version of the game[50] (thus different from the final version), fulfills its purpose: the media realizes the enormous potential of a Disney game made by Square. However, it fails to steal the show from *Final Fantasy X*, which can be played at the publisher's booth (under the name Squaresoft Collection).

October 12, 2001, Tokyo, Tokyo Games Show. Square shows off the big game, not only with a playable beta version—the player's first steps in Traverse Town—at its booth, but also with a long trailer, lasting three minutes and 40 seconds, that's as exciting (the Nomura touch) as it is informative. It's at this time that the media learns concrete details about the concept, with samples of the Deep Jungle, Halloween Town, Agrabah, Atlantica, Neverland, and, of course, some of the Disney characters who inhabit these worlds, in motion. You can catch a glimpse of a few bosses, including the very impressive Cerberus and one of the Titans from *Hercules*. The famous "Disney RPG" starts to take shape. Once again, the video uses *Destati*, heralding a deeper adventure than it would seem at first. While the sound effects appear in the video, the voices are, of course, absent.

Declared by many to be the best game of TGS 2001, *Kingdom Hearts* immediately becomes a highly anticipated game. One surprising fact: while everyone knows that Nomura is involved, no one guesses his actual role (at the time, people didn't really ask that sort of question).

---

50. There are many differences between this beta version and the final version. For starters, the logo was reworked; also, changes were made to textures, scenes, etc. Curiously, the phrase *"Come on, guys! We've got to save Sora!"* appears. At the time, this little phrase caused confusion. People thought that the goal of the game was to save Sora, while in reality is was just an insignificant bit of dialog (probably from Kairi in "a certain passage"), only there to throw people off the scent. One of Nomura's specialties.

November 2001. Square prepares for the Japanese release and a very effective advertising campaign begins. The usual magazines[51] reveal new information and characters bit by bit. Cid in December, Squall and the moogles in January; also announced: the release date, set for March 28. In February, the public learns of the existence of the song by Utada and also of the presence of Cloud in the game (with his new design).

March 28, 2002. Nomura is like a caged lion. Disney has reassured him about the game's potential in the West, but for now, the game is just coming out in Japan and he knows to take nothing for granted. *Kingdom Hearts* may be a multicultural product, but it still remains a game mainly using American licenses. Square is cautious and says that if, eventually, the game reaches 500,000 copies sold, that will be pretty good.

With that said, the game is a total success. Within two days, 415,000 copies of the game are sold. It reaches 465,000 in the first week. These numbers may not mean much to you, so I'll put them in context with the numbers for similar games that came out the same year: *Suikoden III* barely sold almost the same number of copies in six months, *Wild Arms Advanced 3rd* sold half that in nine months, and finally *Grandia II* (the PS2 port) barely sold 10 percent of that (40,000) in the first month. The only game that did better in 2002 was *Onimusha 2*.

The results bolster the team's spirits as they work on the Western version. Goal: Christmas 2002. Disney and Square set up an aggressive communications push. A week after the Japanese release, the official website is online and announces the American version via a trailer. A raffle is also organized for one lucky person to get their name in the game[52]. In May, the list of English-speaking voice talents is unveiled, making a big splash. Nomura says, "I am sure that *Kingdom Hearts* will be well received in the United States." He has no idea how right he is.

---

51. In Japan, publishers mainly use video game media (*Weekly Famitsu*, *PlayStation Famitsu*, and *Dengeki PlayStation*, among others) or weekly manga magazines (*Shōnen Jump*, *Young Jump*, etc.) to reveal new details about their games, as well as to deliver interviews. While this method remains relevant for certain "old-school creators" (including Nomura), the Internet has somewhat weakened this news monopoly...
52. The winner lent his name of the optional boss in Agrabah: Kurt Zisa.

A week later at E3 2002, a new trailer, accompanied by the orchestral version of *Hikari*, gives the game new depth: its main theme[53]. During this time, *Final Fantasy X* comes out in Europe (on May 24, 2002). While it dropped the word *International* from the title, it kept the bonus DVD (with making-of content) and a trailer for *Kingdom Hearts* (the same from E3) that unofficially confirms the game's upcoming European release.

August 28, 2002, a pre-launch soirée in Los Angeles—as would be done for any animated film—demonstrates that Disney is really taking the game seriously.

Monday, September 16, 2002. *Kingdom Hearts* comes out in the United States, with 725,000 units sold in the first week; it remains among the top selling games for several more weeks (behind *Madden 2003* and *GTA Vice City*). The only substantial differences compared to the Japanese version: the addition of several optional bosses (Kurt Zisa, Ice Titan, and Sephiroth), a new level of difficulty, and the secret video *Another Side, Another Story…*

Sunday, November 17, 2002. The European version hits the shelves. It is identical to the American version (including its additions). The reception is more lukewarm, but is quite positive in France and Germany, probably thanks to the efforts made to properly localize the game, including its voices.

Thursday, December 26, 2002. The day after Christmas, Square comes out with the *International* version of *Kingdom Hearts*, called *Final Mix*[54], including the changes from the American version, and then some. In addition to new content (enemies, weapons, accessories, skills) and a few adjustments (basically to the camera and interface[55]),

---

53. Like the *Final Fantasy Main Theme*, written and composed by Nobuo Uematsu, used in the games since the very first episode.
54. *Final Mix* is a title chosen by Nomura to avoid the usage of *International* and thus prevent a war from breaking out. It's a touchy subject, as he said himself: "You can't really call it an international version, it's complicated."
55. In the Japanese version of *Kingdom Hearts*, a chest was opened via the menu. Starting with *Final Mix*, players just had to press the PS TRIANGLE button.

the biggest change is to casting, since *Final Mix* has the American voices with subtitles in Japanese. This decision makes sense and is totally in line with the spirit of *Kingdom Hearts*: a perfect blend of Japanese and Western cultures. However, apparently this is a sore subject for Nomura, who brushes off questions about it: "It's a sensitive subject." It's a strong bet that the success of the American version convinced the higher-ups in Japan to make it the "lead version"[56], although it was largely modified, like a director's cut[57] without the director's name.

Lastly, *Final Mix* offers a new optional boss, the Unknown, that makes a very strong impression. First off, because of his exceptional style: tall, slender, hidden under a black leather cloak, hard to beat, with his own musical theme (*Disappeared*), and also with a combat style reminiscent of that of the Sith lords[58] from *Star Wars*. Better yet, he has no voice and speaks through black boxes[59]. Everything points to him being the real "bad guy" of the story. Which, of course, is very suggestive of a sequel involving him, a chapter with a darker tone. This theory is confirmed by the presence on the disk of *Another Side, Another Story...* and its extended version *[deep dive]*[60]. The new direction taken by the series, the black cloaks, the enigmatic messages: they're all there. The importance of this new City of Darkness too. A countdown that stops at two and the appearance of none other than Mickey Mouse in a black hood dispels all doubt: *Kingdom Hearts II* is indeed on the horizon. At least, everything points fans in this direction... without ever totally confirming or denying it. A very Nomura thing to do.

56. Most of the time, the Japanese start with a Japanese version that gets translated into English; the English translation becomes the "lead version" that is then used for any European translations. Yes, the Japanese games that you play are therefore often poorly translated because of this unfortunate step that sometimes gives the game an ideological bent. In the case of *Kingdom Hearts*, Nomura considers the first chapter to be "unfinished," contrary to what may be suggested by the name *Final Mix*.
57. Director's cut: Basically, it's the director's version. The only one that should be recognized from a creative point of view. Since Nomura always likes to be different, he decided to name his director's cut *Final Mix*, a nod to the term "final cut" used in the film world, but also, above all, suggesting that the American version has the ultimate casting, hence *final mix*.
58. The Sith lords are on the dark side of the Force in the *Star Wars* universe. They oppose the Jedi masters, an order of warrior monks. We'll revisit this later.
59. In movie language, an "intertitle." The transcription of dialog on a background, usually black, as is seen in particular in silent films.
60. More info about *[deep dive]* in Volume II.

End of 2002, it's time to take stock.

Kingdom Hearts sold around 850,000 copies in Japan. It was the third top selling game of the year for PlayStation 2 and the fourth across all platforms. The start of sales for *Final Mix* was huge (over 500,000 copies sold in a week), proving the interest of Japanese audiences in this new series; that or they were lured by the much-talked-about new secret video *[deep dive]*.

In the end, around 1.3 million[61] copies were sold in the Land of the Rising Sun. And to think that Square was only expecting to sell 500,000 units there…

In the United States, it was an unprecedented success: it was Square's most sold game of all time, surpassing all *Final Fantasy* games (even *VII*). Worldwide, it was Square's best-selling game in 2002 (behind *Final Fantasy X*). To this day, it is the tenth best-selling game for PlayStation 2, totaling 6.4 million copies sold (*Final Mix* included), surpassed only by series like *Grand Theft Auto* (*San Andreas* and *Vice City* were the best-selling games for the PS2), *Gran Turismo*, *Need for Speed [Underground 1* and *2]* and *Medal of Honor*, which foreshadowed the success of *Call of Duty*. In other words, what was supposed to be a trial run turned out to be a tour de force.

61. The last known official number dates from 2006. It was 1,215,000 copies sold. Also, we know that the game continued to sell until about 2009. As such, I just rounded to 1,300,000 based on logical assumptions.

THE LEGEND OF
KINGDOM HEARTS

VOLUME 1: CREATION

Genesis of Hearts

CHAPTER III.5 — ONE BECOMES TWO

FINAL FLIGHT OF OSIRIS

Let's backtrack a little bit. In early 2001, Koichi Ishii[1] asked Nomura to help him with the design for *Final Fantasy XI*, but given that it was an MMORPG[2], there was far too much work to be done. As such, Nomura limited himself to creating two essential races of characters: the Humes and the Elvaans (and their respective NPCs). Let's not forget that he was in the middle of developing *Kingdom Hearts*. At the same time, something important was happening behind the scenes: it was time for heads to roll.

In February 2001, Square announced that three of its leading figures were being sanctioned: Hironobu Sakaguchi was stripped of his role as vice president, becoming "just" an executive producer. The company president, Tomoyuki Takeshi, became a contracting consultant and the managing director, Masashi Hiramatsu, was also demoted. It was a cold fury, but the damage was done. Sakaguchi's pet project—creating his film with CGI, incurring serious operating costs (particularly through Square USA)—cost the parent company big time[3]. And Takeshi, his superior, at no time tried to temper his zeal. He was even complicit, most likely smitten with the idea of being the first (chairman) in the video game industry to make a movie: "I thought it was a big accomplishment, so I regret nothing (…) It's as they say: no guts, no glory." It's at this time (April) that Yoichi Wada joined Square. A former management auditor for the Nomura investment bank (no relation), he had no connection to the video game industry and had

1. As we said before, he is responsible for the universe and some of the big ideas in the *Final Fantasy* series. Ishii was also behind *Seiken Densetsu* (of which the second game is better known as *Secret of Mana*). For several years, he served as director for *Final Fantasy XI*, working under Hiromichi Tanaka.
2. *Massively multiplayer online RPG*. Basically, an online role-playing game that can be played with multiple people.
3. The original budget was $40 million. This spiraled out of control, reaching $137 million, three times the original amount. With the movie only making $87 million at the box office, it hit Square hard.

a very pragmatic view of the company. In June, he was appointed as CFO. He then sounded the alarm and froze all external investments (including in *Silent Chaos* from Kalisto and in Square USA; he also froze the shares of DigiCube[4]). The situation was a nightmare: *Final Fantasy IX* did not sell as well as expected, *X* was pushed back and missed fiscal year 2000[5], and *XI* was delayed from the get-go (because of its unsuitable console, the PlayStation 2). However, the worst was yet to come: *The Spirits Within* was one of the biggest flops in movie history. Although Square corrected course a bit in 2001, the company's deficit was estimated at over $143 million. Takeshi resigned from his position, followed a few months later by Sakaguchi because "it's unfair for him alone to pay the price[6]."

Nomura is not the kind of person to get involved with corporate politics. He doesn't even really keep up to date with what's going on in the company. He is only interested in creating video games. He only learned of the departure of his *sensei* much later: "I think I was the last person to find out." Sakaguchi's departure hit the company like a bolt of lightning[7]. Leaving a hangover in its wake. And the cure was harsh; it will be remembered for a long time. All at once, the groggy eyes of other managers opened, looked around at their own company, and discovered that they had been unable to control their champion: "Once Sakaguchi made a decision, that was it," confirms Shinichiro Kajitani (ex-vice president of Square USA). It was a painful wake-up call and, as so often happens, they went from one extreme to the other: "Before, they had no control on costs; then, overnight, that became the priority," explains Yoshihiro Maruyama. The most serious repercussion was, without a doubt, on the company's efficiency. After Sakaguchi's departure, no one wanted to step up to take charge, so every decision required a whole slew of approvals, which took a lot of time. They suffered from "big company syndrome." In short,

---

4. DigiCube was a subsidiary of Square responsible for marketing and distributing Square's tie-in merchandise (toys, action figures, books, CDs) from the late 1990s to the early 2000s.
5. Fiscal year 2000 ended on March 31, 2001.
6. The real person at fault in all of this is Sakaguchi. "Since he bought his studio in Honolulu [in 1998], he has been freely spending money that doesn't belong to him. He is completely out of control," said the vice president of Square USA at the time, Yoshihiro Maruyama.
7. "It's like in *Sangokushi* [the Japanese name for the *Romance of the Three Kingdoms*, a major work of Chinese literature], when the king dies, a civil ware breaks out and everyone starts to fight," explained Tetsuya Nomura, referring to Sakaguchi's departure.

Sakaguchi streamlined things at the cost of excellent management. It's a little late to rewrite history, but if each manager had remained in place, things might be totally different today and Square (likely) might never have merged with Enix. But, "if wishes were fishes, we'd all cast nets." In regards to external relations, the new president, Hisashi Suzuki, took control. In May, he declared that he would rely on the creators themselves and on the *Final Fantasy* series, and in particular on the remakes. This was a way to limit production costs. In June, he announced cooperation with Enix and Namco to develop shared online offerings (to make PlayOnline the Steam of Japan). Rumors at the time suggested that Enix's founder and head honcho, Yasuhiro Fukushima, had another idea in mind... However, balking at Square's financial situation, he eased back on that. He didn't want to buy damaged goods.

SAVIOR

Square needed cash. Fast. Suzuki asked Sony to make an equity investment to avoid bankruptcy. The creator of PlayStation was more than happy to do so (acquiring 18.6 percent of shares). The agreement, considered scandalous, left a bitter taste in shareholders' mouths. They pitilessly and unceremoniously ousted the president less than two months later. He was shown the door on December 1, 2001, and was replaced by Yoichi Wada—officially, to "restructure the company," unofficially, to find a way to get Sony to divest the company and to reconsider Enix's offer with a sales pitch ready. Doing a sort of mating dance and working to secure the company's future as much as possible, the new boss proposed a new strategy: "polymorphic content[8]." He explained: "Traditionally, a sequential series of games relies on one protagonist and a central theme to connect the various installments. However, to this point, we have done things differently. For this reason, we have decided to create sub-series <u>within</u> the bigger

---

8. *Polymorphic content*: different kinds of products all based on the same universe. It has two goals: extend and thus enrich the universe, but also, in particular, reach the broadest audience possible.

series." His reasoning was logical: video games, especially RPGs, are a unique medium where the player spends an enormous amount of time with a protagonist (or hero, or team of protagonists). As a result, the player gradually gets attached to them. Players like to know more about the background and fate of the characters they grow to love. And, the more players are motivated, the more they become fans, and they aren't shy about it. In the early 2000s, they used all means at their disposal, including the emerging internet, to express their love for different video games, especially *Final Fantasy VII*. Not a day went by without Square receiving letters, drawings, entire discussion forums, or photos of people dressed for cosplay[9]. Not a day went by without people thanking Square for creating *Final Fantasy* and clamoring for a sequel to their favorite. "In a way, we just gave them what they wanted," explains Wada. And even if it's an easy argument, it's one that makes sense. Square's new boss was even honest about it: "Above all, we had financial reasons for doing it. In the early 2000s, we were on the verge of bankruptcy. We had to do something. Since our line of thinking concurred with that of fans, we decided to move in that direction." He knew how to make his case. And he wasted no time at all.

As *Final Fantasy X* had been a big success in Japan (around 2 million copies sold), he asked the game's producer, Kitase, to make a "test" for a possible sequel. This test took the form of *Final Fantasy X Another Story: Eternal Calm*, a bonus video in *Final Fantasy X International* (the first I.5 version[10] of a Square game), created with the game's engine and purposely minimalist because it was produced at the last minute. The test was a success: the fans proved to be receptive. That was all Wada needed to call for a sequel, given the modest title *Final Fantasy X-2*. It was produced with three times fewer people and in half the time. It had to be ready before the end of March 2003, for the end of fiscal year 2002. It was the end of an era, both literally and figuratively[11]. It didn't take long for Nomura to join the production team, designing the

---

9 *Cosplay*: portmanteau of *costume* and *play*. Basically, people wear costumes, but it sounds fancier to say "cosplay."
10. While *Final Fantasy VII* had an *International* version before this, the practice became standard for almost all of the company's games starting with *Final Fantasy X*.
11. While work had already started on a number of games before the merger (for example, *Kingdom Hearts II, KH: Chain of Memories, Shinyaku Seiken Densetsu*, and *Drag-on Dragoon*), Final *Fantasy X–2* was the last Square game, chronologically speaking.

characters alongside Tomohiro Hasegawa[12], with support from Fumi Nakashima, as always.

⊰ [INTERLUDE: BAC – BEFORE ADVENT CHILDREN]

In September 2002, CGI was in a moment of crisis at Square. The studio responsible for *Final Fantasy: The Spirits Within* (Square Pictures, based in Hawaii) had folded and Visual Works was starting to show signs of fatigue, or rather weariness. Producing one trailer after another for various games was frustrating given their level of skill. They wanted to do something different. Taking advantage of a lull in business, Kazuyuki Ikumori's[13] studio offered a presentation video (basically a technical demo) to their direct point of contact, Kitase. He really liked the video and encouraged them to come up with something based on *Final Fantasy VII*. After all, Visual Works was created for the purposes of this game in 1997. Kitase lent them Nojima to write a script. Happy to return to this universe[14], Nojima came up with a minimalist drama (without action scenes) in which Cloud receives a letter from Tifa via several children. While pre-production was taking shape, reality came knocking at the door: knock, knock... it's *Final Fantasy X-2*. Reluctantly, Visual Works put its project aside... but not for long.

The end of fiscal year 2001 was fairly encouraging: *Final Fantasy X* was a success and *Kingdom Hearts* was off to an (unexpectedly) excellent start. Following a difficult year, serenity returned to Square. Wada's decisions were starting to pay off and his plan for the future was smart:

12. He started his career at Square as monster designer for *SaGa Frontier* before joining Nomura's "battle team" for *Final Fantasy VIII*. While he didn't participate in the first installment of *Kingdom Hearts*, he joined the Kingdom Team for the second (*Chain of Memories*), thanks to which he went on to lead his own team, co-directing *Subarashiki Kono Sekai* (*The World Ends With You*).
13. Kazuyuki Ikumori: the general manager and creation director for Visual Works. He started by working on video for *Final Fantasy VII* (even though he had never worked in this field before); at the time, he was just a graphic artist.
14. Nojima has a special place in his heart for *Final Fantasy VII*. He has also explained that the game whose development he was most involved in—*Final Fantasy X*—is more or less related to it: Gaia, he claims, is a potentiel future for Spira and the Al Bheds are ancestors of the Shinra people.

— The courting of Enix was on the right track. The only thing left was to have another success with *Final Fantasy X-2* and then the merger would be no more than a formality.

— *Final Fantasy* was more than ever before <u>the heart</u> of Square: each episode could (would) become a potential sub-series and the exceptional nature of the spins-offs could (would) proliferate.

A way of saving the company while preserving enough assets to avoid an acquisition. Clever. "That's nice and all, but what does it have to do with *Kingdom Hearts*?" you might ask. As it happens, everything.

ANOTHER SIDE

Given its—unexpected—success and its broader potential when compared to *Final Fantasy* in the United States, *Kingdom Hearts* immediately became "the action twin" in the mindset of the managers. As such, it received similar treatment: an *International* version with its own test video. Never tired of going against the grain, Nomura used the Western version to do a first test in the form of a cliffhanger[15] 80 seconds long, entirely in CGI: *Another Story, Another Side*[16]. With one difference: he added in a principle of game design—reward[17]. The bonus video became a <u>secret</u> ending and required the player to go above and beyond to access it.

⚜ [INTERLUDE: BBC – BEFORE BEFORE CRISIS]

One night around September 2002, when Nomura had just finished the Western version of *Kingdom Hearts* (and had just started *Final*

---

15. An inconclusive ending intended to build strong anticipation. A technique used particularly in TV series and big movie sagas.
16. On a side note, *ASAS* borrowed the two "bonus names" from *Final Fantasy X. Another Story* is the sub-title for the version from *FFX* with *Eternal Calm* and *The Other Side* is the title of the bonus DVD that came with the original Japanese version (with demos, making-of content, etc.).
17. The foundation of game design is the balance between frustration and reward, between winning and losing. Reward must equal the level of effort made to get it.

Mix), he met with the guys from the brand-new mobile department of Square and asked them: "Could we make an action-RPG on a phone that would use the network?" Kosei Itô[18] started a long discussion with him. The first issue was to determine if it would be fun enough to play. Nomura let a few weeks go by and then came back to Itô with a concept taking place in the *Final Fantasy VII* universe, before the events of the game, in which the player joins the team of Turks and comes face to face with the old AVALANCHE organization (before it was "reactivated" by Barret), a much more violent and terroristic form of the group. Then, a chronology of the universe was established.

Also around September 2002, as he started work on the *International* version of *Kingdom Hearts*, cleverly renamed *Final Mix* (for reasons already explained), Nomura added new content, including the secret video from the Western versions. While he could have been satisfied and stopped there, he decided to go further by adding a new sequence requiring players to face a new bad guy—heralding a possible sequel—to unlock version I.5 of *Another Story, Another Side: [deep dive]*. Longer, better produced, and accompanied by a totally new song (*Another Side*), the video takes place in the same location with the same two hooded characters facing off. However, this time the video ties into *Kingdom Hearts* by referencing Ansem's reports[19], dramatically presented as a countdown that ends with the number II. Then, Mickey Mouse makes a cameo, difficult to recognize because he too is dressed in a black leather cloak. A reveal trailer[20] that does not give the name of the sequel, with three goals:

— Suggest that *Kingdom Hearts II* is already well underway, even though it has not yet started development.

— Get players fantasizing and push them to construct their own theories based on the new information provided by *Final Mix*.

18. Kosei Itō joined Square in the online and marketing department in 1997. He took charge of the mobile branch at the time of its launch in 2002. Today, he is a producer for all of Square Enix's smartphone games, vice president of the mobile branch, and supervisor for the American market.
19. Ansem's reports are a series of notes telling the backstory from the point of view of the bad guy, purposely made to be convoluted in order to spark the player's imagination.
20. As the name suggests, this is a type of trailer used to announce a game.

— Sell his Mickey idea to Disney, because he wanted more than anything to give him a bigger role in the story, and he was ready to fight like hell until Disney gave in.

Ultimately, he transformed a sales gimmick into a totally ingenious game design idea that would become one the unique signatures of the *Kingdom Hearts* series.

◀ [INTERLUDE] THE LOST ANIMATIC

In 2002, Disney asked Seth Kearsley[21], one of its former animators, to make an animatic (an animated storyboard) for a potential animated series based on *Kingdom Hearts*. Kearsley, who loved the game, was delighted to have such an opportunity and gave the task his all, even helping write the script, which he has described as being "incredibly dark."

This pilot starts on the Destiny Islands with Sora, Riku, and Kairi. The two guys are sparring as usual, then meet up with Kairi. They talk casually and are having a good time. Then, all of a sudden, a portal appears in the sky. A group of Heartless invade the island. The three spring into action to repel them, but Riku and Kairi disappear; a Darkside emerges and engulfs Sora with his hand. The hero cries out and wakes with a start, finding himself in a Gummi ship, where he stares at a photo, a relic from a time when they were still together. Meanwhile, at the Hollow Bastion: A narrator explains Riku's situation as a prisoner of Maleficent. It seems that she needs Aladdin's lamp. After dismissing Jafar, she orders Riku to get her the lamp; in exchange, she'll give him back his freedom. In Agrabah, Sora and Goofy are fighting the Heartless and find Riku. Together, they manage to find the lamp. As soon as Riku goes to grab it, Maleficent possesses him. A Darkside appears and carries away Sora.

---

21. Seth Kearsley: Animator specializing in "posing" and "layout." He has worked on projects that include *The Simpsons* and the animated series *The Lion King*. He was also director and producer for the series *Mummies Alive* (for DIC) and, most importantly, for *Eight Crazy Nights*, an animated film starring Adam Sandler. Since 2008, he has managed his own studio, Dojo Productions.

The pilot was seven minutes long and only used (poorly) drawn characters and indications for animations. Kearsley left the backgrounds blank: his idea was to embed the game's protagonists in the backgrounds from each movie. He explained: "For example, when Sora and Riku are fighting in the street, the background would be the street from the movie. When Riku grabs the lamp, the background used would be the same as when Aladdin grabs the lamp in the movie." An excellent idea that Kearsley justified in different ways: "That helps save money, makes it so that you don't have to reinvent the wheel every time, and creates a striking sense of déjà vu!" And, of course, he intended to do this for every setting the characters would pass through. In any case, the adventure never reached that stage because "there was such great respect for the director of the games and too many games already in planning to muck all that up with a TV series." In other words, Kearsley had an interesting proposal, but it was off track and strayed too far from the original game. Given that in 2002 the relationship between Disney and Square was still in its infancy, and thus was fragile, they decided it was better to not get on the bad side of their main game partners, particularly Nomura. This leads us to the question: then why order an animatic in the first place? Was it just a test? Was it out of worry that there would only be one game? Was it an initial attempt to show the Japanese who's boss? We'll never know because Disney, naturally, has no recollection of the subject. In any case, we'll let Kearsley have the final word: "It was the coolest project to never end up becoming reality, not because of the project itself, but rather because of corporate strategizing." Or perhaps thanks to; it depends how you look at it.

LAZY AFTERNOONS

Early 2003. Before starting work on anything, Nomura started by locking down his team as best he could. He had noticed that certain games in development—particularly *Final Fantasy XI*—were "overwhelmed" and would require a movement of team members, and he didn't like that. At all. In addition, he had to deal with a major departure, that of his event director Jun Akiyama, stolen away by Yasumi

Matsuno with the start of production on *Final Fantasy XII* (FYI, just before Sakaguchi's departure); to replace him, Nomura turned to Masaru Oka[22]. For the script, Keiko Nobumoto had already laid out the plot and was no longer needed; in any case, she was too busy (with *Wolf's Rain*). Kazushige Nojima came in from the very beginning of the project after finishing work on *Final Fantasy X-2*.

Other than that, Tomohiro Hasegawa joined the team, bolstering the art department and bringing a bit of change, since he took over textures; Arakawa thus took care of the menu and the interface. One notable fact: at this point, the team became much more structured and hierarchical. It included an army of planners who had to report to "lead planners[23]," who were in turn supervised by the directors of each department, i.e. the "core team" (Tatsuya Kando, Akira Fujii, Tomohiro Kayano, Takeshi Endo, Syuichi Sato, Takeshi Arakawa, Masahide Tanaka, Takayuki Odachi, and the two main programmers, Hiroshi Harata and Kentaro Yasui). Yuuichi Kanemori, still in charge of the battle department, also began managing overall planning. With this dozen or so people, Nomura started by evaluating the strengths and weaknesses of the first installment in order to develop a roadmap for the main changes to be made. Notably, he decided to create a new engine from scratch and make improvements to the system of combat. He explains: "We realized the limitations of the original engine and, given that we wanted to create a better game, we changed everything." They also focused on difficulty because feedback was unanimous: between the platform sequences and the general difficulty of the first, "it's true that we weren't very nice to our players. That's why we made the second more user-friendly by putting in fewer jumping sequences[24] and by lowering the overall level of difficulty a bit." However, multiple levels of difficulty were implemented so that each player could customize their gaming experience. While the story was still a little

---

22. Masaru Oka had been working with Nomura for quite some time, notably on *Final Fantasy VII* and *VIII* (for which he served as map director). He joined the team starting with *Kingdom Hearts II* and, over time, became one of the leading developers for the series, working on writing and events.
23. The "supervisors" who are responsible for the planners, even though they themselves are planners. Among them were Yosuke Shiokawa and Mitsunori Takahashi, two of the most influential members of the team for *Dissidia: Final Fantasy*, and Nobuyuki Matsuoka, who played an important role in designing the battles for the *Final Fantasy XIII* trilogy.
24. "Jumping sequences" is the way that the Japanese refer to "platform sequences."

hazy, it already had several key points: "I had already decided that if one day there was a sequel, it would take place one year later and the atmosphere would change a little because Sora and the others would be a year older. Above all, I wanted the sequel to start in the most intriguing way possible." As always, Nomura was pretending to have his head in the clouds, but he knew where he was heading.

A VERY SMALL WISH

Nomura needed some time to think because, for him, the very concept of a sequel is problematic: "A game that doesn't sell shouldn't have a sequel. To make a sequel, people have to demand it." This was not an issue for *Kingdom Hearts*. However, as the consummate perfectionist, Nomura couldn't imagine a sequel without considering a fundamental question: how could he make it interesting for those who didn't play the first game? This immediately led him to strip Sora of his abilities ("playing a powerful character from the very start doesn't make sense") and to look for an explanation so that this would be coherent. As *KH II* was to take place one year after the end of the first game, Nomura asked himself: "But what actually happened in that year?" This is particularly remarkable given that, initially, "there was absolutely no plan to touch on this subject in *Kingdom Hearts II*." In other words, he was making this big mental effort to justify his own idea to himself. But this wasn't just his neuroses talking.

After the first game came out, he was asked to make a *Kingdom Hearts* for Game Boy Advance. He refused: "I was skeptical about the idea of seeing *Kingdom Hearts* in 2D. So, I said I wouldn't do it." Then, he started receiving requests from his team and from abroad, like, "My kids wish they could play *Kingdom Hearts* on their GBA[25]," more and more frequently. He hated the idea of leaving kids disappointed. So, he starting thinking about a solution. He reconsidered the Game Boy Advance and drew a connection: he would use the "missing year" to develop this much-coveted installment. He thought of absolutely

---

25. His superiors told him, "make a KH for GBA," but he said no. His team told him, "my kids wish they could play it on GBA," and he said yes. An anecdote that says a lot about Nomura.

everything, from the visual style to the story, and even the game systems and, in particular, how to convert the battles to 2D. After several weeks of work, he presented a project book entitled *Kingdom Hearts: Lost Memories* to his team. This invaluable document included dozens of pages of sketches, a basic plot, the card-based game system[26], annotated drawings, and even concept art. Since development of *Kingdom Hearts II* had not yet started in earnest[27] (even though his team was already more or less working on it), he made *Lost Memories* a priority; it was later renamed *Chain of Memories*, because "it has more style and it fits with the plot; also, I just like it." The truth is, you couldn't find a more fitting title given the technical problems, particularly related to memory, that interfered with development.

Nomura's ambitions were totally out of proportion: on top of a long game with a lot of text, he wanted his usual song by Utada and cinematics with dubbing. In other words, an impossible task on a 256-Mb ROM cartridge. It was all the more complicated since his team wasn't familiar with portable consoles; they were used to working on home consoles with a capacity of 4.7 GB. And 256 Mb is a far cry from 4.7 GB. It's time to jog your memory so that you really understand the magnitude of this change.

[A MEMO ON... MEMORY]

T HE *byte* is the unit of measurement for computer memory capacity. Not to be confused with the "bit" (portmanteau of *binary digit*) which refers to the minimum amount of information

---

26. The card game is the battle system in *Kingdom Hearts: Chain of Memories*. We'll come back to that in detail in Volume II.
27. Nomura was very mad at Disney for trying to make *Kingdom Hearts V Cast* behind his back. He was furious when he learned that a mobile "port" (available only on Verizon's service) was being developed by Superscape (which had already produced the awful phone game *Alien vs. Predator*). No one consulted him or asked him to approve anything whatsoever. This may seem like a prideful reaction, but above all, it's a very Japanese way of responding. They don't mess around when it comes to respecting works of art. And if you look at the results (very quickly forgotten by all), you'll agree with him wholeheartedly.

transmitted by a message. 1 bit = 0.125 bytes. A cartridge with 256 megabits = 32 megabytes (around 100 times less than the *Kingdom Hearts* DVD, which has around 2.8 GB). To really put things into perspective, think about the fact that a photo taken with a smartphone takes up between 2.5 and 5 MB and a song in MP3 format takes up between 5 and 7 MB. *Chain of Memories* takes up the equivalent of 5 to 7 songs. As such, it would be impossible to fit an album on the game's ROM cartridge—or the album would have to be very short.

ROM stands for *read-only memory* (memory you can't modify). The only way to write over it (or rewrite it) is if the ROM cartridge has a battery enabling, for example, low-power interactions like saving.

So that you get the full picture, a CD-ROM holds about 700 MB, a DVD-ROM between 4.7 and 8.5 GB (single- or dual-layered). A Blu-ray disc can hold up to 200 GB of data. The game cartridge is actually the medium that offers the least amount of memory: up to 32 GB for Switch cartridges, just under 10 times the size of *Kingdom Hearts II*, but with instantaneous access and lower usage of RAM (*random access memory*, like your brain's working memory).

Since Nomura had absolutely no concept of these equipment-related details and could not care less about them, he categorically refused to give up his ambitions because of "vulgar technical considerations." He thus looked to his direct superior for the series, Shinji Hashimoto, for help. As luck would have it, just after the release of *Kingdom Hearts*, Disney introduced him to one of its contractors, Jupiter Corporation, which at the time was working on *Disney Sports: Motocross* (published by Konami). At the end of their meeting, Jupiter's president, Makoto Nakayama, told him, "if you ever need anything, don't hesitate to contact us[28]." Jupiter seemed to be the solution: they were familiar

---

28. It's most likely at this time, around May 2002, that Hashimoto suggested to Nomura a game for GBA. I have no proof of this theory, but it would be logical, particularly given that the dates are consistent.

with the console, knew how to program for it, and had extensive experience with Nintendo's approval processes (having developed the *Picross* games for Nintendo). All that being said, Nomura wasn't impressed. He wanted to see concretely what they could do. To prove what they were made of, Jupiter had to present a prototype, created in "less than a month's time" by a manager "who was put through hell," according to team director[29] Aguru Tanaka.

Nomura approved the prototype and passed the hot potato to Jupiter. What followed was a long descent into hell for the technicians, particularly the two main programmers Hiroyuki Itô (no relation to the co-director of *Final Fantasy VI* and *IX*) and Masato Furukawa: "We were really under the gun. You need room to fit in events and songs, and the GBA's ROM didn't have much... It was all complicated. We had to test different methods for compressing quality or data," notably for the sound, for which "it was absolute hell to come up with something audible."

The worst part was incorporating videos (which, just to remind you, used dubbing in the Japanese version). After looking at the problem from every angle without finding any viable solutions, they turned to AM3, a company specializing in data compression and using technology developed by a French company[30]. This memory issue was at the heart of all of the game's problems, to the point where Jupiter regularly asked Square Enix to expect fewer facial animations. Daisuke Watanabe has also noted that, indeed, certain characters have no facial animations at all to save space.

On top of this, the 30 or so employees of Jupiter working on the game's development, some performing multiple functions[31], were tasked with "translating" *Kingdom Hearts* into 2D without denaturing anything. This particularly applied to each of the worlds, but also the

---

29. Tanaka had no control over the game himself. However, he was in charge of the Jupiter team that worked on *Chain of Memories*.
30. Although the game credits two former employees of Cryo—Emmanuel Marquez (now CTO at Starbreeze) and Pascal Urro—the technology itself was invented by 4X Technologies, a Paris-based company that later became Mobiclip, which has been part of Nintendo since September 2011. Their latest creations are the NES Mini and SNES Mini, developed under the company acronym NERD.
31. Notably, this was the case for Hidemi Shimomura, who, on top of his role as a graphic artist, wrote the script for the events in the Disney worlds.

Heartless. Jupiter also had to make sure to create the same level of intensity in the battles: "In *Kingdom Hearts*, you feel the impact of each hit and that's impossible to recreate without cheating," said Jun Kominami (VFX designer). Thus, they worked with what they had by mainly focusing on visuals at the moment of impact (stars, white flashes[32], distortions and vibrations of the image) and by using recoil movements and a few clever camera tricks, particularly imitation crash zooms[33]. They came up with lots of ideas for dealing with the weak capacities of the GBA, the team's worst enemy… along with the almost pathologically demanding nature of the Kingdom team: "Someone from Square Enix was at home checking every detail: the characters, textures, colors, menus. Absolutely EVERYTHING." And, to be clear, Nomura regularly had video conferences with the various managers from Jupiter in order to check in and push them to improve quality.

This is because, while Jupiter was actually performing the work, the brains of the operation were, of course, on Nomura's team and they themselves had some serious difficulty adapting to the GBA, especially its damned lack of space. Daisuke Watanabe has said that writing without planning any camera movements was, without a doubt, the hardest part. This was seconded by the events manager, Ryo Tsurumaki: "In 2D, you can't rely on cameras. As such, you have to rack your brains to come up with scenes that are sufficiently interesting and don't seem too long." Everything depended on the animation of the characters, particularly their facial expressions and appearance while in play, but also on the talent of the scriptwriter. More than ever before, Watanabe was put to the test. When he joined the production during Golden Week[34], after finishing work on *Final Fantasy X-2 Last Mission*, everything (or almost everything) had already been decided by Nomura (and Nojima): the story was to take place just after the end of *Kingdom Hearts*, in a new location (Castle Oblivion) where Sora would have to make his way through the 13 levels while confronting a number of bad guys (the members of Organization XIII and the replica of Riku)

32. White flash: a film editing technique where a white-filled image is added between two regular images to create a flash effect.
33. Crash zoom: a cinematic effect intended to create a visual shock in which the camera goes from a wide shot to a close-up very quickly.
34. Four annual national holidays in Japan, all within the same week in early May. As such, Watanabe was contacted during this period in May 2003.

before being offered a crucial choice by Naminé, creating the link with *Kingdom Hearts II*. The main theme of the game was memory.

In other words, there wasn't much room left for Watanabe to add his own voice. The worst part was that the structure allowing the player to visit the worlds in the order of their choosing did not make his job easier, particularly in regards to the relationships between the characters: "I can tell you now, I really felt like I was struggling like a newbie." Nevertheless, he remained concentrated on the game's main point: explaining what Naminé did to Sora. Watanabe also says that the game's last scene got him out of his funk. From there, he saw the bright side of things and recognized: "When there's an actor, they give life to a character using their voice. Since we had no actors this time around, I had to rely on nuances of the characters and carefully choose my words." Additionally, Nomura gave him more freedom with the script for Riku, which made him very happy because he wasn't really happy with how the character was handled at the end of *Kingdom Hearts. Chain of Memories* allowed him to somewhat rehabilitate the image of this character that he loved. To close out this section, I'll give you a little anecdote about Tatsuya Kando, who is the kind of person that really gets invested in the development of a game. For the first *Kingdom Hearts*, he lent his hands to Tinker Bell and his movements to a few Heartless. In *Chain of Memories*, he lent his voice (really just some interjections). Hasegawa has said: "I don't want to name names, but yes, he took care of several characters."

But, what else was happening during all that time? The merger between Square and Enix was announced (on November 26, 2002). However, the agreement was jeopardized because it was found to be unacceptable by the owner of 40 percent of Square's shares, Masafumi Miyamoto. The founder of Square even declared publicly that he would refuse to sign during the next shareholder meeting, set for mid-February 2003. There was trouble afoot. The two companies had to come to an agreement within just a few days[35]. Miyamoto's maneuvering worked: Enix reviewed its (disastrous) position and (slightly)

---

35. You can't outsmart the master. Miyamoto quickly realized that Enix was trying to absorb Square. As such, thanks to his intervention, he helped revalue the exchange ratio from 0.81 to 0.85 shares of Square for 1 of Enix. That may not seem like much, but it's huge in a transaction with a lot of zeros.

revalued the transaction in favor of Square. The merger was then pushed back to April.

February 2003. The first piece of Square's new strategy was almost complete. Sales figures were positive, the end of the fiscal year was fast approaching, and the company was sure that it was going to finish with a spectacular comeback (and, indeed, it did). After a rough start to the year, the merger was set to take place in just a matter of weeks. So, Yoichi Wada decided to shift up a gear before Enix's arrival. He asked his teams to begin the second phase of polymorphic content, truly opening up a whole new world. As Kitase and Nomura worked beautifully together, leaving players blown away by their work and Wada blown away by the yen the company was raking in, Wada made them his secret weapons. He understood that Kitase and Nomura complemented each other: Kitase *is Final Fantasy* and Nomura was the person aiming to *reinvent* it. For this reason, the two of them gained great importance under Wada's reign (and subsequently fell very hard).

[INTERLUDE: FFAC]

As *Final Fantasy X-2* was entering its final weeks of development, Visual Works again found itself with some free time. Now that they had finished with the hard work, they could once again play around a bit, especially because there was nothing on the horizon. As such, it was time to dust off the *"FFVII* technical demo" project. Fairly quickly, they produced a scene with Cloud riding a motorcycle. Just an adjustment to the lighting and Kitase was impressed; he was back in the loop after also finishing work on *Final Fantasy X-2*. Since *Final Fantasy XII* was already in Matsuno's hands and *Kingdom Hearts II* was not likely to start right away, Kitase also had some time and decided to help them out. He soon saw the enormous potential of the visuals, which gave him an idea: make a sequel. He asked Nomura to join in on the project; Nomura said he wasn't thrilled by the idea: Visual Works was "just" a CGI studio and thus didn't have much experience with creating a game and, on top of that, most of the company's resources were tied up in other projects. So, they decided to go back to their original plan, a video. And Nomura was very familiar with videos. He had demon-strated with *[deep dive]* that he wanted to direct action scenes. He started imagining something more exciting, on a bigger scale, inspired by Nojima's initial idea based on Cloud, Tifa, and children. It needed to be seen. He decided that the best form would be a full-length movie that he would co-direct with "his" CGI master, Takeshi Nozue, with support from the legends of old: Kazushige Nojima on the script, Yusuka Naora directing the art department, and Nobuo Uematsu[36] on the music. They decided that it would be a direct-to-DVD film about 60 minutes long. The result was *Final Fantasy VII: Reunion*, which came out on September 14, 2005, under the name *Advent Children*[37]. It was a big success, selling 410,000 copies in a week, 700,000 in three weeks, and over 4.1 million by the end of its run, before the release of the *Complete* version in 2009.

Besides being a success from artistic and commercial standpoints, it was, above all, another piece on Nomura's mental chessboard, notably influencing his way of designing video games thereafter.

End parenthesis.

The final results for fiscal year 2002 (which ended on March 31, 2003) were overwhelmingly positive. With the spectacular sales of *Final Fantasy X* and *Kingdom Hearts*, the take-off of *Final Fantasy XI*, the excellent start for *Final Fantasy X-2*, and the reconciliation with Nintendo[38] after six years of enmity, Square ended the year running on all cylinders, with all-time record profits. Yoichi Wada established his authority. In the days that followed, the 1st of April to be exact, Square and Enix merged. Thanks to his work, Wada was appointed as president and Keiji Honda, the president of Enix, became vice president. Square represented 80 percent of the workforce of the new company. Of course, things don't change overnight and that slowed

36. ... and his group, The Black Mages. It's too bad that Nobuo Uematsu isn't tied to *Kingdom Hearts* because he's an extraordinary guy and there are numerous anecdotes about him. Maybe next time.
37. The title *Advent Children* was chosen by Nomura. *Advent* (from the Latin *adventus*) means "arrival," but it has a second, religious, meaning that evokes the idea of a return (i.e. of Christ). *Children*—suggested by Nojima—comes from one of the film's themes. Thus, the title is a message of hope.
38. With *Chocobo Land: A Game of Dice*, *Final Fantasy Tactics Advance* for GBA, and also, in particular, *Final Fantasy: Crystal Chronicles* for GameCube.

down progress on projects until the summer, when the two companies moved into new offices together in Shinjuku.

[Because it was symbolic: Square and Enix "got married" at about 20 years old (the company was founded in September 1983) and they moved in together within less than six months.]

In spite of the changes, the teams kept working away. Some of them even entered critical months for their projects. This was the case for Kazuhiko Aoki and Akitoshi Kawazu, who were working on *Final Fantasy: Crystal Chronicles*, and for Takashi Tokita, working on *Hanjuku Eiyuu Tai 3D*.

Summer 2003. Going off of *Advent Children*, Kitase and Nomura, with agreement from management, decided to expand the *Final Fantasy VII* universe by launching a project that was the epitome of polymorphic content: *Compilation of Final Fantasy VII*. A multifaceted project with several iterations.

[INTERLUDE: *FFBC*]

Nomura got the ball rolling again on the *Final Fantasy VII* game during a phone call. Itô made significant progress on writing for the project and found a team of about 20 people who were available. He introduced Nomura to Hajime Tabata[39], who had just joined Square Enix. Itô wanted him to serve as director given his experience with video games. Nomura to Tabata: "Can you make a phone game based on the Turks?" Tabata said yes and explained that he already had a few ideas. Development for this game (which was nameless for the time being) was made official and it would become part of *Compilation of Final Fantasy VII*. Kosei Itô served as producer,

---

39. After a career at Tecmo, where he distinguished himself, notably, with *Monster Rancher 2*, he joined Square in the mobile department. He was chosen to direct *Before Crisis: Final Fantasy VII*, then later on, *Crisis Core*. He long continued to work under Nomura (his "creative producer"), ending with their collaboration on *Final Fantasy versus XIII*, after which Tabata took on *Final Fantasy XV*.

Hajime Tabata as director, and Nomura as character designer and creative producer.

Before Crisis: Final Fantasy VII, the game's final title, was a game in 24 episodes whose distribution began on September 24, 2004, on mobile phones using NTT DoCoMo (the number-one network in Japan). The game was never released outside of Japan because it was totally incompatible with Western phones. As *Advent Children* before it, the game was a success: 200,000 subscribers from the first episode. It then became the top selling game at the time, with over 1.6 million users.

FOUR ANECDOTES:

— To choose the composer, an in-house contest was organized. Takeharu Ishimoto[40] won by proposing a rock version of the theme for *Final Fantasy VII* (his favorite game).

— The idea to add telephones to *Advent Children* came from *Before Crisis*, in order to create a link between the two.

— The introductory video and trailer for *Before Crisis* were created by the studio Gainax (responsible for works including *Shin Seiki Evangelion*, *FLCL*, and more recently *Gurren Lagann*). That's why the OAV *Final Fantasy VII: Last Order* (which was supervised by Nomura and came out the same day as *Advent Children*) was assigned to them.

— An American version was considered in 2006, but the project was eventually canceled.

---

40. Hired as an audio integrator (basically, he "translated" compositions for software) at Square in 1999 (for *Legend of Mana*), his first assignment as composer was for *Before Crisis: Final Fantasy VII*. He then "followed" Nomura for most of his productions (*Subarashiki Kono Sekai*, *Crisis Core*, *Dissidia*, *Kingdom Hearts*, *Type–0*, etc.). He was later one of the composers—or rather arrangers—for *Final Fantasy VII Remake*.

✦ [INTERLUDE: *FABULA NOVA CRYSTALLIS*]

Although it was multifaceted, the *Compilation of Final Fantasy VII* project was just considered to be on the side. In Spring 2003, it was high time to start thinking about the next step—*Final Fantasy XII*. Although this project was in a heap of shit, particularly for technical reasons (and in spite of the ingenuity of Taku Murata[41]), at that point in time, it was still set for release in Summer 2004. According to the sacred cycle[42], the next chapter needed to come out at the end of 2006. Once again, Square Enix brushed aside the difficulty in front of them. In line with the new policy, Wada asked his leading men, Kitase and Nomura, to come up with a multifaceted project centered on the next numbered installment, *Final Fantasy XIII*. Assisted by Shinji Hashimoto, they established a new concept: several games around a single central theme, <u>the new story of the crystals</u>. While the *Compilation of Final Fantasy VII* project was, naturally, based on the original game, this time they would create "a new mythology," a series within the series where each event would be a "facet." Each director could thus offer their own vision. They first decided that *Final Fantasy XIII* (for PlayStation 2) would be the anchor, explaining the main points of the new mythology, particularly the relation between the deities and the "mortals." Kitase led these efforts and, naturally, assigned the game to his protégé, Motomu Toriyama, who a few weeks earlier had finished work on *Final Fantasy X-2* with, as we know, great success. Motivated by the idea of doing something other than Disney work in the years to come, Nomura proposed that he would direct the second game, *Final Fantasy versus XIII*: an action-RPG, the "evil twin" to *Kingdom Hearts*, strongly influenced by his work on *Final Fantasy VII Advent Children*. Of course, he waited until completion of *Kingdom Hearts II* to start work on this project, meaning that it

---

41. Main programmer for *Final Fantasy Tactics* and *Vagrant Story*, Murata became one of the leading figures in R&D at Square (Enix). He made major contributions to the implementation of real-time 3D tools and to PlayOnline before becoming one of the main developers of the proprietary engine Crystal Tools until 2013.
42. A new *Final Fantasy* installment comes out every two to three years (sometimes less). Contrary to popular belief, the sacred cycle has always been followed. Yes, even for *Final Fantasy XV* (2016) since *Lightning Returns: Final Fantasy* hit the shelves in 2014, one year after *Final Fantasy XIV: A Realm Reborn*.

would probably have to be for the next generation of consoles. To tie everything together, they asked Nojima to write the mythology for the mini-series. Although he was very busy with *Kingdom Hearts II* (and the rest), Nojima nevertheless completed his bible[43], after additions and modifications from Kitase and Nomura, in February 2004. At the same time development began in earnest for *Final Fantasy XIII*.

End parenthesis.

In 2004, Kitase decided to add a shooter game based on the character Vincent (off of an idea from Nomura)—what would become *Dirge of Cerberus*—and started considering the idea of porting *Before Crisis* to Sony's PlayStation Portable, a port that would eventually become *Crisis Core: Final Fantasy VII*, again directed by Hajime Tabata and the last game included in the *Compilation of Final Fantasy VII* project.

DEARLY BELOVED

Shortly after the move to Shinjuku, Nomura refocused on *Kingdom Hearts II* because he had since received the green light from Disney: he would be able to give Mickey[44] a bigger part! The goal was to finish the story and answer all of the questions left in suspense in the first chapter. Nojima explains: "Tetsu-san gave me a list of loose ends from the plot. I asked him if it was up to me to resolve them and he responded that he already had one or two answers. At that time, I thought that he didn't yet have the answers to all of the questions in his own script." Nomura has clarified this, explaining that he already had half of the answers when developing the first game and the other half came naturally at the very beginning of pre-production. In other words, Nomura knew exactly where he was going and purposely left Nojima in the dark in order to get the greatest creativity possible out of his scriptwriter. To help him in his work, Nomura gave Nojima some guidelines: "He told me that all of the phrases that appeared in the

43. Nojima wrote the *mythos* for *Fabula Nova Crystallis* while taking into account the comments from Kitase, Nomura, and Toriyama. The result was a detailed bible explaining both the origins of the universe and its pantheon. To introduce audiences to this mythology, Yusuke Naora and his team created a video, released in January 2011; the document, however, was finished in 2004. That's when development began in earnest for *Final Fantasy XIII*.
44. I've been told that the negotiations also involved Yen Sid and the world of *Fantasia*; however, given the lack of tangible proof, this is just a theory.

secret video had to be incorporated (...) So, I imagined the situations that might fit with those phrases." Yep, you understood that correctly: *[deep dive]* was really a work document intended for Nomura's team. At the very beginning of development, the Kingdom team knew as much as the players did and had to create the sequel based on speculation. A totally unique way of working.

The central idea of *Kingdom Hearts II* is that it's a sequel that takes place one year later. This had enormous consequences not just for the script, but also for the rest of the game. Particularly for the characters and their animation: "Although it doesn't really look like it, we redid all of the battle animations from scratch. The characters were a year older and so we had to adapt their movements. They had to be less childlike, more self-assured," explains Tatsuya Kando. What's more, thanks to the changes in the combat system, Sora could now use the Keyblade with both hands. As such, all of his movements had to be revised. These kinds of details go totally unnoticed by the average player, but they say a lot about the extreme care given to even the smallest details. Everything has meaning. Nomura confirms this: "We didn't import any data from *Kingdom Hearts*. The second chapter was 100 percent new." The action itself was no longer looked at through the lens of exploration, battles, and events; instead, they went with a more powerful formula: the two teams, each working on their own side of things, were merged together and were placed under the supervision of Yuuichi Kanemori. Exploration and combat were considered to be two sides of the same coin and so they were developed together by the same people. In addition, the console upgrade required models and textures to be improved, particularly in the cutscenes. They especially focused on facial animations, with over a hundred per character. It's for this reason that some players have remarked that even games that came out a dozen years later (off the top of my head, *Mass Effect Andromeda*) don't compare. Kando also says that they had to regulate the number of animations of textures according to the models. As such, the highs (used for close-ups) were less detailed than the middles[45] in order to create transitions that "weren't too crappy," according to Hasegawa.

---

45. The "high models" are those including the most polygons, used in close-ups to provide greater detail. The "middle models" are the most common, used for medium-distance or long shots and thus requiring less precision.

Basically, nothing changed, but everything changed… This approach also applied to the worlds already visited in the first installment: "Even though they were the same places, the connection points were different, so we redid everything," says Takeshi Endo. Odachi explains: "Some of them gave us big problems, like the Disney Castle. In *Kingdom Hearts*, I designed it as an immense castle, but absolutely not as a level[46]." Ah yes, you may not realize it, but that changes everything. The team led by Masahide Tanaka thus had to take into account the original design while implementing changes, some invisible to the naked eye, like alterations to the scale or adjustments to perspective, in order to incorporate level design. Which, it's true, players never notice. Players may have only seen this world in video in the first game, but they figured that it was a world the developers were keeping up their sleeve. In reality, this was not at all the case. Once again, it just goes to show how concern for detail can affect a game. The same was true for the narrative structure. The script for each of the worlds also had to be constructed differently. Thanks to the work on pacing and game situations, it's never noticeable, but *Kingdom Hearts II* is actually broken up into two parts. Masaru Oka explains: "In *Kingdom Hearts*, players could revisit every world after the Hollow Bastion. The only thing that would change was that the enemies were stronger." This time, the developers used the "revisit[47]" to place certain bosses, including some members of Organization XIII. In that way, each world became the setting for an epic duel. However, the events team wasn't satisfied with this: "We decided from the beginning that adding game situations and/or scenes was the best solution." However, that required 800 events, which was two and a half times the number in the first game. A number that they laugh about today: "We actually established a tool at the start of production to help us reduce the number…"

46. The Japanese use English technical jargon in a way that's quite, shall we say, lawless. When Odachi talks about a level, he implies "in terms of *level design*." Similarly, when you see "concept" or "plan," the developers are really referring to game design or to ideas.
47. In game design, a "revisit" is when a player goes back to a level they've already been through in order to finish it thanks to, for example, a new ability.

BLAST OFF

Because of the density of the game, Nomura and Oka agreed to offer regular breathers between major phases. *Kingdom Hearts II* is filled with all sorts of mini-games that add great variety to the gameplay. Some are easy to spot, others less so. This is particularly the case for the skateboard. Originally, the developers only planned on including it in Twilight Town. However, halfway through development, Nomura asked to also make it available elsewhere. "We had to revise certain maps to include it," says Masahide Tanaka. After that, the skateboard was considered a secondary, but important, element in the second game. They went as far as designing multiple boards to fit with the nature of each world, just like the interface. However, Arakawa says that, in the end, they had to remove them from several worlds, like Agrabah, because of comments from Disney. The greatest weakness of *Kingdom Hearts* is, without a doubt, the Gummi ship. There's a rational explanation for this: in the developers' heads, it was just a bonus feature to get the player from point A to point B "in a more fun way." Also, another major factor: it was the work of four people in their free time. "The feedback from players about the Gummi ship [the original] was really bad, so we decided to significantly improve this aspect[48] and make a whole new system," says Nomura. As a result, the Gummi ship in *Kingdom Hearts II* was treated like any other world, with the same level of seriousness and concern for detail. A team was established to focus on it, led by Ryuji Ikeda, one of the programmers: "I'm a fan of shooting, that's actually the reason why I entered the video game world (…) As such, I offered to design this part in addition to coding it. They gave me carte blanche." He was assisted by CG designer Yasushi Kameda. Over time, the two got help from various other people. Their goal was simple: "We wanted to make a real game within the game." "No, even better than the game itself," laughs Ikeda. As such, they stuck with the very spirited rhythm of the second game and at the same time gave it a shot of adrenaline, as well as a dose of staging, using several camera angles. However, their priority was still to make these phases playable

---

48. For more information, see Volume II. You will learn what Nomura thinks of the Gummi ship, a very interesting point of view.

for neophytes. "We wanted them [the players] to say to themselves, 'I finished that level myself? I'm so good.'" Mission accomplished.

In regards to the mini-games and/or the varied gameplay, Yuuichi Kanemori recognizes that they "got carried away with the number." Takeshi Endo adds, "And once again, we ended up chucking out some things because they were too similar or even a pain in the ass." They gave the example of an activity where Sora became an employee at a restaurant and had to cut vegetables (with his Keyblade) with increasing speed. It was a mini-game that took a lot of time and resources. By the time the idea was abandoned, the restaurant had already been finalized and a large number of vegetables had even been designed by Odachi. While this creativity and concern for making the best game possible can be felt in the revamped old material, the same is true for the new creations. Firstly, Nomura wanted a world that would be truly astonishing, even more so than Halloween Town in the first game with its stop-motion animation and its radically different visual style (thanks to Tim Burton). As *Kingdom Hearts* is a "playable cartoon," the most surprising thing would, of course, be to add some "real life." This idea would materialize with the introduction of the *Pirates of the Caribbean* universe (and to a lesser extent, that of *Tron*). However, this was not the original choice: "When I discussed the idea with Disney, I wanted a [live-action video] in particular[49], but they said no. They then asked me to review a list to see if something could take its place, and I chose *Pirates of the Caribbean* knowing that it was a big success." When Nomura informed his team, "they were all really excited and in a hurry to test out the *real capture*[50]."

To obtain an optimal result, the team first spent a lot of time reviewing *The Curse of the Black Pearl*, "tons of times," according to Kando. They would watch the movie and take notes. After these viewings, they held meetings to determine how to get a similar rendering in the game. Nomura established their goal: "We have to make sure that the human characters look as similar as possible to real life, even being exact replicas." It was a titanic task. For Jack Sparrow, for

---

49. Nomura took this denial quite badly. Consequently, he won't say another word about this story and will never reveal his original choice. Several clues point to it being *Roger Rabbit*.
50. *Real capture* is the procedure used to directly model characters with "realistic" proportions. Basically, it's a plug-in.

example, the team watched certain clips over and over again, studying his unique body language. They then mimicked these movements and reworked them until they had a perfect reproduction. "When he [Johnny Depp] saw the results, he told us, 'that's brilliant.' As you can imagine, that motivated us even more."

WORKING TOGETHER

To push themselves harder, the team had a motto: <u>it was out of the question to lose to</u> *Final Fantasy XII*. "We saw their beards and their hair and we refused to create something not as good, so we pushed ourselves into top gear," says Tomohiro Hasegawa with amusement. This led to pursuing constantly higher standards. Oka, for example, no matter what, wanted the events to give the impression that they were filmed by an actual cameraman: "If you look carefully in certain places, we have a mobile camera." Nomura and his team thought about the "specific nature" of Port Royal. This setting then came into focus: it had to play off of chiaroscuro, not only in relation to the game's theme (we'll come back to this later), but also in relation to the film. In it, the darkness reveals the cursed appearance of the pirates and also makes them invincible. An excellent opportunity for game design. But then, what did they do to go from one to the other? "It was trickery. In fact, there are two models at all times: a normal one and a skeletal one. We order the light to make the skeleton disappear with a gradual fade to reveal the normal model, and vice versa for the dark areas." It was meticulous work because they had to verify everything point by point. While the designers didn't have "too much" difficulty with Port Royal, there's one—Nojima—who remembers having some. His task was not easy: he had to write a script for this world, but he was under an NDA[51]. "I would try to watch the movie discreetly at home. When my wife (a big fan of *Pirates of the Caribbean*) asked me why, I told her that I was a fan of Johnny Depp, but she immediately saw through this: 'Oh! You're going to use it in *Kingdom Hearts*!' I tried to throw her off the scent, but it was a lost cause. So, then she told me: 'If you

51. NDA: Non-disclosure agreement

really do use it, you better not screw it up.'" This amusing anecdote aside, Nojima had trouble imagining the "realism" of the situations. He couldn't see the "limits." Should it be more like *Advent Children*, like *Final Fantasy X*, or like a manga? The concept remained blurry, "and so, it was far from easy." However, this was just about the least of his worries given the headaches he had with other subjects. "The worst was still Halloween Town. The movie is a musical with singing that gives its universe a unique atmosphere. Successfully recreating that without singing is a real challenge." And the surprises did not stop there. Nomura asked him to write the lyrics for the songs in Atlantica. This put enormous pressure on Nojima: "Not to sound like a slacker, but if I write a bad line of dialog, it's just one sentence buried in a very long script. A song works differently because it's an end in itself. A song is taken simply for what it is, in its very short duration. As such, working on a song is much more difficult." It was especially difficult because he had to write the lyrics without the music, which was composed after the fact… As he puts it, "It's definitely easier when you do it the other way around." Shimomura agrees with him on this point: "When the lyrics are written first, it's always more difficult. You have to make sure that the melodies are not too simple to fit with the writing, but at the same time, they have to be easy enough to sing (in terms of rhythm). For all three[52], we had to adjust the voices of the voice talents." Ishimoto confirms: "The actress couldn't sing it. So, we had to lower everything a step. It was hell." And this part also made an impression on the animators, as Kando has described: "We really struggled to coordinate the music, voices, and animations. For each action, we needed an animation for success and for failure." But then, why add a world that came with so many problems and that was also largely not well received by the players? "Actually, we wanted a musical section since the first game," explains Masaru Oka. Nomura later confirmed this, explaining that he thought it was necessary given that songs are an essential element of Disney films.

---

52. Out of the five songs in Atlantica, Shimomura wrote three of them: the first, second, and Ursula's song. The two others are *Under the Sea* and *Part of Your World* by Alan Menken (lyrics by Howard Ashman), taken from *The Little Mermaid*, the Disney film by John Musker and Ron Clements, and simply arranged for the purposes of the game.

On top of adapting Shimomura's work[53], Ishimoto had a lot of other work to do. Since he wasn't part of the original team, he first had to set up his work environment: redo all of the patches[54], starting from scratch and making sure that the sound quality was better. With musicians in the room, I'm sure you can imagine how that went.

Ryo Inakura (sound designer) created tens of thousands of sound effects. For the cutscenes alone, there were 20 hours of sound, which is equivalent to about 10 feature-length films! He too pushed the envelope, offering two distinct sound effects (for movement in the air and impact) for each Keyblade, using anything from instruments to coins to create the impact sounds. In certain worlds, like the Timeless River, he added the sound of an old film roll to the background sound: "We copied the old cartoon [*Steamboat Willie*] by pairing actions with musical instruments. For example, a xylophone for footsteps or cymbals for shocks." For Space Paranoids, they based their work on the sounds from the movie *Tron* and tried to replicate the computer sounds from the 70s and 80s. "Generally speaking, the worlds that didn't come from cartoons were a real challenge because we tried to make the sound effects more realistic." What's more, Asako Suga reminds us that *Kingdom Hearts II* also had 120 talking characters, a number two to three times greater than in the first installment. And that too was no walk in the park: "It took us about seven months and the worst part was constantly adjusting, cutting, and re-recording gradually as the script progressed." On a side note, toward the end of development, when she asked the actors to do retakes, they sometimes had totally forgotten to record the passages. As such, Suga's organizational skills were key to making sure that the recording process wasn't a total mess.

Since we're on the subject of voice recordings, I'd like to underscore the fact that, once again, the voice talents were exceptional and unique, no matter the language. They used the same talents as those

---

53. Ishimoto is credited as "synthesizer operator." He was a musician working under Shimomura. He created the sounds that she needed.
54. An electronic sound produced by a synthesizer.

from *Kingdom Hearts*—for the most part[55]—and, of course, added new ones for the brand-new worlds, but also for the new developments in the story. The two new important roles went to—strangely—two rising television stars: Jesse McCartney (Roxas) and Brittany Snow (Naminé). It was also impossible to keep under wraps the participation of Sir Christopher Lee, who lent his voice to the enigmatic DiZ, and of Crispin Freeman (Albedo in *Xenosaga*, Rude in *Final Fantasy VII: Advent Children*, as well as Albel in *Star Ocean: Till the End of Time*) who played Setzer[56]. Organization XIII garnered big names like Robin Atkin Downes (Samanosuke in *Onimusha* and Delita in the PSP version of *Final Fantasy Tactics*), James Patrick Stuart, Kirk Thornton (Black Jack in the eponymous series) and Quinton Flynn, who played Axel and lent his voice to Reno in *Final Fantasy VII: Advent Children* (and to Raiden in *Metal Gear Solid 2*). To play the new bad guy, Xemnas, they chose veteran voice actor Paul St. Peter, who has worked on many games and Japanese series (notably, he did the voices for Joachim and Albert in *Shadow Hearts: Covenant*).

DARKNESS OF THE UNKNOWN

When you think of Xemnas, you probably remember the epic final hour of *Kingdom Hearts II* in which you come face to face with him. And it's good that you remember this, because this final battle (and its various sequences) has an amazing story behind it. Firstly, the idea was devised halfway through development. Nomura went to see his team and told them, "For the final boss, I want the player to feel like they're fighting an entire city." This request left them perplexed and it quickly became a running joke that kept the whole team laughing. After all those giggles, they started to realize that the idea was actually daring enough to present a real challenge and they decided to take it on. When they came to present their idea to Nomura, he was surprised:

55. The most noticeable absence was Billy Zane, who was replaced by Richard Epcar, an expert voice talent (Batou in *Ghost in the Shell*, Ziggy in *Xenosaga*). Why? The contract didn't meet Zane's demands and he had only signed on for one game. One of the risks when making a sequel…
56. Yes, the character from *Final Fantasy VI*—with some design changes to fit with the *KH* universe.

"I didn't think you would do it. To be honest, I just threw it out there thinking that it would be super cool." In other words, he implied that it was just a random thought. Of course, once again, this was a trick by the director, who knew exactly what his team was made of and how they would jump through hoops to please him—or better yet, to impress him. Kentarou Yasui says, "For the phases with Sora and Riku in the ship, the guy in charge of the shooting phases [Ryuji Ikeda] gave us a hand. And he did that on top of his other work until October. He taught us how to make it readable." Syuichi Satō adds, "That was the worst time for my team. We just barely finished in November" (the game came out in December). This last chunk of the game seems to have been an ordeal for everyone, particularly the art director, Takayuki Odachi, who was so far behind schedule that he had to use every minute of his free time. Takeshi Arakawa has an incredible anecdote on this very topic: "We were in the Shinkansen[57] for work, side by side, and it was lunchtime. I sat down and started chowing down. And then, I saw him [Odachi] take out his computer, fold down his tray, and start working on the design for the final boss. I thought to myself, 'Wow, this guy's not fooling around.'" Odachi explains, "That was really the toughest challenge for me and, in hindsight, it was really a very bad way of working."

Another thing about the final battle: the idea to make Riku playable came from the team itself: "It was a surprise from the team working on the final battle. I think that it was just a response to the people who wanted to play as him," says Nomura. Perhaps also to remain perfectly consistent with the direction taken by the series with *Chain of Memories*.

"For many people, *Kingdom Hearts* goes hand in hand with Hikaru Utada, so changing that was not on the table," Nomura tells us. As such, the star again did the main theme, this time called *Passion*; *Sanctuary* in the international version. While previously for the song *Hikari*, she only had "a few video clips and images," this time, Nomura made sure to provide her with a detailed explanation of the story and the characters. She started working by the end of 2003 and came up with a theme that connected the end of *Kingdom Hearts* with

57. Shinkansen: Japan's high-speed train system.

its sequel: if *Hikari* was dawn, then *Passion* was dusk. "The lyrics to *Passion* show how the past, present, and future of the characters are intertwined," she explains. That's why several verses are recorded in reverse and the song leaves you with a floating sensation. The result is a dreamlike, ethereal impression. The track was then shortened to be used in the introduction to *Kingdom Hearts*, *Side A ~ Opening*, revealing the issues faced by its character (who turns out to be Riku); a longer version with a different arrangement was also created, *Side B ~ After the Battle*, "which ties the two parts together and heals the wounds exposed in *Side A*," according to Utada. Nomura explains: "We then decided to use this version for the very last scene. For me, it marks the reunion of Sora and Riku." Nojima confirms this: "The true theme that emerges in this sequel is the rare friendship between Sora and Riku. Such a strong friendship may be common among children, but it's very rare among adults. It could even be embarrassing." The team then began creating the final scene to be set to the song, and I'm sure you've noticed: the synchronization is perfect, but also meaningful. Once again, it's one of the details that make *Kingdom Hearts* a remarkable series. Nomura explains: "In the first installment, the song starts at the exact moment when Sora lets go of Kairi's hand, but this time, they come together." With the video team (including Keiichi Kojima as editor—also for *Advent Children*—and Takashi Nozue as CG director), Nomura pondered over for how long they should show the scene. Against his team's advice, he decided to cut it down: "We left as few images as possible, just enough for people to notice them holding hands." On a side note, the editors told him that he was truly heartless, which still amuses him to this day. In any case, Nojima was very content with the everyday feel of his last piece of dialog: "We're back. — You're home." "If I had to choose something that really represents the script for *Kingdom Hearts II*, it would probably be that (...) Not a definite end, just words that we use every day." Suga remember the emotions it brought out: "This was the very last scene we made. So, we got all of the voice talents together in the same studio. It was very moving." That's another side of *Kingdom Hearts*.

Just as an anecdote, the single *Passion* had a CD+DVD collector's version with a music video directed by Kiriya Kazuaki[58], showing a series of different real-life shots of Beijing, as well as using animation, which was created by Koji Morimoto[59], one of the legends of Japanese animation.

(RE)CONNECT

March 2003. The Japanese website *Quiter* (now dead and gone) revealed in an article that *Kingdom Hearts II* was being developed for PlayStation 2. The source was "anonymous and reliable," according to the website, because the information supposedly came from "someone inside Square Japan." No more details than that. In hindsight, it's possible that the source in question was Hisashi Suzuki, ex-president of Square, canned in 2002. It would be no surprise. After his (brutal) firing, he was quite vocal about the direction taken by his former company and sharply criticized, on multiple occasions, the merger between Square and Enix, going so far as to call it a "real failure." In any case, the rumor did not go unnoticed and probably accelerated the chain of events that followed.

April 1, 2003, in Tokyo. Square merged with Enix. On this occasion, the president of the new entity, Yoichi Wada, announced that *Final Fantasy*, *Dragon Quest*, and… drum roll… *Kingdom Hearts* would be the company's three pillars. With just one game that was less than a year old, *Kingdom Hearts* was promoted to the same rank as two video-game superstars (in their twelfth and eighth installments respectively, almost 20 years old at the time), hinting at a series in the making with everything that comes with that in terms of tie-in merchandise,

---

58. Kiriya Kazuaki was also the director for *Casshern*. He began his career directing music videos for none other than Hikaru Utada. After two years of working with her, they got married. This was a scandal in Japan because at the time she was only 19 and he was 15 years older than her.
59. Koji Morimoto was the director for the segment *Magnetic Rose* in the anthology film *Memories*. An animation expert, he has worked with various big names throughout his career, including Takao Saitō (*Golgo 13*), Katsuhiro Otomo (*Neo Tokyo*, *Robot Carnival*, *Akira*) and Hayao Miyazaki (*Majo no takkyuubin – Kiki's Delivery Service*). He is the founder of the legendary Studio 4 °C.

spin-offs, etc. Wada quickly confirmed this, announcing production of a sequel to the first game.

September 26, 2003, at the Tokyo Games Show. It was a big day for Nomura as he announced, one after the other, *Final Fantasy VII: Advent Children* (at that time only 10 percent complete) and not one, but two *Kingdom Hearts* games: the sequel for PlayStation 2 and *Chain of Memories* for GBA. He made quite a splash, especially because he did not come empty-handed. A trailer that was three minutes and 38 seconds long introduced *Kingdom Hearts II*, relying entirely on a few cutscenes, without voices or sound effects, and accompanied by an orchestral version of *Hikari*, the main theme for *Kingdom Hearts*. The tone was similar to that of the secret video *[deep dive]*. The new game appeared to be a true sequel because everything shown was brand-new, or almost, starting with the background of a never-before-seen town with four characters at the top of a tower, a new type of enemy that moved around in a strange way, and the presence of several "unknowns" (confirming that the unknown boss in *Final Mix* was indeed a teaser). The most surprising part was the reveal of a new hero with two Keyblades, facing off against a black-clad man with wild red hair. And the leader of the group? Another enigmatic character dressed in red, also masked. Lots of mysteries that got the rumor mill churning and almost made people forget about the return of Sora with a new get-up, as well as the appearance of Mickey Mouse who figured at the very end of the trailer, a clear nod to *[deep dive]*. The video ended with the phrase "work in progress," which was frustrating but fair: the game was only two months into development at that point in time. Nomura remained silent about everything in the video, as is his habit, leaving it up to the viewers' imaginations. The crowd simply learned that this sequel would take place one year after *Kingdom Hearts*. In regards to the GBA game, the audience only received information and photos. *Chain of Memories* was to begin immediately after the end of *Kingdom Hearts* and would take place in a new setting: Castle Oblivion. The images revealed that the game would be in 2D and that the new combat system would rely on playing cards. Both games were presented with official illustrations providing enough clues to give rise to all sorts of theories.

October 2003. Square Enix launched the official website for *Chain of Memories* (more than a year before its release).

December 20, 2003, Tokyo. There was a big surprise at the Jump Festa expo: a playable demo for *Chain of Memories,* allowing visitors to get familiar with the (very special) combat system. They also got to see the CGI introduction. It was a stunning performance.

April 2004. After months of silence and just a few weeks before E3, the Japanese media learned that Auron (from *Final Fantasy X*) would be part of the *Final Fantasy* cast to appear in *Kingdom Hearts II*; Hercules and the Beast would also return. Finally, the public learned that the unknown character with red hair was named Axel.

May 15, 2004, Los Angeles. During an E3 expo that went down in history[60], Square Enix offered just the bare minimum with an alternative version of the trailer shown at TGS (again accompanied by the orchestral version of *Hikari*). However, it did reveal more about *Kingdom Hearts II*, particularly regarding the return of certain Disney characters that players encountered in the first game, as well as the presence of a few new ones. What's more, this was the first time that the public got to see phases of the game, notably with Auron, as well as the massive battle with a thousand Heartless. The trailer ended with a bang, using images from *[deep dive],* creating a link between the secret video from *Final Mix* and the new game.

For *Chain of Memories,* the first trailer was revealed (accompanied by *Simple and Clean,* the international version of Utada's *Hikari*). Though the trailer was quite short, it hinted that this installment for GBA would be centered on Sora's memories.

Late August 2004. A few weeks before TGS, Square Enix announced the release date for *Chain of Memories*: November 11 of that year. The

---

60. During its press conference, Nintendo revealed, one after the other, the Nintendo DS and the incredible reveal trailer for *The Legend of Zelda: Twilight Princess,* resulting in the greatest standing ovation of all time (until the announcement of *Final Fantasy VII Remake*). It still gives people chills. Square Enix also left its mark on the expo with *Final Fantasy VII Technical Demo* and reignited rumors that there would be a remake of *Final Fantasy VII* for PlayStation 3.

American media also had the chance to form an opinion about the American version of the game, which was already in preparation, but not yet ready for play. That was all the information offered.

Early September 2004. Nintendo put out a press release to announce a console called the GBA SP[61], accompanied by the release of *Kingdom Hearts: Chain of Memories*.

September 24, 2004, Tokyo Games Show. Square Enix held a press conference on the opening day of the expo. After a brief introduction to the benefits of online games (and to *Final Fantasy XI*), Wada presented a trailer for *Kingdom Hearts II*. The audience could see how the project was moving forward, with improved visuals and new reveals: the return of Aladdin and the world of Agrabah, as well as confirmation on the Kingdom of Hades, the Beast's castle, and a world based on *Mulan*. In the same press conference, the audience learned about Sora's new get-up capable of changing color when he changes "form." However, there was still no release date. *Kingdom Hearts: Chain of Memories* also received a new trailer with much more detail, but still with plenty of mysteries (Riku and Mickey going to meet the enigmatic masked character dressed in red) to keep the theorists busy.

October 2004. To stay relevant through the end of the year (and not miss Christmas), Square Enix redoubled its efforts with an English translation of *Chain of Memories* for the American media and the surprise announcement of its December release date.

November 11, 2004. *Kingdom Hearts: Chain of Memories* was released in Japan with both regular and collector's editions (the latter bundled with the Game Boy Advance SP Deep Silver and a carrying strap).

December 7, 2004, less than a month later, the game hit the shelves in America in the regular edition only. Media around the world hailed

---

61. The Game Boy Advance SPecial was a new model of the GBA. It was different in that it was foldable, helping protect the screen, save battery life, and take up less space. The new format would become a standard for Nintendo.

it as one of the best games ever seen on a portable console and simply one of the top games released in late 2004. Square Enix then used Jump Festa 2005 to promote its new baby by having it available to play at the company's booth, along with a new video for *Kingdom Hearts II* revealing much more, even though it was still just another version of the reveal trailer. Still, the video showed audiences the Wisdom Form, one of Sora's new outfit transformations; the return of Kairi, who was indeed the girl seen in the first trailer; new bosses; and a short sequence with the new Gummi ship. This trailer stoked players' impatience, but the phrase "Coming in 2005" offered some reassurance.

May 2, 2005. *Kingdom Hearts II* received its official website, hinting at the game's release before the end of the year. A few days later, Nomura gave an interview to the magazine *Dorimaga* in which he said that "contrary to what it may seem, *Kingdom Hearts II* was never pushed back. It was simply announced too soon[62]." He also revealed that the game would come out in winter 2005.

May 6, 2005. *Kingdom Hearts: Chain of Memories* was released in its European version.

May 18, 2005, Los Angeles. *Kingdom Hearts II* was one of the stars of the Square Enix booth at E3, notably with a playable demo focusing on two phases: one with Hades and Auron facing off and the other with a swarm of flying enemies in the Land of Dragons. Players discovered the Reaction Commands in a short video shared with the media.

Another video shown during a private session revealed much more, particularly the presence of Jack Sparrow and of a world based on *Pirates of the Caribbean.*

July 21, 2005, Tokyo, PlayStation Meeting. *Kingdom Hearts II* made another appearance in the form of a very powerful trailer about 30 seconds long. It was a compilation of images previously shown. Notably, the video was accompanied by *Another Side* and ended with a battle between Sora and a man in black taking place in the city shown in *[deep*

---

62. Nomura's worst enemy throughout his career: bad timing.

dive]. A few days later, Square Enix confirmed the return of Hikaru Utada for the theme song, *Passion*. However, the theme would be in two separate tracks: the first used for the introduction and the second for the ending. At the same time, promotion of the game began in *Famitsu* with the usual reveals of new characters, including Will Turner and Captain Barbossa. A month later, the magazine focused on the special characteristics of Sora's new outfits linked to a system called Fusion enabling different transformations, with direct consequences for gameplay. The magazine particularly zoomed in on the Wisdom Form, which offered a more fluid way of moving and attacking replaced by shooting from a distance.

September 16, 2005, Tokyo Games Show. Square Enix showed a trailer two and an half minutes long set to *Another Side* that focused on the story (particularly the Nobodies, the new name for the Unknowns). It revealed several new features, including the Timeless River world, the return of Squall and Cloud (now dressed the same way as in *Advent Children*), and the fact that the battle against the thousand Heartless was a playable sequence. This trailer also zoomed in on the Valor and Wisdom Forms, as well as the Reaction Commands. Importantly, the video had voices (but not sound effects) and ended with a definitive release date: December 22.

On October 23, a press release revealed that, in addition to the regular edition of *Kingdom Hearts II*, a set called *Kingdom Hearts Deluxe Limited Edition Package* would be released on the same day. As the name suggested, it included the "trilogy" of *Kingdom Hearts*, *Chain of Memories*, and *Kingdom Hearts II*, as well as a superb illustration created by Tetsuya Nomura himself.

On November 11, 2005, Square Enix launched its American website for *Kingdom Hearts II*, thus confirming the game's release outside of Japan. Of course, this was no surprise, but at the time, any confirmation was considered precious.

December 22, 2005. *Kingdom Hearts II* arrived in stores in Japan in both its regular edition and its collector's edition, *Trinity Master Pieces*

(the new name for the *Deluxe Limited Edition Package*). The only disappointment in the collector's edition was the *Ultimate Hits*[63] version of *Kingdom Hearts*, whereas players rightly expected *Final Mix*.

The game was an instant success (performing better than the first): in just three days, Square Enix had to distribute[64] a million units to meet demand and sold 737,391 copies; this immediately vaulted it to the ninth best selling game of 2005. It passed the threshold of a million within less than a week. For comparison, it was first in its category and sold close to double the number of copies compared to its "direct competitors" released within two weeks either side of it: *Tales of the Abyss* (440,000 copies sold) and *Rogue Galaxy* (around 300,000); it was also way ahead of *Romancing SaGa: Minstrel Song* (which had actually come out in April). I won't even mention *Grandia III* (released in August).

On February 8, 2006, Square Enix unveiled the cast for the English version. Most of the actors came back for their same roles and the press release highlighted the involvement of Christopher Lee (DiZ), Jesse McCartney (Roxas), and Brittany Snow (Naminé), as well as Rachael Leigh Cook and Mena Suvari, who lent their voices to Tifa and Aerith, respectively. Also, the US release date was confirmed: March 28, 2006. Two days before the official US release, Nomura (who attended the launch night party with a crowd of stars who had lent their voices to his characters) declared that "*Kingdom Hearts II* has no difference with the Japanese version besides a few restrictions because of the ESRB[65]."

He was being diplomatic because in the Western version *Kingdom Hearts II* was censored, pure and simple. A few examples:

---

63. In Japan, when a Square Enix game sells over a million copies, it enters the Ultimate Hits collection: games sold at a lower price and in packaging marred by the collection's name. It's equivalent to Microsoft's Platinum Hits.
64. One of the biggest errors made by journalists (or players, but that's not as serious) is confusing *sold* with *shipped*. For obvious sales reasons, the companies, in their press releases, promote the biggest numbers. You should always be wary and check if the number is indeed units sold or just the number put on the shelves (shipped).
65. ESRB or Entertainment Software Rating Board: the body that evaluates the average age required to play a given video game. It's the American equivalent of Europe's PEGI (Pan European Game Information) and Japan's CERO (Computer Entertainment Rating Organization).

— The Hydra's green blood in the Japanese version (taken from the Disney film) was replaced by black smoke in our version.

— When he sacrificed himself, the body of [BEEP] (no spoilers) was consumed by flames—but not for us.

— A sequence in the Disney Castle showed Daisy and Donald squabbling. Daisy pounds on Donald's back with her fists. Removed.

— An attack by Xigbar was completely changed[66].

— The worst was Port Royal. Besides the muskets being replaced by crossbows, there were two really ridiculous changes: when Jack Sparrow[67] is stabbed by Barbossa and when Will threatens to kill himself[68].

A disgrace. However, Square Enix was seriously worried about the idea of making a *Final Mix*, so the director tried to be reassuring. He already had a clear idea of where things would go from there…

March 28, 2006. *Kingdom Hearts II* was released in the United States and was once again met with success. Within three days, it sold 614,000 copies. A week later, Square Enix announced that it had distributed 2.5 million copies in Japan and the United States (1.2 million and 1.3 million respectively, to be exact). Within four weeks, it sold a million copies in the United States alone, a much faster pace than for *Kingdom Hearts*.

September 29, 2006. *Kingdom Hearts II* finally arrived in Europe, distributed by Ubisoft. Before the end of the year, 700,000 copies were distributed; eventually, just over 500,000 were sold. Once again, France and Germany led the way.

By the end of 2006, *Kingdom Hearts II* reached a total of around 1.2 million copies sold in Japan, a number much greater than for the first game. However, less than three weeks later, sales fell (only 200,000

66. In the Japanese version, Xigbar combines his two weapons to create a sniper rifle. When he targets Sora, realistic crosshairs follow the hero. In the adapted version, there's no sniper rifle and the crosshairs are replaced by purple spheres.
67. In the Japanese version, when Jack is stabbed by Barbossa, the sword stays in his body, just as in the film. Not in the Western version of *Kingdom Hearts II*.
68. In the original version, Will threatens to kill himself with a pistol, just as in the film. Not in the Western version, which makes the scene totally inconsistent—and dumb.

copies sold in 2006). It's undeniable that the series was not as strong as *Final Fantasy* (which always sells at least 2 million, or at least that was true at the time), not to mention *Dragon Quest*, whose eighth installment *(Sora to Umi Daichi to Norowareshi Himegimi*, or *Journey of the Cursed King)*—brace yourself, this will leave you dizzy—sold over 3.5 million copies in Japan alone, representing 70 percent of global revenues!

In the United States, the game held its own, but did not pass the symbolic threshold of 2 million units sold. Nonetheless, it was an unprecedented success and the fourth-best-selling game of the year behind *Madden NFL '07*, *New Super Mario Bros.*, and *Gears of War* (just 100,000 units behind); it even beat *Final Fantasy XII* by 400,000 copies. In the end, *Kingdom Hearts II* sold around 4.5 million copies worldwide. This performance was not as strong as for the first game, but there's a good reason for that. The game industry was going through major disruption at the time of its release: the next generation of consoles, launched starting in November 2005 with the Xbox 360, followed a year later by PlayStation 3 and the Wii (which both came out at almost the same time in Japan). In other words, all sales were skewed, especially for the older generation. The PlayStation 2 games took a serious hit: *Final Fantasy XII* sold less than 6 million copies, 2 million less than *Final Fantasy X* and barely a few hundred thousand more than *Final Fantasy X-2*, even though it was a "true" canonical chapter, highly anticipated for a long time—like the Messiah. In any case, we shouldn't be too hard on *Kingdom Hearts II*, which was still one of the best selling RPGs of its time and finished in a solid sixth place for sales in the PlayStation 2 era, behind *Final Fantasy X*, *Kingdom Hearts*, *Final Fantasy XII*, *Final Fantasy X-2*, and *Dragon Quest VIII*. Today, it is still the favorite installment of Japanese players[69].

And where does *Chain of Memories* fall in all of this? It achieved a dazzling score of 400,000 sales in Japan, 900,000 in the United States, and 200,000 in Europe; however, we again need to put these numbers into context because the Nintendo DS came out just 10 days after the Japanese release (on November 21, 2004). There you go. However, across its entire run, the little cartridge ended up with almost 2 million sales, the seventeenth best selling game for GBA. It was the only game

---

69. According to a survey conducted for the fifteenth anniversary of the series, *Kingdom Hearts II Final Mix* was the favorite installment of Japanese players; until *Kingdom Hearts III*?

from a third-party publisher (besides *Finding Nemo*) to climb so high in the rankings. To really help you size up this success, I'll remind you that the top three games were all *Pokémon* games (the best selling being *Ruby/Sapphire* with over 16 million units sold), the fourth was *Mario Kart: Mario Kart: Super Circuit* (around 6 million), and the first *Legend of Zelda* (*A Link to the Past & Four Swords*) only came in thirteenth place, with just a little over 2 million. This says a lot about the performance of *Chain of Memories*.

THE LEGEND OF
KINGDOM HEARTS

VOLUME 1: CREATION
Genesis of Hearts

CHAPTER IV — THE RULE OF (THE) THREES PART 1

A NEW HOPE

Let's backtrack a little bit. In spring 2002, Yoichi Yoshimoto, director of *Brave Fencer Musashi*, discovered *Kingdom Hearts*, which immediately inspired him to do a sequel to his game in full 3D. A samurai-style *Kingdom Hearts*. For scheduling reasons, Square did not immediately follow up on this idea and kept it on the back burner until September 2003. After finishing work on *Hanjuku Eiyuu Tai 3D* and while waiting to start on the first Nintendo DS game from Square Enix (*Egg Monster Hero*), Mr. *Parasite Eve*, Takashi Tokita, had a few months free and was thus the ideal candidate to get things going for *Musashi II*. Yoshimoto formed his team and, naturally, asked Nomura to design the characters. Nomura was very busy with *Final Fantasy VII: Advent Children*, *Kingdom Hearts II*, and *Chain of Memories*, but nevertheless agreed. However, as he does whenever he's overworked, Nomura only designed the main characters and delegated the rest of the work to a number of "his" artists (Takuya Iwasaki, Tomoyuki Sato, and Daigo Tsukada). As they too were busy with other projects, they were joined by a recent defector from Capcom, Gen Kobayashi[1]. *Musashi II* is interesting because it appears to be Square's first game to try to ride the wave of success from *Kingdom Hearts*. This is a very legitimate impression because it was probably through contact with the first *Musashi* (and also *Parasite Eve*) that Nomura developed, or honed, his very action-oriented vision of RPGs. It may be that without these games, *KH* would have looked quite different. Who knows.

1. After doing modeling for Capcom (on *Biohazard Zero*, among others), he found a guru in Nomura while working on *Musashi II* and joined "his" artists, collaborating on *Subarashiki Kono Sekai*, for which he served as a right-hand man, on *Kingdom Hearts: Birth by Sleep*, and on *Final Fantasy Explorers*, alongside his *sensei* and Toshiyuki Itahana, one of the other giants of character design at Square Enix (from *Final Fantasy IX* to *NieR: Automata*).

What's more, it was indeed with *Musashi II* that Nomura changed his style to make it more fluid and modern, moving toward "more manga" imagery. While he maintained his personal touch, his way of drawing did evolve and this influenced all of his work thereafter. This first applies to his projects in 2004, including *Dirge of Cerberus*, the third piece in *Compilation of Final Fantasy VII*. Nomura and the Osaka team got along very well. They had the same direct way of speaking, the same deadpan sense of humor, and they liked spending time together. They got along so well that one day, Nomura told them, "If, one day, I do a *gaiden* (in other words, a spin-off) for *KH*, I'll pass it over to you." He just threw this idea out there, probably under the influence of alcohol, and yet…

In 2004, when *Chain of Memories* was almost ready for release, the team started to show signs of fatigue: indeed, certain team members had been immersed in the wonderful world of Disney for over four years. They watched cartoons over and over, corrected their work according to the guidelines for each universe, and pushed themselves to get the best rendering possible. They had breakfast with Mickey, lunch with Donald, and dinner with Goofy. And yet, the joy was still there. Their tenacity too: "They don't want to stop, even when we reach the end [of development], they keep going all the way through." Although he admired this, Nomura had enough experience to know that he would have to do something, and fast, if he wanted to keep them around and help them grow. This was particularly the case for his esteemed animation director, Tatsuya Kando. When interviewed at the end of development of *Chain of Memories*, he said, "I overwhelmed myself with Disney. I'm a bit saturated. I'd like to work on something more edgy."

TWISTER

In spite of the indifferent attitude of his animation director, Nomura didn't take umbrage with him; instead, he waited for the right moment to respond to his weariness. While debriefing *Chain of Memories* with Jupiter, the two teams thanked each other for always giving support without losing sight of their high expectations, even though development

was often challenging. Indeed, they had developed a sense of mutual respect. Hatao Ogata: "Square Enix's quality policy relies on their high standards for the smallest details. It's a bit of a shock at the beginning, but it's actually a very good thing. It proves that they want to make the best game possible." On the Square Enix side, Hasegawa, heaped praise on the contractor: "They succeeded in getting the game to fit into a 256 Mb cartridge!" Everyone involved left the meeting exhausted, but happy with their fruitful collaboration. Naturally, they wanted to work together again. Nomura intervened and proposed that Kando launch his own project and work with Jupiter, as well as his friends in Tokyo... on condition that the project not interfere with development of *Kingdom Hearts II*. Basically, Nomura offered him a golden opportunity. Kando immediately asked his friend Hasegawa to participate. Neither of them had any project management experience and they spent several days sketching ideas without any real method to their work. As they were struggling, they asked for help from Arakawa, who had barely any more experience than they did, but who at least had already managed schedules and, in particular, was more "structured." The three of them spent several weeks brainstorming what they could possibly do. Finally, during an event in November 2004, they got their idea. To be precise, it was during a showroom event for the Nintendo DS, held a few weeks before its release (on December 2, 2004, in Japan). Arakawa checked out the DS with the demo of *Yoshi Touch & Go* and he couldn't put it down. Right there and then, he declared, "It's awesome. You control below, it responds above." That reverberated in his mind. What would a *Chain of Memories 2* look like on this fantastic console? In fact, the DS was tailor-made for it: the player could manage their deck of cards on the lower screen and follow the action on the upper screen. He shared this idea with Kando and Hasegawa, who said that they felt the need to free themselves from the license, even if only out of respect for their boss and to embrace the liberty that he offered them on a platter. However, it wasn't easy to come up with a setting. So, they decided to start by focusing on the mechanics and quickly finalized a first draft that they submitted in late 2004. Nomura then said to them, "If you're not [really] using both screens, why not make it for PSP?" It was a fair question. Sony's PlayStation Portable had just come out in Japan (on December 12, 2004) and offered not only a bigger screen and greater technical abilities, but also a game interface that they were already very familiar with. However, the trio couldn't let go of the Nintendo DS. They had fallen in love with it and wanted to make "another unprecedented game." With his right-hand men being so determined, Nomura caved and started trying to come up with an idea that "would have to be made for this console." A few minutes later, he told them, "If you really want to make a game for the Nintendo DS, fine, but in that case, you have to use both screens. So use dual-screen battling!" Use what? Did they properly understand this bomb that their boss had just dropped? Kando couldn't believe it: "It's the kind of idea that no one can think of just like that, instinctively, or if you do, you immediately discard it because when you think about it for a couple of seconds, you realize that it's impossible to do." Indeed, no one. Except Nomura, that is. He had just proposed, in all seriousness, that they break the brand-new DS by making the first game in history to have battles on two screens at the same time. And, of course, they did it. They knew that they had something unique. They were just afraid that someone would steal their idea. Arakawa explains: "We kept it secret [implying between Nomura and the three of them] for almost two years" (until a few weeks before TGS 2006, when the game was shown off for the first time). So, starting in January 2005, they got down to work, particularly on the game's universe. Looking at Square Enix's back catalog, they realized that no game used a contemporary setting. Since the closest games were *Parasite Eve* and *Front Mission*, they had a lot of room to propose a game that would be "modern, of our time." Initially, they wanted to depict the entire world (as it was in the early 2000s) by creating a sort of megalopolis with a number of neighborhoods, each with its own landmark: the Tokyo Tower, the Sphinx, etc. They soon realized that this was a pipe dream and they had to come back to reality: they had a tight budget (it was just an experiment without a series license to back it up) and time constraints; let's not forget, they were working simultaneously on *Kingdom Hearts II*. Given the confidence that his *sensei* had in him, Kando refused to give up on his project and sought out a pragmatic solution... only to find that it was right in front of him the whole time. Yamanote[2]. He suggested to his colleagues that

2. Yamanote is the name of the circular train line that goes around the center of Tokyo and serves the city's main neighborhoods, including Shinjuku, Shibuya, Marunouchi, Ueno, and Akihabara.

they just use the different neighborhoods connected by their train line! But, this was still too much. After consideration, they chose to focus solely on the neighborhood of Shibuya: "It's a melting pot. So, we figured that we would create our world entirely there." I'll remind you that the Square Enix offices are in Shinjuku, just 10 minutes from Shibuya, making it easy to travel back and forth as needed during breaks... and thus not neglecting *Kingdom Hearts II*.

Their "location scouting" was conducted mainly in the evenings and on weekends. "We would even go on the roofs of buildings without permission to take photos," they say with amusement. They showed their collection of images to Odachi and asked him for some help. The goal was to have him recreate Shibuya in 2D with a singular style. To achieve this, the *Kingdom Hearts* art director visited there every morning before work. The trio is still amazed: "The most incredible thing is that he did that while we were supposed to be working on *Kingdom Hearts II*." This sheds a whole new light on the Shinkansen[3] anecdote...

I'm telling you about the genesis of this other project, which was baptized as *Subarashiki Kono Sekai* not long thereafter, for several reasons. First, it was strongly influenced[4] by *Chain of Memories*, created by the same team and thus under the auspices of Nomura. Second, it served as a "laboratory" for the team to learn to work with the DS. Finally, its development began during the development of *Kingdom Hearts II* and, as you know, involved more or less the same people. As such, we can say that the two games influenced each other and it was particularly thanks to/because of *Subarashiki* that Twilight Town in *Kingdom Hearts II* has a much more modern look than in the first game (graffiti, urban logos, etc.), even being served by—wait for it—a train. As Odachi was art director for both games, it's perfectly natural that he "self-influenced."

Subarashiki Kono Sekai means "it's a wonderful world." Of course, the game has nothing to do with Disney, but the nod to the company— even if it was unintentional—is too perfect to not mention. By the way, once again, great job translators: the English title *The World Ends With You* loses the biting cynicism of the original title. Anyway, let's move

3. See page 154.
4. A system of badges somewhat reminiscent of the playing cards in *Chain of Memories*.

on. Nomura was not very invested in this project. He designed the main characters, then left the rest of the cast to Kobayashi; impressively, you'd have to be quite clever to discern who did what. Nomura just didn't have time to do much more than that. Although it suffered from no real problems, the development of *Kingdom Hearts II* was intense; also, it was occurring at the same time as the development of *Final Fantasy VII: Advent Children*, in which Nomura was heavily involved, even serving as a motion capture model for Kadaj's fighting[5].

For *Subarashiki*, he just provided general supervision, gave advice, and made sure that his team could work under good conditions. Basically, the work of a producer. And yet, he was casually learning to master the Nintendo DS. Was this in anticipation of future projects? That would make Nintendo happy: they had been harassing him for quite some time about creating a *Kingdom Hearts* for the DS... So this digression is actually essential. *The World Ends with You* is part of the *Kingdom Hearts* ecosystem. What's more, there's a good reason why, later on, a portion of the game's cast showed up in *Kingdom Hearts: Dream Drop Distance* <u>instead</u> of the usual transfers from *Final Fantasy*. This is even a very strong sign, but we'll come back to that later. Working together on multiple projects inevitably leads to new ideas... that are sometimes unexpected. For example, this was the case with a fighting mode in *Kingdom Hearts II*. Nomura started with a simple idea: he wanted to recreate the energy of the battle between Cloud and Sephiroth (a crucial scene in *Advent Children*). He soon realized that it would be absurd to see Donald, Goofy, or Mickey throwing punches. So, he decided to abandon the idea. When asked in early 2006 about a potential sequel, after the release of *Kingdom Hearts II*, Nomura was clear: "We dedicated all of these years to *Kingdom Hearts*; now we're going to take a break and work on something else" (he was referring to *Final Fantasy versus XIII* without mentioning its name, of course). This statement was—purposely—deceiving because it did not mean that he was going to put *Kingdom Hearts* on pause. Quite the opposite...

---

5. The main antagonist in *Final Fantasy VII: Advent Children*, going up against Cloud for the entire film, leading up to the ultimate duel, in which Nomura played him via motion capture.

◂ [INTERLUDE: B/CC – BEFORE CRISIS CORE]

In 2005, with the *Before Crisis* "series" already off to a good start in Japan, Square Enix had the American market well in mind, even announcing the game's release there (during E3). However, before long, the project foundered because Western phones were far behind their Japanese counterparts. Keiji Fujita[6] explains: "*Before Crisis* is a network-based game. Only the latest-generation Japanese phones have the features needed for the game to work. There is no chance of porting it for American phones because they're not powerful enough." Yep, it sounds dumb, but this was well before the advent of smart-phones, which didn't come until two years later with the release of the iPhone (in June 2007).

Since the phone market wasn't ready, Kitase considered a port for PSP. He decided to talk over this idea with the game's original initiator. As always with Nomura, the project broadened its scope. Since they were going to port it to a real gaming platform, he figured they should revise the game's systems and make it into something more dynamic (namely, an A-RPG). Still, the script was originally planned to precisely replicate the conflict between Avalanche and the Turks. Since it was essentially a remake, Nomura named it *Before Crisis Core*. At the same time, he was in the middle of production of *Advent Children* and super-vising visuals for the short film *The Last Order*, which told the story of the Nibelheim incident "as seen by Zack." This gave him the idea to shine a spotlight on the unsung hero of *Final Fantasy VII*, especially because his backstory had been quietly hiding in Nojima's files since 1997. The project then turned in a new direction and became a full-on game dedicated to Zack. Renamed *Crisis Core* to round out the *Compilation of Final Fantasy VII* (*AC*, *BC*, *CC*, and *DC* for *Advent Children*, *Before Crisis*, *Crisis Core*, and *Dirge of Cerberus*), it most importantly served as a link between the chapters of the *Compilation*. Originally planned as a remake of *Before Crisis*, the core team in charge was pretty much the same. They had Tabata as director, Naora as art director, and

---

6. A Taito employee who joined Square Enix when his company was acquired in 2004. After three years of loyal service, he was transferred to the United States to work in the mobile department, specifically on Taito products.

Ishimoto in charge of music. Nojima used his notes from the phone game to write the script, while Nomura did character design on top of his duties as creative producer. Hideki Imaizumi[7] served as producer.

Crisis Core: Final Fantasy VII came out in Japan on September 13, 2007, for PSP. It was the tenth best-selling game for the console, with 3.18 million copies sold, about the same success as *God of War: Chains of Olympus*.

FOUR ANECDOTES:

— The reveal trailer at E3 2005 only used images from *The Last Order*.

— The "Digital Mind Wave" system, a sort of slot machine that appears randomly on the screen to grant bonuses, was inspired by pachinko. It was an idea that Nomura and Kitase came up with together. The purpose was to underscore the theme of the game (fate, an uncontrollable aspect that influences battles).

— For the theme song to *Dirge of Cerberus*, Nomura suggested they contact Gackt Kamui, a former singer from the group Malice Mizer, of which Nomura is a fan. Nomura proposed that they offer Gackt a role to thank him for his participation. Contrary to what you may think, the importance of Genesis (the character) was absolutely not one of Nomura's whims; it was a decision from producer Hideki Imaizumi, who simply wanted a link between *CC* and *DC*. Seeing Gackt fully invested in the creation of his character (his physical appearance, voice, personality, attitude, and even his clothing), Imaizumi was moved and made him into one of the main characters.

— Nomura was very involved in the final scene. He even designed the storyboard himself and insisted (i.e. was a royal pain in the ass) on every detail, including the presence of blood to drive home the tragedy and brutality of the scene. This decision created some debate because Kitase disagreed. We know how that turned out.

---

7. He joined Square in 1999, where he immediately took on the role of production manager for *Legend of Mana*. After that, he became associate producer for *Final Fantasy X*, and then for *X–2*. *Crisis Core* was the only game he was significantly involved with, notably signing Gackt. Just FYI, he is credited in the "special thanks" section for every *Kingdom Hearts* (except *Re: coded*, for which he was project manager).

SUNSET HORIZONS

Nomura had absolutely no intention of abandoning *Kingdom Hearts*. He even had an idea for what would come next, or rather before: the childhood of Sora and Riku. From that starting point, he came up with a new chapter in the series. Contrary to his usual method, he first worked on the plot, then thought about the mechanics. He "saw" two scenes in particular: an unknown designates Riku as the inheritor of the Keyblade and a female character meets Sora and Riku while they're still just young boys. Nomura wanted so badly to see these two scenes become reality that he started to get some ideas down on paper. This was the starting point for *Episode 0*. The only problem was that, at that time (early 2005), he had zero time to dedicate to this project. His team was working hard on *Kingdom Hearts II* and his future was already laid out for him (the US and European versions of *KH2*, then *Final Fantasy versus XIII*). In other words, they wouldn't be able to come back to *Kingdom Hearts* for at least five years. Already at that time, he knew that his *Episode 0* would be based on the worlds of the three princesses (from the past). He had wanted to do something of this sort since the beginning of the series. However, once again, he had to resign himself to seeing his dream put on the back burner because of a lack of available personnel.

June 2005. The release of *Musashi II* was imminent[8]. Yoichi Yoshimoto finally eased back a bit on work and, during a night out, asked Nomura, "Why don't we do something together?" Nomura then thought about his project in standby mode. He realized that this experienced, well put-together, skilled group who he got along well with was available. Could this be the B team he'd been searching for? Had fate struck again? He answered Yoshimoto: "What would you say to a *Kingdom Hearts*? As Yoshimoto tells it, "We had a hard time believing it because we're all fans here. We said yes right away."

However, nothing is ever simple for the loyal subjects of Kingdom Hearts. They had to prove themselves worthy. To get up to speed,

8. *Musashiden II: Blade Master* first came out in the United States in March 2005 under the name *Musashi: Samurai Legend*, then on July 7 of the same year in Japan.

Osaka got a beta version of *Kingdom Hearts II* and started "training" on it before producing a technical demo for PlayStation 2. However, that wasn't enough. It's one thing to boast, "we're the best, you won't regret it," you still have to prove it. Yoshimoto passed the hot potato to a planner who had experience from working on *Vagrant Story* and who had distinguished himself while working on *Musashi II*, a certain Tai Yasue[9]. His mission: create something just as good from a technical standpoint as the very experienced Tokyo team. After weeks of work, they showed their demo to Nomura. It involved Sora, Donald, and Goofy and, technically speaking, was similar to *Kingdom Hearts II*. They rose to the occasion. Now, it was time for Nomura to tell them more about *Episode 0*. The story was to take place ten years before the first installment. It would involve a new cast with a new trio of heroes. Lastly, the game was to be for PSP. It was a surprising choice, but one that made sense. Just before E3 2005, Sony and Microsoft unveiled their newest generation of consoles: PlayStation 3 and Xbox 360. As such, in September 2005, all eyes were looking toward the future. In this context, it was problematic to plan a new installment for the aging PlayStation 2, especially because, at that time, *Kingdom Hearts II* had still not yet been released. So, what about the new generation of consoles? The Japanese were, as always, stunned by the new hardware. If that wasn't enough, the new consoles were hell to program for. As a tell-tale sign of this, Square Enix, which had become the top Japanese third-party publisher, had no launch titles for the Xbox 360. Worse yet, they didn't produce a single game for the console until two years later with *Infinite Undiscovery*, a game created by tri-Ace (so, not even an in-house product). Also, it's no accident that Gotanda[10] and his team were regularly called upon to help out during this generation of consoles, even for *Final Fantasy XIII*.

The big-name studios had run out of steam and any of the smaller ones who could produce some decent 3D graphics were propelled

9. The key player on the B team, who went on to become a valuable right-hand-man for Nomura on the *Kingdom Hearts* series. Tai Yasue joined Square just after finishing his studies. He came in as a planner and proposed backgrounds for *Vagrant Story*, then for *Musashi II*. Yoshimoto took notice of him and offered him the chance of a lifetime.
10. Yoshiharu Gotanda is the creator of the *Tales of* series, but he had his baby taken away by Namco. To "get revenge," he founded tri-Ace and created, among others, *Star Ocean* and *Valkyrie Profile*.

to the forefront of the industry, with tri-Ace first and foremost, but also Level-5, PlatinumGames, CyberConnect2, and FromSoftware. In hindsight, they were overvalued, but at the time, they were the only ones who were using the technology (more or less) properly. That just goes to show how bad everyone else was. I'm not going to lie: over the next decade (starting in 2006), the Japanese went through a terrible dry spell. Their survival was completely tied to their ability to adapt. Being pragmatic, most of them bet on the rapidly expanding smartphone market while continuing to honor portable consoles. There are two reasons for this: the games for these devices were cheaper to produce and made use of technical skills that they'd already mastered. As such, the most reasonable option for a game of *Kingdom Hearts* caliber was to produce it for a portable console. Nomura immediately opted for the PSP for two reasons brimming with logic: "It was the only way to make sure that controls and graphics would be similar to the first two games." OK, but why not for the DS then? Nintendo had been openly pursuing Nomura for months asking for an installment for the DS; however, making a DS game would require revamping the controls and designing the game differently. He was waiting to come up with the right concept. After a false start with the PlayStation 2, the Osaka team started R&D[11] for PSP in late September 2005.

The twin game, *Crisis Core*, whose development had begun a few weeks earlier, was floundering due to a heap of technical difficulties and initial ambitions—over a hundred hours of gameplay—that were out of step with the actual capabilities offered by the PSP. Nomura presented Osaka's work to them: "This is what we can do with a PSP." While he was being a smartass, he had only just started writing *Episode 0* and was himself floundering a bit… At least, that's what he let his B team believe. In reality, he already had a roadmap and, as always, very clear ideas for certain scenes. There was one in particular: a pivotal scene, in every sense of the word. It was so key that he decided to turn it into a <u>secret ending</u> for *Kingdom Hearts II*. This time, it was meant to be a teaser: "I wasn't sure about doing anything at all [with *Another Side, Another Story*]. I just had a fairly vague idea. In this case, I know exactly where it's headed." As such, each shot was perfectly planned out.

11. Research and development.

Three characters in armor are in a Keyblade cemetery, the only marker of a terrible battle. Around them, a desert landscape stretches as far as the eye can see. Then, in front of them, a mysterious and menacing silhouette emerges from a sandstorm and moves toward them. Entitled *The Gathering*, this video is as enigmatic as can possibly be. Every effort was made to leave the player troubled and surprised. Once again. None of the protagonists are identifiable, the location is totally new, and the tone—melancholy—is unique. *Kingdom Hearts* had transformed itself again. As in *[deep dive]*, the video used Ansem's reports and a series of fairly explicit keywords (Master of Keyblade, The lost two, Memory of Xehanort, Chasers, Keyblade War), which ends with the very puzzling phrase: *"It all began with… birth by sleep."* This was all it took to get people wildly speculating and it again proved the fans' powers of observation, their obsession with details, and their emotional investment. A number of harebrained theories sprouted up, even referring to *Dragon Ball Z* and suggesting that the three characters were like Super Saiyans, coming from a faraway land to find their master and begin the destruction of the world. It's true that the video's style was reminiscent of certain OAVs. The most common theory was that it was not an announcement for *Kingdom Hearts III*, but rather for a potential episode zero, telling the origin story of Xehanort. At this point, the saga took on a scope that no one had ever expected (because they couldn't have): *Kingdom Hearts* was much more than the adventures of Sora. However, the excitement was tempered by the total lack of communication from Nomura who, once again, chose to keep his secrets and say as little as possible about the video. There were enough hints to spark imagination, but not enough for understanding. What did he really have in mind? When asked before the end of development of *Kingdom Hearts II*, the team in charge of the video admitted that they were in the same boat as everyone else: "Totally in the dark. We don't know who is who or who does what, but whatever, we're used to it," said Takeshi Nozue. Nojima said that he had no idea what it was even talking about. Hasegawa went further: "When I asked him [Nomura] what the armor should look like, he answered: 'Not made of iron, more like crystal, but we absolutely must not see their faces.'" And for good reason: at that time, they did not exist, even if doubts remain.

The Gathering left the team speechless. Shimomura explains: "For *Sunset Horizons* [the new song that accompanied the video], the only directive that he gave me was to make it a memorable melody. Besides that, he gave me carte blanche." Masaru Oka concludes: "I suppose that if we were to redo a *Kingdom Hearts*, we would need a scene to explain all that[12]." An interesting detail is that Oka said this in January 2006. That suggests that the Kingdom Team itself had absolutely no idea where things were going. The boss was inscrutable. Yet, they could have suspected what was up because toward the end of development of *Kingdom Hearts II*, Nomura had them add a very meaningful bit of dialog. Just before the fight between Sora and Xigbar, the latter tells Sora: "You don't look like you're half the hero the others were," implying the existence of other heroes <u>before</u> Sora. This was a serious hint about the next game: the time period in which it would take place, as well as the bigger role that would be played by the character Braig.

Kingdom Hearts II was released on December 22, 2005, in Japan. Then, it was time for localization. While they didn't plan on adding any content, a few weeks later, Nomura decided that there were not enough links with the next episode(s). So, the solution was to make a *Final Mix* version, but that was absolutely not on Square Enix's agenda. The director would not admit defeat. He made a big counteroffer to win them over: a port of *Chain of Memories* as a bonus feature. After all, the GBA game was a segue in the larger story and not everyone owned the portable Nintendo system. He hit the nail on the head with his proposal. However, there was an issue that needed to be resolved: how could they do all this work at the same time? That's where Nomura decided to play his trump card: Osaka. He asked them to halt development of *Episode 0*, which was no longer a priority, so that they could concentrate on the appropriately named *Re: Chain of Memories*. Two birds with one stone: he got the thumbs-up to assuage his pathological perfectionism and could put his new team to the test working on a remake. And he did not pull any punches, imposing on

---

12. And yet, everything is fairly explicit. The setting, the heroes (who seem to be following different paths and converge on this key location), and their common enemy. The words that pop up on the screen establish the background and even reveal the future title, *Birth by Sleep*.

them many requirements, including that they had to finish the game in a year! It was January 2006 and the small team (of about 40 people) began preparing to take on this enormous challenge. Yoshimoto began recruiting reinforcements, including an artist from France (an important detail for future events). Nomura immediately set a plan in motion to find the best way to "translate" *Chain of Memories* for PlayStation 2. The initial idea was to do a simple "HD port," with the game remaining in 2D. During preliminary discussions, this idea was abandoned as they preferred to do a true remake in 3D. In that case, Nomura wanted to revise the structure of the levels and use the *Kingdom Hearts* camera. After several tests, Osaka told him that would be impossible within such a short time frame. So, they decided to keep the "rooms," but also added more interactions with objects. Aware of the magnitude of the task, Nomura reshuffled his deck and brought the Kingdom Team on-board to supervise and handle directing according to the standards required for the series[13]. Thus, the Osaka team was left to handle "only the game part" of the project; along the way, they learned what it meant to work on this series. Yasue remembers, "We regularly had video conferences with each of the managers (…) That's when we realized the differences in procedures between Tokyo and Osaka and the higher standards imposed." There was no time to play around. *Re: Chain of Memories* came with a very steep learning curve. It was a symbolic passing of the baton aiming to ensure the best future possible for *Kingdom Hearts* while limiting the involvement of the original team as much as possible. And for good reason: *Final Fantasy versus XIII* was turning out to be more and more ambitious[14] as its release date drew closer and thus it required the most experienced developers.

13. With a voice-over and real scene production. In the case of *Re: Chain of Memories*, only the transitional scenes received this treatment. The dialog in the worlds was quite basic and displayed as speech bubbles.
14. While no concrete work had started, Nomura was building the game's universe and talking with Nojima about the story, characters, and script. And their ideas, all combined together, quickly added up to something huge.

Somnus

At the very end of 2005, knowing that they were being sidelined[15], the youngest members of Nomura's team came to him asking if they could work on another RPG, hoping that he would do them the honor of serving as director. Nomura thought to himself that maybe it was time to push them out of their comfort zone: "From a creative point of view, they're excellent, but I want them to grow, to become responsible, and to understand why it's important to know how to manage a team." So, he decided to purposely take a step back. That being said, there was no way he was going to abandon them: "I want to see them succeed." Like a coach, he tried to come up with a project that would be neither too ambitious nor not ambitious enough, "immediately ruling out an RPG" because, from experience, he knew that this was the most difficult genre to work on and thus the easiest way to screw things up. Then, he remembered throwing out the brawl mode for *Kingdom Hearts II* because it would have been ridiculous to see the Disney characters fighting. He was suddenly struck with inspiration: replace them with *Final Fantasy*[16] characters. He did some tests with the struggle tournament in Twilight Town and was pleasantly surprised with the results. Before long, this idea was joined by an older idea that had never become reality: a 3D action game with the heroes from each installment of *Final Fantasy*, following their systems and facing off against their antagonists. In other words, he had a whole roster[17] of characters ready.

The twentieth anniversary of *Final Fantasy* was approaching. The project, named *Dissidia Final Fantasy*, ticked all the boxes for an anniversary game. It was also a golden opportunity to put the group of young staffers to the test: creating a spin-off from this flagship series was a great privilege, but also a big responsibility. Once the project started taking shape, Kitase and Imaizumi were added to the team,

---

15. The young staffers may have been creative, but the *versus XIII* team was composed entirely of veterans who had been in the trenches for *Final Fantasy VII* and *VIII*. At least, this was the case at first. So, they had to keep them busy.
16. Let's not forget that a number of years earlier, Nomura was on the team for *Ehrgeiz* (see page 40).
17. A term from the world of sports; in e-sports, in the context of fighting games, it refers to the list of playable characters.

if for no other reason than to make sure that the original works were respected. In addition to designing all of the characters, not without difficulty[18], Nomura again took on the role of creative producer. However, he kept his word and remained in the background. He entrusted the key creative position to the young team members[19] and made sure they were supported by his lieutenants, first and foremost Takeshi Arakawa, the most fitting person to be director.

January 2006. The Kingdom Team was busy working on the American version of the second game, while the young staffers (and the planners) were making plans for *Dissidia*. Kando and Hasegawa continued to focus on *Subarashiki Kono Sekai* and Arakawa split his time between all three. Osaka, as you already know, got the order to focus on *Re: Chain of Memories*. During this time, Square Enix was a flurry of activity. The E3 bogeyman was approaching, and with it the unveiling of the *Fabula Nova Crystallis* project, which marked Square Enix's disastrous debut for PlayStation 3. While *Agito XIII*, still in the beginning stages of development, didn't need to be presented (after all, it was just a mobile game), *Final Fantasy XIII* and *versus XIII* needed to show what Square Enix was made of, so as to make up for being late coming to the grown-ups' table, and to stick it to everyone. As such, the company's top brass asked the projects' lead creators, Toriyama and Nomura, to develop a reveal trailer. The only problem was that both projects were still in their infancy[20]. Toriyama had a clear idea of

18. Nomura was not very comfortable with the idea of proposing his own vision of Amano's work, a feeling he had previously admitted in regards to Vivi in *Kingdom Hearts II*. On a side note, certain choices sparked debate, notably Vaan from *Final Fantasy XII*. Some team members preferred Balthier instead, but for "canonical" reasons they went with the youngster. This may be why the "Han Solo" of *XII* was added to the PSP version of *Final Fantasy Tactics*. While Lightning was initially included, she was pulled from the cast to avoid pulling the rug out from under *Final Fantasy XIII*. It would have been absurd for players to encounter her for the first time in a spin-off game instead of the game where she's the heroine.
19. Mitsunori Takahashi (lead battle designer for *Kingdom Hearts II*) and Yosuke Shiokawa (lead world designer for *Kingdom Hearts II*) became the leaders of the young staffers and directed battles and graphics, respectively. Writing was handled by Harunori Sakemi who, along with Sachie Hirano, represented the new generation of scriptwriters at Square Enix, under the supervision of veterans Daisuke Watanabe and Motomu Toriyama.
20. Originally, *Final Fantasy XIII* was planned for release in 2006 for PlayStation 2. However, *Final Fantasy XII* was two years behind schedule (it was planned for 2004, but didn't come out until March 2006, and not until February 2007 in Europe). In the meantime, Sony released its PS3 development kit in late 2004/early 2005. While waiting, Toriyama's team instead worked on a technical demo for *Final Fantasy VII*... and then there was no turning back. Work done on *Final Fantasy XIII* for PS2 was thrown out (besides the script and the universe) and development started over from square one. There you go.

how battles would occur, so he decided to give audiences a taste while making them think that they were seeing the actual game. The illusion was a success. However, once his intentions were revealed, he could no longer backtrack and absolutely had to deliver the same level of quality in the game. To do this, he needed a very flexible engine. This may seem like a trivial detail, but it would have huge consequences...

Final Fantasy versus XIII was even less advanced in its development. Although he was obsessed with his future game, Nomura was caught off guard by the trailer request. As he later admitted with unease, he was forced to make his trailer haphazardly. And he hates that. When he received the order, he had not yet finalized the design of his protagonist and still only had a somewhat vague concept of the game itself. He just knew that it would be like *Kingdom Hearts*, but darker. He "saw" one scene in particular: a modern-day prince, dressed in black, descends the stairs of his palace and uses a series of phantasmagorical swords to single-handedly fight an army, in the rain. Classic Nomura. We'll never know whether or not this is true, but it's said that this scene appeared to him in a dream years before. And it was that dream, in particular, that supposedly gave him the idea for *versus XIII*. Was this just great storytelling? One detail suggests that's not the case. The title for his next *Kingdom Hearts* was *Birth by Sleep*[21]. So, of course, that could be just a huge coincidence, but we know Nomura well enough to see that combining references is part of his creative process and that he loves codes and other symbols. The fact is that the title *Birth by Sleep* could be connected—subconsciously or not—to the game that had been haunting him for almost a year: *versus XIII*. In any case, let's get back to the facts.

At E3, the trailers for *Final Fantasy XIII* and *versus XIII* were — naturally—very well received. Nomura's trailer even almost stole the show from the canonical game. By clearly positioning the game as an alternative, which thus would not be subject to the series' strict specifications, Nomura could let his creativity run wild and finally realize the dream he'd harbored for years: to make a playable *Advent Children*.

---

21. In Volume II, I'll go back to explain each title because, indeed, they do have meaning, some even have double meanings. Each title will have its own dedicated section of explanation because, indeed, they have meaning, even double meanings. Each and every one.

Inevitably, *XIII*, in spite of the brilliant song *Defiers of Fate* by Masashi Hamauzu[22] and the reveal of the magnificent Lightning, almost paled in comparison because it was more "classic." However, Square Enix's victory was short-lived and their troubles were just getting started: the reveal was followed by a decade-long breakdown in communication, with terrible consequences for human resources, as well as, above all, for the company's image. We'll come back to this later.

❖ [INTERLUDE: ACC]

Summer 2006. After a fairly rough start for the Blu-ray format, all systems were go; the only console with a reader for the new disks, the PlayStation 3, made a great impression at E3. That was all Square Enix needed to start developing a Blu-ray version of *Final Fantasy VII: Advent Children*. In other words, a new technology showcase. The timing was good: Visual Works had finished its work on *Final Fantasy XII* and had already made good progress on *Crisis Core: Final Fantasy VII*. Basically, they were (more or less) available. Since the movie had to be entirely remastered, Nomura took that opportunity to propose a <u>true</u> director's cut: almost 25 additional minutes, around a hundred modified shots and several brand-new bonus features, including a short film based on Nojima's book *On the Way to a Smile*, entitled *Episode: Denzel*. This version was named *Advent Children Complete*. Symbolically, that says it all.

With the PAL version of *Kingdom Hearts II* set for release in late September, Nomura started development of the *Final Mix* version, which he approached in the same way as the first: additional narrative and playable scenes and a few gameplay surprises, intended to make it the ultimate version of his game. However, this time, he left it up to his team: "I wasn't even aware of several changes." Of course, he forgot

---

22. Masashi Hamauzu is one of Square Enix's star composers. He started his career at Square working on *Front Mission* and *Tobal No. 1*, for which, notably, he collaborated with Junya Nakano and Kenji Ito. He was then asked to replace Ito on *SaGa Frontier 2*, after which he worked on *Final Fantasy X* and then, naturally, *Final Fantasy XIII*, but not before serving on *Unlimited SaGa* and *Musashi II*.

to mention that the most important additions came from him: the Limit form, based on the Sora from the first *KH*; the Mushroom XIII[23] side-quest; and the famous battle against Roxas, probably one of the best (in every way) in video game history, in the form of a cinematic in the original version. According to legend, it was the absence of this playable battle that made Nomura push so hard for *Kingdom Hearts II Final Mix*. It was also (above all) an opportunity to connect it to the future of the series, particularly the story of Roxas (*358/2 Days*), but also the origin story (*Birth by Sleep*), with the famous scene where Xemnas pays a visit to "his friend," one of the (motionless) suits of armor from *The Gathering*, and the dialog between Zexion and Xigbar that brings up two mysterious rooms, one of which is supposedly in Castle Oblivion (the setting for the events of *Chain of Memories*). Best of all, he added a secret boss and a new secret ending modeled off of *Kingdom Hearts Final Mix*, i.e. linked to the next chapter in the story. The difference was, this time, the video was a direct sequel to *The Gathering*, entitled *Birth by Sleep*. In it, we find out what happens to the armored trio and the silhouette in an intense battle, in which a fifth person joins—also a brand-new character. A notable fact: with the exception of the still-mysterious new arrival, players got to see the faces of all of the characters. It was not just a teaser, but rather a scene, about three minutes long, from the future game, which wouldn't be released for another three years. It was a huge spoiler, even though at that time things were still not written in stone: "We didn't really know what we could include in a PSP game, nor how long it would be. We didn't know if the scene would be at the end or at the beginning or if we would even manage to fit it in." Time has shown that they did, but using the game's engine.

[WARNING: Since the beginning of this book, the goal has been clear: allow you to experience the development and the creative process from a daily perspective, making you feel like you were actually there. Up until now, things have been fairly simple. Take a deep breath because

---

23. A group of Heartless with a very peculiar design, scattered across each of the worlds. The way to vanquish them is unique. Already having appeared in the first game, they are now dressed in black cloaks to show their affiliation with Organization XIII, even if they're not actually part of it. It's just in reference.

they're about to get complicated. We will now look at the creation of three games almost at the same time, for three different consoles, handled by three different teams. As such, I will use new identifying codes. At the beginning of each section, I will indicate which game it will cover. This will make things easier to follow and, I hope, will make it more interesting.]

WELCOME TO WONDERLAND
[CODED: CONCEPT]

Summer 2006. Nomura was busy working on his first phone game, *Monotone*. It was an unpretentious, but quite original little RPG where the player had to restore sounds and colors to the world. A Kodak-inspired game with battles in the form of puzzles. It was a testing ground for a potential *Kingdom Hearts* mobile game, and that concept took shape a few weeks later. "It all started with Nomura who, one night, came to us[24] to talk about a concept for a mobile game, using a chalkboard and his phone," says Hajime Tabata (co-director). Jun Kato (lead planner) adds, "He told us that he wanted to make a sort of virtual amusement park." At that point in time, Nomura just had an idea and wanted to see what his colleagues thought. Nothing more, nothing less. Tabata listened attentively to the proposal and loved it. He was even the one to suggest that it be a *Kingdom Hearts*: "He proposed that we make it a Disneyland," says Nomura. This simple conversation evolved into an impromptu work meeting. By the end of the night, many things had been decided: the basic concept was to build a platform for *Kingdom Hearts* fans with different activities, the main one being a new chapter of the story that would interact with the other activities. They were already planning to have a wide variety of situations "like side-scrolling and inward-scrolling[25]. The idea was to play off of nostalgia," says Kato.

It was the very beginning of 2007 and Nomura was like a caged lion. He was waiting impatiently to start *versus XIII*. And when Nomura

---

24. The mobile department of Square Enix.
25. Unlike side-scrolling games where the camera follows a character from left to right, the scrolling goes toward the "interior."

gets bored, his mind starts to wander. As he was in mobile mode at that time, he started coming up with a new game with Aya Brea (*Parasite Eve*) as the heroine. His initial idea was to make a TPS[26] in an episodic format: "Like an American TV series that relies on cliffhangers. I was pondering if we could do the same thing with a game." Given the setting and the fantasy/horror nature of the series, *Parasite Eve* was the ideal guinea pig. Nomura then created a threat—the Twisted, a race of monsters that were both hostile and intelligent—and the way to fight them, the Overdrive. It was a wild idea where Aya would be an astral body capable of inhabiting any other body and, in so doing, taking on the body's special characteristics (e.g. stats, gear, weapons). A brilliant idea. He decided to bring it up with Square Enix and the concept soon became the project *The 3rd Birthday*. Because of his packed schedule, Nomura handed off directing to Tabata, because "he trusts him and they work well together," and for the music he chose Shimomura. Because of his previous experience with a TPS (*Dirge of Cerberus*), Kitase produced the game and even lent his talents to level design. Finally, writing was entrusted to Motomu Toriyama. While the origins of this project are interesting, I won't go further into the details. That's not the subject of this book. However, it was necessary to touch on this game because, as I'm sure you can guess, there was once again cross-influencing occurring between the games.

February 2007. The release date for *Kingdom Hearts II Final Mix + * was approaching; the A team (Tokyo) and B team (Osaka) were once again available. While the B team was supposed to pick up development of *Episode 0* where they'd left off, the A team was to start development on *Final Fantasy versus XIII*. But (because there's always a but), Crystal Tools, the special engine for the two flagship components of the *Fabula Nova Crystallis* project, was not ready. In fact, it was way behind schedule and had put *Final Fantasy XIII* in a difficult situation. Considered to be a <u>post</u>-*Final Fantasy XIII* spin-off, *versus* was not a priority and thus would have to wait. This was a setback for Nomura, who could already imagine the consequences: a team whose morale would dwindle over the weeks, or even months. On other words, he had to give his team something as soon as possible

26. TPS: *Third-person shooter*. An action game with an "over-the-shoulder" camera. This is opposed to the FPS, *first-person shooter*.

or else he would see them reassigned elsewhere. While he was a free agent and didn't belong to any department of Square Enix, the others were regular old employees. As such, the publisher had all the power over them and could take away his Kingdom Team at any moment. Naturally, he hated that idea. Perhaps it was time to give in to Nintendo's harassment, he thought.

CRITICAL DRIVE
[358/2 DAYS: CONCEPT]

This DS game had been in his thoughts for quite a while. The idea took root between 2005 and 2006 during development of *Subarashiki Kono Sekai* to alleviate a frustration. The team in charge, led by Kando, set the goal for themselves of taking advantage of all of the possibilities offered by the Nintendo DS. As such, they used the dual screens and the touchscreen capabilities like no one before them, but the concept of the game itself did not allow for the incorporation of a multi-player mode. They felt like they had fallen short. That's when Nomura got the idea to base his DS *Kingdom Hearts* on this untapped feature. He decided to make it a collaborative multi-player game. Given his packed schedule, he decided to keep the concept at the back of his mind and develop it gradually over time, by talking it over with his team. In late 2006, when he saw the first prototype for *Dissidia Final Fantasy*, he got the idea to adapt the concept to the members of Organization XIII. Let's not forget that *Dissidia* originally came from the versus mode that was rejected for *Kingdom Hearts II*. So, why come back to it? "These guys [Organization XIII] are connected to Disney, but they belong first and foremost to the *Kingdom Hearts* universe. We figured that it would be accepted more easily. And then their weapons and attributes also make it possible to make them distinctive and thus incorporate them into a multi-player concept." On other words, he had 13 unique characters. The only problem was he didn't want a *second* fighting game. So, he decided to make a "true" multi-player *Kingdom Hearts*.

Days came from a persistent request from Nintendo and *Coded* was in response to one of Disney's needs. So, don't be surprised by their, shall we say, unusual treatment in the compilations *I.5* and *II.5*...

In early spring 2007, Nomura gathered his team to explain his plan. Hasegawa tells the story: "He told us we were going to make three *KH* at the same time[27]. One for **PSP**, another for **DS**, and the other for phones. He already had the general concept [for each]." He then gave them, for the very first time, the plan for *Birth by Sleep* (although it still appeared under the code name *Episode 0*): "When I showed them what I was preparing for Osaka, they all told me they absolutely wanted to work on it." In spite of the difficulties surrounding *versus XIII*, they showed proof of their support and, above all, their affection for *Kingdom Hearts*. Nomura is still moved by their reaction to this day. One of his most treasured memories.

THE PROMISED BEGINNING
[*BIRTH BY SLEEP*: PRE-PROD]

In 10 years of existence, Square Enix's Product Team 5 (Osaka) hadn't changed much, if at all. For the needs of *Musashi II* and then *Re: Chain of Memories*, they had done (a little) recruiting, but almost all of the studio was made up of former Konami employees who had followed their boss, Yoichi Yoshimoto. In all, they had fewer than 50 people. This was too few for a game of this magnitude, which would require at least double that number; and then, they also had to be capable of "handling" the client. I'll remind you that *Kingdom Hearts* is a Disney trademark and that everything must be approved by the studio. So, Nomura decided to maintain the same dynamic as for *Re: Chain of Memories* by having Osaka and Tokyo collaborate, as Yasue tells us: "At the very beginning [March 2007], he gave us the guidelines for the project. We handled battles and Tokyo handled the rest." When we say Tokyo, we imply not only Product Team 1 (the Kingdom Team), but also the indispensable CGI studio Visual Works and AVANT Inc., a crucial

---

27. And there was a good reason for this: Nomura wanted to unveil all three at the same time at the TGS in September.

contractor at the time working with just about everyone, from Disney to Capcom, from Konami to, obviously, Square Enix (particularly for *NieR*). This organization of work came with a number of changes in the series' staffing, particularly because some team members were already "reserved" for *Final Fantasy versus XIII* and had been assigned for several months to *Dissidia Final Fantasy*. Just waiting. This was the case for Takayuki Odachi, who gave up his position as art director to Takeshi Fujimoto, a veteran from Konami (who had worked on games including *Metal Gear 2: Snake's Revenge* and *Parodius*), and the two main programmers for the series, Hiroshi Hirata and Kentaro Yasui, who were replaced by veteran Tamotsu Goto and the young Masashi Nakamichi. Most departments had a director in each city. For example, animation was the responsibility of Munenori Shingawa in Tokyo and Koji Hamada in Osaka, both supervised by Tatsuya Kando. And the same goes for all other positions. Everything was controlled by the "board," composed of managers from the Kingdom Team (Kando, Kayano, Arakawa, Hasegawa, Endo, Tanaka, Sato, and Oka), who were in turn under Nomura. Since he couldn't manage the day-to-day work of both studios, the position of co-director was given to Tai Yasue. Careful though, the job title is deceiving. It does not in any way mean that they shared the same duties. Yasue was very important, because he was "a creative force," but no more so than the rest of the studio, and more specifically his boss, Yoshimoto. His decision-making powers for a game were limited to making sure the Osaka team's work was moving forward; his real job was, "above all, to follow Nomura's ideas to a T and implement them in the game, getting them as close as possible to what he had in mind (…) If he tells us, 'I want this,' or, 'do this like that,' we have to find solutions to make it happen." For *Birth by Sleep*, the director wanted "an elevated *Kingdom Hearts*." Which they did not understand at first. What he really meant was a straightforward adventure like *Kingdom Hearts*, with lots of interactions like *Kingdom Hearts II*, that would use and improve the systems from *Kingdom Hearts: Chain of Memories*. In other words, on paper, he had the makings of the ultimate game.

In any case, this *Episode 0* was special to Nomura and he wanted time to design and write it. It's one of the things (in addition to those

previously mentioned) that pushed him to get work started on *Re: Chain of Memories*. Three birds with one stone: he would save time, observe changes in the card system, and simultaneously assess if the B team really had what it took to live up to his standards. He had, once again, planned it all out. And that's quite fitting because it's precisely the theme of *Birth by Sleep*: "Fate is inevitable." The subtext is that the events of the series all have an explanation, contrary to what they might have led you to believe up to this point. For example, Kairi meeting Sora and Riku was not purely by chance. That being said, at that time (April 2007), the plot was still in its infancy. Indeed, Daisuke Watanabe, the co-scriptwriter, was much too busy elsewhere (*Final Fantasy XIII* and *Dissidia*). Thankfully, Nomura's plan was already complete enough to start work: he had already planned out all of the game systems. This starts with the Command Deck, in which each skill becomes a card in a deck that the player can create however they see fit. And no matter what, Nomura wanted 512. Yasue and Yoshimoto thought this was absurd: "We immediately thought that it was impossible and that he was going too far." However, the concept was well thought-out as it included all of the original commands and their potential evolutions, based on a new system, the Command Board, "a sort of board game inspired by *sugoroku* (…) where you want to play to gain power." Yoshimoto remembers, "That's how he presented it to us." His reaction was fitting for the strangeness of the request: "Hopeless. We spent a lot of time trying to understand what exactly he had in mind. We had to go back to the drawing board numerous times before we produced something right." Nomura continued to present his ideas, including the Shotlock, which says a lot about his constantly renewed desire to add shooting to his series[28]. Finally, he presented the Dimension Link (or D-Link), a system created in response to a major issue related to the console: "In *KH* and *KH II*, Donald and Goofy [and guests] fight alongside Sora. On the PSP, it was impossible to have several characters on the screen, for many reasons. So, instead of being side by side, you simply borrow their powers remotely. You're 'connected' to them." Yoshimoto doesn't hide his feelings about it:

28. Examples include the Gummi ship, the controllable robots in the world of *Toy Story* (*Kingdom Hearts III*), and the Wisdom Form in *KH II*.

"Honestly, when he explained the concept to me, I didn't get it at all." Yasue understood better, but still poorly: he imagined a connection between players, which was nothing like what his boss had in mind. We'll come back to this later.

Although their director had them motivated, they had a very hard time getting (back) to work on it. That said, they would bend over backwards to please him, and much more…

RESULTS AND REWARDS
[358/2 DAYS: PRE-PROD]

With the PSP part of the plan on track, it was time to tackle the DS game. The initial idea was to make it in 2D like *Chain of Memories* and *Subarashiki Kono Sekai*. However, an external factor turned the situation on its head. It was the mid-2000s and the gaming market was in the doldrums. Gamers were sulking because, bit by bit, they were being replaced by what is derisively referred to as the "mass market." The new trend was "serious gaming[29]," notably *Tōhoku Daigaku Mirai Kagaku Gijutsu Kyōdō Kenkyū Center Kawashima Ryūta Kyūju Kanshu — Nō o kitaeru Otona no DS Training* (simply known as *Dr. Kawashima* in many places; *Brain Age* in the US market). It was an unexpected hit that suited the Japanese game industry well, as they were suffering at that time. Everyone was content to lean on this new trend, but not Nomura, who found it incredibly wearisome. He wanted to make a video game "without beating around the bush." So, he decided to attempt an exploit: a real game; and what's more, it would be in full 3D. At least, that's what he was hoping for because, knowing nothing about the technical aspects, he had no idea whether or not it would be possible on the Nintendo DS. He needed the opinion of someone with expertise on the subject. Naturally, he first thought of Jupiter, but they had neither the skills (3D and wireless) nor the time. Instead, the solution came from Square Enix. He was told to ask h.a.n.d., based in Sapporo. This studio had already proven its skill, having just

---

29. A game with an educational or serious intention behind it. This designation quickly became an effective marketing tool.

finished the great game *Chocobo To Maho no Ehon* (*Final Fantasy Fables: Chocobo Tales*), a *Pokémon*-like game that had the merit of also offering a true multi-player mode. Koji Yamamoto (team director) explains, "They really liked our way of creating 3D for the DS. So, they asked us to think about how we could do that for a *Kingdom Hearts* (…) We couldn't believe it. When you get a chance like that in your career, you can't say no." Koji Tokuyama (graphic director) took it as a personal challenge and wanted to "prove that a *Kingdom Hearts* in 3D for the DS is possible." After weeks of work, h.a.n.d. presented a demo with Sora, Donald, and Goofy fighting a group of Heartless. "A little prototype," Tokuyama notes. It may have been little, but it was enough to convince Nomura, who immediately issued instructions: "[Mr. Nomura] explained to us his expectations (…) particularly the multi-player mode with the members of Organization XIII," explains Yamamoto. I'm sure you've noted the politeness and respect that he shows Nomura. He continued by saying, "I was also surprised to see that Organization XIII had a fourteenth member." That's classic Nomura: the character in question was conceived of more than two years before that, "while we were putting the finishing touches on *Kingdom Hearts II*," as Nomura explains. "[Dans *KH II*] Roxas leaves the Organization. We wondered why (…) it probably had something to do with a girl his age."

Yamamoto didn't have all the answers, but he got to work. After the demo got the thumbs-up, h.a.n.d. focused its attention on the reason they were hired in the first place: to figure out how many characters could be displayed simultaneously on a DS screen. Nomura took this opportunity to introduce the concept of Panels. In sum, the first steps for *KH* DS were purely technical, as is often the case in Japanese game development. Artistry was far down the list of priorities at this point. For example, in spring 2007, the script was still non-existent. In fact, Nomura was only just starting to think about it. His first order of business was to situate the game within the series' chronology, particularly because, as he always reminds people, "there is but one, that's it." As the new game was to be based on Organization XIII, he had no choice but to have the story take place between the first two installments. As *Kingdom Hearts* games are "always written by a team," he started looking for a scriptwriter who knew the series like the back of their hand. Everything pointed to Watanabe, but he was heavily involved with *Final Fantasy XIII* and co-writing *Dissidia*[30] —with Harunori Sakemi. Also, more generally, he was tasked with supervising the script for *Birth by Sleep* (not long after, in addition, he supervised the scripts for the DS and mobile games). In other words, he was swamped with work. So, Nomura had to turn elsewhere. Ultimately, the solution was to be found outside the company. Once again, Nomura's pragmatism hit a bull's-eye: he contacted Tomoko Kanemaki[31]. Since 2005, she had been adapting every *Kingdom Hearts* installment into novels. Nomura liked her work and decided that, in the end, she was the woman for the job: she wrote well, she knew the series backward and forward, and, as luck would have it, she was available because she had just finished work on the fourth and final volume of the *Kingdom Hearts II* adaptation. It was fate.

Nomura organized a meeting with Watanabe, Ishida[32], and Kanemaki, during which he laid out the setting: the DS game would end where *Kingdom Hearts II* begins; thus, they would be <u>connected</u>. For this reason, the main role was given to Roxas. He was the best choice because he was a member of the Organization, but also because "he would provide an easier entry to the series' universe for new players." It was logical. A Nintendo DS owner would not necessarily have played the previous games. At the same time, fans would not be offended because this new installment would give them a better understanding of the rest of the series. Also, how could they not get excited at the idea of playing the bad guys? That is, if we can even call them that because, as we all know, their story is more tragic than anything else.

This new angle on the series would require a new approach. Nomura explained that he wanted to depict the everyday experiences of the members of Organization XIII during the 358 days of Roxas' existence. He clarified: "The title should resonate like a countdown (...) with

---

30. The story of *Final Fantasy XIII* and its narrative concept were the work of Motomu Toriyama. That being said, the actual writing (including the dialog) was done by Daisuke Watanabe, Harunori Sakemi, and Sachie Hirano.
31. Tomoko (or Tomoco) Kanemaki is a successful novelist. She has written around 40 books. She started working for Square by adapting *Legend of Mana* into books before being asked to do the same for *Kingdom Hearts*.
32. Yukari Ishida is an events specialist. She first did events for *Kingdom Hearts II*, then for *Subarashiki Kono Sekai*. For *358/2 Days*, she again was in charge of events, while also working on the script, particularly the parts that took place in the Disney worlds.

Roxas, as the player already knows, condemned." It was an excellent opportunity to comment on how things can change dramatically, and it also happened to be a poignant story. Fleshing out his idea further, he imagined the game having a serial format: each day would have its own mission while maintaining a running plot line, "the girl who causes the split between Roxas and the Organization." Her original name was No.i[33], as Ishida tells us. Always playing around, Nomura decided to give her the same features as Kairi, only changing her hair color "to deceive players." "Could she be Kairi's Nobody? If not, then who is she? Or rather, what is she?" he adds, laughing. "I really wanted people to ask themselves these questions."

With the characters, the concept, and the big ideas set, the only thing left was to actually write the script. Kanemaki took charge of the plot and soon realized that writing a book and writing a game are two radically different beasts. It's likely because she was struggling that Nomura decided to write the entire script himself, dialog included. Which he had never done before. It was a painful experience, he says: "I don't want to do that ever again." His nature as a workaholic certainly didn't help. For two weeks, he saw no one, barely went out, and only ate canned foods. By the time he put the final touches on it, he was exhausted. Conscientious about not being a career scriptwriter, he gave the manuscript to Kanemaki and Ishida so that they could make corrections. Each had her own specialty: Kanemaki fixed the dialog while Ishida worked on improving the cohesiveness of the script overall using her experience. And she had her work cut out for her because Nomura had not slacked and had made numerous changes to the initial plan. In particular, he realized that 358 missions was a bit too much, so he significantly reduced the number, only using 150. He also introduced, after each mission, a dialog where the main characters discuss more or less existential questions over ice cream, the Disney version of coworkers going out for drinks after work. Of course, the concept went further than that: "I wanted Roxas to learn

---

33. No.i has several meanings. In English, it's read as the words "no I." A suggestion of non-existence. It is also a reference to the imaginary unit i in mathematics, an "inconceivable number" (its square is negative), as it was called in the 16th century. No.i was then renamed Xion to make people think that she was the Nobody of Kairi; "Xion" follows the Organization's naming rules, being an anagram of "No.i" with an added X, the symbol of the Organization.

something each time." So, he asked Kanemaki and Ishida to include this aspect in the script for each mission: "They're the ones who wrote those parts, I just reviewed them and asked for changes." Meanwhile, Xion became his Rorschach test[34]: each protagonist saw her differently. This was again intended to make players think: "We wanted people to be shocked when Xion's hood appears and disappears depending on the shot, or for her to change faces (…) When I finished writing the script, I asked Ishida to plan some events, because I didn't think it would be clear enough in the game."

The h.a.n.d. team finished its technical tests. A portion of the Tokyo team joined them, "ten people tops, counting supervision and sound," according to Tomohiro Hasegawa. He had just finished work on *Subarashiki Kono Sekai* and was appointed co-director for *Kingdom Hearts* DS, which had been renamed *358/2 Days*. His role was the same as Yasue's on *Birth by Sleep*: make suggestions, yes, but most importantly to make sure his boss' orders were followed. Having just arrived, he was surprised by the project's progress: "[The demo] surpassed our original expectations." However, the team was far from resting easy: "We were worried that we wouldn't be able to replicate the gradation of textures that is so characteristic of the design of *KH*." This was because of the more limited color palette of the DS. Hasegawa: "[But] when we saw the Beast's Castle, which perfectly reproduced the series' typical design, we realized that we would get results that were almost the same as those for the PS2." With that concern put to rest, Nomura was able to move on to other matters, namely the mobile game.

FORBIDDEN SECRET
[CODED: PRE-PROD]

A reminder of the facts: one night in late 2006, Nomura was discussing his desire to create a "virtual amusement park[35]" with the Square

---

34. A Rorschach test is a psychological assessment where a person must interpret asymmetrical ink blots. In their graphic novel *Watchmen*, Alan Moore and Dave Gibbons made a character called Rorschach with a mask based on this test. In a certain way, Xion was inspired by this.
35. From the very first mention of it, *Kingdom Hearts Mobile* was described as a hub for "attractions," including mini-games, downloadable bonuses, personalized avatars… and the pièce de résistance: a whole new *Kingdom Hearts* episode.

Enix mobile team, which included Hajime Tabata and Jun Kato. It would be an online portal for cell phones with a new *KH* installment as the main attraction. They left it there because the project was much too ambitious and they all had other things to worry about. Nomura revived the idea six months later, which was no accident: he found the "right device."

Code name: P–01A, the flagship of the new FOMA line[36] from NTT DoCoMo; in plain English, at that time (2007) it was the most powerful cell phone in the world. With its PEAKS processor enabling HD, its 5.1-megapixel camera, and its VIERA flippable screen, it blew the competition out of the water (including the nascent iPhone). And to top it all off, it could be connected to a TV. In other words, it was the dream platform for a *Kingdom Hearts* for cell phones. However, the device was still in production at Panasonic plants. Square Enix saw in this phone a golden opportunity to do a launch game. Better yet, with the pre-installed i-appli[37] as headliner. However, there was a problem that needed to be solved: the Prime series, headed by the P–01A, was set for release in November 2008. In other words, very soon, and the game had to be ready for that date. The Square Enix team panicked. To take that pointless pressure off, Nomura decided to use the episodic format that he's a champion of (first used with *Before Crisis*, then *The 3rd Birthday*). The model had been proven effective, it reduced the pressure on the team in charge, and, above all, it would allow them to establish their priorities. This was necessary because the announcement was already planned for the TGS just three months away. There was no time to lose: the concept had to be established as quickly as possible. Right off the bat, Nomura stressed the "casual" nature of this installment. He wanted it to be "light" and to target, first and foremost, the mass market. Sora was the natural choice to be the hero.

Nomura's old obsessions then resurfaced, particularly his first principle: "Playing a powerful character from the get-go makes no sense." To explain the "forgetting of powers," he once again used <u>memory as</u>

---

36. *Freedom of Mobile Multimedia Access*, a W-CDMA (*Wideband Code Division Multiple Access*) phone network. It was the world's first operational 3G network.
37. The name for the applications (using Java ME, for Micro Edition) on NTT DoCoMo phones.

a device[38]. After memory loss (*Chain of Memories*) and reconstruction (*KH II*), there was still another unexplored facet: saving memory. The rest came naturally: a virtual hero in a virtual world facing a virtual threat. In other words, Data-Sora in the Datascape (the digital version of the journal that tells of his past adventures) threatened by bugs[39] altering the memory of the worlds previously explored. This all led to a new approach, a brand-new game system, and, of course, a title that would anchor the concept: *coded*. And when you put things in context, this idea makes perfect sense because, I'll remind you, it was the main attraction in the virtual world of *Kingdom Hearts Mobile*. Nomura went from a "light and casual" game to creating a metaconcept that was profound on many levels[40], even becoming the new shining light of combining references[41].

With the concept of *coded* established, Nomura just had to find a co-director to see it through to successful completion. Nomura once again decided to turn to Hajime Tabata. Not only for his experience with phone games, but also, particularly, because Nomura trusted him. A fun fact: Nomura had to beg Kitase to entrust *The 3rd Birthday* to Tabata. Good thing Kitase trusted his instincts.

FIGHT AND AWAY
[*358/2 DAYS*: DEVELOPMENT]

When development was just barely beginning, h.a.n.d. encountered its old nemesis: memory, both read-only and working.

---

38. Memory is one of the main narrative devices in the series. We'll come back to this in the analytical part of the book (Volume II).
39. The Datascape in *coded* is a "buggy" version of the first *Kingdom Hearts*, whose main inspiration was, as I've said, *Super Mario 64*. In it, the bugs are represented by blocks. It all comes full circle.
40. We'll review in detail what such a decision really involves in Volume II.
41. If you think about it a few seconds, the concept of *coded* is not so different from that of *The 3rd Birthday*. In the latter, Aya is an avatar in a virtual past, generated by a computer to eradicate a virus. Incidentally, the idea of taking action in the past to prevent the future (i.e. the game's present) comes from Motomu Toriyama. And what did he write in 2010 (three years later)? *Final Fantasy XIII–2*. I'll let you mull that over.

READ-ONLY

Kingdom Hearts 358/2 Days was contained on a 256-MB ROM (read-only memory) cartridge, which was double the capacity for *Subarashiki Kono Sekai* and quadruple the capacity of the previous h.a.n.d.-made game, *Chocobo To Maho no Ehon*. It was a comfortable capacity to work with, but also a limited one given the project's ambitions. Nomura didn't want just an *omake*[42]. He would do whatever it took to get his way, including numerous cutscenes... with dubbing[43]. The capacity of a ROM cartridge is not extendable and the space would be entirely occupied by the game itself, requiring the team to adapt everything else (music, lighting, etc.). Thankfully, the Tokyo team quickly found a fantastic encoding solution that would allow them to significantly reduce the size of files while maintaining their quality. Thanks to this, the modus operandi didn't change: the scenes were made with CGI (just like for PS2), then were compressed. This explains their exceptional rendering for a DS game. The team breathed a big sigh of relief. Hasegawa recognizes that without the technicians, he would have had to lower his ambitions and include two times less video.

WORKING

The real nightmare for h.a.n.d. was the "working memory," the information (i.e. data) processed by the console in real time. Yoshikazu Hosoda, main programmer, says, "We had problems all throughout development (...) The worst was when I realized that we needed to display things on the lower screen when we were already using all of the RAM on the upper screen." This caused consternation. Being too focused on their graphic performance, h.a.n.d. had totally spaced on the whole dual screen thing. Hosoda remembers it almost with embarrassment: "We even looked for an excuse to say that it was impossible." However, he knew that in this nation of men proud as peacocks, there

---

42. *Omake*: a Japanese term meaning "bonus, extra."
43. When it came out in 2008, it had more cutscenes than any other DS game. A little over 2 hours and 20 minutes of video.

was no room for weakness, fragility, or despair. And Nomura is not the kind of person to cut corners on anything, especially not the usage of the lower screen, which was needed specially for communication with the Panel System and with the other players (via a sort of PictoChat[44]).

After struggling for some time with what to do about it, h.a.n.d. changed its approach to the game and faced the hard truth by throwing out a big portion of their prep work and reducing all of their ambitions for visuals. Not one to mince words, Kyohei Suzuki (battle planner) declared: "It's useless to have awesome graphics if the game lags and is unreadable." I'd gladly give him credit for this if he had made this point from the very beginning instead of offering it out of disillusionment. Nevertheless, h.a.n.d. had the right attitude and started searching for a workaround. At first, they focused their attention on the animation. Once again they were struck by the curse of memory, which this time was saturated by the movements of the characters and their interactions with the environments. This was another blow to the team.

❖ [INTERLUDE: *DAYS*]

I'm going to go on a little tangent here because it's necessary to understand the essence of *Days* in order to get why the development team encountered so many issues. All backgrounds, items, characters, and enemies had to be designed for both solo mode and multi-player mode. Already suffering from memory (ROM) problems, the team had to settle for making two versions of each world: a superior version, rich in details, for solo mode and an inferior version to enable action in four-player mode. It was a pragmatic choice: design each parameter to be used with four simultaneous players and too bad if overall there was a big downgrade of visuals. Nomura recognizes it himself: "Recreating the *Kingdom Hearts* world so that four players can play together on the DS was probably one of the worst pitfalls." But not the worst. I'll save that for later. In any case, these various memory problems had

---

44. Simplified communication software that allows you to both write and draw. It was incorporated into the DS family of consoles and was a precursor to the Miiverse.

a significant impact: *Days* was but a shadow of what had originally been planned. So, the team had no choice but to double down on the gameplay to limit the damage. Nomura told them to beef up the battles, adding desperate moves called "Limit Breaks." Suzuki explains: "So, we changed course (...) The new goal was to focus on the intensity of battles and recreate the sensations experienced in certain duels [from the previous games]." While the technicians in Sapporo were struggling, the Tokyo team was constructing the worlds. In response to the particular structure of the game (a hub and missions), level design became the leading factor. Each world thus served a <u>function</u>. Agrabah was built high up to enable "acrobatic" gameplay, Olympus Coliseum was centered on its arena, the Beast's Castle was made for exploration, and Neverland was totally revamped as an "open world" to allow free flying. Nomura explains that the "most open" levels were the hardest to design, for example, Twilight Town: "Creating this type of area without hurting the experience for the player is a real challenge." It's probably because designing this world was such a pain that it became his favorite in *Days*, but also because it's a "memorable place because of what happens there." On a side note, they had planned on creating a Pinocchio world with a circus setting. Nomura says, "It was a really sad part of the story where Roxas and Xion realize, while observing Pinocchio, that they have no hearts." I don't need to explain why it was thrown out. Memory and all that. After designing each of the worlds, the Kingdom Team made a list of game situations and distributed them across the 150 missions "so that the player wouldn't have to do the same thing from one level to the next," says Hiroyuki Itô, lead planner for the missions. Everything seemed to be going smoothly, but Nomura reminded his team that he really wanted players to be able to "redo missions as many times as they wanted." This was a big challenge: they had to find a way to make sure that players wouldn't get bored and to make them want to go back. That's when Yasuhiro Sato, lead planner for battles, dug up an idea that had been abandoned in pre-production: offer several challenges per mission, some of which would be impossible to complete until the player reached a certain level of mastery of game mechanics. The idea was unanimously accepted and led to the creation of the famous Holo-Missions. However, Hasegawa remained concerned about the balancing that, in his opinion, would cause issues sooner or later...

BIG RACE
[BIRTH BY SLEEP: DEVELOPMENT]

In Osaka, the team was still trying to grasp what Nomura wanted with his Command Deck, Command Board, Shotlock, and D-Link. After two months of working on these, Yasue and Yoshimoto finally came up with a solution: "We figured it would be easier to understand if we made a single system where all of the commands would interact with each other." Meanwhile, the rest of the team was tinkering away. The animators and graphic artists were watching DVDs of old Disney movies over and over to get in the spirit, taking notes and doing tests. The programmers were busy trying to master the PSP. Basically, they were deep in pre-production, a comfortable period that encourages reflection rather than action; a calm that was, nonetheless, disturbed in June by a request from the boss: he needed about 20 seconds of game for a reveal trailer that would be part of a larger presentation on the future of the series, planned for the TGS. They had three months until then and the request caused a wave of panic. At that point, they had nothing concrete, just a model of Terra and the prep work for the three starting worlds. The priority was to breathe life into these disparate pieces, starting with Terra, the main character for the future demo, but also the game's brand-new enemy, the Unversed. The team worked together to note down keywords that would best describe all of the animated elements. In the case of Terra, for example, they noted that he is powerful and that must be felt in the way he carries himself, how he walks, runs, and also how he attacks. This was then translated into a dozen variations for each movement. "We got skeletons from modelers that we modified or even reconstructed using 3D tools to make the animation easier. Then, we tried out the movements. Nothing too complicated. Where it did get much more complicated was when we tried to reflect a character's personality in, for example, their way of striking." While Terra posed no real problems, and was

in the hands of a key animator[45], the new enemy, the Unversed, was much more difficult to create.

Nomura explains: "The idea was to create a race of enemies that would no longer exist after *BBS*." He then got the idea to link them to Vanitas. Since it had been decided when the plot was written that Vanitas would be vanquished, the Unversed could disappear with him. As Vanitas was, in a certain way, an amalgam of feelings (sometimes paradoxical), Nomura decided to give meaning to his new race of enemies, even in their appearances: "The concept behind their design was based on emotions. That's why some are smiling, others have expressions of anger or sadness." Even their mark incorporates this idea: "A heart that expresses emotions." Once again, nothing was left up to chance. Koji Hamada was responsible for translating all of that into animation(s): "My first goal was to differentiate them from the Heartless and the Nobodies with their fluid movements. For the Unversed, we needed to create different mannerisms." Namely, very jerky and peculiar ones: "Big jumps, sudden stops in the middle of sequences, to the point where several times we asked ourselves, 'who would move like that?'" Hamada showed his team's work to Tetsuya Kando, the animation supervisor, and to Tai Yasue so that they could choose from among the various proposals and offer any changes or adjustments. Before submitting it all to Nomura. A problem remained: they had a lot of difficulty testing their work with a high resolution. The reason was that they were going forward without a rendering engine. When they recovered the one used by *Crisis Core* a few weeks later (in early summer), their relief was short-lived because they realized that it would take some time to get the engine to do what they wanted: *Birth by Sleep* was not *Crisis Core*. However, this gave Nomura an idea: include Zack as a guest star. That said, the reason he put forward was much simpler: "*BBS* takes place in the past of *KH*, so we had to choose a character from *Final Fantasy* who belonged to the past. This was the case for Zack in *Final Fantasy VII*. He was the ideal character. There

---

45. Each main character is produced by a key animator and one or more assistants. Hamada was just following the normal procedure for an animated film.

were other options, but since they'll appear in other games[46] that have not yet been announced...". He then had the idea to connect Zack to Olympus Coliseum: "It's true that this world is in each *Kingdom Hearts* game, but we had never shown young Hercules, even though his growth is central to the movie."

It took several months of work (to the end of 2007, actually) to completely adapt the *Crisis Core* engine to the needs of this production. In other words, the 20 seconds of gameplay shown in the trailer at the TGS came from preliminary work without any way of verifying the "final" rendering. It was a small miracle... After the TGS came two intense years of development with one mindset: make the "elevated" first *Kingdom Hearts* just like Nomura wanted. It was a challenge; no, a struggle. Against the game itself and its huge volume, "similar to a *Final Fantasy*," as its creator explains. The game was three adventures in one. A key figure that became a common denominator: three characters with varying levels of difficulty, three ways of playing and approaching a single world, and three different paths to discover all of these things. It was a task much more difficult than for *Re: Chain of Memories*, as Yasue can attest: "The rooms [in *Re: Chain of Memories*] adapted to the actions of the player. This time, the maps were three-dimensional and complex." Initially, Osaka proposed vast, semi-open settings like in *Kingdom Hearts II*, much easier to negotiate for battles. However, "Nomura told us that he wanted smaller fields with a lot of variation." Basically, he wouldn't settle for a *KH II* for PSP. Instead of letting the player get lost in an open world and losing sight of the narration, he wanted to create a lot of stuff within limited areas. Working with Tokyo, Osaka put all of their efforts into level design: heights, multiple paths, spontaneous events, the goal being to create interaction everywhere possible. Kaname Miyazaki and his team started designing the maps and held nothing back. Yoshimoto explains: "They

---

46. Nomura may be resistant in interviews, but he is calculating with everything he says or reveals. In this instance, he's teasing like, "oops, I said that, but I shouldn't have." What's more, since he is very uncomfortable with the idea of using Amano's characters in "his" games, we know it must be one of "his own characters." That just leaves Laguna Loire, a "past" character from *Final Fantasy VIII* who has not yet appeared in *KH*. Knowing that this character was incorporated into *Dissidia 012 Final Fantasy*, which came out in 2011, two years after this statement was made, we can conclude that Laguna is indeed who he was talking about. This was confirmed a few years later when Nomura revealed that he was supposed to be the "final boss" in the Mirage Arena.

started providing us with very precise plans, which allowed us to fine-tune our ideas (...) Honestly, it's thanks to them that the levels were so fun and interesting to explore." He made his own small contribution by deciding to change the position of the treasure chests—and their contents—according to the character being played. Better yet, the rewards were made to match the effort given: "We purposely placed certain chests in difficult-to-reach places and adapted the reward so that it would be worth the trouble." They had come to understand Nomura's style of video game creation: a player's freedom is measured by the gameplay possibilities offered to them. Thus, the player can experiment and choose how they want to have fun. And it didn't take long for them to discover the unexpected results of the *Kingdom Hearts* equation: the absence of limits between the fields and arenas; basically, blending together exploration and battles. For example, the QA[47] department realized that an attack (Sliding Dash), when used wisely, would allow the player to reach certain chests intended to be reached much later in the game. Yasue says of this, "Initially, we only planned for this movement to be used to get around quickly in battle. We didn't imagine it would be used like that." Nomura told them to not touch a thing: "If the player demonstrates creativity in using the game mechanics, we shouldn't deprive them of that reward." After this discovery, Osaka started to truly "see" the game as it *really* was and began to take advantage: "For a somewhat high platform, the player doesn't necessarily need the High Jump, we provided other ways to reach it."

The system was so complex that the more they checked the effects, the more they were left pulling their hair out. Yoshimoto explains: "There were so many possible combinations that we found ourselves facing a load of stuff we hadn't thought about." And they had to check everything, even (particularly) the least used commands because "that's often where something unexpected occurs." Overwhelmed by their volume of work, they decided to rely on the expertise of the QA

---

47. QA: quality assurance. A department made up of veteran testers who inspect every nook and cranny, test every game system, and try their hardest to push those game systems to their absolute limits. They then prepare reports for the development team to correct the bugs, better balance battles, etc. All too often forgotten, or even scorned, they are nonetheless absolutely crucial for the success of a game. And if the gameplay of Japanese games is so incredible, it's, generally speaking, because they benefit from the best QA testers in the world.

department. "We have [at Square Enix] a unit of testers that specialize in battles; they are crucial for verifying the balance of games," says Nomura. "I really feel like I'm abused. No matter the enemy, they always find a flaw," Yasue explains tragically before adding jokingly, "after ten tries." "So, our enemies can't be that weak," Yoshimoto thunders, a little peeved. As we know, he was largely responsible for the "elevated" side of the battles in *Birth by Sleep*, so he doesn't really appreciate people talking smack about "his" enemies, or even people doing them "too much" harm: "I recommend that players use Mega Flare in moderation," he jokes. Yasue explains that they paid particular attention to the strength of the bosses and that they worked a lot with the QA department so that the bosses would be difficult to beat, but would have weaknesses that could be exploited using certain commands. It's then up to the player to master the system. However, Nomura reminds us that the game is as challenging as the individual player makes it and, in accordance with tradition, he included a secret boss "with demonic power, similar to Todomarishi Shinen [Lingering Will, the secret boss in *Kingdom Hearts II Final Mix*]." Of course, he was referring to Vanitas no Shinen (Vanitas Remnant in English), who has left many a player with tears of frustration. He concludes: "When I was in Osaka to test him, I couldn't beat him." So, he gave the green light: "If I had succeeded in beating him, that would have meant that he wasn't strong enough. In this case, he was perfect."

BIBBIDI-BOBBIDI-BOO
[*BIRTH BY SLEEP*: DEVELOPMENT]

Now, let's take a look at the artists. For them, it all seemed too easy. They had no prep work to deliver because they had a sizable bank of data already put together for the previous games. They worked off of DVDs of cartoons, which they watched over and over again "in order to recreate, as faithfully as possible, the worlds in 3D." When certain details were missing, like for the world inspired by *Lilo and Stitch*, they asked Disney for help: "In the movie, you never see the back of the giant ship Durgon. So, we had to ask for complete views and scenarios." That works for a film from 2002... but what did they do about the

starting worlds, given that *Snow White* dates back to 1937, *Cinderella* to 1950, and *Sleeping Beauty* to 1959? Disney has vast archives, but time was not on their side. It was a shame, but most of the members of the original teams for the films were already gone, either too old or, in some cases, deceased. For the world of *Cinderella*, for example, the team had to create certain backgrounds from scratch. Takeshi Fujimoto (art director) says: "In that level, Ven is the size of a mouse and thus can travel inside walls. That doesn't exist in the movie. So, we did a lot of research on rococo[48] style to be faithful to the time period." For *Snow White* and *Sleeping Beauty*, they got a helping hand from fate… From July 15 to September 24, 2006, the National Museum of Modern Art in Tokyo hosted an exhibition entitled *The Art of Disney*, made up of no less than 550 boards, sketches, paintings, preparatory drawings, and old celluloids, half of which had been "lost" for close to 50 years.

It was an incredible story. In 1960, for the release of *Sleeping Beauty* in Japan, Walt Disney organized an exhibition to travel across the country. He personally selected 200 works from several of his films, first and foremost *Sleeping Beauty*, but also *Flowers and Trees* (1932), the first-ever winner of an Oscar for an animated short, and *The Three Little Pigs* (1933). What was his goal? To explain the animation process through the various stages of production. After a fantastic tour (that went through 17 stores across the entire country), the pieces were given to the National Museum of Modern Art in Tokyo. They were then lent to Chiba University for the purposes of anatomical research. Upon their arrival there, they were carefully stored in a janitor's closet, where they stayed until 2002! When they were rediscovered, they showed the effects of aging after 42 years in the dark. However, it was a unique treasure trove. Lella Smith, Creative Director of Disney's Animation Research Library and conservator of Disney's heritage, was interviewed by the *New York Times*, which reported: "Today animation art is prized by collectors, a top-quality Earle[49] background from 'Sleeping Beauty' might sell for $20,000 to $30,000. Given the rarity of

---

48. A European art movement from the 18th century that spread to all of the arts (architecture, painting, sculpture, etc.). It started in France and then spread to the rest of Europe. The term comes from combining the words "baroque" and "rocaille" (a French word meaning "stony ground" and also a decorative style from the same period).
49. Eyvind Earle: A Disney legend, known for his work on *Sleeping Beauty*. In particular, he designed and colored all of the backgrounds for the film.

some of the pieces, it is hard to assign a dollar value to the collection over all, because nothing comparable has been offered for sale." Ms. Smith told the newspaper, "There is no way to put a price on these works—they represent our artistic heritage." Perhaps, but nonetheless, Disney thanked Chiba University by giving them high-resolution digital copies of each of these relics, along with a million dollars to be given out as scholarships.

After years of restoration by the technicians in her department, Lella Smith sent the pieces back to Japan, accompanied by 350 additional pieces for the famous exhibition *The Art of Disney*. And of course, the two teams (Tokyo and Osaka) working on *Birth by Sleep* took in every bit of it. After several visits, they bought the exhibition catalog, a "wonderful book" with miniature versions of each work. Later, they bought the DVD version. "It was one of our most useful reference materials," says Fujimoto.

Besides the exhibition, Osaka had another ace up their sleeve: a Frenchman who, like all Westerners, grew up with Disney films—which is not the case with most Japanese for reasons previously explained. He's a bit of a shadowy figure who we should shed some light on. Mark Vigouroux is the creator and illustrator of the series *Trigs* and *Miss*, published by Les Humanoïdes Associés. He was hired by the Osaka team in 2006 for the purposes of *Re: Chain of Memories*, "probably because the legendary Mœbius[50] worked for the same publisher as me (…) It had nothing to do with my skills," he jokes. After learning the ropes on *Re:CoM*, for *Birth by Sleep*, he was tasked with modeling, designing objects, creating textures, and also assisting with UI[51] design for VFX[52], and sometimes even feedback[53]. He says, "For everyone, it was a huge workload with the difficulties that go hand in hand with major projects." That being said, "it was as fascinating as it was fun." Vigouroux turned out to be an asset for Osaka, a studio made up only of technicians; he was "their creative type." The liaison to the Tokyo team. It's funny to think about when you consider the fact that he

50. "His aura radiated well beyond France. We don't fully realize the enormous influence he had in Japan," he said off the record. This fact is supported by the many connections drawn between the works of Mœbius (a.k.a. Jean Giraud) and Hayao Miyazaki in the 2000s.
51. UI: user interface.
52. VFX: visual effects.
53. Feedback: visual signals that indicate to the player what they're doing.

was hired in spite of a language mix-up: the day of his interview, "my future boss asked me if I was interested in the world of video games. I misunderstood the question and answered 'no.' Having doubts, I looked in my dictionary and then quickly corrected myself, 'yes, yes, of course.' We laughed about it and then I was hired."

In spite of these many advantages, the art design for *Birth by Sleep* was not all sunshine and rainbows. Once again, they ran up against technical difficulties, more specifically, memory related. Fujimoto explains: "*Kingdom Hearts* is fun thanks to its dynamic action and its very rhythmic battles. It would be much less fun if the game started to lag with more than two enemies on the screen." Thanks, Captain Obvious. Since the PSP didn't have as much memory as a home console, certain adjustments (or even sacrifices) had to be made; in particular, they had to reduce the number of polygons and textures for certain background items because changing the characters was out of the question. However, as a consequence, "lowering the resolution ended up making the image blurry." To mask this, Fujimoto and his team did some improvising: "We reworked it several times and adjusted the colors and the contrast as much as we could." I'll remind you that, for six months, they had no way to check their work in high resolution. As such, it was difficult to plan out anything... They moved forward while fumbling around, reducing the number of polygons according to calculations. For that reason, in late 2007, when the rendering engine from *Crisis Core* was finally adapted to the needs of *Birth by Sleep*, the team went back over it. They could finally get a rendering and found out how they had been too hasty in cutting things out. They started reincorporating details, re-increased the number of polygons, and improved the textures. They even realized that they could create very big maps, like those in Rumble Racing.

SECRET OF NEVERLAND
[358/2 DAYS: DEVELOPMENT, CONTINUED]

For several months, Tomohiro Hasegawa (co-director) and Yasuhiro Sato (lead planner for battles) had been stressing about the Panel System envisioned by Nomura. Yet, the original goal was simple: allow any character (in any game mode) to assume the skills previously acquired. In addition, it was supposed to establish a link between the story and the multi-player mode and make it so that players wouldn't have to "develop" each character individually. The system went through numerous iterations before reaching its final form: "We totally revamped it halfway through." After examining the problem from every angle, Sato finally decided that they needed to follow one of Nomura's guiding principles: "Add gameplay as soon as possible." So, he transformed the Panel System—tied to character growth, a subject near and dear to Nomura—into a sort of *Tetris* where the player must arrange the Panels in question (which are really skills) in a backpack represented by a grid. To explain it more simply, it was an—unlikely— combination of the inventory from *Resident Evil 4* and the junction system from *Final Fantasy VIII*, allowing magic to be connected to the characters' stats. There were multiple advantages to the Panels: not only did they make managing your character and inventory more "playable" than ever, but they were also one of the key balancing elements (at least in Critical Mode). "We arranged missions that were intentionally difficult to force the player to pay attention to their Panels," says Hasegawa. Sato adds, "Like the one where you face the Antlion in Agrabah to learn how to use the Dodge Roll." Force them without forcing them. After numerous unsuccessful attempts, the player realizes that perhaps their failure is due to their poor usage of the Panels. At that point, they try something new, which will probably lead them to understand the extent of the system and how pivotal it is. All the rest stems from there, starting with the enemies. Most of them are crafty, or even quite tenacious, with a basic configuration. However, because they are susceptible to certain skills, they are actually quite easy to beat if you use the system wisely. So, if a player gets stuck, it's probably because they don't have the right skills yet. In that case, they can redo old missions (via the Holo-Missions) or even tackle challenges to experiment with new combinations. Sato has the last word on the subject: "Honestly, in Proud Mode, it is impossible to succeed without using Limit Breaks and, especially, an optimal configuration of the Panels." While the mechanics were well-designed and worked, Nomura was not content because there remained a sizable problem: the handling. "Given the limits imposed by the material specifications of

the DS, recreating the controls was really difficult," he stated. Hasegawa confirms this: "The number of buttons was a real problem." What they mean is that not having the two joysticks and two buttons (L2 and R2) of the PlayStation controller was a real thorn in their side. To deal with the issue, they had to assign different functions to the same button while keeping things clear and not allowing this to impede the fluidity required by the pacing of the game, especially in battles. It was a real puzzle. Once again, h.a.n.d. was tasked with coming up with a solution. Koji Yamamoto (team director at h.a.n.d.) confirms that it was not easy and that it took them a long time to come up with the solution because they "considered every possibility for using the buttons available," even creating several specific configurations and clever shortcuts with portability in mind so as to recreate the feeling of the previous games. Still, the team found that playing on the DS was quite complicated and they decided to focus on tutorials. Hiroyuki Itô (lead planner for missions) explains that this came, in particular, from a frustration related to *Chain of Memories*: "We all regretted the fact that the tutorial was so short. So, we decided to explain the game system in detail using the prologue." However, these training missions turned out to be fairly difficult to design, and it's little wonder why: before mission 25, Roxas can't leave Twilight Town, and you have to come up with a reason for that. Itô continues: "We thought of a lot of things, like alternative paths so that the player wouldn't get bored and stop right away." Yukari Ishida (scenario & planning director for events) says, "Given the game's structure, we made a sort of calendar so that the entire team would be on the same page. With Itô, we noted things like 'you can't reach such-and-such world before such-and-such moment in the script' or 'you can't finish this mission until after you acquire such-and-such skill.'" In addition to establishing this practical tool, she suggested that they make use of the members of Organization XIII who go to Castle Oblivion to train Roxas: "Given that they leave on the twenty-second day (and never come back), they were hardly seen in the game and I really wanted to use them in the story. So, I asked Itô to modify the prologue missions" to add this little something extra. All agreed that it was an excellent idea. Itô, in turn, added the possibility of going back to each tutorial via the Holo-Missions, in addition to a special tutorial menu that would always be accessible. He concludes, laughing, "It certainly would have been easier if he could reach the other worlds earlier." Needless to say, many more negative effects resulted from the limitations of the console. The limited memory that posed a problem for all aspects of the game inevitably meant fewer sounds. Yakuhiro Seta (sound editor) explains: "The DS doesn't have a lot of memory. Honestly, if we had wanted to use the same sounds as for the PS2, we would have used up ALL of the memory," not just the portion allocated to sounds. He laughs grudgingly: "So, we had to redo everything from scratch (…) and when I found out the number of weapons, I panicked. I immediately realized that giving variations to each one would be a hell of a challenge." Starting with Zexion who, unlike in *Chain of Memories* and *KH II FM+*, this time used his book to fight: "And you might think that a book doesn't make much noise." Ryo Inakura (sound designer) clarifies: "In the end, we created over 4,000 sounds. That's a lot for the DS, but when you compare that to the tens of thousands of sounds for *KH II*…" And there was good reason for the reduction: "If we had thrown in too many sounds, we would have had to cut back on the videos." This led to a new project for the programmers, including Tatsuya Shoji (sound programmer). "It's really thanks to his work that the quality was not too far off from the PS2," confirms Inakura. In spite of a significantly reduced number of tracks (13 in total, including eight new ones and five newly arranged), Shimomura has some painful memories of her work for *Days*, especially because of the console: "On the DS, you have to fiddle with each note, whereas if I'm doing variations on a real piano I just have to press the keys harder or use the pedals. Inevitably, the overall quality goes down and that did not please Tetsuya. So, that was very hard." This was the case for Xion's theme, in particular. Nomura told her, "You should be able to pick out Kairi's theme if you listen carefully, but I don't want it to be obvious." When she had him listen to her first version, he insisted, "I told you, 'if you listen carefully,'" thus suggesting that her composition lacked subtlety. So, she spent a lot of time trying to satisfy him, and she notes, smiling, "I couldn't even ask the people around me for their opinion because we were all under NDA[54]." *Vector to the Heavens* (the magnificent track for the final battle) was also a challenge:

---

54. Non-disclosure agreement.

"One of Tetsuya's ideas. He told me, 'I want something really intense on the piano [for the battle against the final boss].' I tried to tell him that we couldn't do that on the DS, but he wouldn't hear of it. So, it was Noda [first name Hirosato, synthesizer operator] who got stuck making it work," she laughs. But, the worst was probably adapting *Another Side*: "When he told me that he wanted to use the track for the battle against Riku, I thought about the fact that we had recorded it with real instruments. It was going to be hell to make a DS version. I found myself wondering why they always ask me to do these impossible things."

For the voices, Asako Suga explains that the actors worked hard so that people wouldn't notice the difference: "Of course, it's not the same equipment or the same studio or the same recording conditions [as for *KH II*], but you can hardly hear the difference between the two." However, she encountered an unexpected problem: "When they were making *KH II*, the voice actor for Roxas [Kôki Uchiyama] was in middle school. Now, he was in high school. So, his voice sounded different. We had him listen to his old dialog [from *KH II*] over and over again so that he could get as close as possible." Since then, Uchiyama has started a career as a voice actor: he played Neku in *Subarashiki Kono Sekai* and also the title role in the anime series *Soul Eater* (produced by Square Enix); more recently, he played Akira, the hero in *Devilman Crybaby*. He also explains that Roxas was the only character where he was really himself: "I wasn't really acting, actually, I just thought about what I would do if I were him (...) I just had to raise my voice a bit to get closer to my voice in *KH II*... without it sounding weird." Nomura, who never tires of giving his team challenges, told them to use the onomatopoeias from *Subarashiki Kono Sekai* during the dialog scenes (except for cutscenes). Suga explains: "We were halfway through development, so we had to hurry." She gave the actors keywords, like "anger" or "joy," that they had to express in a sound; in the end, each actor recorded over 30 of these. It's the same obsessive attention to detail found throughout the games, even covering the sound that the characters make when eating ice cream. Inakura says, "When it was time to record the ice cream part, I thought to myself, 'there must be a recording out there of a guy eating ice cream,' and I discovered that there was not. So, I bought a bunch of ice cream and we recorded ourselves eating it (…) What's more, it was a struggle to find enough ice cream because it was fall." They went so far as to record different sounds for each character: "We bit into it with the front teeth, then back teeth, with varying strength. For example, it was more gentle for Xion." Seta jumps in: "Yeah, and then we had to use very specific ice creams so that it would make enough noise," suggesting that there were several unsuccessful recording sessions. Inakura says, "What's more, I yelled at Seta and asked him to make more noise when he eats." The two laugh like crazy at this. Inakura concludes, "In any case, we are going to be very careful to preserve those recordings because there might be another game with people eating ice cream."

ON THE DEBUG!
[CODED: DEVELOPMENT, CONTINUATION AND CONCLUSION]

Alas, we don't know much about the development of *coded*. Because of its unique format and (probably) because it was a direct order from Disney, Nomura remained very discreet about the game. All we know is that he came up with the foundational ideas, like the "debug" phases and the plot. Most of the writing was done by Harunori Sakemi[55], with support from Yukari Ishida on the *cutscenes* and Daisuke Watanabe providing supervision.

As could be expected, Jun Kato (lead planner) got most of the work done with newly arrived planners and by relying on contractors. From there, it's not a big stretch to say that it was a "side" project handed off to a backup team, but we won't go there. Nevertheless, while it may not have been a priority, *coded* was not a second-rate production. What's more, it was one of the first games to offer such a high quality of visuals on phones thanks to its 3D engine, the MascotCapsule Eruption. Just FYI, this engine, compatible with Java and OpenGL ES, is a powerful little piece of software that has enabled, among others, the port of

---

55. He joined Square Enix in 2005, mainly writing secondary dialog for *KH II*. As part of the group of "dynamic young people," he joined the *Dissidia* team and became Watanabe's protégé. Watanabe also had him work on *Final Fantasy XIII* and *coded*.

Resident Evil 4 for the iPhone. It has also been one of the keys to the migration of Japanese gamers toward the mobile market. Eruption was created by Hi Corporation, a Japanese leader for middleware and a specialist of mobile UI and UX[56].

In 2009, the engine's creators said of it, "we do not think that either Ideaworks3D's Airplay [or] Unity Technologies' Unity are competing products," this thanks to Eruption's "flexible and highly scalable functionalities, such as bump mapping, camera animation, light animation, morphing, motion blending, particle system, shadow mapping, skeletal animation, and skinning." It also includes graphics-oriented development tools, including preview plug-ins for Autodesk 3ds Max, Maya, and Softimage, as well as New Tek's Lightwave 3D. In other words, *Kingdom Hearts coded* was bound to make a splash thanks to its built-in technology that, moreover, cut both development time and the staff required in half. Besides the work for the usual cutscenes, which required the same number of designers and animators as for a "normal" game in the series, *coded* was really just the work of a dozen people, led by Jun Kato. The portal (*Kingdom Hearts Mobile*) was entrusted to Mobile & Game Studio[57], founded in 2004 by Masanobu Endo, a former Namco legend responsible for games including *Xevious* and *Tower of Druaga*; and to SERIALGAMES, which has since become one of Square Enix's top partners[58]. Character development for the Avatar Kingdom was entrusted to Monster Octopus (real name Atsuhiro Tsuchiya), an artist who was already famous in Japan for, among other things, creating Clinoppe, a mascot for Japanese social network GREE, and who later went on to do exceptional work for the *Theatrhythm* series (which we will come back to later).

On November 19, 2008, the P01-A phone came out in Japan with the *Kingdom Hearts coded* preview episode pre-installed. This was necessary for Square Enix to be able to collect feedback before the real first episode. Less than a month later, the *Kingdom Hearts Mobile* portal was online. Also in December (on the 18th), *Dissidia Final Fantasy* was

---

56. UI and UX: user interface and user experience.
57. Now known as Game Studio, they are the developer for many Square Enix games, including the *Lord of Vermilion* series and, more recently, *Dragon Quest of the Stars* and *Figureheads*.
58. Responsible for, among other things, the network portion of *Dissidia Final Fantasy Opera Omnia* and of *Final Fantasy Legends II*.

released in Japan. However, the team had no down time because they immediately started work on a "true" Western version in collaboration with their Los Angeles and London offices. This resulted in some big modifications to the gameplay, new events, a new mode, a shortened tutorial, new attacks, etc. To make a long story short, there was a lot of new content. This Western version, which was actually a director's cut, was later released in Japan (on November 1, 2009) under the name *Dissidia Final Fantasy: Universal Tuning* with a special feature very typical of *KH*: the choice of voice talent (both English and Japanese).

CROSSING TO NEVERLAND
[*358/2 DAYS*: DEVELOPMENT, CONTINUATION AND CONCLUSION]

In early 2009, *Kingdom Hearts 358/2 Days* entered its final phase of development. At this point, the Tokyo team realized that they could no longer ramp up the number of teleconferences. So, Itô and Sato were sent to Sapporo to handle the final details. Itô recounts: "I spent two months in a Sapporo hotel located across the street from h.a.n.d." Apparently, the work was so intense that his daily routing consisted of waking up, crossing the street to go to the office, then crossing the street again at the end of the day to go back to the hotel. He explains, "I would just stop by a convenience store and I ate food bought off the shelf almost every day." And Sato? "I have a funny memory from our time in Hokkaido[59]. One day, we were on a snow-covered street. One of the planners jumped and imitated Roxas' pose in midair, yelling, 'Roxas *jump!*'... and he tore the seat of his pants. We were dying with laughter. Toward the end, when things got really tough, I would remember that moment and I would feel much better," he says, beaming. Straying from the usual pattern, Nomura did not plan a secret ending at the last minute: since *358/2 Days* was, in a certain way, the prologue to *Kingdom Hearts II*, "it would have been difficult to make a 'preview video' like we did for the previous games," says Hasegawa. "Since this time our goal was multi-player

59. Hokkaido is a prefecture, region, and island in the north of Japan. Sapporo is its capital.

fun, we decided to add hidden characters instead." These included King Mickey and Sora, chosen by the Tokyo team. On the other hand, h.a.n.d. insisted on including Donald and Goofy. Tokuyama (graphic director) explains: "Originally, there was no plan to include them, but we thought their way of moving was funny and since they're very popular, they let us incorporate them as secret characters. Koji Yamamoto (team director) says, laughing, "And Tokuyama put his foot down from the beginning of development: 'If I can't control Xion, I'm not buying the game.'" That made Nomura laugh. The director then told him that there was no need to worry because, of course, they couldn't skip over the game's key character.

Kingdom Hearts 358/2 Days came out on May 30, 2009. Less than 10 days later, owners of the new P–01A phone got to explore the first episode of *coded*. The only thing left was to finalize *Birth by Sleep* and then Nomura would have successfully completed his (triple) challenge.

ENTER THE DARKNESS
[*BIRTH BY SLEEP*: DEVELOPMENT, CONTINUATION AND CONCLUSION]

A reminder of the facts. At the very beginning of development, Nomura went to present all of the fundamental concepts of *Birth by Sleep* to his B team in Osaka. When he brought up the Dimension Link, they couldn't immediately wrap their heads around what he had in mind. Tai Yasue imagined that it was a system "linking" players together; he misunderstood. That being said, Nomura kept this idea, finding it interesting: "Allowing players to 'connect' with each other is particularly fitting because it goes perfectly with the main theme [of the series]." So, he decided to incorporate it into the "plan" in the form of a specific world: the Mirage Arena. However, since Yasue was the one responsible, he left the decisions up to him. The co-director waited to finish everything else before giving it serious thought. As usual, he had Yoshimoto assist him. When they presented the idea to the programmers, their reaction was frosty: "The wireless connection is a bad idea. You're just asking for bugs." However, Yasue was confident about his idea and decided to disregard their warning, even though he recognized that "the concern with a wireless connection is that it can get cut off, no matter what you do"; and, of course, there was no way they could let the game suffer like that. This was a big problem that required a lot of work from the programmers "right up until the very end of development." Yoshimoto and Yasue understood that, in spite of their best efforts, they would never manage to get the same visual quality in a wireless mode as with the single-player mode or on the PS2. So, they decided to compensate for this with the gameplay by "taking full advantage of the gaming possibilities offered by the PSP"; basically, by offering several types of activities. Given the amount of time left for development, they played it safe by creating multi-player modes for the Command Deck and Rumble Racing. Then, they went big by creating a versus mode allowing up to six players to face off. Finally, they added an arena mode and missions with varied goals that could be played solo or in cooperative multi-player mode. For the purposes of these feature, they slightly adapted the controls while creating group outcomes and a devastating special move whose gauge was the "link" created with the other players. In agreement with Nomura, Yasue decided that using the multi-player mode should be rewarded, as seen in the power of the players' combined forces and the famous attack resulting from that union. Clever. Especially because it was perfectly in line with the philosophy of the Dimension Link as imagined by Nomura. Killing two birds with one stone. On this subject, Nomura says, "The idea of the D-Link between Ventus and Vanitas during their final battle also came from them. I like how they managed to incorporate the system into the story. I think they did excellent work." And yet, he didn't do much to make that work any easier... If you remember, from the beginning, he gave them nearly-in-surmountable challenges, like having to include a grand total of 512 skills. Yasue hasn't forgotten this and laughs about it: "Frankly, at the time, I thought it was absolutely absurd, but then I realized that, in the end, we almost did double that! Which really surprised me." This feat was achieved without him realizing it thanks to Yoshimoto's methods. Starting in 2008, Yoshimoto made lists for all of the moves, skills, commands, attacks, etc. Essentially, he registered and sorted absolutely everything so that they could "properly distribute the skills across each [of the heroes] and verify that there was a good balance."

However, he forgot one detail: he gave code names to each of the items and the entire team worked with them for over a year; so, of course, when Nomura went and renamed ALL of the commands (in summer 2009), they all felt lost: "We didn't know what we were talking about anymore," laughs Yasue. Yoshimoto remembers, "There were so many times where we asked each other questions like, '*Snipe Burning*, does anyone know what that's supposed to be?'" This little mistake due to a lack of experience with this type of production could have cost them big time...

As always, Shimomura was put through hell. She may have only had around 40 tracks to produce (much less than for a canonical game), but Nomura was just as inflexible as usual. The director's top goal was to create a link between *Birth by Sleep* and the rest of the series via the music. This meant not only arrangements of old songs, but also new tracks "reminiscent of others." Shimomura calls this "combo music": an original melody peppered with specific phrases taken from other songs. This was especially the case with the themes for the main characters. Shimomura based them on *Fate of the Unknown*, the music from the secret ending *The Birth by Sleep* in *Kingdom Hearts II Final Mix* (and from the battle against the game's secret boss). She pulled out the must "dramatic" phrase to create Aqua's theme and the most "powerful" phrase for Terra's theme. For Ven, she proposed a totally new theme, but Nomura told her to go back to the drawing board: "He told me that he wanted 'a whole-new melody that would bring together Sora's and Roxas' themes without it being too obvious.' He could have told me that from the start," she grumbles with a smile. He also asked her to put it in context: "Mr. Tetsu's orders often seem impossible at first. So many times I've said to myself, 'Him and his damn obsessions!'" she says, laughing. However, when she sees her music in context, it all makes sense: "When I see my songs used in the game, I can see that it's really well thought-out and he knows exactly how and where to use them."

Because of her heavy workload, she got a helping hand from Tsuyoshi Sekito. He took several arrangements off her plate, including the excellent *Radiant Garden* and "lighter" tracks such as *Big Race, Hero or Heel?*

(Captain Dark's theme), and *Fresh Fruit Balls*, which bears a certain resemblance to his (extraordinary) OST for *Brave Fencer Musashi*. So, it all came full circle: a return to the series' roots... in Osaka. However, Sekito didn't stop there and wrote several tracks himself, including the excellent song *Black Powder* (the theme of the battle against Braig). And he has nothing but good things to say about Shimomura: "It's so motivating to work with her. If the opportunity presents itself again, call me." While it wasn't initially planned, Takeharu Ishimoto also lent a hand to his former boss: "Kawamori[60] [Keiji, synthesizer operator] called me and asked me to help." I'll remind you that before becoming a stand-out composer (*Crisis Core*, *Subarashiki Kono Sekai*, *Dissidia*, and later *Final Fantasy Type-0*) at Square Enix, Ishimoto learned the ropes working under Shimomura as a synthesizer operator for *Kingdom Hearts II*. So, it was only natural that his successor would call on him for help. However, Ishimoto was picky: "I told him that I would agree on condition that I would only work on the things I wanted." It should be said that he knew what he was up against, having been in this situation before: "I know that Nomura has very precise ideas about what he wants. And it's not that I don't like rules, but they are always too restrictive for my creative work." So, he took on the most "free" work, including the themes for Vanitas (*Unbreakable Chains* and *Enter the Darkness*). Being the curmudgeon that he is, it's worth noting that this time, Shimomura was not his superior. Essentially, she couldn't say a word about his work. Perhaps that's why his are the worst tracks in *BBS*? To each his own, you might say, but even he has recognized, in hindsight, that he "really missed the mark for a *Kingdom Hearts*, even though the compositions are, on their own, excellent." Goddamn Ishimoto. On a side note, he recently announced his departure from Square Enix. Good luck to him, though apparently he remains on good terms with his former employer and there is still a possibility that, like many composers before him, he will continue working with the company as a freelancer.

Around September 2009. Nomura entered the final straight and realized that the game's ending was just too dark. Between Terra being

---

60. Joining Square in the late 90s, he quickly became the lead sound programmer for *Final Fantasy* (starting with *VIII*). He was also the bass player in the musical group Black Mages.

possessed by Xehanort, Ventus' eternal coma, and Aqua disappearing into the Darkness (the original ending to his script), you might say that he laid it on a little too thick. "So, we decided to add a final episode and a bit of hope"; this meant, in particular, the scenes where Sora and Riku are talking on the beach, which "absolutely were not part of the original plan." In late October, the director commented: "I still have a ton of things to do. On my desk, I have five *Birth by Sleep* files, four *coded* files, and seven for the rest." Scripts, ideas, plans, things to correct or approve, and, of course, designs. Also, he was very aware of the fact that the packaging for *Birth by Sleep* was becoming an urgent matter. But, all in good time: he was already scheduled to be at the editing studio on October 28, 2009, to work on the credits for the end of each game. He explains: "We had a bit of experience with double [credits] from *Chain of Memories*, but it was much more complicated this time." With Nomura-style credits, the music determines the rest, not the other way around. This led to some headaches for him as he juggled three games with distinct scenes. The hardest part was, without a doubt, timing them. This was meticulous work. However, it was almost like a joke to him, noting that he really had to hurry on the videos because the editor wouldn't be available forever and because "next week, we have to work on *Final Fantasy XIII*." He counted with amusement everything that he still had to do: "We still have the promotional videos, the intro and the secret ending [*Blank Points*, to be precise], but we'll do that another day." However, he had already planned ahead by writing and creating draft storyboards for each video. In regards to the introductory video, he knew that he couldn't do the same thing that he did for *Kingdom Hearts II*. *Birth by Sleep* was the first episode in the series; chronologically, "nothing happened before." An astute observation. So, he had to devise the intro the same way that he did for *Kingdom Hearts*: "I talked with Nozue[61] about the opening movie, and we decided that we wanted the movie to show what would happen during the story."

Regarding *Blank Points*, he just followed the series' tradition. However, he notes that, unlike the normal pattern, the title "doesn't necessarily"

---

61. On a side note, if you read translations of interviews where he is mentioned, you will see his name transformed into Nomatsu. This is a crude translation error.

reflect the content of the video, it's more "a way to reveal a few gray areas to better 'connect' *Birth by Sleep* to the rest of the series, and particularly to Sora." He explains, "In that scene, the ones who are calling for 'Sora' are the ones who have already disappeared from the world, but in the world of *Kingdom Hearts*, there is no concept of death [...] they are just sleeping. If you can just wake them up, they'll be able to return to the world, they would thus be *born from sleep*." Of course, I'll come back to this to give a thorough explanation, but *Blank Points* is crucial for understanding the chain of events that followed. You may not realize it, but its very end takes place just before *KH III* (yes, in 2010). Nomura and the video team didn't have much time left to tie up all the loose ends before the game's release. Barely two months. The countdown had started.

Those last few weeks were extremely trying for everyone, of course for the Tokyo team, but also, in particular, for the Osaka team, which was not used to such a hectic pace of work. They entered the delicate and tiring phase of debugging. Yasue remembers, "Toward the end, we holed ourselves up in the office for days on end." And yet, no one complained. Everyone was going full speed ahead, driven by an incredible state of mind: "When a bug was found, nobody blamed anybody else and everyone worked together to fix it." Yoshimoto adds, "I think that the team went through an extraordinary transformation at that time. They would spontaneously check their work and the work of others and they helped me on multiple occasions without asking anything in exchange." Holding back tears, he says, "The theme of *Kingdom Hearts* is the 'connection [of hearts]' and I think that same idea applies to my team as well," tight-knit and capable of moving mountains. They had finally understood this. Yasue concludes, "Nomura had warned me from the beginning: 'You'll see, *Kingdom Hearts* is a special series, the magic always happens at the end.' At the time, I didn't understand what he meant. Toward the end [of development], I told myself, 'I can't go on, I'll never make it[62],' and it was thanks to the strength I got from the team that I never gave up. That's when

---

62. The part of the game using a wireless connection really gave them a hard time. The problem was solved thanks to the effort and talent of the programmers just a few days before the release. At the time, Yasue said that Yoshimoto and he were in a panic. They didn't think they would get it done on time.

I said to myself, that's the magic. And that's when I realized, 'Oh, so that's what he meant.'"

They came out of the experience galvanized and hoping, naturally, that Nomura would call on them again in the future because they had "new ideas and were motivated to do even better the next time," said Yoshimoto after the game's release. They didn't yet know that they wouldn't have to wait long...

Nomura succeeded with his big challenge: three (exceptional) games for three different platforms, created by three different teams, all while carrying out other experiments at the same time (*Subarashiki Kono Sekai*, *Dissidia*, *The 3rd Birthday*) preparing for his greatest obsession: *Final Fantasy versus XIII*. About this experience, he says, "It was difficult, but really positive. I tried some things out and learned a lot. What type of gameplay should I choose for each system? For example, a PSP game is similar to a PS2 game, so we'll try to stick as close to that as possible. For the DS, the lack of a joystick requires us to make more modifications and it's difficult to make a *Kingdom Hearts* for phones with simple controls. All of that will be useful for me in the future."

(RE)CONNECT

[Note to readers] The normal (re)Connect section will also be adapted to cover all of the different games Nomura worked on during this period. I'm going to mix everything together (communications plans, descriptions of trailers, and numbers) while being as clear and precise as possible.

April 2007. Following the release of *Kingdom Hearts II Final Mix +*, Nomura was forced to divulge a few bits of information about the mysterious "knights in shining armor," particularly the hidden boss, Todomarishi Shinen (Lingering Will): yes, all of that is indeed linked to a future *Kingdom Hearts*.

May 2007. In letters to the editor published in the magazine *Disney Adventures*, a young 13-year-old fan asked if there would be a *Kingdom*

Hearts III, and if so, when? The magazine cited Nomura (of course, we don't know whether or not the quotation was real or not): "We have made no announcements regarding any sequels. However, I can tell you that a new project related to *Kingdom Hearts* is in the works." A few days later, in an interview, Nomura said a little more on the subject: this project will focus on characters other than Sora and aims to clarify certain gray areas in the story. For example, "how Mickey obtains the Keyblade of the Realm of Darkness or Riku's fierce battle to protect Sora while he slept." What's more, he suggested that Sora could be the main character of another game in the future, but for the moment, his priority was using Roxas again. Finally, he clarified that "project does not necessarily mean [a] game."

July 27, 2007. *Subarashiki Kono Sekai* is released in Japan, selling 200,000 units, a very respectable performance, especially for a new game not connected to any existing media. Alas, it never really took off, but did ultimately sell 800,000 copies worldwide (including barely 40,000 in Europe, by the way). On a side note, the game was later ported for the iPad and was released in its final form for the Switch in 2018. If you made the mistake of not giving it a try back in the day, you can now get caught up.

Thursday, September 13, 2007. *Crisis Core: Final Fantasy VII* was released in Japan.

September 19, 2007, at the Tokyo Game Show. For several days before, rumors had been swirling. It was believed that Square Enix was about to announce an episode zero. No one could have suspected at that point that they would actually announce three spin-offs. The media were invited to check out the publisher's line-up at the usual Closed Mega Theater, a pop-up movie theater closed to the public and where taking videos and photos is prohibited. A video began playing: *KINGDOM HEARTS NEW TITLES, NEW CONCEPTS.* So, there would be multiple games? The video opened with a quick introduction recapping the end of *Kingdom Hearts II*, then, in a very "Nomurian" style, displayed several phrases: *"Flow of time"*, *"The secret is solved"*, and *"The world extends."* Jiminy Cricket then told of how, following their adventure in Castle Oblivion (*Chain of Memories*), the first of his journals recounting

Sora's journeys was wiped totally clean. Just one sentence remained: "Thank Naminé[63]." Flipping through the journal, he discovered with amazement that another sentence had appeared at the end of the book[64]. He immediately went to inform King Mickey. The king determined that only one person could straighten this matter out: Sora, who, the audience discovered in the next scene, had teleported to the Destiny Islands. The sequence that followed was composed solely of game footage. With the interface shown in the video, there was no doubt: it had to be a cell phone game. The journalists couldn't believe their eyes: how could it be possible to make a game with such great graphics for a phone? Moreover, the game portion of the video seemed to be on par with the rest of the series. The video ended with the scene in which Sora and Pluto meet before Sora comes across Mickey who claims that he must tell him the "truth." The game was called *Kingdom Hearts: coded* and would be for cell phones. However, the video gave no information about the phone that was supposed to host the game. At the time, journalists reckoned that it was an initial show of strength for the iPhone, which had just come out (in June 2007). On a side note, *Vay*, the first RPG for the iPhone, wasn't announced until a year later and was nothing more than a crude port of a Sega CD game and thus had retro graphics. In other words, *Kingdom Hearts: coded* was truly revolutionary.

A second trailer began with the ending of *Kingdom Hearts Re: Chain of Memories*. Sora was gradually regaining his memory and several phrases appeared on the screen: *"The other side returning to Sora to sleep," "Whenever crossing the mind comes back."* Viewers could immediately recognize the background music, the great track *The Other Promise*. It's a theme tied to Roxas, who then appeared in the video talking with Axel at the top of the clock tower in Twilight Town. After that, Roxas was showed being introduced to the members of Organization XIII as their new recruit. In the two scenes that followed, viewers discovered that the new game would reveal more about the events in Castle Oblivion, as well as about both Mickey and Riku. Perhaps the game

---

63. Which, to remind you, was already known at the start of *Kingdom Hearts II*.
64. "We must return to free them from their torment." I won't say anything more about this for the moment because it's one of the series' big plot twists. We'll come back to it in detail in Volume II.

would take place at the same time as *Chain of Memories*? The montage of game footage confirmed that the game would be a "true" episode: Roxas was seen moving around and fighting on slightly pixelated 3D backgrounds. A DS game? All doubt was erased with the appearance of four screens, typical of announcements for multi-player modes for the Nintendo DS. Viewers understood that it was indeed a whole new episode where you would be able to play cooperatively with the members of the Organization (Axel, Saïx, and Xigbar shown in the video). The trailer kept a surprise for the end: the reveal of a fourteenth member (?) and an enigmatic phrase from Roxas to conclude: "I will disappear from this world in 151 days." *Kingdom Hearts 358/2 Days* would be the new game for the DS.

Before the audience knew what was happening, a third trailer began playing. This one opened with the ending of *Kingdom Hearts*, then did a fantastic rewind to the opening. The video then followed the same MO as the other videos: *"Sleep gives way to hidden fate."* Could it be the famous Episode 0? The video then showed two characters (previously seen in different get-ups in *Birth by Sleep*, the secret movie from *Kingdom Hearts II Final Mix*): the first resembled Roxas, the second looked like Zack (*Final Fantasy VII*). Certain clever members of the crowd already knew that his name was Terra (thanks to a leak revealed by *Famitsu*). Terra called his companion Ven. Fans could immediately recognize the theme song playing: *Fate of the Unknown*. This dispelled all doubts: it was indeed the much-hyped Episode 0. The video then showed Terra facing off against the old sorcerer dressed like Ansem previously seen in *Birth by Sleep*. His name was Xehanort. Terra invokes his Keyblade just like Todomarishi Shinen (Lingering Will, the secret boss in *KH II FM*). This was followed by 20 seconds of gameplay showing that rumors of the game being for the PSP were probably true. What's more, Terra was indeed the hero and the Disney worlds were tied to fairy tales (*Sleeping Beauty* and *Cinderella* shown in the video). Next, the video showed Xehanort facing off against Ven in Olympus Coliseum. Xehanort revealed to Ven that they know each other, which troubled the young man, who in the next shot was knocked to the ground by another character, a "biker" with a helmet and an outfit reminiscent of Riku's when he was possessed by Ansem in *Kingdom Hearts*. Mickey intervenes to protect Ven. In the next scene, Terra is in

the Destiny Islands, watching two kids (who you should know) fighting with wooden swords! Xehanort asks someone (unseen, of course) to fix his mistakes. The last shot shows Ven asking a friend (who is also unseen, of course) to erase him. Finally, it is confirmed: the game was *Kingdom Hearts: Birth by Sleep* for PSP.

Three spin-offs for the price of one, on three different platforms, with three new heroes, and shedding light on three different periods: the past (*BBS*), the present (*Days*), and the future (*coded*). The "new project" that had been announced previously was taking shape. Moreover, each new game was a true episode with undeniable technical quality and gameplay just as a.) insane, b.) fantastic, and c.) incredible (circle all that apply) as the previous games. This publicity event was worthy of a case study. The three reveal trailers were incredibly well-executed: they each told different stories in their own ways. They were connected and comprehensible enough to spark imagination without real understanding. Each was structured to scrupulously follow the "rules" of giving the who, what, when, where, and how.

Each of the trailers opened with the ending of an episode to which it was connected, indicating its place in the series chronology. Each trailer revealed its game's purpose (to tie up a loose end) and introduced its cast (in the case of *BBS*, having all-new characters) or presented key plot points (the new sentence that appeared in Jiminy's book for *coded*, Roxas' induction into the Organization for *Days*). Also, each trailer had a section of game footage reminding viewers that these were, above all, games with fighting governed by complex mechanics. Each trailer made sure to distinguish its game from the other two. Finally, each trailer ended with a question suggesting where its game's story would lead… In each case, this left viewers both confused and excited, and also not really understanding why. The best part about this story is that Nomura made the exact same move as in 2003 when he revealed, one after the other, *Kingdom Hearts II* and *Chain of Memories*. When I tell you that there's method to his madness and that he sticks to his own principles, you better believe it… In the weeks following the TGS, more information was given without really revealing anything. Square Enix also distributed images and maintained the excitement built up by their presentation. Nothing was left up to chance, everything had meaning, everything was calculated down to the smallest detail, proving that a lot of thought had gone into it...

October 2007. Short videos taken on the fly at the TGS began to appear online, notably four seconds of gameplay for *358/2 Days*. This was enough to get fans dreaming for days.

December 3, 2007. The official website for Jump Festa '08 had pages dedicated to each of the new *Kingdom Hearts* games, suggesting new reveals, or at least that they would make appearances at the expo. Two weeks later, the magazine *V-Jump* revealed new images.

December 22, 2007, at Jump Festa '08. Like every year, the convention sponsored by publisher Shueisha hosted video game publishers, including Square Enix, with great fanfare. The three new *Kingdom Hearts* games each got a "new" trailer, only shown to professionals; they were really extended versions of the trailers shown at the TGS. The trailer for *coded* showed a few new scenes, notably one with Riku, thus indicating that he would appear in the game. Most importantly, the trailer revealed the game's device and a window for its release: the game would come out in late 2008 for an NTT DoCoMo FOMA phone. It was all starting to make sense. Given that the new phone had been announced for the following winter, the game could be a launch title for the new FOMA line. The *Birth by Sleep* trailer revealed a world from *Snow White* and confirmed that Ven would be a second playable character thanks to a few in-game sequences. Finally, the trailer for *Days* announced a release window: summer 2008. Little new information was revealed, but there was a playable demo allowing expo attendees to try out the famous cooperative multi-player mode.

February 2008. Shimomura announced *Drammatica*, a compilation of her work to be released on March 26. The album included, of course, many tracks from *Kingdom Hearts*.

Also, Nomura announced that *Kingdom Hearts* would not appear at the next E3.

June 2008. Square Enix announced their DK–3713[65] Private Party 2008. Nomura provided clarification in the days that followed, revealing that *BBS* would appear there in playable form. A rumor about a *Kingdom Hearts* anime appeared online.

July 23, 2008. The official website for *Days* was launched. *Shonen Jump* shared the first info on the Shotlock in *Birth by Sleep*.

August 2, 2008, at the DK–3713 Private Party 2008. Square Enix's private event took place at the Quest Building in Tokyo's Harajuku neighborhood over two days. The event was full of announcements, trailers, and playable demos. A Square Enix party hiding its true purpose. It was the second big event in the publicity plan for the future *Kingdom Hearts* games. In particular, during the event, the company revealed *Kingdom Hearts Mobile*, an interactive online portal allowing users to create customizable avatars (basically, you could make a Sora in Riku clothing) and control them in the Avatar Kingdom, a virtual amusement park with various "booths" providing news, goodies, and even mini-games. A format that would totally revolutionize navigation. All three games got new versions of their old trailers, incorporating new scenes. The *coded* trailer was beefed up with in-game sequences. These included views of exploration, dialog, battles, a boss, and even of the 2D platform, which was unusual for a *KH*. The trailer also revealed that the blocks were called "bugs" and that they played a real role in the story. The *Days* trailer was four minutes long and was made up almost entirely of brand-new scenes, one of which showed Naminé and DiZ in the basement of the Old Mansion, in which Sora was asleep. This showed that the game would take place before *Kingdom Hearts II*. The trailer was structured around gameplay phases that showed in passing three new worlds (the Beast's Castle, Olympus Coliseum, and Wonderland), as well as Larxene and Xaldin in action. Viewers learned that in solo mode, Roxas could collaborate with members of Organization XIII (including the famous number XIV), just like Sora with the Disney characters in the first two *KH* games. The sequence ended

---

65. D for *Dissidia*, K for *Kingdom Hearts*, Σ for *Sigma Harmonics*, 3 for *The 3rd Birthday*, 7 for *Final Fantasy VII ACC*, and 13 for *Fabula Nova Crystallis*. A name likely devised by Nomura…

with a sort of ranking. So, viewers could infer that multi-player mode involved a series of missions separate from solo mode. A new scene revealed that the fourteenth member was a girl who, moreover, carried a Keyblade and faced off against Riku (blindfolded). Finally, Naminé revealed the name of the new girl: Xion. And this Xion began removing her hood, but (of course) the scene cut out before viewers could see her face. And so the mystery continued on. The *Kingdom Hearts 358/2 Days* trailer concluded by revealing the game's new launch window: winter 2008. Finally, the trailer for *Birth by Sleep* relied on previously-revealed scenes, but also introduced a new character: Aqua. A girl with blue hair (also present, wearing armor, in *Birth by Sleep*, the secret movie in *Kingdom Hearts II Final Mix*). Viewers assumed that she was a playable character, but the trailer did not confirm this. However, it was clear that she was important to the story because she interacted with Terra and Ven and seemed, like them, to be looking for a certain Master Xehanort. Maleficent again played an antagonistic role and appeared to use Terra to kidnap the first Princesses of Heart, including Aurora (*Sleeping Beauty*), Snow White, and Cinderella, who all appeared in the trailer. As a final flourish, the trailer showed Aqua facing off against Maleficent, transformed into a dragon. This trailer was important because it positioned *Kingdom Hearts: Birth by Sleep* as an heir (strange for a prequel) to *Kingdom Hearts* while adopting the darker tone of *Kingdom Hearts II*. It was announced for a 2009 release.

There was a new demo for *358/2 Days* and *Birth by Sleep* was, as promised, playable for the first time. Event attendees could play as Terra and Ven in two different episodes!

DK–3713 Private Party 2008 also revealed that *The 3rd Birthday* and *Final Fantasy Agito XIII* had been canceled as cell phone games, instead moved to the PSP. Interestingly, 90 percent of the products presented at the party were developed under Nomura. In fact, all received treatment similar to *Kingdom Hearts*, like *Dissidia Final Fantasy*, for example. All this being said, the big feature was the first real trailer for *Final Fantasy versus XIII*.

September 2008. The *PlayStation UK* official magazine revealed that *Kingdom Hearts III* would supposedly be announced at the next TGS.

October 2008.

On the 2nd, Nintendo unveiled the Nintendo DSi. Yes, that's important.

On the 6th, the official website for *Kingdom Hearts Mobile* (and for *coded*) was launched.

On the 9th, the Tokyo Game Show 2008 was held. Like every year, Square Enix's Closed Mega Theater was one of the expo's main attractions. For the 2008 edition, the titles shown were more or less the same as those shown at DK–3713 and *Dissidia* was the centerpiece. This was logical because it was THE release for the publisher for the end of the year. *The 3rd Birthday* got a new trailer, but still showed no gameplay. This was also the first time that audiences got to see *Final Fantasy Agito XIII*. It came with a reveal trailer entirely in CGI.

Kingdom Hearts remained a big feature and, as usual, a series of new trailers was unveiled. The *coded* trailer focused on the story and, as a central theme, showed a stranger encountering our digitized hero several times. Could this stranger be the person behind the "bugs"? This was followed by a longer version of the DK–3713 trailer for *Birth by Sleep*. Aqua was the main attraction. All of the new scenes involved her, notably one where she was preparing, apparently, to face the Queen's mirror (from *Snow White*). It was also confirmed that she would be a playable character, as shown in several in-game sequences, thus becoming the series' first female playable character! That was a big deal. Given the special attention that Nomura has given to his female characters since the beginning of his career, there was no doubt that she would be developed with the same seriousness as her male comrades. In battle, she appeared quite graceful, with fairly magic-focused attacks, and resolutely different from Disney's strong female characters in the game: Maleficent and the Queen. The longest and most illuminating of the three trailers was once again the *Days* trailer, which revealed a lot more about Xion. Viewers finally got to see what she looked like. She showed up in almost every shot and increasingly appeared to be the plot's key character. The gameplay phases revealed two new worlds (Agrabah and Halloween Town) and two new playable members of the Organization: Marluxia and Lexaeus. Finally, the trailer ended on a sad note, with Xion questioning whether she really existed. The new release window was February 2009. All three games could be played during the expo. This was nothing new for *BBS* since it was the same demo from DK–3713. The *358/2 Days* demo, on the other hand, allowed players to try out Marluxia in multi-player mode and check out Halloween Town in solo mode. The *coded* demo unveiled its (future) preview version and was located at the NTT DoCoMo booth.

November 1, 2008. The Nintendo DSi was released in Japan. The design version was more understated, but had a somewhat more powerful performance and, above all, was now equipped with a built-in camera allowing users to take photos with their devices. Undoubtedly, this was a prideful reaction by Nintendo against the invading iPhone, which shamelessly reused the touchscreen concept made popular by the DS.

November 18, 2008. With 500,000 units produced, the Panasonic P–01A hit the shelves in Japan. As previously announced, a playable demo of *Kingdom Hearts: coded* was pre-installed on the devices, allowing players to try out *Olympus Coliseum — Side Episode* and *Traverse Town — Special Edit version*. The first involved a series of battles in the arena, helping players get familiar with the controls. The second offered a full experience of the game (exploration, dialog, platforms, puzzles, battles), but of course, it was just a sneak peek. On a side note, *coded* was the star of the "i-applis," along with *Layton-kyōju to Fushigi na Machi* (*Professor Layton and the Curious Village*), a somewhat toned-down port of the famous puzzle game developed by the studio Level-5.

December 2008.

On the 2ⁿᵈ, Square-Enix revealed that the three new *Kingdom Hearts* games would be present (and playable) at Jump Festa '09. Disney Interactive confirmed an international release for *Kingdom Hearts 358/2 Days*.

On the 5ᵗʰ, the official website for *Kingdom Hearts Mobile* was online. Ten days later, the service itself was launched for all NTT DoCoMo models. However, to use it, a monthly subscription was needed (between 315 and 1,050 yen, the equivalent of $2.85 to $9.50 in 2019).

On the 18ᵗʰ, *Dissidia Final Fantasy* was released, asserting the strength of the *FF* brand (and benefiting from a Christmas sales bump).

Ultimately, 2.5 million copies were sold worldwide. This was a feat for a new game, especially since it "suffered from piracy," according to its director, Takeshi Arakawa.

On the 20th, it was time for Jump Festa '09. The upcoming *Kingdom Hearts* games were, of course, present. That said, *coded*, *Mobile*, and *Birth by Sleep* just reused their material from the TGS. Indeed, Square Enix decided to focus their efforts on *Kingdom Hearts 358/2 Days* with a long trailer, running for six minutes, that was actually the launch trailer, though they didn't say so at the time. How do we know this? Because of its artistic style, which became the standard for all advertisements thereafter, no matter the market. *The Other Promise*, which had been the theme regularly used in the trailers up to that point, was replaced by *Passion*. Moreover, the trailer wasn't made available to the general public until a few months later. This launch trailer (since we can now call it that) had a combination of old and new scenes and was again focused on Xion. However, it reintroduced Roxas and Axel and even portrayed the three characters as a trio comparable to Sora, Riku, and Kairi, even showing them together in the Destiny Islands. The gameplay part of the trailer revealed the world of *Peter Pan* (Neverland), several bosses, as well as Demyx and Luxord in action. It then ended with a final mystery. *Kingdom Hearts 358/2 Days* was given a release window in spring 2009. In other words, it was once again pushed back...

March 6, 2009. Square Enix confirmed the final release date for *Kingdom Hearts 358/2 Days*: May 30, 2009. A bundle including the game and a limited-edition Nintendo DSi would be released the same day. In addition, Square Enix started promoting the game by regularly adding content to the official website, but also, as usual, by passing information to Japanese magazines (*V-Jump*, *Famitsu*, *Shonen Jump*, *Dengeki*, *Nintendo Dream*, etc.).

April 2009. Square Enix announced that *Kingdom Hearts* had sold over 12 million copies worldwide, all games in the series included. This news solidified the series as the third pillar of Square Enix, behind *Dragon Quest* (47 million copies) and, of course, *Final Fantasy* (over 85 million).

May 30, 2009. *Kingdom Hearts 358/2 Days* hit the shelves in Japan, available on its own or in a *bundle* with a Nintendo DSi decked out for the occasion in a fantastic *KH* skin (which Nomura himself was responsible for). The game was a success, selling around 300,000 copies in two days, by far the best-selling game that month for any console. It maintained its top spot in the rankings the next week, selling 100,000 more units. Just FYI, the first PS3 game came in third place (*Shin Sangoku Musō 5: Empires*). By the end of the year, it had sold around 600,000 copies in Japan, ending up the twelfth best-selling game of the year. To put things in context, the top three games were from Nintendo (led, of course, by a *Pokémon* game, in this case *Heart Gold/Soul Silver*) and the first game from a third-party publisher was in sixth place: *Final Fantasy XIII*, which sold around 1.5 million copies. In other words, *Kingdom Hearts 358/2 Days* has nothing to be ashamed of.

June 3, 2009, at E3. At its annual pre-E3 press conference, Nintendo revealed the US release date for *Kingdom Hearts 358/2 Days*: September 29. The official American website was launched immediately after.

This was also an important day because the *Kingdom Hearts: coded* "series" began its distribution of an episode each month. They would remain available for download until 2013.

June 3, Episode 1 — *Destiny Islands*
July 8, Episode 2 — *Traverse Town*
August 5, Episode 3 — *Wonderland*
September 17, Episode 4 — *Olympus Coliseum*
October 15, Episode 5 — *Agrabah*
November 26, Episode 6 — *Hollow Bastion part 1*
December 26, Episode 7 — *Hollow Bastion part 2*
January 28, 2010, Episode 8 — *Castle Oblivion*

Late August 2009. Nomura announced that the release date for *Kingdom Hearts: Birth by Sleep* had still not been determined and depended on *Final Fantasy XIII*, whose potential Square Enix didn't want to hurt. Additionally, *Famitsu* revealed a new world in *Birth by Sleep* based on *Lilo and Stitch*.

September 4, 2009. The official website for *Kingdom Hearts: Birth by Sleep* went online. *V-Jump* revealed Neverland.

September 25, 2009, at the Tokyo Game Show. In line with Nomura's declaration in August, *Birth by Sleep* was announced for a release in January 2010 (since *Final Fantasy XIII* would come out December 17, 2009). As such, the game entered the final straight of its publicity campaign, which naturally meant a new trailer with all the makings of a launch trailer.

Running four minutes long, it included brand-new shots. It started with a key phrase: *"There is no coincidence in fate."* In the first scene, Aqua is speaking to Terra and Ven. She gives them Wayfinders, talismans that will connect them no matter what happens. Next, Terra and Aqua are taking an exam to become Keyblade Masters, with a new samurai-looking character judging their performance. He is most likely their master. Master Xehanort, who is apparently a friend of the unknown character, had made the trip to observe the exam. New scenes revealed Mickey in a new get-up, a world based on *Peter Pan*, and interactions between the heroes and Disney characters like Captain Hook. They could also be seen interacting with the stories of the Disney films, for example, Aqua trying on the glass slipper in the world based on *Cinderella*! Viewers also got to see, for the first time, a world based on *Lilo and Stitch*. The gameplay phases were just as interesting. One of the heroes in armor can be seen perched on some sort of flying vehicle out in space, seemingly in the middle of a battle. This is followed by a succession of bosses, including the Queen's mirror (from *Snow White*). Then, viewers see a board game-like sequence with characters moving across the spaces like in a game from the *Itadaki Street* (Fortune Street) series. This seemed to be a mini-game. Next, viewers see the heroes in armor in some sort of arena, several special moves, and the Shotlock. The trailer then returned to the story with Ven again facing the mysterious "biker." After that, Terra is in the middle of a conversation with Master Xehanort, talking about controlling the Darkness. Also seen are several of Ansem's apprentices at a time when they were human. Finally, the trailer ends with the meeting of the five main characters in the Keyblade Graveyard, a scene similar to the beginning of the secret movie in *Kingdom Hearts II Final Mix*. Before this scene finishes, Master Xehanort reveals to his opponents that they are on an ancient battlefield where the Keyblade War took place. TGS visitors also got to try out the new playable demo and, in particular, play as Aqua in a part of the story related to *Snow White*. They also got to check out the multi-player arena mode. In it, the other characters were in armor, to the delight of the expo attendees.

September 29, 2009. *Kingdom Hearts 358/2 Days* was released in the United States. 300,000 units were sold within just a few days, but the game still didn't reach the top 10 for sales. Ten days later, on October 9, the game was released in Europe. In the end, around 2 million copies were sold worldwide, making it the sixty-second best-selling game for the Nintendo DS. To really give that some context, Nintendo monopolized the top thirteen spots (led by *New Super Mario Bros.*, with 30 million copies sold... crazy, right?). The top game from a third-party publisher was *Dragon Quest IX* with 5.8 million copies sold. While *Final Fantasy III* was just fifty-sixth.

October 14, 2009. The magazine *Jump* provided some clarification about the samurai in the latest trailer. He was the master of Aqua, Terra, and Ven, and his name was Eraqus. What's more, they all lived in a brand-new world: the Land of Departure. That same week, *V-Jump* revealed that the masked man (the "biker") was named Vanitas and that he was the apprentice of Master Xehanort.

October 21, 2009. Square Enix announced the release date for *Kingdom Hearts: Birth by Sleep* as January 9, 2010, about three weeks after *Final Fantasy XIII*.

January 9, 2010. *Kingdom Hearts: Birth by Sleep* finally hit the shelves in Japan. And it was a big success, selling around 500,000 copies within two days. This was a strong performance for a **PSP** game, although the console was gaining steam again in Japan, particularly thanks to the popularity of *Monster Hunter*. *Birth by Sleep* ultimately sold 760,000 copies in Japan alone. In the rest of the world, well, that's another story. To be continued...

THE LEGEND OF
KINGDOM HEARTS

VOLUME 1: CREATION

Genesis of Hearts

Chapter IV.5 — The Rule of (the) Threes Part 2

IN RESPONSE TO CHANGES

Let's check in on how Square Enix was doing business-wise. I think this will help you really understand what you read in the last section and lay the groundwork for future sections by putting things into perspective.

In the 2005 fiscal year[1], Square-Enix was humming along. All was well thanks to the release of *Final Fantasy XII*. While it would be responsible for all the chaos to come, it was still the hit it was expected to be, with around 2.5 million copies sold in Japan alone within less than a month. *Kingdom Hearts II* solidified the international strength of the series with around a combined 2.5 million units sold in Japan and the United States (with 1.3 million sold in the US in just three days). And despite already having given four years of faithful service, *Final Fantasy XI Online* continued to remain the heart and soul of Square Enix with its 500,000 paid subscribers, whose interest was constantly sustained by expansions like *Chains of Promathia*. The ports of *Dragon Quest* and *Final Fantasy* for cell phones were big hits and the magazine *Shônen Gangan* was an undeniable success, in part thanks to the serial publication of its star manga, *Fullmetal Alchemist*. Finally, *Final Fantasy VII: Advent Children* was a hit in Japan, with around a million units sold (DVD and UMD[2] combined). It also pulled in over $15 million in the United States, surprisingly ending up as the best-selling anime in this market in 2006[3], ahead of the Hayao Miyazaki film *Howl's Moving Castle*.

All was well.

---

1. From April 1, 2005, to March 31, 2006.
2. Universal Media Disc. A Sony proprietary format exclusively for the PSP.
3. According to the Nielsen ratings.

Yoichi Wada was satisfied with his company's performance, but he knew that it wouldn't last; they wouldn't have "million-seller" games in stores every year. He also saw that it would be difficult to move over to the new generation of consoles as it would require a major human and financial investment and need a lot of R&D. Incidentally, to anticipate future needs as much as possible, he launched development of the company's first in-house engine, the White Engine[4]. However, this was not his top concern. "The video game is on the verge of a revolution," he said before declaring 2005 "year zero for the video game industry." He explained, "Up to this point, we have only had the console video game industry (...), however, the prerequisites for maintaining this [reassuring] ecosystem are eroding away." The implication being that the internet would change everything, on the one hand due to the decline of physical media in favor of a new form of (digital) distribution, and on the other hand because "the business models themselves" would be affected, as Wada noted. The following year, he made a realistic assessment of the situation: "The [historic] gaming companies are no longer the only players in the [video game] industry." In other words, "casual gaming" was gaining ground, allowing companies that had nothing to do with video games to take up an increasing amount of space in the market. This was a real source of concern for the "historic" Japanese players in the industry, stuck in their "old models" that were more costly and limiting, and only in touch with a minor target audience. And the worst was yet to come[5]. Wada declared, "There is no future for those who bet on the [old-school] gaming market unless they can break out of their habits and adapt their strategies." What he meant was that the "100 percent home console" publishers would have a rude awakening. It was time to reassess, or better yet to make sure they had more than one iron in the fire.

Wada's change of tone says a lot about the doubts shaking the Japanese video game industry in the mid-2000s. Even in the darkest of

---

4. After a change in direction in April 2006, the engine was introduced in its first version in September 2007 under the name Crystal Tools. It was partly responsible for the delay of *Final Fantasy XIII*, the failure of *Final Fantasy XIV*, and the cancellation of *Final Fantasy versus XIII*. We'll come back to this later.
5. In the late 2000s to early 2010s, "casual gaming" evolved into "social gaming," particularly thanks to Zynga (*Farmville*, among others) and PopCap (*Peggle*), but also the rise of Facebook. It might seem crazy to you, but that was less than a decade ago.

times, Square had never considered the potential "no future" scenario. Their boss was able to see things clearly. Almost exactly one year after this declaration, on top of the proprietary engine, Wada gave the green light to start work on *Final Fantasy XIV*. The goal was to "relieve *Final Fantasy XI*," which is to say, to get rid of it: "We are far too dependent [on *Final Fantasy XI*] and that's a problem," he stated frankly. While everyone was rushing into the race for HD, he remained cautious. In spite of conventional wisdom, there was no way they could immediately move to the next generation of consoles because "to get their best visual performance and use their network access, you have to have a strong enough connection and an HD screen." He was being realistic; this same line of thinking pushed Satoru Iwata (the late and former president of Nintendo) to make a console—the Wii—that was quite inferior to its HD competitors from a technical standpoint. In 2006, he retorted to journalists, "[Japanese] households don't have the right equipment yet."

So, Square Enix pursued a different strategy with two major facets.

1. They bluffed. At E3 2006, the publisher led everyone to believe that two huge blockbusters were in development: *Final Fantasy XIII*, to be the next episode in the flagship series (a "multi-million seller"), and *Final Fantasy versus XIII*, a *Kingdom Hearts*-style take on *Final Fantasy*. Two windows into the future of Square Enix led, once again, by the dynamic duo of Kitase and Nomura. You already know what happened from there: it was just an illusion because no work had actually begun. Of course, this was reprehensible for a host of reasons, but Wada believed he was doing what had to be done. He had no choice but to position the company as a leading player in this market that was home to the core of its target audience. When your name is Square Enix, you have to keep up appearances, no matter the situation. Exposing your weaknesses means getting eaten alive. Brandishing weapons, imaginary though they may be, means survival. What's more, PlayStation 3 was not the big hit that had been expected and Sony put pressure on its allies[6] to produce ammunition, even if

6. Let's not forget that Sony was one of the biggest shareholders (with around 9,520 shares, or about 8.25 percent) of Square Enix until 2014. They then sold their shares, making room for fun new investors like Goldman Sachs and, more recently, JPMorgan.

they turned out to be duds. From there, it wouldn't be a stretch to suggest there may have been a quid pro quo, but I won't go there. In any case, the announcements at E3 were a total lie because, behind the scenes, the company's true ambitions were much more confidential and sensible.

2. They decided to go all-in on portable consoles because, unlike home consoles, "they stand on their own and don't need a special environment," said Wada. In other words, the consumer benefit would be immediate. It was ironclad pragmatism. To avoid taking any risks, he had already launched two test cases: *Final Fantasy III* and *Dragon Quest Monsters: Joker*. The mission of these two games was to test the waters, especially with Wi-Fi. The results were spectacular. Both sold like hotcakes (1.5 million copies sold in Japan and the US for the former and the same amount in Japan alone for the latter). Moreover, with 5.6 million different users, *Dragon Quest Monsters: Joker* became extremely popular. It was a good move. Time to flood the market. It must be understood however that this was just an interim strategy: "This strategy will only be used in this transitional period. Square Enix will not rely solely on portable console games in the future." Basically, they were biding their time as "the years to come will be used to restructure in order to offer cutting-edge technology for the next generation of consoles... and PCs." All the same.

Square Enix unleashed a veritable tidal wave of games between 2006 and 2009. And of course, to ensure success, they relied heavily on their three pillars.

— *Final Fantasy*. After their successful test with *FFIII* (while continuing to supply ammunition for the GBA with episodes *V* and *VI*), the juggernaut got going with spin-offs (*Final Fantasy XII: Revenant Wings*, *Final Fantasy Crystal Chronicles: Ring of Fates* and *Echoes of Time* for the DS, and *Crisis Core: Final Fantasy VII* for the PSP), remakes (*Final Fantasy, Final Fantasy II, Final Fantasy Tactics: The War of Lions* for PSP, *Final Fantasy IV* for the DS), sequels (*Final Fantasy Tactics A2: Grimoire of the Rift*), and even all-new games, including *Dissidia Final Fantasy* for the PSP, joined a year later by *Final Fantasy: The Four Heroes of Light* for the DS, which, as we all know, later gave rise to the series *Bravely Default*.

— *Dragon Quest*. First off, the remakes of *Dragon Quest IV* and *V* for the DS, which paved the way for a brand-new, DS-exclusive game, *Dragon Quest IX: Hoshizora no Mamoribito (Sentinels of the Starry Skies)*.

— And, of course, *Kingdom Hearts*, with a game for the DS (*358/2 Days*), another for the PSP (*Birth by Sleep*), and a third for cell phones (*coded*).

Square Enix also took the opportunity to try to reactivate its less successful licenses like *Front Mission* (DS), *Seiken Densetsu* (*Children of Mana* and *Heroes of Mana* for the DS), *Valkyrie Profile* (*Lenneth* for the PSP, *Covenant of the Plume* for the DS), *Star Ocean* (*First Departure* and *Second Evolution*, both for the PSP), *Bahamut* (*Blood of Bahamut* for the DS), among others. On the side, they tried to please "old fans" with the port of *Chrono Trigger* for the DS and a—welcome—remake of *SaGa2* entitled *Hihô Densetsu Goddess of Destiny*, in addition to new experiments like *Subarashiki Kono Sekai* and *Sigma Harmonics*.

In short, for around four years, Square Enix largely produced games for portable consoles, with no less than 40 games for the Nintendo DS and 12 for the PSP. However, the company was simply in survival mode: *Final Fantasy* and *Dragon Quest* represented "less than 50 percent of the company's profits," and any new attempt at originality was brushed aside by consumers. As a Square Enix employee (who insisted on remaining anonymous) very astutely observed: "Players always say they want new, original games, but paradoxically, they mostly buy remakes while waiting for sequels." For that very reason, in the middle of a fiscal year, Square Enix brought up the possibility of transforming *Final Fantasy versus XIII* into *Final Fantasy XV*. No matter what the game may have to offer, a new numbered installment will always curry more favor with audiences than an original game, even if it has *Final Fantasy* stamped on the front. Likely burnt by the flurry of spin-off series like *Crystal Chronicles* and *The Four Heroes of Light*, the publisher had pushed the brand's power beyond its limits and so they wanted to refocus on the main franchise. But that's another story. *Versus XIII* had to wait patiently for development of

Final Fantasy XIII to finish before launching. And Nomura did not make their job easy. While the company leaders had ambitions from a sales perspective, he saw things from a creative perspective. And he knew that a numbered installment would mean that he would have to stick to guidelines and he hadn't proposed *Versus XIII* to then get stuck following a formula. That's not really his thing. But, for the time being, the idea of a "transfer" remained dormant. The question was, for how long?

As of March 31, 2009, the situation for Square Enix became alarming:

1. Square Enix still had not resolved the problem of *Final Fantasy XI*, which was no longer the breadwinner that it had been (after seven years of heroic service, it should be said). *Front Mission Online* was a failure.

2. The few forays into new-generation consoles (*Infinite Undiscovery*, *The Last Remnant* and *Star Ocean: The Last Hope*) turned out to be duds. No million-sellers.

3. Development of the in-house engine required a lot of resources (both financial and human) and encountered numerous problems, hindering the development of *Final Fantasy XIII* and *Final Fantasy XIV*.

4. In April, Square Enix acquired the British publisher Eidos for a mere 12.1 billion yen ($110 million today), mainly for their technical skills and their corporate culture of collaboration, but also, in particular, "because it was probably one of the only Western companies that owned all of its own IP," said Yoichi Wada. This was particularly important so that the company could "increase the number of ways to reach consumers." In plain language, this implied tie-in products like movies, comics, action figures, etc. In addition, Square Enix wanted to boost its reputation by reactivating one of the most valuable licenses in the market, *Deus Ex*. Let's just say that it would take some time for the acquisition to become profitable.

5. Because of all of the previously mentioned problems, blockbusters were conspicuously absent. *Final Fantasy XIII*, *Final Fantasy XIV*, and *Dragon Quest IX* missed the deadline for the 2008 fiscal year. That gave the company's president some real headaches.

6. Wada caused the bankruptcy of GRIN, a Swedish studio which, in total secrecy, had been working for two years on the project called

Fortress, which was submitted to the publisher and then branded as a *Final Fantasy*.

Now, let's get back to less tedious matters.

[WARNING] Nomura again pulled off the hat trick with three games at one time. So, I will use a labeling system fairly similar to the one in the previous section to facilitate reading.

WONDER OF ELECTRON
[RE: CODED: DEVELOPMENT]

Fall 2009. The fourth episode of *Kingdom Hearts: coded* had been out for about 10 days. There had been a decent number of downloads, but not nearly enough for Tokyo. The problem was the game's device, the P–01A. Since it was a technological jewel, there weren't many out there and it was expensive (over $700, unheard of at the time) and, in particular, it crushed the competition from a technical standpoint, the iPhone included. Above all, it was the only phone capable of running *coded*. It was impossible to distribute the game on other, more common models and "in particular, foreign fans are deprived," said Nomura. Déjà vu[7]. To prevent history from repeating itself, he proposed a port for a game console.

Given the original ambitions of the game, their choices were limited. The first option was to release the game on WiiWare[8], maintaining its episodic format, but the desire to make it accessible to all was stronger. They didn't want to make things too complicated. The Nintendo DS was the best-selling console. Note that, at that time, Nintendo dominated the world portable console market with a 68.3 percent share for the entire "DS family[9]." It was easy math. Also, the P–01A and DS had many things in common, like a horizontal screen and similar forms and ergonomics. In other words, they were "twins" in their uniqueness,

---

7. A similar problem existed previously (see page 175) preventing Western players from playing *Before Crisis: Final Fantasy VII*.
8. WiiWare is the Wii's download platform, originally designed to allow independent developers to easily produce games without using a lot of resources.
9. Nintendo DS, DS Lite, and DSi.

which would largely facilitate porting of the game. Or at least, that's what they thought.

Having set their sights on the promised land of the DS, they needed a guide. The obvious choice was, of course, Hajime Tabata, the co-director of *Kingdom Hearts: coded*, but he was completely overbooked[10]. The second most obvious choice was to give it to a member of the Kingdom Team, but that would have been counterproductive. Nomura had been deprived of his team for several months, so he wasn't going to shoot himself in the foot by giving them a "side project" while he had been waiting impatiently to get them back so that they could resume work on *Final Fantasy versus XIII*. One solution remained: turn to people who could bring something new to the table. So, Nomura decided to split the responsibilities between Jun Kato, lead planner for *coded*, and Hiroyuki Itô, one of the leaders on *Kingdom Hearts 358/2 Days*, which by then was mission accomplished since it had been released in all regions. As a result, h.a.n.d. had its hands free[11] and so the port of *coded* for the Nintendo DS was entrusted to them.

Nomura wasted no time and "reserved" the Sapporo-based studio[12]. Koji Yamamoto (team director) estimated that they would need a year for development. They began work in October 2009. The project may have been a "simple port as-is," as Nomura described it, but there were still many matters that needed to be reviewed. For example, you don't play games the same way on a phone as you do on a console, especially when the console has two screens, one of which is a touchscreen. So, the top priority was to redevelop the manner of play. Kato and Itô realized that this would be more complicated than expected because the question of playability covered a whole host of other issues. Because Nomura always designs his games based on their devices, and since a phone is not primarily intended to be a game machine (while that is the only purpose of a console), the approach to the video game was totally different. *Kingdom Hearts: coded* was clearly not up

10. In late 2009, Tabata was simultaneously working on *The 3rd Birthday* and *Final Fantasy Type-0* (formerly *Final Fantasy XIII Agito*), both of which had become PSP games a year earlier. Quite a bad experience for him. Poor thing.
11. I know, I'm hilarious. It helps when you have such an easy set-up.
12. h.a.n.d. is not part of Square Enix. It's a totally independent company that, as such, is free to do whatever it pleases. To work with them, you have to coordinate schedules.

to Nintendo DS standards. So, it had to evolve. Since h.a.n.d. had already been involved in a *Kingdom Hearts* in 3D, Nomura wondered if maybe the solution was ultimately to do a remake in full 3D[13]. This choice would come with many consequences because it would require redoing "everything," or almost everything.

The game was renamed *Kingdom Hearts Re: coded*, a naming convention that—up to that point—had been reserved for *Re: Chain of Memories*. This was not in any way a random choice: Nomura had a <u>true</u> remake in mind. He started by re-establishing the lexicon of the game's universe, adapting it to computer terminology. However, he had some doubts: would this be too complicated to understand? Nonetheless, he ultimately stuck to the idea: "This is my only opportunity to incorporate this type of vocabulary into a *Kingdom Hearts*." Might as well take advantage. Daisuke Watanabe was dismayed: "And I thought there wouldn't be much to do because it was a port…" You almost want to say to him, "Bad luck, buddy!" He continues, "In the end, I had to come up with a lot of names for objects and skills, and even write explanations for each one," but he was reassured by the fact that the biggest chunk of work went to the technicians. First off, they had to create the backgrounds: "How am I going to bring out the charm of *coded* on the DS?" wondered Ry to Shinzato (lead designer BG). While he had the raw materials needed, he wasn't content with doing "just" a port. Still, he tried to save time by reusing the assets from *Kingdom Hearts 358/2 Days*. He quickly realized that this was a waste of time and had to start again from scratch. He was not happy about that. That said, he improved absolutely everything, from polygon collisions to camera movements. In the end, it was like *358/2 Days* had just been a draft for *Re: coded*. In connection with the computer code theme, he came up with dozens of different "bug blocks" before ultimately only keeping seven of them because with "the others, it would have been too many and too complicated." Using 3D graphics also meant doing new modeling of the characters. Satoshi Otani (art director for the 3D characters) worked off of the models from *Kingdom Hearts*, mainly Sora and Riku. His goal? "Make them more attractive by maintaining their visual quality, particularly their faces and hair." This was delicate

13. *Kingdom Hearts: coded* was in 2D.

work because the difference in power between the two consoles (the PS2 and the DS) required that he reduce the number of polygons by at least fivefold. He explained that the Disney characters were "the most problematic because of their rounded shapes," and to recreate them faithfully, you need to use a large number of polygons. As a consequence, you then have to reduce the presence of enemies on the screen by a corresponding amount. It was a puzzle and, once again, the result of a pesky memory problem. On a side note, Otani says that Cloud was the character who gave him the hardest time because of "his pointy hair and his numerous accessories." All this said, some people were delighted by the introduction of 3D graphics: "I'll finally be able to incorporate the effects I wanted for the Keyblade and the enemy attacks," exclaimed Koichi Akiyama (art director); he had been forced to abandon these features in the phone game because, in spite of having better screen resolution than the Nintendo DS, the P-01A "handles 3D very poorly." Could that be the reason why the cutscenes in *Re: coded* aren't like the ones in *Days*? "Partly," says Masaru Oka (event director). His initial intention was to reproduce the same type of events, but he wasn't satisfied with the results. "Because of the capacities of the DS, no matter what we tried to show, the facial expressions were much too limited," says Nomura, who then proposed that they do something simpler with basic animation using different poses of the characters prerendered in 2D[14]: "That gives you a whole range of expressions that are consistent with what the characters are feeling," he concluded. Mai Okauchi (art director for 2D characters) explains that over 400 drawings (front and back views) were created, including 55 just for Sora and Mickey. "Then, we collaborated with the animation team to make the characters as lifelike as possible," says Oka. This approach was not headache-free. They particularly had trouble when three or four characters were talking at the same time, which quickly overwhelmed the screen; "a real head-scratcher," as he puts it. Munenori Shinagawa (animation director) was unsure of his work: "Early in development, late at night, I showed a scene to Nomura to see if I was on the right track." He held his breath, but there was no need: the director loved it and immediately gave his approval. This was a great memory for Shinagawa, who put

14. A pre-rendering in 2D means that the image is first created in high resolution before being reduced and incorporated into the game.

enormous pressure on himself: "I wanted to identically reproduce the movements of the characters from *Kingdom Hearts*," he says. Note that he says "reproduce," not "reuse." He also recognizes that he gave h.a.n.d. a hell of a time, sending them numerous comments and modifications. He says that he worked harder on *Kingdom Hearts Re: coded* than probably any other game in the series. From there, it's not much of a stretch to deduce that Tatsuya Kando (animation supervisor) began to ease off a bit, but, again, I won't go there. I will, however, note that with the many setbacks for *versus XIII*, he had no intention of twiddling his thumbs when he could be moving forward. So, he continued supervising while, nevertheless, placing trust in his deputy.

With the game now in full 3D and Tokyo and h.a.n.d. making progress working closely together, Nomura decided that the gameplay also needed to be refreshed. This, again, came with a heap of consequences, particularly for interactions. "Initially, I was going to reuse my code from *Kingdom Hearts 358/2 Days* and simply adapt it, but I soon realized that there were too many differences, even just in the bug blocks... I had to go back to square one," Naoyuki Ohashi (main programmer) moans. It's funny to note that they all tried to "reproduce" *358/2 Days*, without success. That made Nomura smile, especially because *Re: coded* was shaping up to be a mix of the past three games. In addition, his priority was to add a character development system that would be simple, effective, and fun. So, why not reuse the Panels from *Days*? He also wanted to introduce a difficulty control that the player could activate at their leisure, like in *Subarashiki Kono Sekai*, if for no other reason than to avoid the criticisms leveled against *Kingdom Hearts 358/2 Days*: "The goal was to make some waves [against the flavor of the week, casual gaming] with a game with some real character. Apparently, it had too much," he jokes, "many found it too hard." He had also learned his lesson about the D-pad of the DS being too rigid and thus wanted to "avoid technical battles as much as possible"... and blisters, he might have added. Since designing these systems would require time that he didn't have[15], "in January, he asked

---

15. Nomura was burning the candle at both ends. He was involved in several projects at once as creative producer and character designer, including *Dissidia Duodecim* and *The 3rd Birthday*. He was particularly focused on *Final Fantasy versus XIII* because he finally got his core team back. And 2010 was supposed to be a key year.

me to work on the battles and the character development system," says Tai Yasue. At that point, *Birth by Sleep* had only been out for a very short time. Yasue was taking a break, but he never balks at a challenge, especially when his boss calls him in to save the day. Every day, he considers himself even more lucky to be working alongside Nomura. He immediately got to work drafting into his team the few people who weren't on leave (there were literally three of them). He very soon came up with the idea for a character development system much like an electronic circuit[16]. It was original, interactive, colorful, fun, inspired by childhood, and embraced both the Panels concept from *Days* and the virtual universe of *Re: coded*; it checked all the boxes. However, Nomura was skeptical. While he thought the idea was brilliant, he was worried about its readability. It was when he saw a design that accompanied the "plan" that he finally gave his approval. In fact, he did better than approve: he made it the backbone of *Re: coded*. Once again, he decided to place his trust in Yasue by appointing him as planning supervisor.

Nomura was able to adapt to the situation by being smart about dividing up the work: programming was handled by h.a.n.d., creation by Tokyo, and management and battles by Osaka. Ohashi notes: "Before we knew what was happening, we were doing a complete revamp. However, the thing that never changed was the planning." By taking advantage of the strengths of the three studios, Nomura was able to effectively stick to the timing that he sold to his superiors without dropping the ball on everything else: it was already late January and for Osaka (at least), that meant it was time to get down to business on the localization of *Birth by Sleep*.

DARK IMPETUS
[*BIRTH BY SLEEP*: DEVELOPMENT]

The Western version of *Kingdom Hearts: Birth by Sleep* was only to have a few new features. A new Command Board, a new mini-game

---

16. Inspired by electronic learning kits for children, also called "electronic building blocks" or "snap circuits."

(stickers), a new track for Rumble Racing, and two brand-new Keyblades (including one in response to players' grumbling[17]). There were also a few adjustments to the cutscenes and a rebalancing of certain skills, notably Mega Flare, which was found to be too power-ful. The biggest additions were to the D-Link (with Captain Dark) and, especially, a brand-new secret boss in keeping with tradition, an Unknown for that matter. The big issue with the choice of an Unknown was the why and, particularly, how, given that Organization XIII didn't exist yet. Nomura was purposely muddying the waters: "The fact that [this battle] takes place at this moment is impossible. And yet…" Nomura gloats. This is a point in common with Lingering Will in *Kingdom Hearts II Final Mix* while, like Xemnas in *Kingdom Hearts Final Mix*, EM[18] introduces the main bad guy of the next installment. In other words, Nomura was messing with players' heads by playing around with his own conventions.

Finally, Critical Mode was added, with a difficulty even higher than the usual Proud Mode. But, out of curiosity, why do the non-Japanese versions always offer a greater challenge? Nomura's answer stings: "On average, the Japanese are much more casual gamers than Westerners. Moreover, they generally find [Western] games to be too hard." So, the difficulty is adapted to the region. This also explains the systematic addition of a new secret boss that is always very hard to beat. Far too difficult, according to most Japanese. Nomura says that he had a sample[19] of Japanese players try out EM and their feedback was decisive: he was so difficult that they never wanted to try again. Enlightening, no? Above all, it debunks an old myth. No, the Japanese are not superhuman gamers and, no, they are not better than Westerners. OK, they have some exceptionally talented players among them, but they are a tiny minority. And these "pure bloods," as some people call them (or PGs[20], depending on who you talk to), like

---

17. Players complained about the Vanitas Remnant. In their opinion, this boss was too hard and, in particular, didn't give them anything. This injustice was corrected in the localized version, with players getting the Void Gear (in its monochrome version) for winning the battle.
18. EM for Enigmatic Man, the name given to him by fans.
19. It was really a focus group. Square Enix invites players of different stripes to try out a product not yet available in stores, with the goal of obtaining comments based on their experiences. This allows them to test an idea on representatives of the public or to determine the orientation of a publicity campaign.
20. PG for "pro gamer." A term for a professional gamer competing in e-sports or, more generally, for an excellent, very experienced player.

Kingdom Hearts and want to take on the same level of difficulty as the Whites[21].

The *Final Mix*-es are, in a way, dedicated to them. Besides Nomura's pathological perfectionism, this also explains why he adds new dogmatic content like more hardcore new bossesand new secret endings. It's his way of rewarding them for standing out from the crowd. The question was, would Nomura have a chance to do the same this time? As previously explained, the company's strategy for that fiscal year was to bide their time, and this was not the right moment for Nomura to go asking for an "expendable" version, especially one for a console that was on its last legs. And then, as Nomura said himself: *"Kingdom Hearts Re: Chain of Memories* was enough to justify *Kingdom Hearts II Final Mix +*, but we won't be able to do the same thing again this time."* No surprise there. It's hard to beat a bonus game (and what a game it was). It seemed like a lost cause, but Nomura hadn't given up just yet. He took some time to think before bringing it up with his bosses. He knew he just needed a spectacular idea to get them to give in. Particularly as there were no issues with either the organization or money: the whole production would take no more than three to four months, it would only require a reduced number of people, and what's more, the American voice work was almost complete.

Which leads us to a (delightful) side note on that very subject, because *Birth by Sleep* may have been a PSP game, but it was treated like a "numbered" episode and its cast proves it.

UNFORGETTABLE
[*BIRTH BY SLEEP*: DUBBING]

Before we get into the details, I'd like to have a moment of silence (please, just play along).

In memory of those actors and actresses no longer with us who lent their voices to Disney characters.

---

21. Don't get out your torches and pitchforks: the term "Whites" in Asian countries is an informal way of referring to Westerners. It's a little like how we refer to them collectively as "Asians."

Just after finishing the recording of voices for *Kingdom Hearts 358/2 Days*, Wayne Allwine, the sixth official voice of Mickey Mouse (for over 30 years) passed away due to complications with diabetes. It was a tragedy... but of no consequence for the games. It's almost cruel, but he was replaced within less than a week by an illustrator named Bret Iwan. As a side note, the first voice of Mickey was Walt Disney himself; for example, he's the one you hear whistling in *Steamboat Willie*.

Birth by Sleep is special in that it used several worlds from older Disney movies. As such, the (first) three Princesses of Heart were not played by their original actresses. Ilene Woods (Cinderella) suffered from Alzheimer's and died from the disease (in July of the same year *Birth by Sleep* was released). Mary Costa (Aurora) was 80 years old and thus wasn't capable of taking part. Jennifer Hale[22] played both of their parts. Adriana Caselotti (Snow White), who passed away in 1997, was replaced by Carolyn Gardner, who called it quits after *Birth by Sleep*.

Facing off against the three Princesses of Heart, there was just one voice artist. She played Maleficent, the Queen-Witch, and Lady Tremaine, the stepmother in *Cinderella*. She is THE voice of Disney's female villains: Susanne Blakeslee. Next, I should mention Disney's prolific voice talents, including Corey Burton, the only man capable of playing Yen Sid, Grumpy, the Magic Mirror... and Ansem the Wise. Indeed, he had to replace Christopher Lee, who got too old. One of his colleagues, Rob Paulsen, provided the voices for Jaq and the Grand Duke from *Cinderella*. I'll also mention, in no particular order, Jeff Bennett, Russi Taylor, Tress MacNeille, and James Woods, the perfect Hades. The list goes on. Some of the Organization XIII voice actors also returned, including James Patrick Stuart, alias Braig/Xigbar, who played a significantly larger role in this game. Richard Epcar (Ansem) and Meaghan Jette Martin (Naminé) were there as well. Finally, Rick Gomez, just as in *Crisis Core: Final Fantasy VII*, lent his voice to Zack. And the leading roles? Nomura explains that Disney did the legwork for him by creating a list of experienced actors: "Usually I select the

---

22. Jennifer Hale is a star voice actress. She has participated in a vast number of productions and works a lot in the video game industry. Notably, she is the voice of female Commandant Shepard in *Mass Effect*, Naomi Hunter in *Metal Gear Solid*, and Samus Aran in *Metroid Prime*.

voice that's closest to the Japanese voice. However, this time, I wanted the voices to match the characters." As such, Terra was played by Jason Dohring, a television series actor (including, most prominently, in *Veronica Mars*). Willa Holland (Speedy in *Arrow*) lent her voice to Aqua. By giving the roles of Ventus to Jesse McCartney (Roxas) and of Vanitas to Haley Joel Osment (Sora), Nomura knew that he would sow confusion among fans of the series. The question is, <u>why</u>? "It may mean something (...) and Miyu Irino (the Japanese voice of Sora) wanted to play a bad guy." Thank you, Mr. Director, for clarifying that. Nevertheless, as we know, nothing Nomura does is random. Everything is always well thought-out and calculated[23]. What's more, there's reason to believe that the choices of voices for the two masters had deeper meanings. Nomura says, "For them, it was an easy choice. They were made to play Master Eraqus and Master Xehanort, and I must admit that I was being a bit crafty." He has no idea how right he is. Mark Hamill versus Leonard Nimoy; Luke Skywalker versus Mr. Spock. *Star Wars* versus *Star Trek* in a Disney and *Final Fantasy* mash-up. Yes, it's totally out of left field, but it makes sense. Both are fantastic voice actors. Hamill is an even better voice actor than live-action actor, as proven in his role as Joker in the *Batman* cartoons and his extensive video game experience (from Adrian Ripburger in *Full Throttle* to Goro Majima in *Yakuza*). Leonard Nimoy has lent his voice to Optimus Prime (*Transformers*).

The Japanese voices were just as impressive. Eraqus was played by Makio Inoue, a huge star who has played Goemon Ishikawa (*Rupan Sansei*) and, especially, Harlock (*Space Pirate Captain Harlock*), having filled this role since the original series in 1978! Playing opposite him, Xehanort was voiced by Chikao Otsuka, a.k.a. Dr. Robotnik (*Sonic the Hedgehog*), as well as Jagi (*Hokuto no Ken*), Mercenary Tao (*Dragon Ball*), and the official voice of Captain Hook in Japan! Fun fact: the *seiyū* for Terra-Xehanort was his own son, Akio Otsuka, who was already the official voice of Ansem, as well as of Big Boss/Snake (*Metal Gear Solid*), Batou (*Ghost in the Shell*), and Gabranth (*Final Fantasy XII*). The foursome of Ventus/Roxas and Vanitas/Sora was also given life by well-known actors: Koki Uchiyama and Miyu Irino. Ryôtarô

23. We'll come back to that in Volume II.

Okiayu, who previously played Setzer in *Kingdom Hearts II*—as well as Zero (*Rockman*), Alucard (*Castlevania*), and Ronfar (*Lunar 2*)—voiced Terra. Finally, Aqua was played by Megumi Toyoguchi, who notably played Paine in *Final Fantasy X-2* and in *Kingdom Hearts II*. On a side note, she also played Dawn (*Pokémon*) and Junko (*Danganronpa*).

The actors and actresses who give life to characters while making us forget that it's just acting are unsung heroes. We thank them.

STORM DIVER
[*KH3D*: CONCEPT]

Let's backtrack a little bit. In the middle of development of *Kingdom Hearts: Birth by Sleep*, Nomura was already thinking about the next step. This is a habit for him, having always operated this way for each game in the series. However, this time, his considerations went deeper. You might even say he was questioning. This was because of a very trying summer 2009: he could no longer move forward with *Final Fantasy versus XIII* which, because of company priorities, was taken away from his team by management so that they could provide support for *Final Fantasy XIII*, which was mired with Crystal Tools problems. What's more, friction had started to become apparent between Disney and Hikaru Utada, the Japanese pop star so closely connected to *Kingdom Hearts*. Even though her statements remained reserved, she suggested that she would "probably no longer" participate in the series. Her father/manager/producer, Teruzane Utada, took the opportunity to settle a score with the American company, saying that "Disney doesn't pay." That's not quite true. Hikaru explains that with each new song, she always writes two versions (a Japanese one and an American one), which suggests that Disney pulled a fast one by only paying her for one version each time. We can also imagine that each time the theme songs were reused in each of the spin-offs, she was not sufficiently compensated. We'll never know the full truth of this story, so we'll just have to stick with these assumptions. In any case, these declarations worried Nomura, who knew that he would have to fight to keep her on board. He was stuck in the reality of business, which he hates. To alleviate his fears, he decided to concentrate on his role as a creator. He continued to pursue the same objective: create a successful game along the lines of *Advent Children*. He knew that salvation would not come from *Final Fantasy versus XIII*. He had already realized some time before that he could not fight the menace of it being turned into a numbered episode forever. Which, from a creative perspective, meant abandoning his grandiose ambitions and conforming to various requirements. His only option was to change the *Kingdom Hearts* paradigm. Take a different approach to his series and distinguish it even further from its twin, *Final Fantasy*. With hindsight, he found the series to be too conventional, lacking some zest or even zaniness, particularly in the exploration phases. Overall, it seemed too mundane. Weighing the pros and cons, he realized that he was chiefly responsible because he had placed restrictions on himself that the universe never required. Indeed, the cartoonish identity of *Kingdom Hearts* would let him do absolutely anything: "[*Kingdom Hearts*], above all, is about daring actions that would be impossible for a realistic character," Nomura says. The time had come for him to break the chains holding back both him and his series. The only limits should be imagination and enjoyment of the game. He "saw" the possibility of adding a vertical dimension to gameplay by allowing the characters to run on walls and jump impossible heights and by intensifying interactions with the environment. He wanted it to be fast-paced and fluid, both more and better than in the past, and that went for both exploration and battles, above all. He called this new (or revamped) style *Free-Flow Action*. This would now be the heart of *Kingdom Hearts*. Furthermore, Nomura wanted to take the time to fully develop this approach with a (or several) last game(s) before the grand finale, the culmination of a decade of reflection: *Kingdom Hearts III*. The possibilities were exciting, but, for the time being, he had to come back down to earth to face reality, particularly Square Enix's strategy for the current fiscal year (2009). The thing was, no portable console would allow for the grand vision he wanted to make a reality. The home consoles would potentially work, but it wasn't the right time for *Kingdom Hearts III* and, in any case, *Final Fantasy versus XIII* had waited long enough; it was without a doubt its turn. Nonetheless, Nomura began sketching out a plot that, logically, would

fit into the canon after *Re: coded*, allowing for the return of Sora that fans had been clamoring for[24].

However, for some time[25] he had wanted to dedicate an episode to Riku and depict "how he turns the darkness inside of him into a strength." It would be foolish to not have them share the lead, as had already been done in *Chain of Memories*. What's more, the friendship between Sora and Riku remains one of the most important symbols in the series, "light and dark sides of the heart," thus "connecting" this hypothetical game to the rest of the series. The only thing missing was a link to *Birth by Sleep*. Given the context, the two heroes would have to prepare to face Xehanort. So, they would have a final challenge to overcome, the Mark of Mastery exam they would need to become Keyblade Masters. With that, he had everything he needed for a new installment. The only thing left was to wait for the right opportunity and the right console.

January 2009, in Kyoto. Nintendo was thinking about its next portable console. How could they surprise consumers? What technology should they use? One of the programmers suggested, "Why not 3D?" An old hobbyhorse that goes back to the 1980s. Back to 1987, to be exact, when Nintendo produced glasses with shutters called the Famicom 3D System, an accessory for the Famicom Disk System. Compatible games included *Famicom Grand Prix II: 3D Hot Rally*[26], which marked the first collaboration between Shigeru Miyamoto and Satoru Iwata (who was just a programmer at HAL Laboratory at the time).

After that, Nintendo held onto hopes of trying 3D again, doing so with the Virtual Boy in 1995, which was probably the company's greatest failure ever (yes, even worse than the Wii U). In spite of all that, the Nintendo president at the time, Hiroshi Yamauchi, continued to believe in the potential of the amazing technology. He even pressed Shigeru Miyamoto to do another test. That's why the GameCube had a 3D system built into it. *Luigi's Mansion*, the console's first game, was originally designed with stereo imaging[27]. According to Miyamoto, it

24. According to a survey conducted for the series' fifteenth anniversary, Sora and Aqua are the most popular characters. More details to come.
25. Since 2007. See page 227.
26. Developed by HAL Laboratory for the Famicom Disk System and released in 1988.
27. Now you understand better why Nintendo put so much energy and passion into producing *Luigi's Mansion 2* for the Nintendo 3DS. Perhaps it was their way of chasing an old ghost…

worked very well with glasses. That being said, having a game depend on an accessory was out of the question: "Let's assume that only 10 percent of users buy the glasses offered optionally; in that case, you end up making games in 3D for only that 10 percent," he explains. For a time, Nintendo considered building a screen into the console, but abandoned the idea because it was far too risky and, above all, very expensive. Never giving up, they held onto the idea of 3D and did another test a few months later. This time, they tried to incorporate an autostereoscopic (or auto-3D, not requiring any additional peripheral) screen to the Game Boy Advance SP. This was definitely the right method, but the resolution was far too weak. Defeated, the engineers threw in the towel... until that fateful meeting in 2009. Finally, all systems were go. Nintendo dominated both the home console (Wii) AND portable console (DS) markets, prices had dropped, and, in particular, they could produce the 3D console very quickly. All they had to do was work off of the Nintendo DS, improve its specs, and give it an autostereoscopic screen with good resolution, a subject that most people are unfamiliar with. So, I'll explain the basics. Yes, this is important for the next step of the journey because, though it may never seem like it at first, all roads lead to... *Kingdom Hearts*.

➵ MEMO ON RESOLUTION

R esolution is not determined by the (physical) size of the screen, but rather by the number of dots (called pixels in digital terms) that it can display. A more appropriate term would actually be "screen definition." For example, the LCD (*liquid crystal display*) screen of the Game Boy can display 160 × 144 pixels. If you still have one, as well as a magnifying glass and some time to kill, you can check for yourself and you will see that, indeed, the screen is 160 dots wide by 144 dots tall. The Game Boy Advance is called that because its screen supports 16-bit colors (32,768 colors per pixel) and its definition is 50

percent greater than that of its predecessor, at 240 × 160 px. However, that wasn't enough for Nintendo, which was testing the famous, previously mentioned autostereoscopic LCD screen for the GBA SP. This test screen also displayed 240 × 160 px, or rather 120 × 2 × 160, since the resolution was split in two and equally distributed across both eyes to generate the intended 3D effect. This resolution was far too weak, resulting in what's referred to in technical language as "pixel soup." The test was a failure and the screen was rejected. For the Nintendo DS, the company still chose not to go for a higher resolution and settled on two LCD screens (one being a touchscreen), each displaying 256 × 192 px. This was a slight improvement from the GBA. They didn't seriously consider the idea of 3D again until the Nintendo 3DS. First and foremost, the issue was the price. They ultimately decided to use an LCD touchscreen with a definition of 320 × 240 px (thus greater than the original DS screen) for the lower screen and an autostereoscopic LCD screen that was 800 × 240 px for the upper screen. Once again, the resolution of the upper screen was divided in two to generate the 3D image (400 × 2 × 240 px). That's less than the PSP (480 × 272 px), but it was not a glaring difference. For the first time, a Nintendo console could display an image that was "practically" on par with the PlayStation 2. Indeed, you get similar image quality between a small screen with good resolution and a big screen, even one that has a definition up to two times greater. How can this be? It's just a matter of ratios, with help from an optical illusion. It's the very principle used by the Switch, Nintendo's latest console. To put things in perspective, consider that the smallest Apple Watch, whose screen measures 38 mm, can display 272 × 340 pixels. Yep, they keep getting better and better.

In early 2010, there was already an initial version of the SDK[28], but it was only available in-house at Nintendo and at The Pokémon Company. As such, a number of games were already being planned, such as *Mario Kart 7*, *Nintendogs+Cats*, the remakes of *The Legend of Zelda: Ocarina of Time* and *Starfox 64*, and of course *Kid Icarus Uprising*, the console's leading launch title[29]. While Nintendo had its various prestigious licenses to rely on, it had to boost its line-up with games from third-party publishers. They had specific ideas about what they wanted, particularly a *Tekken*, a *Metal Gear Solid*, and a *Kingdom Hearts*. In the weeks that followed, they got to work trying to convince certain creators[30] selected as the best of the best.

This led them to try to win over Square Enix, or rather Nomura. When he learned about the Nintendo 3DS for the first time, he immediately fell in love with the autostereoscopic effect: "I thought it would be much more finicky. It's amazing how everything seems so solid and three-dimensional." He also noticed that the screen's definition, significantly better than that of the original DS, was close to that of the PSP, which made him happy because he wouldn't have to cut corners on quality. That was a big plus. Even better was the joystick (called a "Circle Pad"). Nomura said, "[Analog controls] are crucial in action games." This was a big relief to him, having suffered with the Nintendo DS, to the point of being forced to simplify the battles in *Re: coded*.

He really liked this "very bold" console. It had everything: great visuals, functions, and controls, as well as lots of originality. As you might expect, he began trying to imagine a system that would be perfectly suited to the new console's "incredible sensation of depth." That's when he came up with "Dive Mode," a mini-game in which the player controls the character in a free fall while shooting and demonstrating skill, the objective being to reach the goal ring for their next

28. SDK stands for "software development kit." It's a software package intended to facilitate programming, for example, on a new console.
29. On a side note, after a few months of negotiations and aimless work (initially, this game by Masahiro Sakurai was an original story being developed by a team of only eight people), development of *Kid Icarus Uprising* officially began in March 2009, the same time that development officially began on the 3DS itself. Not having the SDK, for a long time, the team developed the game for the Wii and PC!
30. Including Square Enix, Konami, Level-5, Capcom, Koei Tecmo, SEGA, and Bandai Namco.

destination. The idea had two main purposes: it replaced the usual Gummi ship journey (the weakest part of the series) while making reference to the falls that opened the previous episodes[31]. To make a long story short, it was an idea with substance. This Nintendo 3DS was the console he'd been waiting for. It would allow him to experiment with his new philosophy,, "Free-Flow Action,", and improve it before *Kingdom Hearts III*. In other words, Nintendo passed its Mark of Mastery exam with flying colors: the *Kingdom Hearts 3D* project was on.

[INTERLUDE: *TRFF*]

For Ichirô Hazama[32], the Nintendo 3DS was also a godsend. It would bring an end to four years of frustration for him. Working alongside Nomura on *Final Fantasy VII: Advent Children* changed his way of seeing the world. In late 2005, he was thinking about his future. He wanted to make video games, in spite of the fact that he was just a merchandising guy and had no idea how to do so. After talking with Nomura, who encouraged him to pursue his dream, he decided to go for it. He then got the idea for a musical game based on the *Final Fantasy* universe. Being a total novice, he asked for help from Masanobu Suzui, one of his former underlings. This was not just a random choice: Suzui was a big fan of *Final Fantasy*[33] who also happened to have his own company, Indieszero, known for *Electroplankton*[34]. They worked together to write the concept. Before long, the game was planned for the Nintendo DS. However, it was relatively new at the time and its abilities were still too limited for the game. Before any development could begin, the project was canceled.

---

31. The scene that always opens each different episode in the series: the entry into the dream of the protagonist via a fall into the Chamber of Waking, a key location in the series. We'll come back to it in detail in Volume II.
32. Ichirô Hazama started his career in Bandai's procurement department. Poached by Shinji Hashimoto, he joined Square, where he became head of merchandising. His first "assisting" experience was with Tetsuya Nomura on *Final Fantasy VII: Advent Children*, for which he served as associate producer.
33. Before leading Indieszero, Masanobu Suzui cut his teeth with Hazama at Bandai, where, notably, he was in charge of the *Final Fantasy Trading Cards*.
34. *Electroplankton* is a creative musical game for the Nintendo DS created by artist Toshio Iwai, directed by Indieszero, and produced by Nintendo.

Crushed, Hazama returned to selling action figures until in 2010 one fine day restored his hopes: "Yes! We'll finally be able to do it," he exclaimed. It was an unexpected opportunity that he wasn't going to let pass him by. That very same day, he went to Indieszero to finalize his concept. He then submitted it and got the green light from Nomura, who took on the role of creative producer. And that position was not undeserved: he ultimately played a key role in the game's development. Firstly, he made the concept original by insisting that they give it an RPG flavor by adding battles and a character development system. In addition, he came up with the title, *Theatrhythm Final Fantasy*[35], and the tagline, "play your memories." He also took charge of a portion of the publicity by creating the cover art for the box himself and supervising the trailers. Nomura also advised Hazama to create a demo, telling him, "If we get people to try it, they will see for themselves how good it is." This was a very smart idea because otherwise it would have been difficult to see the enormous potential of *Theatrhythm*, partly because of its VERY particular visual style, which was created by the character designer for *Kingdom Hearts Mobile*, Atsuhiro Tsuchiya, a.k.a. Monster Octopus. At the time, he was working on the Avatar Menu and, moreover, the 800 pieces of gear for *Kingdom Hearts Re: coded*.

Ten bucks says you didn't see this transition coming. By the way, what ever happened to h.a.n.d.?

NO MORE BUGS!
[*RE: CODED*: DEVELOPMENT (CONTINUED)]

It was an exciting time in Sapporo, where they had just reached the halfway point in development. In other words, they had just six months left. Since time was not on their side, you might expect that they would be in panic mode or that everything would be falling apart. Nothing of the sort was happening; in fact, it was the complete opposite. The organization was perfect; each person knew what they

---

35. A simple contraction of "theater" and "rhythm." With such an unpronounceable name, it should be no surprise who came up with it.

had to do, worked fast, and worked well. Even communication between the studios, which is often complicated, was optimal. Every member of the team remembers how they came together to succeed. On several occasions, h.a.n.d. made its concerns known: terrified by the scope of the project, they were afraid that they wouldn't be able to meet their deadlines. The director's response could not have been more pragmatic. Halfway through development, he sent most of the important decision-makers (the co-director, planning director, etc.) to Sapporo for the remaining duration (six months) with just one mission: get the job done. In short, from a human resources perspective, everything was under control. The difficulty was to be found elsewhere. Besides the very tight timing, the game itself was no walk in the park. Beneath its nice spin-off veneer, it was actually the most incongruous game in the series. Each world was different, "like attractions in an amusement park," remembers Takahito Ebato (planning director), and the game situations were extremely varied. They included 3D A-RPG, 2D RPG with turns, puzzle games, 2D platformer with a few eccentricities like scrolling, as well as amazing inward/outward phases[36]; *Kingdom Hearts Re: Coded* incorporated many different genres. That's hard enough to handle on a normal timeline, but with such tight deadlines, it was nearly impossible. Naoyuki Ohashi (main programmer) says that he "felt like he was working on several games at once because the content was so varied."

And his work was far from over because it was time to add a key piece of the puzzle: the System Sectors. A series of secret rooms, scattered throughout the Datascape and teeming with the viruses responsible for bugs and other "reality" alterations." They are the very essence of the Datascape, in the form of data, without the mask of the various worlds explored. Since the team didn't get what Nomura wanted, Ryôto Shinzato (lead BG designer) created a prototype background to show what he had in mind. In doing this, he drew inspiration from *Tron* and from the image that people imagine of the "visual universe that could be a real world inside a computer." This approach was not unlike that used in many works from Disney, including *Tron*, yes, but

36. Inward/outward: The protagonist flees a pursuer by going toward the top of the screen or toward the bottom, and thus toward the player. It's a technique in game design.

also *Wreck-It Ralph* and many others... Another comparison would be *The Matrix*[37]. He tried to visually depict the work of an antivirus. Yes, this game is much deeper than you might think[38], but we'll come back to that later. For the audio identity of the System Sectors, "he [Nomura] wanted two new themes in a very old-school techno style," says Shimomura, who left that work to Hirosato Noda (synthesizer director), who in turn was honored to be trusted with such a project: "I will never forget the opportunity that she gave me to create my own arrangements." Finally, Yuki Hirose (sound designer) also received a request to create "computer sounds," of which he had to make around a hundred, on top of everything else. "It was a lot," he says, but he had a trick up his sleeve: "This is a secret, but most of the audio data are those from *Birth by Sleep*, just slightly reworked." Very clever.

In any case, the concept of the Sectors was not totally new. Nomura had already sketched out the idea for *coded*. So, why didn't he add them in the original game? "A combination of factors," he says. Perhaps demanding rooms with hundreds of levels from a team of newbies is reason enough? "When I told them that I wanted a hundred levels, they couldn't believe it," he says, as if he's the one who can't understand. Unsurprisingly, "Most of the members of the team for the phone version had never worked on a *Kingdom Hearts* before," says Koichi Akiyama (art director), not to mention on a phone and in 2008. In any case, the System Sectors, besides being the central feature of the adventure, also come in the form of imitation VR Missions (from *Metal Gear Solid*) or a knock-off *Bloody Palace* (from *Devil May Cry*, a tower with 9,999 levels; yep, that's the Japanese for you) in the Avatar Menu, a feature dedicated to interplayer communication, part of the legacy of *Kingdom Hearts Mobile*.

With the starting point for *Kingdom Hearts 3D* decided, Nomura considered the possibility of making a teaser for it in the form of a secret ending in *Re: coded*.

---

37. The immensely popular trilogy of films from sisters Lana and Lilly Wachowski, one of the top inspirations for *Kingdom Hearts*. We'll come back to that in Volume II.
38. *Re: coded* is a remarkable meta-game, as well as a profound "*mise en abyme*."

GETTING BACK IN THE GAME
[BUSINESS REVIEW]

Fiscal year 2009 (which ended on March 31, 2010). The risks the company took paid off. Square Enix naturally returned to its position as a leader among the strongest third-party publishers, ranked fourth, just behind SEGA Sammy (at the top were two huge Chinese companies, including Tencent[39], which was totally untouchable). *Final Fantasy XIII* had been released in all regions and sold 5.5 million units worldwide[40]. *Dragon Quest IX* reached a record 4.26 million units in Japan alone. And the icing on the cake, the acquisition of Eidos was already profitable thanks to *Batman: Arkham Asylum* and its 3.24 million copies sold worldwide. Square Enix was enjoying renewed success, but, in the process of achieving that success, had wrung all the potential out of the Nintendo DS. So, the company decided to change tack and go after the fast-growing smartphone market. It was a smart move: the port of *Final Fantasy* (of course) reached number one on the App Store. Encouraged by this, Square Enix decided to double-down on the smartphone market with a brand-new game, *Chaos Rings*, relying on Media.Vision, the studio behind *Wild Arms*, for its production. Finally, the publishing department boosted its sales with a new in-house series, *Soul Eater*. Wada knew that he was playing all of his cards at once, which is dangerous, but he was unfazed because his ultimate weapon, *Final Fantasy XIV*, was set for release in the next fiscal year. Failure was unimaginable.

39. This Chinese giant is, first and foremost, a purveyor of internet services, including several social networks and an instant messenger. Starting in 2007, Tencent established itself as a new player in the video game industry, by acquiring several South Korean licenses, distributing the very popular *League of Legends* and *Clash of Clans* in China, and implementing its very aggressive business models, including the sale of virtual assets. In 2009, it became the number-one video game company in the world (in terms of revenue).
40. At that point, it had only been available for three weeks in the United States and Europe, suggesting that it would sell many more copies. Which was indeed the case.

READY TO RUSH
[*KH3D*: PRE-PROD]

On March 23, Nintendo announced the development of the Nintendo 3DS in a brief press release, simply promising to reveal much more at E3. Why did they do things this way? To get shareholders excited. And why at that moment? Because it was just before the end of the fiscal year. When you review the facts, that's the only possible explanation; otherwise, it makes no sense from a communications perspective. To be perfectly honest, it remains a mystery to this day.

For its pre-E3 press conference, Nintendo was like a boxer. A left hook of self-congratulation (of course), followed by a straight right with big current-gen announcements, including *The Legend of Zelda: Skyward Sword*, *Donkey Kong Country Returns*, *GoldenEye* and *Epic Mickey*[41]. Finally, to KO the competition, Nintendo delivered an upper-cut with the Nintendo 3DS and its strong line-up of third-party titles, including a *Metal Gear Solid*, a *Tekken*, and a *Kingdom Hearts* (leading people to imagine a *Final Fantasy* as well).

It was an impressive plan, but nothing was ready just yet. Nintendo, as usual, was behind schedule. What's more, they were slow to warn the third-party publishers. A month before the event, Nintendo asked them if they had demos for their games, if only to beef up their private presentations. Square Enix, of course, responded no, but we're already familiar with their exceptional ability to respond fast. And in this case, they really didn't have a choice. They HAD TO respond. Since E3 2006, their reputation had been tarnished. This was due to several communications errors, as well as too many delays on games like *Final Fantasy XIV*, or *Dragon Quest IX* before that, not to mention *Final Fantasy versus XIII*, which had totally evaporated. The public had gradually lost confidence in Square Enix. It was such a huge problem that Wada, starting in 2009, began blaming their marketing, which he considered a real Achilles heel for the company. As such, an autostereoscopic demo would be welcome, or better yet was a necessity. It

---

41. *Epic Mickey*: that time Disney tried to make "their own" *Kingdom Hearts*, by their own admission. It's a game of great interest for this book and we'll come back to it in Volume II.

would serve as more evidence of Square Enix's spectacular economic comeback and prove, more than ever before, that they were embracing the innovation arms race. It was a chance to reverse the trend, but they needed to hurry because E3 was almost upon them. And once again, acting as the company's champion, Nomura was "persuaded" to come up with an initial teaser trailer for *Kingdom Hearts 3D*. This was no real problem because he already had everything more or less laid out. He just had to determine who would be involved. The Kingdom Team, freed from *Final Fantasy XIII* a few weeks previously? No, because they were FINALLY focused on *Final Fantasy versus XIII*, which had just barely started pre-production. The younger generation? No, they were off working on *Dissidia Duodecim*, led by their young prodigy Mitsunori Takahashi and guided by their master, Takeshi Arakawa. So, what about h.a.n.d.?? No, they were just a contractor. It's true, they often worked with Nomura, but at that point in time they were very busy with *Re: coded* and they had no experience with the kind of graphics needed. There weren't many people left to choose from. In any case, from the time he began planning out *KH3D*, Nomura knew that he wouldn't make it with anyone but the Osaka team. They may have been busy, but Nomura trusted them and knew that they could get it done. However, there was still a problem to be resolved. He needed time and resources. Designers, modelers, texture artists, programmers, the list goes on. He needed as many technicians as possible. However, they were busy finalizing the international version of *Birth by Sleep*. That meant a smaller staff. Nevertheless, Nomura went to Yoshimoto and asked him to reassign people according to his needs. It was a matter of priority. They needed to maximize their chances in a minimal amount of time. He wrote and storyboarded the teaser to save some time, then went to Osaka with Shinji Hashimoto. The boss' presence was crucial for underscoring the fact that the request was coming straight from corporate. In other words, to put some pressure on the Osaka team.

Here's how things went. It was June 1 and there were exactly 14 days remaining until E3. Nomura laid out the future of the series for Tai Yasue: The story of *Kingdom Hearts* was going to take a new turn thanks to *Free-Flow Action*. Then, Nomura presented to him the *Kingdom Hearts 3D* project overall and all of the planning he had done for it. Yasue loved Nomura's ideas and the new direction the series was going to take. However, Nomura explained to Yasue that development wouldn't start until September. For the time being, they had to make a 3D video about a minute long in less than 10 days. Hashimoto returned to Tokyo while Nomura remained in Osaka to direct the teaser. They needed to quickly come up with solutions to meticulously follow what Nomura had written. Given the exceptional nature of the project, the technicians suggested that they use the *Birth by Sleep* engine to make the work faster. Whether they modeled or textured Sora instead of Ventus was of little importance. The assets (backgrounds, characters, enemies, and FX) and the animations were developed as "spin-offs" from *Birth by Sleep*[42], then converted to 3D. After all, it wasn't an actual game yet; they were just making a video. There was nothing too complicated in and of itself. Their allotted time was needed, in particular, to create a story to match Nomura's ambitions, and all of the corrections and steps of approval that come with that. There was nothing new about this method; it's the same one used by the film industry. Even today, there aren't many films written for, not to mention produced in, 3D. Most of the time, movies are produced in a traditional fashion and it's only afterward, in post-production, that the footage is modified to add depth. The first film to really buck the trend was James Cameron's *Avatar* (in 2009) and that was only thanks to the inventiveness (and genius) of the director. To create the 3D effect, he created his own tools himself by connecting (and tinkering with) two Sony HDC-F950 HD cameras, which (today) cost over $120,000 each.

Osaka completed its mission stupendously. *Kingdom Hearts 3D* had the word DEMO attached to it so as not to put out any false advertising. In any case, it was just a temporary title because even 3D ended up being just an acronym for the game's future subtitle. It may sound silly, but for a Japanese person, 3D is pronounced *Three Dee* (thus, the same as in English) and literally implies three words starting with D;

---

42. The creation of assets for *Kingdom Hearts 3D* left some traces in the data for *Kingdom Hearts: Birth by Sleep Final Mix*. If you dig down a bit, you'll find character models for Sora, Riku, Kairi, and certain enemies, including the Twilight Thorn (from *KH II*), but also Ansem and Xemnas (who appear in the first "real" trailer shown to the public in January 2011), as well as animation sets with the movements of the characters seen in the teaser.

in other words, Why Do Things the Easy Way When You Can Do Them the Hard Way, episode 372.

Hashimoto and Nomura went to Los Angeles. Nomura was already in a bad mood even before E3 began, thanks to the promo days that he hates and his nervousness about the audience's reaction. But, when it came down to it, he didn't really give a damn because that wasn't why he was there.

TREASURED MEMORIES
[HD I.5 REMIX]

Nomura was called to a meeting with Steve Wadsworth, the head of Disney Interactive Studios, who was on his way out[43]. This is no big revelation, but I think it's safe to say that Wadsworth took Nomura's appearance at E3 as an opportunity to see him one last time. It's only right to give advance warning to a longtime partner who you've had a fruitful relationship with, don't you think?

Nomura took the opportunity to bring up the tenth anniversary of *Kingdom Hearts*, which was fast approaching. Before getting to the heart of the matter, he stated a fact. A lot of things had happened in the past decade; in particular, video game audiences had been in constant flux. The numbers said it all: the portable games in the series sold well, but not as well as the "numbered" episodes. While there may have been a faithful core target audience that bought each installment, they were a minority; those who showed no interest in the portable episodes, often simply because they didn't have the necessary console(s), passed judgment solely based on whether there was a number behind the name or considered spin-offs to be just a sales ploy. Whatever the case, the results were the same: they only played *Kingdom Hearts* and *Kingdom Hearts II*. What's more, other players

---

43. Wadsworth left the company in September to work on new projects, particularly the free web radio *Slacker* and to lead Tapjoy, one of the first companies to use the "freemium" game model. He is also a board member at Entertainment Partners, a leader in integrated production management solutions for the entertainment industry. He was replaced at Disney Interactive in October 2010 by John Pleasants and James Pitaro.

had joined the bandwagon along the way and it was hard for them to understand what was going on in the story or to get their hands on the first episodes which, although they had aged quite well, used outmoded technology and a 4:3 aspect ratio. As such, the players of *Kingdom Hearts* were not all in the same boat and it would be hard to continue the story (with *Kingdom Hearts III*) unless everyone was brought up to speed. So, Nomura proposed that they make a compilation of the six games released up to that point, but in HD. And the tenth anniversary of the series was the perfect opportunity. Nomura was so persistent in his proposal that Disney gave the OK[44]. What's interesting about this decision is that *Kingdom Hearts* continued to forge its own path without the need to "do the same thing as *Final Fantasy.*" In fact, the opposite was happening, since *Final Fantasy* went on to follow the trend started by *KH*. And there's a good reason for that: the remake of *X/X-2* (which then led to the remake of *XII*) was an initiative brought forward by none other than Tetsuya Nomura. In the meantime, Osaka took advantage of his absence to put the finishing touches on *Birth by Sleep*. Or so they thought.

HUNTER OF THE DARK
[BBS FINAL MIX]

Upon his return to Japan, Nomura convinced the upper management of Square Enix that they needed a *Kingdom Hearts: Birth by Sleep Final Mix*. One can imagine that the fiscal year's strong performance and several days spent with Hashimoto in the United States were both decisive factors…

Of course, there was also the bold and enticing proposal advanced by Nomura: a <u>playable</u> secret ending. Come again? You read that right. He wanted to continue the story of Aqua's journey through he…[45] I mean, umm, the Realm of Darkness. Initially, he wanted this "episode,"

---

44. Nomura may have been the creator of *Kingdom Hearts*, but the IP belonged to Disney. As such, for all the, shall we say, crucial decisions, Nomura had to ask for permission/consent from the American company, sometimes even traveling to do so in person.
45. Oops! Apparently I'm itching to write the final chapter. Bad news for me: there's still a long road (to Calvary) to travel before the end. Just kill me now.

as he called it, to be in the form of a "classic[46] video," but he soon realized that would not be enough to justify a *Final Mix*. And he was <u>really</u> set on the idea. That's when inspiration struck: allow the player to BECOME Aqua for the secret ending. Though he didn't invent the idea, this was probably one of the first examples of a DLC scenario[47], with the difference that it was tagged onto an improved final version of *Kingdom Hearts: Birth by Sleep*. Indeed, *Final Mix* incorporated all of the content added to the Western version and even brought in some new quirks.

For example, there were new command styles like Illusion, a sort of Blue Magic[48] allowing the player to transform into different kinds of Unversed and <u>use their attacks</u>. Another such new command style was Rhythm Mixer. You might be wondering where he got such an idea (and name). I'll give you a clue: you'll find the answer on page 268. What's more, Nomura decided to add side missions (like in *Kingdom Hearts II Final Mix*) that were little challenges, often with time limits. He and the Osaka team mutually agreed that the Mirage Arena was the weakest part and that they needed to add more interactions between the players to push them to play more cooperatively. This involved new Friendship Commands, as well as two new secret bosses: the Armor of the Master (i.e. Eraqus) and No Heart, which appears to be Xehanort's armor[49], both "much harder to defeat than the Unknown, or even nearly impossible to beat alone." The secret bosses are purposely hardcore to push players to cooperate.

To create a greater impact, the team created introductory scenes for each one, but Nomura turned them down, explaining that these two secret bosses "had no part in the story, they were only in the Arena." Simple cutscenes, without a word from them, would suffice. He wanted to avoid creating any more confusion, explaining honestly with a laugh: "The game is already hard enough to understand." Finally, he

---

46. *Kingdom Hearts* sets the bar so high that a secret ending can be considered "classic." If you just look around the rest of the market, you'll see that having a secret ending is still quite exceptional. Not at all normal or standard.
47. DLC: downloadable content. In video game jargon, the word "scenario" is added after DLC to distinguish an extended game experience from ordinary extra options.
48. The ability to use enemy techniques, something *Final Fantasy* players are quite familiar with.
49. Though this has never been confirmed. In any case, No Heart is definitely the "knight" form of Xemnas during the final battle in *Kingdom Hearts II*; however, his cape was taken away because it caused too many problems for the animators.

absolutely wanted another Disney boss, a huge one. He first thought about reusing one of the Titans from *Hercules*. Osaka then suggested to him a more original idea: Monstro, the sperm whale from *Pinocchio*, which Nomura gladly agreed to.

PRETTY PRETTY ABILITIES
[RE: CODED: DEVELOPMENT (CONTINUATION AND CONCLUSION)]

At the end of June, development of *Kingdom Hearts Re: coded* was 80 percent complete. What remained were a few odds and ends for each department to figure out, in particular the *Matrix* system, i.e. the backbone of the remake. The Osaka team was working fast and diligently, but there was only so much they could do at one time. So, with the international version of *Birth by Sleep* finalized and *Final Mix* underway, they decided to reassign a score of people to finish up *Re: coded*.

[INTERLUDE: HOW THE OSAKA TEAM WORKS]

When I say "Osaka," I'm referring to Square Enix Osaka, an entity with between 50 and 70 people with varying statuses: employees, *freelancers* (regular and otherwise), and even some bosses of micro-enterprises. For a long time, Osaka was an afterthought at Square. So, Yoichi Yoshimoto decided to feed them more work by finding opportunities elsewhere, meaning providing services to other publishers. Since Osaka had some pretty good technicians, some of their programmers, modelers, and other technical people were assigned to outside productions. In fact, many games are produced this way, a method called 360°. These games are basically "assembled" from parts made by people from several companies. This was the case for *Mario Hoops 3-on-3*, which involved people from Tecmo, Square Enix, Capcom, and Nintendo collaborating together. There's also *Mario Sports Mix*, which involved not only "star programmers" Kenro Tsujimoto and Tatsuo Fujii, but also experienced modelers and graphic

artists, not to mention Gen Kobayashi as the art director. At the time of *Re:coded*'s development, Yoshimoto was getting ready to direct the PSP version of *Final Fantasy IV: The After Years* (and *The Complete Collection*) with the studio Bullets (which went on to develop *Uppers* and *Senran Kagura: New Link*, among others) working under him. Now you know why that remake was one of the best.

However, just because these employees work on games for other publishers does not mean that they're not part of the Osaka "entity" and that they don't take an interest in what their colleagues are up to. Rather, they often help each other out in little ways, giving a few hours, days, or even weeks of their time. They are then included in the credits according to the nature and/or duration of their involvement, either added to the famous "Special Thanks" section or to the main team… even though they may have only worked on the game for a grand total of two weeks. The advantage of this is that it inflates the number of people involved, giving the impression of a huge production with 300 people, while that's not necessarily the case. In any event, you should really see a game studio as a living being. The people in the studio talk with each other, collaborate, smoke and eat together, stay late, and help each other out. That's not the case everywhere, but it's quite common, especially in Japan where a job still tends to be seen as a calling in life, more so than in Europe. Long story short, that's how Tai Yasue got reinforcements to finish work on *Kingdom Hearts Re: coded*. I can imagine it now: Yasue working in a dark office; a guy comes to wish him a good evening, then, seeing his boss drowning in work, takes off his coat and asks how he can help. That's also how the video game world works. Or at least, that's how it should be. I know perfectly well that this sort of information is a side note, or even completely off topic, but in my view, it really enriches the narrative, besides being necessary to understand what the video game industry is like and how it operates. End parenthesis.

In Tokyo, the team of graphic artists was struggling with certain backgrounds, including for Olympus Coliseum: "It's more difficult than expected because of the large number of different zones," explained Ryôto Shinzato (lead BG designer), adding that they would probably have to "adjust things until the end." It was also time for Masaru Oka (cutscene director) to replace Chip and Dale, which were used as placeholders[50] for the dialogs and are sources of a number of funny anecdotes: "In the scene where Cerberus arrives, Sora was shaking like a leaf before... Chip," says Oka. The team had a good laugh at that. Scriptwriter Daisuke Watanabe says that he too had to make some adjustments because, up to that point, the Unknown in Castle Oblivion wasn't supposed to be Roxas... but instead Axel! So, everyone was putting on their final touches before the debugging phase. It was the ideal time to add a final big piece of content. Nomura had his heart set on teasing *Kingdom Hearts 3D* with a secret ending, but "*Re: coded* had a lot of video scenes (...) and there was almost no space available." He changed tack: "Since there's not enough room left for a surprise scene, we'll have to shock people with dialog," he decided. He traded in his original ambitions for an ordinary scene of dialog between Mickey and Yen Sid where the old master makes a major revelation "connecting" *Re: coded* not only to *Kingdom Hearts 3D*, but also to *Birth by Sleep*. It all came full circle.

Although it's a little-known (and undervalued) game, for the people who worked on *Kingdom Hearts Re: coded*, to this day, it is the source of some of their fondest memories. During the game's development, they experienced some serious life moments that will remain etched in their minds (and hearts). Takeshi Ebato (planning director) remembers, for example, huge, delicious pieces of sashimi shared with his colleagues while they were on assignment in Sapporo. Watanabe remembers "a real feeling of unity, in spite of a smaller team size." Koichi Akiyama says that he got "goosebumps when he read the script." I'm sure the particular conditions of the game's development played an important role, but these exaggerated emotions hide a truth, something pure and precious. The most senior team members are nostalgic about the project. For example, Yuki Hirose (sound designer) says, "For certain sounds, we had to search through the audio files for *Kingdom Hearts*, some of which were exactly 10 years old," evoking a strong emotion in him, somewhere between joy and melancholy. Similarly, Mai Okauchi says, "For Jiminy's journal, we reused the 3D model that we made for *Kingdom Hearts II*." In the game, for each world debugged, a new

---

50. A placeholder can be any substitute while waiting for something to be made (a title, a logo, etc.).

journal page was added with a key phrase. As such, "we would add and turn the pages, which brought back all sorts of memories for me." A metaphor for her own experiences. She began by designing textures alongside Tomohiro Hasegawa. Today, she serves as art and character director. She's come quite a long way! To conclude this lovely little paragraph, Hirose, truly inspired, had this to say: "We were checking the music in each cutscene up until the last minute. When I looked around me, I said to myself that I had the best team in the whole company. Mickey says at one point, 'Never forget, you don't fight alone. Your friends are there for you.' That's exactly how I felt, but in real life." What else is there to say?

That's the magic of *Kingdom Hearts*.

MASTER, TELL ME THE TRUTH
[BBS FINAL MIX]

While people in the West were just playing *Birth by Sleep* for the first time, a portion of the Osaka team was already approaching the end of development of *Final Mix*. At the end of September, all that was left was to finish up the secret episode, which would take place between episode 0 (*Birth by Sleep*) and episode 1 (*Kingdom Hearts*), hence its name, *0.5*[51]. As planned, it would allow players to play as Aqua in the Realm of Darkness. Although it was shorter than a normal world, it maintained the normal game patterns, including searching for chests and a final boss, who was totally unexpected. Unlike the usual secret ending, it was not a reward requiring the player to go above and beyond. Rather, it was actually—interestingly enough—accessible to anyone who finished the game, even at the lowest level of difficulty. That says a lot about the intentions behind it. Nomura didn't want <u>anyone</u> to miss out on the story in his famous secret episode. A bit of mercy on his part? No, it was a trap in the form of a new secret ending entitled *A fragmentary passage*. It was a video, with *Destati* as the background music, composed of several brand-new scenes and ending with the very enigmatic words *Birth by Sleep — Volume Two*. Once again, the

---

51. See Volume II.

director was toying with his audience, hoping to surprise players and leave them wanting more. He was aware that fans would know that the only possible sequel to **BBS** was *Kingdom Hearts*. Unless... What if there was a sequel to Aqua's adventures in the Realm of Darkness, as implied by the emergence of the Castle of Dreams before her at the start of the video? The second scene also raised questions, with Mickey also appearing in the Realm of Darkness. Could it be that he met Aqua and, thanks to her, found the Keyblade that he uses at the end of *Kingdom Hearts*? Did they work together? If that's the case, why didn't she "wake up"? So many questions, so few answers. Players were snared in the trap. It was exactly what Nomura wanted and why he was determined to create the secret episode[52] and make it accessible to all. Further proof of how unique he is.

The worst part about it is that he <u>already</u> knew that there wouldn't be a *Birth by Sleep 2*, even though he avoided questions about it on several occasions. In reality, he was using a play on words. *A fragmentary passage* or "*Volume Two*" is not the secret ending of *Birth by Sleep*, but rather that of *0.5*, i.e. <u>the secret episode</u>. In turn, *0.5* is the "first episode" of *Zero point*[53]. This implied that there would be others and, if you follow the same logic, it should be called *0.2*, read as "*Zero Point Two*." Since Nomura had presented *Birth by Sleep* as a prelude to *Kingdom Hearts III* since 2009, there was room for doubt. Could it be that everything was already written out? Could this supposed episode *0.2* already be planned out as a prologue to the final episode? Nothing is out of the question, especially when it comes to Nomura! Nomura's *A fragmentary passage* trick was not unlike the *Birth by Sleep* trick, but took it even further: the video produced four years before the game that it would come from and, disturbingly, the actual game in question both turned out to be one and the same. *MINDFUCK*? Could he be messing with us again with the **SAME GAME** using a mirror image? OK.

---

52. You can probably find another reason on page 263.
53. It's very interesting that no one ever pays attention to this intertitle in the phase that introduces the secret episode. And yet, there it is in black and white: "*Zero point*." A code for the parallel story of Aqua in the Realm of Darkness where, as we know, time doesn't pass. I'll let you mull that over.

Calm down. Let's not jump to conclusions, we don't have enough information about the development of *Kingdom Hearts III* to say for sure. So, we'll have to settle for a guess… for now. Now, as I was saying. In October, Megumi Toyoguchi, a.k.a. Aqua, recorded the few lines of extra dialog for *0.5,*, which was also the only part of the game only dubbed in Japanese, while the rest let you choose the language, as in *Kingdom Hearts II Final Mix*. The end of development of *Kingdom Hearts: Birth by Sleep Final Mix* brought a definitive end to an adventure that had started five years previously.

Symbolically, the "rule of threes" ends here. *Kingdom Hearts* was thus ready to serenely begin its final act, crowned by its new style (*Free-Flow Action*), orchestrated by its visionary <u>architect</u>, and made possible by the team that, in summer 2005, dared to tell him, "We're the best, you won't regret it."

(RE)CONNECT

January 2010.
The 28th**.** Release of *Kingdom Hearts: coded Episode 8 Castle Oblivion*.

February 2010. Nomura revealed his plan for the years to come: "We would really like to release a *Kingdom Hearts* every year." Unbelievable though it may see, he kept his word and a game in the series indeed came out every[54] year. Incidentally, that's always been the case since *Kingdom Hearts: Chain of Memories*.

In the same conversation, he said that he was considering a "mystery" game connected to the rest of the series and "probably more canon than spin-off." We'll never know exactly what he was referring to because the project in question was canceled, giving way to *KH3D*. However, several clues point to it being the famous *Zero point* (or *Birth by Sleep II*), focused entirely on Aqua's odyssey through the Realm of Darkness. It's probably one of the factors that pushed him to make the secret episode in *Kingdom Hearts: Birth by Sleep Final Mix*. This is just an assumption because Nomura has always avoided questions on the subject.

54. Except in 2016, which *Kingdom Hearts HD 2.8 Final Chapter Prologue* missed by 12 days.

The 20th. A fan sent an email to Eddie Carroll asking him if he planned on lending his voice again to Jiminy Cricket. The actor answered affirmatively. Given that he was not involved in *Birth by Sleep* and that was the only *KH* coming out in 2010, his response suggested there would be a surprise game.

March 2010.

The 16th. *Kingdom Hearts: Birth by Sleep* was officially announced for release in the USA. However, fans had to settle for a vague "summer 2010" as the release date. The official website was launched on the same day. The same was done for Europe the next day.

The 23rd. Nintendo announced the Nintendo 3DS in a press release.

The 24th. Fans learned that, besides *Kingdom Hearts III*, two new episodes were being developed. Nomura also made clear that the *Kingdom Hearts* series would not end with *KH III*. Finally, he expressed his desire to launch a brand-new game with multiple protagonists, probably in 2011.

April 2010.

The 6th. Eddie Carroll passed away due to a brain tumor. May he rest in peace. He was very quickly replaced by Phil Snyder, a regular performer at The Comedy Store in Los Angeles.

May 2010.

Italian illustrator Roberto Ferrari joined the *Final Fantasy versus XIII* team.

The 14th. Release of the first official US video for *Kingdom Hearts: Birth by Sleep*. It was a "cut[55]" of the Japanese launch trailer, about 40 seconds long, beginning with the tagline *"Destiny is never left to chance"* and ending with a monologue delivered by Leonard Nimoy, then revealing the release date for the American market: September 7. Three days later, a localized version of the same trailer also revealed the European release date: September 10.

Square Enix confirmed that the game would be released on its own, but also in a collector's bundle with a "Mystic Silver" PSP–3000

---

55. In video game jargon, a shortened version.

customized for *Kingdom Hearts*, a 4-GB memory stick, and a movie on a UMD (indeed, there was one).

The 19th. Phil Snyder inadvertently revealed that his first performance as Jiminy Cricket would be for *Kingdom Hearts Recoded* (yes, he made a mistake in the spelling). This was a surprise for all since no one had ever heard mention of it.

June 2010.

Very early in June, a Japanese journalist asked Nomura if a *Kingdom Hearts: Birth by Sleep Final Mix* was a possibility. The director answered that his top concern was finalizing the international version.

The 1st. Shinji Hashimoto tweeted about a meeting in Osaka with Nomura to plan for an "incredible new title whose direction has been established."

The 8th. Accompanied on his trip to E3 by Nomura, Hashimoto implies in a tweet that there would be a "shocking announcement." The next day, Square Enix Europe announced on social media a remake of *Kingdom Hearts: coded* for the Nintendo DS, renamed *Re: coded*.

The 15th. *Kingdom Hearts 3D DEMO* was announced in the line-up for the Nintendo 3DS during Nintendo's pre-E3 press conference. Later, Hashimoto explained on Twitter that, although the game wouldn't be available to play at any booth during E3, Square Enix had created a 3D video. "It all starts with [this video]," he noted. Of course, it was only shown during private sessions and was never distributed to the public. So, I'll tell you what it contained.

Sora and Riku were leaning against the paopu tree in the Destiny Islands. With a strange flash, Riku disappears. Sora, panicking, startes to run across the island in search of his friend. Riku awakes in Traverse Town where he is soon challenged by some Heartless. He tries to shake them off, but then stops dead in his tracks and looks up. Shocked, he sees it's raining sleeping Soras, literally. One of them reaches the ground and awakes, then takes on all the Heartless, who had banded together around him. The trailer ended with Sora facing off against a Twilight Thorn (the enormous Nobody from the prologue to *Kingdom Hearts II*). As Nomura clarified, this video was, above all, symbolic. E3 began just a few days later. With it, the first trailer for *Birth by Sleep* entirely dubbed in English (without sound effects) was released. It was nearly identical to the Japanese launch trailer. Only its "game footage" was different, showing, among other things, a brand-new boss, though it was yet another unknown. Also released at E3 was the first trailer for *Kingdom Hearts Re: coded*, entitled *Special Trailer*. It was three minutes long with *Destati* as its background music. The trailer had incredibly perfect pacing. It included a good number of events to show a variety of new dialog and game scenes, including some surprises. The trailer ended with a significant revelation: a "virtual" unknown that managed to teleport into the Realm of Light. At that point, there were no voices or sound effects and the only release date given was "Coming Soon." A week later, Nomura said, "I'm aware of fans' increasingly fervent demands for worlds from Pixar films [Pixar having been acquired by Disney]." He couldn't guarantee anything at that time, but he added, "maybe someday…"

The 29th. Europeans got their trailer for *Kingdom Hearts: Birth by Sleep*. It was a very strange creation that did nothing but present the three heroes and reiterate the release date. This trailer was then used for all promotions thereafter (ads on TV, in stores, etc.).

The 30th. Nomura announced that all of the creative aspects (e.g. universe, script, character design) for *Final Fantasy versus XIII* were finished.

July 2010.

The 1st. Launch of the official website for *Kingdom Hearts Re: coded*, the main channel for communications about the game. It was then regularly updated with news and little videos to explain the changes made compared to *coded*. A few days after the website launch, the release date was revealed by media outlets: October 7, 2010.

The 21th. Square Enix France announced a special collector's edition for *Kingdom Hearts: Birth by Sleep* with a 48-page mini art book and a packet of postcards.

August 2010.

On the 27th, the public learned that there would not be a digitized version of *Kingdom Hearts: Birth by Sleep* and thus it would not be playable on the newly released **PSP Go**. The reason was not given at the time. It was later learned that it was simply an issue of IP rights belonging to Disney and Utada.

The 17th. Just a day before Gamescom, Square Enix created a Facebook page for *Re: coded*. This was interesting for two reasons: first, because of the game's theme, and second, because of what it says about the gradual incorporation of this new way of communicating.

The 18th. At the second annual Gamescom, the European gaming trade show in Cologne, Germany, *Kingdom Hearts: Birth by Sleep* prepared for its release with a long trailer, lasting seven minutes, that's referred to in the video game industry as an "overview[56]." It was really an adaptation of the Japanese trailer created for Jump Festa '10, dubbed entirely in English and with the new content from the Western version added. Shortly thereafter, *Kingdom Hearts* got a Twitter account. Since the job of "community manager" didn't exist at that time, Nomura and Yasue took turns managing the account.

The 26th. Just before summer ended, Square Enix announced that *Re: coded* would be available to play at the TGS!

September 2010.

The 7th. *Kingdom Hearts: Birth by Sleep* boosted PSP sales a bit in the United States with 225,000 copies sold. It was a decent number that made it the sixth best-selling game for the month in the US, all the more impressive given that *BBS* was only released in a physical format[57], unlike its biggest competitors. Three days later, it hit the shelves in Europe, lagging behind the rest of the world as always (particularly because of Ubisoft's[58] totally crappy communications).

---

56. As the name suggests, this type of trailer gives a look at all of the game's features. It's very common among Japanese studios, who have an almost pathological need to always explain everything.
57. *Birth by Sleep* was only released in a UMD version and was never made available for download from PSN. As such, it couldn't be played on the PSP Go (a totally laughable approach). It was because of legal issues related to Disney and Utada.
58. Indeed, I'll remind you that, at the time, Ubisoft was in charge of European distribution for Square Enix. This explains why they would regularly give nods to one another.

By the end of 2010, the game sold over 1.3 million units worldwide. It ultimately sold over 2 million copies, becoming the best-selling of the series' three spin-off games and the twentieth best-selling game for the PSP, just behind *Metal Gear Solid: Peace Walker*. On a side note, the number-one best-selling game was *GTA: Liberty City Stories* with around 8 million. *Monster Hunter Portable 2ⁿᵈ G* (*Freedom Unite* in Europe and North America) came in second with 5.5 million units. Finally, *Birth by Sleep*'s "twin," *Crisis Core*, came in ninth with 3.2 million units sold.

The 14ᵗʰ. *Kingdom Hearts: Birth by Sleep Final Mix* was announced for the Japanese market. The next day, at Sony's pre-TGS press conference, the audience got to see the game's first trailer. It was a revamped version of the most recent trailer, showing off the new features from the European version, particularly the D-Link with Captain Justice, the new courses in Rumble Racing, and the battle with the Unknown. The trailer also showed off the features specific to *Final Mix*, like the battle against Monstro. The trailer ended with the reveal of a new suit of armor (Eraqus' armor) facing off against the game's heroes, as well as a release window (January 2011).

Square Enix also announced that preorders would come with a download code for a *Kingdom Hearts*-style skin for Cloud in *Dissidia Duodecim*.

The 16ᵗʰ. At the Tokyo Games Show, Square Enix announced that the Fabula Nova Crystallis Conference would take place on January 11, 2011. It was to be an event where the publisher would provide information on, among other things, *Final Fantasy XIII Agito* and *Final Fantasy versus XIII*, of which very brief extracts were shown at the TGS.

The TGS also featured the Japanese launch trailer for *Kingdom Hearts Re: coded*. In addition to the story to introduce the game's plot, the trailer showed off the Matrix system, the Avatar Menu (and its special features related to surprise encounters), the System Sectors, and its unique combat system and level design. A fun fact: the trailer used *Hikari* as the background music... probably as a reminder that it was a rewrite of *Kingdom Hearts*. While not all of it was dubbed, it delivered the most important piece of information: its release date, October 7.

The 28th. Nintendo held a press conference to reveal more about the Nintendo 3DS, specifically its release date, its price, and its features. There in person, Nomura said that he was considering "several other titles for the Nintendo 3DS," in addition to *Kingdom Hearts 3D*.

October 2010.

The 6th. Launch of the American and European websites for *Kingdom Hearts Re: coded*. Both announced their release date: January 14, 2011.

The 7th. *Kingdom Hearts Re: coded* was released in Japan. It sold 105,000 copies in the first week. You have to put that number in context because the last few months of 2010 were quite slow. To illustrate that point, even with "so few" sales, it still ranked third on the Japanese charts, which were dominated by *Pokémon Black*, which sold "only" 235,000 copies that same week. In the last three months of the year, few games managed to do better than 300,000 units in a week, which was quite worrisome. *Re: coded* never really took off and ended 2010 at 300,000 copies sold.

November 2010.

The 24th. The official website for *Kingdom Hearts: Birth by Sleep Final Mix* was launched.

December 2010.

The 13th. Square Enix announced that the Fabula Nova Crystallis Conference was to be called instead the Square Enix 1st Production Department Premiere and was moved back to January 18. The new name suggested that the event's scope might be broadened to *Kingdom Hearts*.

The 19th. Audiences in the West finally got to see *Kingdom Hearts Re: coded* thanks to a new launch trailer that was identical to the Japanese version, except for the voices, of course.

The 22th. Release of *The 3rd Birthday* in the Japanese market. Kitase was hoping to sell 500,000 copies. He achieved that, in spite of a rather slow start in Japan (barely 140,000 in the first week).

The 27th. At Jump Festa, Square Enix unveiled the launch trailer for *Kingdom Hearts: Birth by Sleep Final Mix*, with *Simple & Clean PlanitB Mix* as the background music. Unsurprisingly, the trailer focused entirely on the new features (however, without revealing the secret episode) and introduced, at the end, No Heart.

January 2011.

The 8th. Instead of appearing at the CES, Nintendo organized its own three-day conference, Nintendo World, where it presented the first 32 games and applications for the Nintendo 3DS. Of course, *Kingdom Hearts 3D* was not far enough along in development to offer anything more than a very short 10-second extract taken from the video shown to journalists at the previous E3. It was enough to get fans pumped up. I should mention that no one (other than a few "chosen" journalists) had seen that E3 video yet.

The 14th. *Kingdom Hearts Re: coded* was released in both the United States and Europe. Once again, sales were disappointing. Only 72,000 copies were sold in the first week in the US. It wasn't much, but it was enough for the game to be ranked the seventh best-seller. FYI, all of the games ahead of it were casual-gaming titles like *Wii Sports* and *Just Dance*, as well as *Call of Duty Black Ops*. And let's not forget that people were already waiting for the 3DS. I'll let you draw the obvious conclusions. In any case, by the end of its run, *Re: coded* crossed the threshold of 500,000 copies sold in the United States. It sold a little over 100,000 units in Europe (which is ridiculous). So, if you add those numbers to the number of units sold in Japan, it didn't manage to reach the one million mark.

The 18th. The Square Enix 1st Production Department Premiere took place as planned at the TOHO Cinemas in Roppongi Hills, Tokyo. The conference held multiple surprises. First off, the *Fabula Nova Crystallis* project was smashed to pieces. Seven years of bad luck?

Final Fantasy XIII Agito was no more, becoming instead *Type-0*, the starting point for a new "side" series that would be more realistic, according to its director, Hajime Tabata. *Final Fantasy XIII* was to become its own full-fledged series with a sequel, modestly dubbed *Final Fantasy XIII-2*. Finally, there was the first true trailer for *Final Fantasy versus XIII*, which dropped so many bombs that it placated absolutely everyone. Not only was it long (seven minutes), but it also revealed all of Nomura's intentions: a visual styling similar to *Parasite*

Eve, gameplay relying on collaboration between the four heroes, and insane phases very similar to *Kingdom Hearts*, all in a semi-open environment that would allow players to drive vehicles. Nomura was delivering *Kingdom Hearts'* twin, but this time, it was according to HIS precepts. He was turning the situation on its head!

In addition to this shocking reveal, the event also featured the first trailer for *Kingdom Hearts 3D* which, incidentally, had changed names, gaining a sub-title with three words beginning with D: *Dream Drop Distance*. The trailer revealed lots of new information. It started by drawing connections with *Kingdom Hearts II*, *Re: coded*, and *Birth by Sleep*. Then, it finally showed the game (in its alpha version) with some real demonstrations of gameplay. The action shown was FLUID. Sora moved at high speed, bouncing off of the walls, using pieces of the background to perform acrobatics... Basically, it was nuts. And Riku was playable! He was seen bouncing straight from one wall to the next at incredible speed. After that, the trailer gave a glimpse of the first brand-new world, which looked like Notre Dame Cathedral in Paris. Finally, the trailer concluded by showcasing Sora and Riku facing off against their sworn enemies, Xemnas and Ansem. It was cleverly written, remarkably produced, and used *Destati* as the background music. Those two minutes and 38 seconds were like a fantastic dream. Square Enix took the opportunity to launch the game's official website.

The 19th. A day before *Final Mix* was released into the wild, Square Enix released an alternative version of the launch trailer from Jump Festa '11. While it's major points were the same, this time it had an extract from the battle between the three heroes and No Heart, as well as, in particular, a glimpse of the secret episode with Aqua.

The next day, *Kingdom Hearts: Birth by Sleep Final Mix* hit the shelves in Japan, selling around 80,000 copies. It succeeded in dethroning the unbeatable *Monster Hunter Portable 3rd*, which had dominated Japanese sales for almost two months. *BBS FM* thus took the top spot on the charts, but the next week it began a steady decline, ultimately selling less than 160,000 units. Another big disappointment for Square Enix. It wasn't really worth fretting over. It seems that the PSP was not the right console for taking such a risk, as Nomura's intuition had told him. But no matter: he made a choice that valued creativity over sales potential. One thing is certain: the future of the *Final Mix* appeared to be seriously jeopardized. Could it be the end of an era?

THE LEGEND OF
KINGDOM HEARTS

VOLUME 1: CREATION

Genesis of Hearts

CHAPTER V
BETWEEN DREAM AND NIGHTMARE

"**A** story focusing on the Mark of Mastery exam with Riku as the hero (…), *Kingdom Hearts: Birth by Sleep* on steroids, developed in 3D, and connected to *Kingdom Hearts III*.*" That's how Nomura presented *Kingdom Hearts 3D* to his Osaka team in early June before having them get to work on the demo. He didn't burden them with more details than that because, for the time being, they needed to stay concentrated on *Kingdom Hearts Re: coded*, *Birth by Sleep Final Mix*… and now *Kingdom Hearts 3D DEMO*. The full version would come later. Anyway, Nomura had to jet off to the United States to meet with fans and Disney… and he also had to finalize the universe for *Final Fantasy versus XIII*. Slow but steady wins the race.

ONE FOR ALL
[*KH3D*: PRE-PROD]

In early summer, pre-production was fast approaching. Nomura was looking at the core of *Kingdom Hearts 3D*, with the goal of having a workable plan by September. As we know, he's a very sensitive creator. Ideas come to him from all sides and even sometimes in quite surprising forms. In this instance, he "saw" black and pink. That's no surprise since every episode in the series has had its own color scheme, apparently loaded with symbolism. However, this time, the color scheme was the starting point and would have a real influence on the rest of the game, which is quite unusual, according to Nomura. OK, cool, but that still doesn't tell us where the idea came from. Well, don't ask him, because even he doesn't know. We can probably chalk it up to inspiration, that quasi-mystical superpower. Unless, of course, there's a more ordinary explanation, probably related to his biggest concerns at the time. After all, his games are just <u>extensions of himself</u> and <u>adapt to his state of mind</u>. He has implicitly recognized this: *"Final Fantasy versus XIII* certainly influenced me on several occasions." As it turns out, he really needed this 3DS game: "The characters in *versus XIII* are serious and experience situations that are so dramatic that sometimes I can't take it anymore, I need to take a break," he says, laughing. A story that might ring a bell[1].

So, what story did he want to tell? That of Sora's and Riku's Mark of Mastery exam. However, at this point, Nomura was a little frustrated because he didn't have the bigger context for the story. As this episode was supposed to be the first stage of a comeback, he wanted to avoid repetition at all costs. That being said, there were some things he specifically wanted, like incorporating the world of Pinocchio again, as it had been unjustly eliminated from *Kingdom Hearts 358/2 Days*, and another world based on *Fantasia*, which had long been a dream of his. But, he still had to come up with the context and justify it to himself. Although he had liberated himself from corporate constraints just a few weeks earlier, he remained a victim of his own pathological need to "connect" everything. Reflecting on the origins of the exam in question, he went back to *Birth by Sleep*. Sleep. One of the key themes in the series and also, interestingly enough, in *Final Fantasy versus XIII*[2]. But, what happens when we fall asleep? Well, we enter the world of dreams…

His starting point was to be otherworldly. The colors he had imagined were replaced by ideas and he began to adjust his past reflections. It was like pieces of a mysterious puzzle coming together. As if everything had been planned out without him even knowing where he was going.

Such a unique approach is worth examining.

The starting point: dream. The first of the three D words in the title of *Kingdom Hearts 3D*. And the second D? Why not "drop," particularly since it evokes the sensation of "falling asleep," which relates perfectly

---

1. Remember the reason behind *Final Fantasy VIII*? See page 41.
2. The illustration in the logo for *Final Fantasy versus XIII* (reused with a slight modification for *Final Fantasy XV*), created by Yoshitaka Amano, shows a person sleeping. Once again, the connection with *Kingdom Hearts* is striking. We'll come back to this in Volume II.

to the very first idea he had about using 3D: free-falling. The game's protagonists would literally fall into the dreams of sleeping worlds. It was all starting to make sense, but it wasn't enough for someone like Nomura, who is constantly inundated with new ideas. Why Do Things the Easy Way When You Can Do Them the Hard Way, episode 372. "Drop" became the name for the system where the player switches from Sora to Riku via… sleep. It all came full circle. That said, he later went ahead and added several levels of meaning that were much more complex[3], even changing the main plot line. During the exam, Sora falls into the trap of a new threat that "plunges him into his worst nightmare," from which he will be saved at the last moment by Riku, who completes his training and redeems himself all at the same time. It was like *Inception* (but much more intelligent) combined with a new concept: "the distance you fall in your dreams."

Nomura is hopeless. He really can't stop himself. He even managed to justify the insanity of his new gameplay, using dreams as the context. He does whatever he wants. At the same time, he got himself an excellent laboratory for testing his famous "Free-Flow Action." He wanted to test it, expand it, and improve it with just one goal in mind: perfect it for *Kingdom Hearts III*. The combination of gameplay and narration was set, the levels of meaning were there, everything was coherent because it was "connected." The only thing left was to solve a problem, which he deliberately set aside because of his schedule: the undetermined third word starting with D "that still hadn't come to him," which he was not happy about.

ALL FOR ONE
[*KH3D*: PRE-PROD]

It was time to do some R&D because, though it may not seem like it at first glance, the team had a steep climb ahead of them: "The Osaka team had only worked on a Nintendo DS game one time and, as for that, they only designed the character development system for *Kingdom*

---

3. You'll have to keep holding your horses. This isn't the right time to get into that sort of detail. See Volume II. .

Hearts Re: coded," Nomura reminds us. They lacked experience with this kind of console. *Kingdom Hearts 3D* was thus an important first for them, imposing some serious technical challenges, including the touchscreen and, especially, the autostereoscopic imaging. Producing a 2D video amplified in 3D is one thing, but programming a game entirely planned and designed with depth is different and much more complex. A number of technical staff members from Tokyo and Osaka would learn this lesson the hard way. By September, they were already investigating the hardware in order to prepare their work environment and avoid time-consuming technical problems once the rest of the team (which was finalizing *Birth by Sleep Final Mix*) joined them between October and November.

Tamotsu Goto (main programmer) explains that the main problem with 3D is that it "requires expanding the fields," which is hard enough on its own, but it was made all the more difficult by the Free-Flow Action, "becoming difficult to analyze the performance required. Thankfully, Nakamichi did everything he could to help me [with this aspect]." He was referring to his partner, Masashi Nakamichi (main programmer), who in turn explains that "creating the system allowing you to view all of the scenes in 3D (...) is very difficult. If there's a graphical error somewhere, it had repercussions elsewhere." Other departments had similar difficulties, having to revamp their methods. For example, this was the case for special effects: "If you have to show something far away in a cutscene, there are tricks for simulating that effect. Instead of placing it far away, you can make it small, for example. But, that doesn't work in 3D," explains Yasuhiko Onishi (art director – VFX). Sometimes, the effects were even more problematic: "For the cutscenes, the subtitles are difficult to read, for example," says Masaru Oka (cutscene director). That's why *Kingdom Hearts 3D* was the first game in the series to include an option allowing players to activate and deactivate them. To make a long story short, working in 3D is no walk in the park. Nakamichi sums up the situation perfectly, joking, "New hardware, new game, short time for development. I'll never forget [developing this game]. Thank you to everyone who worked with me."

THE SORCERER'S APPRENTICE
[*KH3D*: PRE-PROD]

November 2010. *Birth by Sleep Final Mix* was reaching the end of development and its team was, naturally, moving on to *Kingdom Hearts 3D*. Tai Yasue was among the new arrivals to the project and he discovered that the plan had changed since June. The concept was now a bold action game where the player has to feel free to try anything. No restrictions of any kind. That included a new vertical dimension to gameplay and more interactions with the backgrounds, like bouncing several times in a row off a single wall in order to reach jaw-dropping heights. "The team did not like that at all," says Nomura, laughing. That's understandable because they knew what that much freedom of action requires: if the player can try anything, they have to anticipate every little movement and establish all possible actions. That would be a challenge under normal conditions, so for an action game that was so fluid, or even supercharged, the task was that much more diffi-cult. Take a few seconds to think about how you handle a camera, the properties of each surface, propulsive force, where to place the treasure chests, or even how to take advantage of them in battles, and you'll have a good idea of the enormous challenge they faced. And, indeed, the team pouted over it. Nomura, however, was inflexible: this was his new style, the famous Free-Flow Action. They had to get used to it because this was just the beginning.

Next, he presented them with the story, which would be divided between Sora and Riku, but with no pauses in between. They would visit the same worlds, but not in the same order. Their journeys would differ, they wouldn't necessarily meet the same characters and would face different bosses. Like in *Chain of Memories*, each one would have his own specific set of actions and the two would not be played in the same manner. And the difference between the two would be significant because it was part of the plot: the two protagonists wouldn't have the same goals.

To make this alternation exciting, "a new system requiring the player to switch from one hero to the other suddenly and automati-cally was established," says Nomura with an evil grin. He wanted to throw players for a loop, offer them an experience that would shake them. "When he told us that he wanted us to create a system that would force the player to switch the character being played, he really scared me," admits Yasue, holding back his laughter. It was a decision that was surprising in how much it changed the normal rhythm, or even dynamic of the *Kingdom Hearts* series. Moreover, it was a huge risk to take with players. Nomura was aware of all of this, but didn't back down because it came from a choice he made: "Taking away the sense of security for players who know that the system will force them to change characters can bring out strong emotions." <u>Once again, he didn't want to make players' lives easier. He wanted to surprise them</u>. To assert his point of view, he made an irrefutable argument: "It's like that special moment where you don't have enough HP, giving you the chills." He's referring to those battles that remain etched in players' memories, where the entire team is dead except the hero, who doesn't have much HP left. He's at death's door, but hangs on just long enough to deliver a deadly blow to a boss. There's no greater thrill in an RPG than that experience of "it's you or me." So, in addition to his Free-Flow Action, Nomura wanted to incorporate a second system to excite players. He was able to fit it perfectly into the context by making it unavoidable, since the character being played would fall asleep, forcing the player to switch.

However, the team resisted. Most of the planners objected. They found the system to be abstruse and frustrating. Osaka was in panic mode. They were scared by both of the key systems in this new game. Having already anticipated their reaction, Nomura had a plan to turn their attention elsewhere in order to get his way. He would reward them for their frustration. "He asked us to come up with a system that would involve the lower screen for something other than the map and would connect it with the upper screen and with battles," Yasue explains excitedly. Better yet, he suggested that they help him choose the worlds for the game. He had just a few requirements: a world based on *Fantasia*, a new look for Traverse Town, reincorporating the amusement park from Pinocchio, and, <u>no matter what</u>, they couldn't forget about The World That Never Was. The meeting ended with something along the lines of, "yep, you have a little over a year left to get it all done, bye." I joke, but that really is pretty much how it went.

LINK TO ALL
[*KH3D*: DEVELOPMENT]

The priority was to develop the heart of the game, Free-Flow Action, which became known as "Flowmotion" for this particular game. Using examples from Nomura, Yasue extrapolated and thought about adding movements using poles (know what I'm referring to?) or even "rails" in the backgrounds. So, why not test these new ideas out in Traverse Town, since it had to be renovated? The planners started to understand where Nomura was going: they had free rein to suggest crazy ideas. "Using the data from *Birth by Sleep*, we came up with a solid plan in two or three days that came to life within a few weeks," says Yasue. Takeshi Fujimoto (art director) got roped in. Once he saw the new style of the game, he declared that they absolutely had to revise the typical dimensions of the game fields: "The small areas could be crossed in no time, so I expanded them as much as possible while directly incorporating the new possibilities for interaction." He was referring to Traverse Town, of course. In this world, he and his team worked together to rebuild the second and third neighborhoods for an in-house demo[4].

Yasue explains, "I think that the team really understood what we wanted to do from there. That really sped things along." Koji Hamada (animation director) confirms, "When I saw the Free-Flow Action on screen, I was really surprised. From there, Yasue asked us for invigorating, stimulating action." Basically, the co-director was making the demo to convince himself. He implicitly admits as much: "It was really when I saw [things] becoming reality that I understood that this system was a natural evolution of *Kingdom Hearts*." About time. It took him a month to realize this, but no matter, that doesn't mean that time was wasted. The team was now fully on-board with the approach and feeling more motivated than ever before. Nomura finds this amusing: "They tell me that the old episodes seem slow in comparison, or they say things like, 'once you go Free-Flow Action, you can't go back,' or, 'a *Kingdom Hearts* where you can't bounce off the walls is not a

---

4. Upon seeing the results, Nomura pulled out a few short game phases that he incorporated into the first real trailer for *KH3D*, shared in January 2011.

Kingdom Hearts.'" He loved hearing that. Above all, that boded well for the next steps. The team selected the worlds and how they would be played. The first was La Cité des Cloches, in response to a request from players. Yasue explains: *"The Hunchback of Notre Dame is very popular and fans often asked for it."* Munenori Shinagawa (animation director) remembers creating the backgrounds for this world: "Reproducing movie scenes can be difficult. When Quasimodo swooped down from the cathedral toward the square to save Esmeralda, there weren't enough walls to create a course similar to that used in the film. I had a heck of a time with that."

Next, they adapted Traverse Town for the new style as requested by Nomura. However, they maintained the same gameplay: "In the proposed version, we had Cid, Leon, and others, but I don't think that worked anymore. I wanted something <u>really</u> different that would fit with the future of the series," explains the director. And, as the saying goes, if you want something done right, do it yourself. So, Nomura corrected the plan and replaced the *Final Fantasy* characters with characters from *Subarashiki Kono Sekai*: "I figured that the encounter between city kids and country kids could produce some interesting results," especially given that "Traverse Town is a place where you always learn a lot in *Kingdom Hearts*, and Joshua was the perfect choice to fulfill that <u>function</u>." This use of the word "function" has a very particular meaning because it echoes the first *Kingdom Hearts*. I'll remind you, in 2001, Nomura used this word to justify the presence of *Final Fantasy* characters, particularly Squall as Sora's mentor. I'm sure it was subconscious, but as the series developed, it increasingly moved away from the specter of *Final Fantasy*, to the point of completely eliminating it in this installment. The fact that the *FF* characters were replaced by characters from a game for which he was the originator and master sends a clear signal. And the Free-Flow Action, which resulted from a re-assessment, is only further proof of this distancing. There are other examples. In a conversation, he brought up the possible influence of *Final Fantasy versus XIII*. Basically, creating young adults deeply rooted in "a fantasy based on reality" and characters who were now adolescents that were supposed to be living on an island perhaps made him want to bring these two universes together. In a way, perhaps he was at a point in his life where he was taking stock of his own life.

Or perhaps he was simply trying to honor the members of his team, some of whom played an important role in making *Subarashiki Kono Sekai*, first and foremost its director, Tatsuya Kando (animation supervisor for *KH3D*): "I'll never forget the numerous times he checked and rechecked to make sure that everything was just right for the animation of the characters. At one point, he told me, 'Rhyme is much cuter than that,' and to help me understand, he did an impression of her. It was hilarious," Shinagawa says. Gen Kobayashi (art director for the characters in *KH3D*), as co-creator of the characters (alongside Nomura), was brought to tears when he saw them in 3D. And let's not forget that *Kingdom Hearts 3D* got the benefit of three composers, including Takeharu Ishimoto, who also created the music for *Subarashiki Kono Sekai*. He took the opportunity to do several arrangements for which he personally re-recorded the acoustic guitar parts, for *TWISTER*, for example. Also, he found singers Stephanie and OLIVIA on the internet because "Japanese artists have trouble singing in English." Some great fun facts. Adding some *SKS* into *Kingdom Hearts* surprised the Osaka team. "That was the last thing we ever expected," says Yasue. You have to put things in context: he had just seen his plan for Traverse Town rejected and so he was a little shocked to see such a dramatic change. That said, he immediately fell in love with the idea and saw it as a real opportunity to give this key world a new image. He readjusted the sizes of the buildings, added graffiti, and more generally gave it a look closer to that of Shibuya. When he took a step back to look at his work, he said, "Finally, a very good choice. That really refreshes the universe."

Now it was his turn to choose! In collaboration with his team, he chose the direct-to-DVD movie *Mickey, Donald, Goofy: The Three Musketeers*, "just to see them dressed differently," he says. The three Disney heroes in a different setting, in keeping with the past. Nomura liked the idea, immediately seeing an episode in Mickey's story at a time "when he's trying to obtain knowledge." Basically, in another life.

Next, it was Nomura's turn to choose again. There's not much to say about Pinocchio's world which, after its removal from *Kingdom Hearts 358/2 Days*, had been waiting patiently in a drawer. And there was enough material there to turn it into something spectacular.

For example, the amusement park was already there. The only thing left was to adapt it to the new style and then Nomura's turn was over. On the other hand, no work had been done yet on the world that he wanted more than anything: the world from the 1940 masterpiece film *Fantasia*, which the director had been dreaming of working with since the beginning of the series. You could even say that *Fantasia* is closely linked to *Kingdom Hearts*[5].

Since his first dream (creating worlds based on fairy tales) had become reality with *Birth by Sleep*, he allowed himself to give in to his fantasy with *Kingdom Hearts 3D* which, coincidentally (or not), shared the same universe of dreams. In the initial plan, Osaka intended to incorporate both *Fantasia* and *Fantasia 2000*, with Sora visiting the first and Riku visiting the second. However, after meticulously studying both, Yasue came to a decision: "As it turns out, there are enough different locations and music in the original. It has very rich content." In keeping with the concept of two complementary adventures, Yasue suggested to Nomura that the "sequences[6]" be split between Sora and Riku. The director thought it was an excellent idea and evaluated each sketch. He particularly considered the ways in which they could incorporate interesting game scenarios and mechanics. He ultimately chose only four (two "sections" per character): *The Sorcerer's Apprentice* and *The Pastoral Symphony* for Sora, *The Nutcracker Suite* and *Night on Bald Mountain* for Riku. I have to admit, I'm sad they didn't use *Toccata and Fugue in D Minor* after seeing how faithful they were to the other classical pieces and how they showcased them. I can just imagine the amazing things they would have done with that extraordinary piece by Johann Sebastian Bach...

To bring the *Fantasia* world to life without distorting its original poetry, they needed some clever ideas... that ended up being difficult to implement. For example, that was the case for the sudden weather change in the *Pastoral Symphony* section, which raised a lot of problems for You Miyazaki (planning director): "When the weather

---

5. In the very first game, he used Chernabog.
6. *Fantasia* is an anthology film, i.e. a film composed of several segments, each with the vision of a different director but based around a single theme. The best examples of anthology films are *Neo Tokyo*, *Robot Carnival*, *Memories* and *The Animatrix*. They are animated masterpieces that everyone should have on their shelf.

changed, a huge amount of data had to change too." When he started working on the background for this segment, his colleagues regularly pointed out to him that it was unreadable. Of course, lightning, torrential rains, and their effects on the lighting of a background seem super simple today with all of the tools we have available, but imagine doing the same thing back in 2010 for the Nintendo 3DS. Not so simple anymore, is it? Ryo Inakura (sound designer) also faced some serious difficulties: "What's different about *Fantasia* is that it had neither voices nor sound effects, just classical music. Which is incredibly hard to work with in a video game." Yep, unfortunately for him, he had to create the sound effects without interfering too much with the music. That's when he got the idea to involve the player: "They're the one who will create the atmosphere of sound with their actions." In other words, he associated musical instruments with the various hits. This was a method quite similar to the one he used for the Timeless River, if you remember[7].

For The Grid, the world based on *Tron: Legacy*, Yasue explains, "Actually, it was the first one we thought of because we really wanted a futuristic world." OK, but why this one and not the world from *Treasure Planet*[8], for example? There are several good reasons.

1. The *Tron* universe is already "connected" to *Kingdom Hearts* via Space Paranoids, one of the "surprise" worlds in *Kingdom Hearts II*.

2. Up to that point, they had only worked with cartoons. It was only natural that they would be excited about trying out "real" material.

3. Maybe the developers were just impatient to see the film because, at that point in time, it still hadn't come out in theaters.

4. By the way, Japan had an exclusive world premiere (on November 30, 2010), around two weeks before the United States, if you'll believe it. That's unusual enough that it's worth noting. From there, it's not much of a stretch to imagine Disney pushing them in that direction.

---

7. See page 152.
8. If you pick through the data for *KH3D*, you'll find the plans for a ship that resembles the *Legacy* from… *Treasure Planet*. Perhaps they're keeping it for *Kingdom Hearts III*, where it would fit perfectly?

In any case, it was not an inconsequential decision. First off, from a technical standpoint. Takeshi Fujimoto (art director) says that he had huge issues replicating the "glass" effect: "We had to work with transparent polygons and we noticed shimmering mixed in with the other effects. It was really not good for the rendering. If we wanted to keep the natural appearance, we would have to resort to more subtle techniques." And we'll never know what those were because like all good magicians, he never reveals his secrets. What's more, the team encountered a major problem, but it was one so ordinary as to seem totally out of place. Satoshi Otani (art director for character modeling) says, "When we started working on it, the film was still in theaters and there was no DVD. So, we had to make regular trips to the movie theater to watch it." You read that right. They had forgotten about this "detail" and didn't have the DVD they needed to do their work. And these are the people who are used to watching their various DVDs over and over again. This time, they found themselves empty-handed. This made their work extremely difficult. I can just imagine them going to the movie theater armed with pads of paper. It was a totally absurd situation that they brought on themselves: "We really struggled until halfway through development," in April 2011, when the movie was finally released on DVD. Did you get that? They waited for the movie to become legally available before getting their hands on it. Dreaming might have been the theme of the game, but I assure you, you're not dreaming. The Japanese don't "steal." That's how they're brought up, having respect for works and the people who create them. Yes, we have a lot to learn from Japan about these ideas that today we consider totally hackneyed. That's also the main reason that leads me to believe that *Tron: Legacy* was truly chosen out of love, given all that they endured to include it. And I think I can explain why they loved it. In addition to the very "manga" visual style of the film, its original soundtrack was composed by Daft Punk, the world-famous French electronic musical duo that has many ties to Japan[9].

9. Electronic music, of course, but also *Interstella 5555*, an animated film produced by Toei Animation, presented at the prestigious Cannes Film Festival in 2003, and for which the Daft Punk duo (Thomas Bangalter and Guy-Manuel de Homem-Christo) co-wrote the script and, particularly, composed all of the music. Of note, legendary anime creator Leiji Matsumoto supervised the VFX himself.

Of course, the game didn't get the benefit of their talents for licensing reasons (it was too expensive). So, they had to compensate. "Sekito and I received a list of the tracks that were still open. When I saw *Tron* on the list, I immediately put down that I wouldn't do it," says Takeharu Ishimoto. While normally he puts himself out there, this time he was not going to play the hero. Following Daft Punk is a difficult challenge: "At first, the very strong identity of the music was a problem"; his very personal way of admitting that he lacked self-assurance. "However, I used my talent and my uniqueness to do it in my own way." One hell of a guy. And you have to give him credit because the themes he created for The Grid are excellent.

On a side note, initially, this world was designed differently. Like for *Fantasia* and *Fantasia 2000*, Sora was supposed to visit *Tron* and Riku was supposed to visit *Tron: Legacy*.

SACRED DISTANCE
[*KH3D*: DEVELOPMENT]

Two months of development had passed. Everyone had their hearts set on releasing the game for the series' tenth anniversary. That meant they had just one year to get everything done. This resulted in an extremely tight schedule that led to some mishaps. Masashi Nakamishi (main programmer) explains: "Work on the design documents and assets started very early and, as a result, we hadn't had enough time to finalize the system." So, for the programmers, the start of development was hell. They were totally overwhelmed with the amount of data they had to integrate. Tamotsu Goto (main programmer) confirms this: "Producing a game in one year is extremely difficult. Thankfully, we were able to rely on the engine from *Birth by Sleep*, but only up to a certain point. We had a lot of new things to create. The hardest part was incorporating the data from the planners and artists at the same time." They too were struggling to keep up, particularly in designing the system that was supposed to use the lower screen. Several proposals were made, but Yasue ultimately chose Reality Shift, based off of an idea from Nakamichi: a sort of mini-game on the touchscreen where, basically, the player swipes[10] to interact with the upper screen while in battle, but also sometimes just to interact with the background. It was an original idea in that the activity would change from world to world. For example, in the *Fantasia* world, Reality Shift directly influences progress; in the world of *The Three Musketeers*, however, the player interacts with a sort of comic strip.

Still, there was a major problem that needed to be solved: the Drop System. The Osaka team was very critical of this new concept: "They thought it didn't make sense," says Nomura. So, they suggested making it totally optional. Nomura countered that proposal with a good argument: "In that case, the people who only want to play Sora or Riku will be able to do so and one of the two will become much too strong," and that was absolutely out of the question because the game's narrative depended on the alternation between the characters. Nomura thus rejected their proposal, but agreed to tone it down a bit. It was up to them to transform the test system. **The director was right, but the Osaka team**

WHAT? I didn't finish that last sentence? Indeed, I deliberately and brutally cut it off. From here on out, I'm going to adapt the text to mimic the Drop System from *KH3D*. That means I'm going to "force you to change characters." At the risk of unsettling and frustrating you. To make this game more fun, I'm going to warn you with a countdown in the margin and I'll always re-establish the context at the start of each section so that you don't end up completely lost. Come on, show a little enthusiasm. You probably didn't notice, but I've done the same thing before without announcing it, adapting the text to the systems of narration of the games previously discussed. I think these theatrics add a bit of spice to this extensive text. And then there's also the fact that, as I warned you, I'm a gamer and I like to play around.

---

10. Swipe means to slide your finger on a touchscreen to perform an action.

⚷ [DROP] > *L'Eminenza Oscura I*

Context: Nomura did not agree with the Osaka team about his Drop System. Above all, he wanted to spark emotions in players, or even destabilize them.

In any case, he wasn't going to enter into a debate with them, especially because he trusted them and knew that they would propose something better. Nomura didn't want to waste any more energy because it was <u>finally</u> time to begin development of *Final Fantasy versus XIII*. Well, theoretically.

Let's briefly review (since it's a bit complicated).

2003 — Kitase, Nomura, and Hashimoto conceived of *Fabula Nova Crystallis*, a new multifaceted project for Square Enix, an evolution of the concept of *Compilation of Final Fantasy VII* whose first component would be *Final Fantasy XIII*. Nomura suggested an A-RPG called *Final Fantasy versus XIII* that he offered to direct himself once he had finished *Kingdom Hearts II*, i.e. not until 2006.

2006 — Nomura began coming up with the story and creating the main character. However, he had to drop what he was doing to create a trailer for E3. The goal was to reassure people about Square Enix's intentions for new-generation consoles and respond to a discreet request from Sony, who needed to reassure PlayStation 3 owners.

2007 — Nomura was waiting for the special engine, Crystal Tools, to be ready, but *Final Fantasy XIII* was, in any case, the priority. Since he wanted to keep control of his team, he launched several projects related to *Kingdom Hearts*.

2008 — Two people from Visual Works (a digital artist and a modeler) worked with him to create a trailer around five minutes long, of which a few seconds were real footage and the rest was CGI.

2009 — While he was supposed to get more human resources, he had to make do with his core team, with which he worked to figure out what the game should be like. The team was busy with *Final Fantasy XIII*, which was stuck in the quagmire of Crystal Tools.

2010 — He got back his core team and a portion of the team from *Final Fantasy XIII*[11] starting in February and March. This finally

---

11. Of the 400 people working on *Final Fantasy XIII*, a little over 250 moved on to *Final Fantasy XIII–2*.

allowed him to start pre-production... Or so he thought. As it turned out, there was no way the Universal Engine[12] would fit his needs. It was solely designed for *Final Fantasy XIII* and thus absolutely not for a semi-open world, which was the direction in which *Final Fantasy versus XIII* was heading. What's more, Kitase recognized at the time that it was absurd to develop an engine at the same time as a game. That explains a lot, both about *Final Fantasy XIII* and about this period of time in general.

In May, Roberto Ferrari, a very experienced Italian designer who, notably, has worked for Tatsunoko[13] and Namco, joined the team to work alongside Nomura. He created the characters Aranea and Arden (Ardyn), and later Gentiana, allowing Nomura to concentrate entirely on writing the script and finalizing the universe by late June. That summer, Nomura started casting for the voices of the characters. In October, the goal was to grow the team by recruiting highly qualified individuals, including battle planners and level designers "with experience using 3D for both the PlayStation 3 and Xbox 360," according to the job posting. In late November, it was <u>finally</u> time to start development of *Final Fantasy versus XIII*. Well, theoretically: behind the scenes, a new plot twist was taking shape... A big one.

[DROP] > *KH3D*

The director was right, but the Osaka team was still bothered by this totally "unpredictable" system. No matter: they would try to transform it. At first, they tried to make the idea more exciting by adding a countdown so as to warn the player that the Drop was inevitable. However, they were still just as unsatisfied. They planned to mitigate their concerns by playing off of the most important notion in game design: the balance between frustration and satisfaction. They made the change optional by going through the menu, while still controlling the player's progress: one character can't get too far ahead of the

---

12. The name given to the Crystal Tools engine, having been modified by the *Final Fantasy XIII* team to fit their needs.
13. The legendary Japanese animation studio responsible for *Speed Racer*, *Science Ninja Team Gatchaman*, *Samurai Pizza Cats*, and much later *Beyblade*.

other; if they do, they automatically fall asleep. However, playing by the rules would win the player bonuses that would apply to the other character after the next Drop. "It's much more user-friendly," Yasue commented, breathing a sigh of relief, because, "the Drop System was one of the hardest aspects to deal with." And it's clear that the original idea adjusted in this way, although it was still somewhat abrupt, turned out great. When you manage to defeat a boss at the last second while forestalling the signals indicating that the next Drop is coming, the victory is that much more rewarding. Yasue then became the standard-bearer for his director's idea: "Can you really achieve satisfaction without frustration?" As he made progress with Oka on the scripts for each of the worlds, Nomura eventually found his third D: Distance, which "expresses the separation between Sora and Riku, both physically and from the viewpoint of the story," explains Nomura. And so, once again, it all came full circle and the title evolved into its final form: *Kingdom Hearts 3D: Dream Drop Distance*.

The next year, 2011, began, and with it came the Square Enix 1st Production Department Premiere. It was an event whose title was, for once, quite clear. During the Premiere, the first "real trailer" for *Kingdom Hearts 3D: Dream Drop Distance* was shown to the public. As always, Nomura avoided socializing and instead observed the audience's reactions in silence. He learned a lot from this.

First lesson: the outfits of Sora and Riku were a point of confusion. Some thought that *KH3D* was a 3D remake of *Kingdom Hearts* for the Nintendo 3DS. Other than proving that they had the intelligence of an amoeba, it alerted Nomura about the issue and he decided to change their attire once again. In spite of not having designed anything yet, he had to go back to the drawing board. He dusted off several sketches that dated back to sometime between *Kingdom Hearts* and *Kingdom Hearts II*, showed them to the Osaka team, and let them decide. Then, he adjusted the designs to tie them into the script. I'm sure I sound like a broken record, but every detail, no matter how small, always has a meaning in *Kingdom Hearts*. The new designs definitely affected the artistic departments. Munenori Shinagawa (animation director) explains, "For Riku, for example, the new cut of his clothes meant that his movements would be closer to those in *Kingdom Hearts II*." So, he reduced the size of Riku's head to make it "more realistic" and thus in line with the evolution of his design throughout the series. Satoshi Otani (art director for character modeling) adds, "In fact, the human characters have bodies more like in *Kingdom Hearts* with heads, indeed, of the same size as in *Kingdom Hearts II*." He then notes that he used five to six times more polygons compared to *Re: coded* and doubled all of the models, with a high version for the cutscenes and a middle version for during gameplay.

Second lesson: the few seconds of gameplay revealed definitely made a strong impression. However, players weren't sure about the playability: how could they handle characters moving so quickly? Nomura was aware of this concern; it even amused him: "For the time being, only the programmer is capable of doing that [referring to Riku bouncing off the walls], we still have a long phase of testing[14] to complete to make that accessible."

Even more importantly, when taking a step back to take stock, he realized that the game changed everything, or almost everything, but still kept the Heartless and the Nobodies. This didn't work in the context and "since I decided that the story would take place in the world of dreams, I've been trying to come up with an idea to develop enemies and make them fight alongside the protagonists[15]. Which doesn't make sense with the Heartless." That's when he got another idea.

[DROP] > *L'EMINENZA OSCURA I (CONTINUED)*

Since spring 2010, everyone knew that *Final Fantasy XIV* was heading for disaster. The first signs came from "the most devoted players of *Final Fantasy XI*, who were invited specially to play the alpha version" and deplored the lack of content, empty backgrounds, an unstable frame rate, a ridiculous battle system, and a confusing interface. Is that all? To make a long story short, the only thing everyone liked was the visual quality. Naturally, they would need to redo everything,

---

14. Using trial and error, a basic methodology used in video game creation.
15. Given that Nomura worked on *Final Fantasy XIII–2*, which also allowed players to capture monsters and use them in battles, the coincidence is too great to not mention, once again, cross-influencing between games.

but that was impossible because the main problem was the engine itself, Crystal Tools. It was not at all designed for an open (or blue) world with so many characters on the screen. Not so smart for an MMORPG. The second sign of trouble was that the beta version kept getting pushed back, to the point of being just three weeks before the game's release date. The feedback was still negative and the outlook was pessimistic. That said, amazingly, *Final Fantasy XIV* was indeed released on September 30. Yoichi Wada had promised investors that his protégé would bring the biggest success of the fiscal year and he couldn't go back on his word, disregarding common sense and many people at the company who spoke up to try to prevent irreparable damage, including Hiromichi Tanaka[16], the game's producer. As expected, *Final Fantasy XIV* was obliterated by the media and players. In addition to the aforementioned problems, there weren't enough servers and they got so overloaded that there were 400 crashes per day. Given that the game's business model relied on subscriptions, buyers felt like they'd been swindled, and with good reason. By trying to force the hand of fate and telling himself, "it's OK, we'll patch that later," Yoichi Wada sent *Final Fantasy* to the gallows. And his responsibility doesn't stop there: let's not forget that he was the one who ordered the creation of White Engine, which became Crystal Tools and was largely responsible for the mess they found themselves in. What's more, he decided to respond by making another gamble: fix the first version as a placeholder while waiting for a real total revamp to come out later. Tanaka alone assumed responsibility for the failure to protect his team and keep around director Nobuaki Komoto, who was demoted to lead game designer. The new director, personally appointed by Wada, was Naoki Yoshida, a little-known team member who had been working for some time on *Dragon Quest X*, the first online installment in the series. **It didn't take long for him to establish his carefree style.**

16. Hiromichi Tanaka: I'll remind you that before he was dragged through the mud by a horde of angry MMORPG players, and thus resigned from his position, this great man was one of the pillars of Square. He was one of their first employees, alongside Sakaguchi, I might add, and was the game designer for *Final Fantasy I* through *III*. The dynamic duo he formed with Koichi Ishii was responsible for the development of the A-RPG branch of Square with the series *Seiken Densetsu*, without which there might never have been a *Kingdom Hearts*. Later, the duo was responsible for the incredible success of *Final Fantasy XI*. In the PlayStation era, he produced games including *Xenogears* and *Chrono Cross*. It's funny how quickly people forget.

꩜ **[DROP]** > *KH3D*

So, what would replacements for the Heartless look like in the context of a dream world? Perhaps monsters that devour dreams? Dream Eaters. He got the idea while thinking about his childhood pet dogs and cats. He remembered how much he loved them. For a long time, he thought how it was too bad that he couldn't recreate that same natural relationship in a video game. That is, until he discovered *Nintendogs*[17]: "I'd never seen anything like it before. The way that game brought the user and the animal together had a very strong impact on me," he says. However, Nomura was still the same old Nomura and <u>his biggest neurosis is to always relate everything to battles</u>. In addition, "when I would go out with my 3DS and I would come across other dogs with StreetPass, I would say to myself, 'it's too bad that we can't make them fight each other.'" Since the developers of *Nintendogs* had, for obvious reasons, never planned on anything of the sort, he told himself that maybe one day he would have the opportunity to be the first to do something like that.

SWEET SPIRITS
[*KH3D*: DEVELOPMENT]

As he started planning out *KH3D*, he asked himself if the idea was worth a try. What's more, he wanted to be the first to do it in an action game. And so it was that the Spirits were created. He drew the first of them, Meow Wow, a cat-dog hybrid, and showed it to Yasue: "I recoiled. I wondered if he was messing with me. Him designing that sort of thing, I couldn't believe it (…) But no, he wasn't joking, he had even already come up with its moves. It would bounce on the ground and Sora would be able to ride it." Indeed, Nomura was totally serious. He wanted to replace the usual Heartless with Nightmares, which would be demonic versions of Spirits. Meanwhile, the player would be able to create and raise Spirits, then make them fight alongside

17. *Nintendogs* is a Nintendo game in which you raise virtual dogs. It was released for the Nintendo DS in 2005.

the protagonists. The proposal caught Osaka totally off guard. And, as usual, they had their doubts. However, it didn't take them long to see the potential in the idea, as Yasue explains: "When I saw the final results [modeled, textured, and animated], Meow Wow had a very particular charm. I said to myself, 'Nomura, that sun of a gun.'" Mai Okauchi, who performed that work, adds that the palette of colors for Meow Wow was initially different, and that she preferred the older version. Of course, the director wasn't going to stop at just one speci- men. He asked his team to draw inspiration from Meow Wow to create several other species. However, he had one rule: "I want bizarre and not necessarily attractive creatures, but they must have something unusual about them that makes them lovable." Gen Kobayashi (art director for characters) says, "There were four of us designing them, three women and me. The women handled the smallest and cutest ones. I handled the bigger, more menacing ones." The first round of proposed Spirits was not good enough. Nomura thought that they had a serious lack of variety: "So, I asked them to make me 50 or so."

[DROP] > *L'Eminenza Oscura I*

It didn't take long for him to establish his carefree style with a <u>candidness</u> not often seen from Japanese people. Yoshi-P (as those close to him call him) explained point by point where the game went wrong using a sly old trick: bring others down to boost yourself up. The problem is that he has a habit of fibbing. In 2015, for example, no one knew anything about his career, which annoyed him. To show that he was an industry veteran, he claimed to have 19 years of experience and, in an interview, said that he had worked on presti- gious titles like *Tengai Makyô (Far East of Eden)* and on the legendary NEC TurboGrafx-16: a lie of omission because he never worked on this game from Red Company, or at least he didn't play a big enough role to be credited. The same is true for the NEC console and, what's more, its production stopped two years before he even started working for Hudson Soft. It's possible that he's just bad at math and that he actually had over 20 years of experience. In that case, it would be possible that he had worked on the last game in the *Tengai Makyô* series (for the

TurboGrafx-CD), *Tengai Makyô Deden no Den*, a sort of *Bomberman* starring Kabuki Danjuro, one of the heroes of the series. Which is not exactly the same as what he claimed. Let's be clear, Mr. Yoshida. If you're going to go around scorning other video game makers, you yourself need to be beyond reproach. Because, indeed, he scorns "old-school video games" and even derides work he considers "too artisanal" and thus behind the times. He was out to prove that the master craftsmen[18], as they were called at Square Enix, were dinosaurs and that it was time to make room for ambitious "young" people with more modern methods. Objectively speaking, he wasn't totally wrong: reforms were needed for certain productions. However, that didn't give him the right to go around insulting people. He even went as far as lying to discredit certain artists: he called out their obsession with visual quality and explained, for example, that they put just as much effort into a flower pot as they did into a playable character, with a thousand polygons and 150 lines of shaders[19]. The public found this hilarious. Those has-been creators are such idiots!

But, it was an outrageous lie because the characters in *Final Fantasy XIV* were made up of between 15,000 and 30,000 polygons and were remarkably optimized. Maybe he got the numbers wrong; you've probably noticed that he's not great with math. That is, unless he was trying to manipulate public opinion in order to get support: "At least this guy tells us stuff. He even writes us letters and plays with us. This guy's pretty awesome." I can understand how players, especially MMORPG players, might not have the brain power to see through his charade; however, it's astounding to me how the media fell into his trap and allowed themselves to be taken in by his easily debunked cock-and-bull story. It's inexcusable for a director/producer to take such brazen liberties with the truth in a press conference where he excoriates people who made major contributions to video game history. It says a lot about his opportunism. Yoshida is a businessman, as he enjoys saying himself, with an acute sense of communications who will stop at nothing to achieve his ambitions. That being said, you

18. "Master craftsmen" is what Square Enix calls the exceptional, meticulous, gifted artists who made Square Enix untouchable in the era of the first two PlayStations.
19. "Shaders": computer code for the rendering of graphics, used, for example, to represent different materials.

can't blame him. Wada gave him free rein: what Yoshida wanted, Yoshida got. So, as soon as he stepped into the new role, he hoarded the resources (both financial and human[20]) that had originally been intended for the company's other productions.

Why such favoritism? The truth is that Wada didn't really have a choice, particularly because of Square Enix's powerful investors, first and foremost Yasuhiko Fukushima, the sly old fox from Enix who, armed with 20 percent of the combined company's share capital, had been lying in wait for the man who prevented him from seizing control of Square to make a false move. Wada <u>had to</u> bail out *Final Fantasy XIV*, no matter the cost. He was willing to destabilize the entire company for a year if needed. MMO games are a very significant and long-term source of revenue. Given the importance of *Final Fantasy XI* in the past, he knew that Square Enix couldn't do without it. Of course, he was responsible for the failure of *XIV*. His drive for the company to have its own engine and an **MMORPG**, without dedicating the resources to compete with *World of Warcraft* was a big mistake, but he told himself it was just a rough patch. Thanks to his remarkable reading of the market, he had already anticipated the next stage. In 2010, he hired Julien Merceron, a young prodigy from France who had already managed to get Eidos afloat once again. Merceron's job was to help out the Japanese by making modern, customized tools for them. In addition, a number of former members of the **Sonic Team** (yes, from SEGA) were hired, including Yoshihisa Hashimoto, a highly-qualified lighting expert who previously helped create an engine[21] for *Sonic Unleashed*. This marked the start of a collaboration that would slowly but surely lead to a new engine, Luminous Studio[22].

20. At the height of its development, *Final Fantasy XIV* had over 500 people working on it in-house, not to mention the hundreds of people from contractors working on it. This was unprecedented for a Square Enix production.
21. When he was at SEGA, Hashimoto developed Hedgehog Engine, which included, notably, a global illumination algorithm and an in-house "light field" system, a mixer that makes light appear to reflect around naturally.
22. A powerful engine compatible with DirectX 11 technology that incorporates a range of tools (including a cutscene editor), libraries, and all sorts of algorithms. Its architecture is similar to that of Epic Games' Unreal Engine, but is really adapted to the needs of the Japanese style of video game.

10

9

8

7

6

5

4

3

2

1

To get himself out of hot water, Wada blamed the management of *Final Fantasy XIV*, namely Hiromichi Tanaka, for all of the problems. It was Tanaka's bitter reward after everything he had done for Square Enix. No matter that he had sustained the company for almost 10 years with his extraordinary *Final Fantasy XI*; someone had to pay. That ~~didn't factor~~ no longer factored into the equation. There remained a riddle to solve: how do you shoot a collateral victim at point-blank range when you already poisoned them, while at the same time embracing the cause of the first sweet-talker who comes along? The business *voices* were resolutely inscrutable. Anyway, *Final Fantasy XIV* is not the subject of this book, so I'll stop there. However, its failure had consequences, particularly for *Final Fantasy versus XIII*. What does that have to do with *Kingdom Hearts*? As the name of this section, L'Eminenza Oscura I, suggests, the story will be continued. And you're going to laugh at this:

[DROP] > *KH3D*

Ideas started pouring forth from the planners, who based the Spirits off of real animals, "even the alpaca and other species that I didn't even know," says Kobayashi. Gradually, the magic started to take over. The full development team (Osaka and Tokyo) fell in love with the little creatures which had "a unique charm to them." Everyone wanted to participate with ideas or designs, or by proposing moves, so that they could be the "parent" of one or more Spirits. For example, Satoshi Otani regrets that he wasn't personally responsible for Me Me Bunny. In other words, the team members did all they could to make the creatures as lovable as possible. First off, from a technical stand-point. A newcomer to the team, Takashi Itai (art director for character models), explains that in spite of everyone's best efforts, no Spirit came close to being as great as Meow Wow. So, he wanted to help make the other Spirits less dull. To do this, he gave a larger-than-normal number of polygons to their eyes: "I wanted to help make them as lifelike as possible," he says. His efforts gained him the gratitude of Koji Hamada (animation director): "The modelers and programmers did me a huge favor. I can animate the eyes and mouths of the Dream Eaters (...) in

addition to their battle moves, they'll express emotions. You'll be able to see if they're happy or sad." Ryo Inakura (sound designer) added his two cents: "We're really creating a special tool where we can use all sort of materials. The goal is to give them original sounds." The designers decided to make their own contribution by establishing that every creature would get a distinct personality. "A single type [of Dream Eater] can have four characteristics," Nomura declared. This significantly influenced how they behaved for the player: "That really depends on the creature. It may fall asleep and be useless or, conversely, it may be super angry and attack all the time," says Yasue. Mamoru Ohashi (planning director for battles) says on this subject that he assigned the behaviors in battle according to the nature of the animals that served as models. For example, a sheep puts you to sleep and fish can poison you. He also gave them attacks "according to their inclinations." All in all, the Spirit or Nightmare of the same Dream Eater have slight differences, like a few moves. Yasue adds that a lot of work was done on artificial intelligence and that the system is totally different from the *Birth by Sleep* system, which was much more scripted. What's more, as the relationships between Sora/Riku and their monsters deepened, the AI would become more, well, intelligent, according to Ohashi. Additionally, Tomokazu Shibata (battle director) used a "simple chart in a spreadsheet to compare the status for each of the Spirits" in order to balance the strengths of each one so that no single Spirit would be too dominant. Alright, cool, all the Spirits have a "charm that makes it so you can't hate them," as Nomura put it, each has a personality, and they fight against Nightmares... Is that it? If that's what you think, then you don't know Nomura very well. The Dream Eaters were at the heart of every system:

— Relationship-building system reminiscent of *Nintendogs*. The goal was to raise them and take care of them by performing different activities (feeding them, petting them, playing with them, etc.) showcasing the special features of the Nintendo 3DS, like augmented reality and the touchscreen.

— A system specific to character development: as the Spirits' relationship with Sora and Riku developed, the protagonists would be able to "grow." Basically, their fate was closely tied to their creatures. Each had very specific skills (both passive and active) distributed across a sort of "game board" similar to *Birth by Sleep*. As you took care of a Spirit, the reward would multiply, from an emotional point of view, but also, especially, from a purely gaming point of view. Once again, nothing was left up to chance. Nomura wanted to force the player to love and care for their companions, otherwise they wouldn't be able to advance through the game. *Well played.* With that established, Kobayashi wondered whether or not he should plan for the Spirits to evolve one or more times to become much more attractive, but he decided against this: they weren't designed to be cute only to then push the player to strive for the opposite.

— An assistance system during battles; incidentally, the Spirits were more or less useful depending on their personalities. However, they all had gauges that would fill as they exchanged hits. When a gauge was filled, the played could trigger a Spirit Link, a high-powered attack mode. This system did not work the same way for both protagonists. Indeed, Sora had a physical connection with his Spirits and could, for example, ride them, whereas Riku absorbed the powers of his Spirits and transformed himself while maintaining the option to continue using his normal abilities. The system itself could be powered up if the player then performed a Dual Link; of course, each Spirit had its own special characteristics which, when mixed with those of another, produced totally different results.

— Finally, the Spirits were used in a mini-game called Flick Rush, basically monster tournaments in an arena (the realization of Nomura's vision he had while playing *Nintendogs*), based on a "speed card game," according to the creator.

Finally, to conclude the discussion of Dream Eaters,

[DROP] > *L'EMINENZA OSCURA I (CONTINUATION AND CONCLUSION)*

And you're going to laugh at this: not only did Square Enix not learn its lesson from *FFXIV*, but the company went on to repeat the SAME mistake and this time, *Kingdom Hearts* was not spared. But, we'll come back to that later. For now, we'll focus on the end of the

2010 fiscal year (March 31, 2011) and look at how Yoichi Wada handled the investors. Unsurprisingly, performance for the year was "significantly below the level forecast at the beginning of the fiscal year and the lowest level in the history of our company has been reached," he admitted. There were several reasons for this. Of course, the problem with *Final Fantasy XIV* was number one: "We failed with the launch of this title in which we had placed all of our hopes," Wada stated, after explaining that a revamp was already underway. However, he also figured that it was important to note that *FFXIV* was not the only poor performer. Indeed, almost all of their titles were duds, with the exception of *Kane & Lynch 2: Dog Days* and *Dragon Quest Monsters: Joker 2*, two little million-sellers. He blamed poor sales of home consoles and portable consoles reaching the end of their lifespans. Totally defeated, Wada declared, "It is now out of the question to release an important title hastily." This resulted in *Deus Ex: Human Revolution* being pushed back, as it was not yet on par. The only bright spot was the exponential growth of social gaming, particularly benefiting *Sengoku IXA*, a browser-based game produced in partnership with Yahoo! Japan, and *Nicotto Town*, a social game similar to *The Sims* or *Animal Crossing* (with 700,000 subscriptions, I might add). Wada nevertheless decided to cancel several games in development to rebalance things[23] and concentrate solely on a dozen licenses "to be brought up to the level of *Final Fantasy*."

To do this, he intended to make internal reforms by boosting the management of development teams (essentially, put more pressure on them to make their games faster), breaking the chains of company hierarchy by allowing the upper management to communicate directly with lower-level employees, and ensuring as much flexibility as possible in the "change of existing IP," while avoiding disputes with game creators as much as possible. In other words, the company was taking control of its business and bypassing the creative types to impose its own way of thinking. **This policy of austerity was then reinforced by a tragic event.**

---

23. He fired around 800 people and then went on to hire 300 more highly qualified people. It was a net decrease of 457 employees, to be exact.

[DROP] > *KH3D*

Finally, to conclude the discussion on Dream Eaters, Tsuyoshi Sekito was responsible for their musical themes. He was given just one instruction: "Think *Kingdom Hearts*, but don't take it too seriously." The composer laughs about this: "It's easy to say, but in reality that made me nervous, like I was taking a test." Still, he produced four battle tracks "that make you want to fight," and two other tracks for the menus that were very "unusual and particularly difficult to create." The tracks were *kawaii* music, typical of Japanese anime.

HAND TO HAND
[*KH3D*: DEVELOPMENT]

Speaking of music, what ever happened to Yoko Shimomura? Why is it that for the last two or three episodes she's been sharing her composer duties? Let's not forget that she'd been working for some time on *Final Fantasy versus XIII*, for which Nomura was, as usual, very demanding (i.e. maddening). Additionally, since 2003, she hadn't been an employee of Square Enix, instead working freelance. As such, she took on other contracts. She made her dear Tetsu a priority, of course, but she still had responsibilities elsewhere. Moreover, some of her other contracts were long-term endeavors since they were often RPGs like *Xenoblade Chronicles*, *Last Ranker*, and *Radiant Historia*. With so much going on, it was hard for her to keep the same level of quality for *KH*. So, she needed help, which is where Ishimoto and Sekito came in, with their differing styles creating a more heterogeneous soundtrack. Her status was never questioned: Shimomura remained and shall always remain the series' regular lead composer. Moreover, for this episode, she handled almost everything[24] and set the tone using the word "dream" as a basis. To push the 3D in *Kingdom Hearts 3D*, she also used a "dreamlike" style of composition using

---

24. Except for The Grid and the themes related to *Subarashiki Kono Sekai*, which were handled by Ishimoto. The Drops, Dream Eaters, and certain bosses were assigned to Sekito. Finally, Shimomura didn't have to worry about the Symphony of Sorcery world. Obviously.

ternary form and triple meter. Basically, like a waltz. 1–2–3, 1–2–3. It's a relatively rare way of composing these days, but it's very common in classical music. It wasn't a random choice and had real meaning to it. She chose to do away with a simple or linear rhythm and instead used an odd number of beats in order to create music with dimension to it that destabilizes the listener… This fit perfectly with the loss of visual points of reference caused by the autostereoscopic imaging. From a technical point of view, Shimomura says that she was thrilled with the 3DS because it finally allowed her to use streaming audio, offering compositions with better quality.

Takeshi Nozue (cinematic movie director) also considered this anniversary game very important: "Of all the *Kingdom Hearts* games, this is the one where I feel the most pressure and I fully intend to give it my all to meet everyone's expectations." What a commitment! Perhaps that's because he was fully in charge of his department. Indeed, Nomura didn't intervene this time and gave him carte blanche: "He knows what he's doing and, given his enthusiasm, we can expect something great." Nozue's initial idea was to have a perfect anime Mickey Mouse on the lower screen whose movements would be "connected" to the upper screen. To get the desired quality, he had to go outside of his area of expertise and use traditional animation. Unless someone can prove to me otherwise, I have to say that it doesn't get better than celluloid animation[25]. Recognizing that he had zero knowledge in this area, he asked for help from a living legend from Telecom Animation Film, Nobuo Tomizawa[26]. The results they produced, with help from Disney, were phenomenal. As Nomura put it, "Mickey moves so well that you would think it was CGI!"

However, Nozue didn't stop there. He gave himself a second challenge: to create a scene constructed like a pop-up book[27]. It was a real pain

---

25. Celluloid is a transparent sheet that graphic artists for animated films draw on. Movement is then created by superimposing different celluloids. That's where the term "cel shading" comes from.

26. Nobuo Tomizawa is a student of Miyazaki who has been working in animation since the 1970s. He has held all sorts of positions and worked on numerous series, including *Meitantei Conan* (*Case Closed*), *Meitantei Hōmuzu* (*Sherlock Hound*), and *Lupin III*. Additionally, he was animation director for the film *Little Nemo: Adventures in Slumberland*, then later he was creator for several *shōjo* series.

27. You know, pop-up books. Those children's books where certain pages have parts that are folded down but stand up when deployed by a mechanism. In this way, the image "comes to life" and the reader can even interact with it using things like pull tabs.

to make. The request surprised Visual Works. Although they were not used to that kind of approach, they didn't let themselves get discouraged and even earned themselves the admiration of their leader: "They're so energized and motivated, it's incredible to see." Naturally, this difficult work required some "adjustments" to schedules. Such an extraordinary opening requires time, concentration, and… sacrifice. Nozue, for example, had to work over Golden Week. In spite of that, he was happy: "I found myself alone at the office, in the dark, working while listening to the orchestral version of *Hikari* on full blast." It was a very good memory, as shown by his big grin while telling the story.

It was at about the same time, in spring 2011, that stalwart team member Asako Suga (dialog editor) started working on the game. At first, she was stuck watching the movies from which the game's new worlds were taken from, over and over again, so that she could adjust each dialog "and get the tone as close as possible to their movies. A huge task," she says. But, she had to hurry because with the *Kingdom Hearts* games, the voices are always recorded using the storyboards. The cutscenes are then created afterward so that the animation of the characters can be adjusted, particularly performing lip syncing. Suga was delighted because "this time, they promised me they would use all of my voices and so I won't be left crying from them cutting any out in editing." So, if the cutscenes have to wait until after the voices are recorded, what was Masaru Oka (event director) up to? Once again, I want to dispel the notion that anyone was just twiddling their thumbs. A production takes time to prepare. Oka's job was to plan out the scenes and storyboard them, with approval from Nomura. As such, the proposed camera angles, direction, and dialogs were all integral parts of his job. As Oka puts it, "Filming isn't a big deal. The biggest part of the work is the planning and preparation beforehand." And let's not forget that he was also scenario director. Essentially, he assisted Nomura in writing what happens in the Disney worlds, since the general plot was mostly the boss' work. Besides that, Oka wrote all of the descriptions (of items, for example), which was an enormous undertaking. And for *KH3D*, he was also in charge of the "Mementos": a new system offering, among other things, summaries of previous episodes in order to refresh players' memories, as well as, according to Nomura, "to allow them to discover new clues

to facilitate understanding" because of the complexity of *Kingdom Hearts 3D: Dream Drop Distance*. The Mementos menu became a source for information. On a side note, initially they planned to instead have a souvenir photo mode, but the idea was abandoned in favor of text: "The advantage [of text] is that you can go back over information immediately," says the director. What's more, thanks to the Mementos, players could see any game scene whenever they wanted. Nomura explains: "I've always thought that to allow players to follow a deep story, you have to increase the number of cutscenes," maybe too much, according to some. This has been a long-standing debate: Does *Kingdom Hearts* systematically use too many cutscenes and, in so doing, break its own rhythm? Let's just say that it's a firm position taken that can become a liability, especially when players aren't allowed to skip the cutscenes. Nomura is aware of this criticism: "[With *KH3D*], we are testing a new approach. Those who want to keep the action going can skip [the cutscenes] and watch them later." Hallelujah. It was a smart decision because *Kingdom Hearts* can sometimes be hardcore and you end up dying a lot, especially when fighting bosses. If after a game over you can face the boss again without having to sit through a cutscene that can sometimes last several minutes, that's not just an improvement, it's a revolution. And of course, this approach was given due consideration and became a new standard for the series. That was a big relief for players, allowing them to better appreciate, if at all possible, *Kingdom Hearts* in all its glory.

By early summer 2011, Nomura was anxious. He had presented the various scenarios to Disney, but "it's hard for them to take it all in at once," as he explains it. So, he patiently explained to them, point by point, the reasons behind his different choices and how you have to see things as a whole because each element has its own importance and connects to the series. Could this be the first consequence of Steve Wadsworth's departure from Disney? Nomura was floundering and he needed approval to move forward. He counted on his allies at Disney to help him dig his way out of the situation: "A number of people at Disney like *Kingdom Hearts* and support me." Still, this hiccup in his plan led him to take stock of the project's progress. Development was about halfway through, but they had very tight deadlines and no more than seven months remaining. They were still on schedule, but they couldn't dawdle. It was time to tackle dubbing and cutscenes.

JUST WONDERING
[*KH HD 1.5 REMIX*: TEST]

At the same time, Nomura was asking the programmers in Osaka if they thought that a re-release of *Kingdom Hearts* would be possible for the PlayStation 3. Given that there was good progress on *Kingdom Hearts 3D*, Tamotsu Goto freed up one of his programmers, Sumio Nasu, and reassigned him to this new task. When he took a look at the program, he realized that it wasn't going to be easy: "He told me that it was so old that almost all of the data were lost. They had disappeared," Nomura laments. So, what could they do? Salvage whatever they could and recreate almost everything working off of the most recent games, particularly *Kingdom Hearts 3D*. Kenro Tsujimoto, who was more experienced, joined Nasu and they started working on it together. They soon found themselves struggling, as their boss explains: "The trouble was that they had to recreate everything based on a program that wasn't theirs." Nasu confirms this: "Since [the program] was 10 years old, no one remembered how they did things back in the day." Tired of wasting their time, they finally decided to "analyze the PS2 code and rewrite it entirely so that it would work on the PS3, while saving as much data as possible." This was a huge, time-consuming task.

Returning to *KH3D*. The task at hand was to "polish" certain backgrounds and items for a new trailer for the TGS, the second major stage in publicity for the game. The new trailer would reveal a good portion of the game's features. **However, an external event disturbed the director's normal serenity...**

🜸 [DROP] > *L'EMINENZA OSCURA*

This policy of austerity was then reinforced by a tragic event. On March 11, 2011, at 2:46 pm local time, the Pacific coast of Tohoku was

hit by the worst earthquake in Japan's history (magnitude 8.9). It was also the world's seventh most powerful earthquake ever recorded. It was a terrible natural disaster that resulted in thousands of deaths and shook buildings in Tokyo, even though they were 380 km (236 miles) from the epicenter. A major tsunami alert was immediately issued for the entire Pacific region. An hour later, over 6,000 people were evacuated from the area around the Fukushima nuclear power plant. Everyone feared the worst: a leak from one of the reactors, or worse yet, several of them. Around 8:00 pm, another earthquake, this time magnitude 6.6, hit somewhere between Tokyo and Nagano. Around 11:00 pm, the prime minister asked the population within a 10-km radius around the Fukushima plant to evacuate due to radioactivity eight-times greater than normal. You know the rest: the worst nuclear disaster of the 21st century. End parenthesis. I'll give you a second to just breathe.

I bring up this painful memory because, of course, it had major consequences for Square Enix. To be clear, the effects on Square Enix were <u>nothing</u> in comparison to the suffering of others; I would never compare the loss of money to the loss of human life. But, the facts remain. Wada explains: "The Tohoku earthquake cost Square Enix 570 million yen." Naturally, this was because of destroyed production plants, the need to save energy, online services that had to be suspended, and also more basic reasons, particularly absences from work. You'd think that 2011 was truly a cursed year.

L'EMINENZA OSCURA II

In this context that shook (pardon the pun) Japan for weeks, even months, *Final Fantasy versus XIII* found itself in an anemic state. I chose that term for a good reason. Yoshida the vampire swooped in to feast on the production and take what he needed, even stealing some of the managers, including Jun Akiyama, who Nomura had a heck of a time getting on board (after the development of *Final Fantasy XII*) and Syuuichi Sato, his precious VFX director. Nomura was furious. He developed a rare dislike for Yoshida. The *Final Fantasy XIV* producer, however, did not care. He even went so far as to order a "light" version of Luminous Studio, the engine being developed, I'll remind you, to get *Final Fantasy versus XIII* out of its slump. In spite of this backstabbing, Nomura persisted. In spring 2011, his team was growing, becoming several hundred people strong. It was now or never. They had to move forward. He asked the programmers to fix Crystal Tools to make it more malleable to fit their needs, without considering this an end in and of itself. Ebony[28] was the name given to the result. It was just a stopgap engine while they waited for the famous Luminous Studio, on which significant progress had already been made, particularly in regards to its lighting technology, which the programmers decided to incorporate into Ebony. From there, development progressed at a mediocre pace, but at the end of the summer, there was another dramatic turn of events: Sony introduced its next console, the PlayStation 4. It was the straw that broke the camel's back.

All that had been done up to that point—through blood, sweat, and tears—was for nothing. The *versus XIII* dream, which had already been quite dark for about a year, turned into a nightmare and the *Final Fantasy XV* vulture began to circle overhead. That said, Sony's SDK was not yet available, so they had to return to toiling away on a product that would end up being useless. Nomura had to digest the news. After putting up a good front at the TGS and giving a final interview, he went totally silent for about six months.

Likely alarmed by Square Enix's fragile situation, Disney Interactive began quietly plotting a betrayal by making its own *Kingdom Hearts*. No surprise there. First, they have the right to do so since the brand and the trio of heroes belong to them. Second, the more or less insidious threat had always been there: don't forget the *V-CAST*[29] game or *Epic Mickey*[30]. Only this time, it was serious as they were talking about using Sora in a new adventure.

---

28. Since their conception in 2003, *Final Fantasy XIII* and *Final Fantasy versus XIII* were associated with white and black, respectively. Two brothers who were opposites in almost every way. Since *XIII* was the priority, the engine intended for the development of both games was called the "White Engine." So, the *Versus* engine was called "Ebony" in keeping with the theme, but internally, it was known as the "Black Engine."
29. See page 134.
30. See page 273.

In summer 2011, Disney contacted Go For Launch Productions[31], a design studio. Their mission: to come up with a formal proposal for a spin-off game for smartphones. The studio produced 145 pieces of concept art and other design documents for the would-be worlds where Sora and a female character, presumably Kairi, were supposed to travel to: *Alice in Wonderland*, *Snow White*, *Aladdin*, *Tron*, and *Lilo and Stitch*, but this time in Hawaii. There was also a *Peter Pan* world where a good portion of the action would take place on the rooftops of London, as shown in a quite detailed storyboard of what appeared to be a cutscene with Sora and Kairi facing off against an Unknown.

Certain illustrations gave glimpses of new destinations based on works like *Wreck-It Ralph* and the animated series *Star Wars: Clone Wars*. Finally, a handful of backgrounds from *Rapunzel* and *Frozen* showed that they were the last ones the team had worked on and that there hadn't been enough time to finish them before the end of the production. In addition to the Disney worlds, the proposal didn't burden itself with acting ethically, choosing to offer a reinterpretation of some of Nomura's original creations: the Destiny Islands, Traverse Town, and Twilight Town. That said, they also proposed brand-new settings like New Town, a "hub city" with a castle and its adjacent village (that was reminiscent of Radiant Garden and the Hollow Bastion), as well as a never-before-seen evil tower, probably the hideout of the bad guys and the last world in the game. The low level of detail in the illustrations and the sometimes troubling resemblance to Square Enix's work long led some to believe that it was a project created from scratch by a fan website that had gotten the scoop. It wouldn't be the first time that *Kingdom Hearts* aficionados had taken on a big production[32] requiring lots of help, especially to excite a certain group of fans who aren't very good at checking their sources. You'll also notice that the media

31. A design studio specializing in animation, managed by the Crudens (Philip and Lorraine), animation legends who together have 45 years of experience. They have worked on numerous anime series, as well as feature films, notably ones directed by Don Bluth (*Anastasia* and *Titan A.E.*). Basically, high-level stuff.
32. *Kingdom Hearts* fans are very productive when it comes to trying to unravel the mysteries of the series and take on the challenges given (traps laid) by Nomura. Also, one of the latest amusing fan creation was the construction of a city only mentioned in a fan event (and of which a piece of concept art has been floating around since *Birth by Sleep*) in the game *Minecraft*. This sort of project is a group effort requiring sometimes months, or even years, of work. This particular fascination is also to thank for the series' survival and its (still) exceptional popularity 15 years later.

didn't stop to think for a second before sharing the information, at best shielding themselves by calling it a rumor...

There's no surprise there because it is quite an incredible story. The website that discovered the illustrations, allegedly on the official website of Go For Launch Productions, is now the only one that has them because the studio has, apparently, deleted the evidence. There still remains a troubling fact: Philip Cruden, the Creative Director at GFLP, says on his LinkedIn profile that he worked on a *Kingdom Hearts* game for Disney Interactive. If you dig a little bit, you'll find that he's not the only one and that the game even had a code name—*Kingdom Hearts: Forgotten Keys*, according to its technical director (at Disney Interactive), Tom Ketola. So, what should we think of all this? It's hard to not think that it was a hoax. As of now, it's impossible to say for sure one way or the other. Cruden chose not to respond to my numerous requests for an interview. As such, I remain suspicious. It may well be that Disney Interactive ordered a game between September 2011 and March 2013. In that case, Disney would have canceled this game that was—apparently (really)—called *Kingdom Hearts: Forgotten Keys*. Assuming that this whole story is true... the question is, what was Square Enix's reaction?! Also, a second and more important question: could this story of a love child with another studio have had consequences related to what happened in 2013 with Nomura and the development of *Kingdom Hearts III*? To be continued.

[DROP] > *KH3D*

However, an external event disturbed the director's normal serenity... putting him behind schedule for designing the "key art," the first real illustration for *Kingdom Hearts 3D: Dream Drop Distance*. Nevertheless, he managed to finish it at the last minute, just before the TGS.

MY HEART'S DESCENT
[*KH3D*: DEVELOPMENT, CONTINUATION AND CONCLUSION]

In October, development entered its final stages. Technically, there were only three of four months of work remaining. Takeshi Fujimoto was more frustrated than ever before with The World That Never Was: "This world is hell because the backgrounds change all the time, with buildings that cut off, turn around, that sort of thing. It's a headache to optimize the memory allocated to the graphics." Tamotsu Goto says, "It's kind of my fault. At the start of development, I opened my big mouth and said 'that's fine, we have plenty of memory to do that,' but now we're crying because we're starting to have big memory problems." Meanwhile, Nomura insisted on changing the boss that Riku fights at the end of The World That Never Was: "Originally, it was supposed to be a Nightmare version of Meow Wow," explains Mai Okauchi. In the end, this enemy became the <u>Anti Black Coat</u>, a humanoid, hooded Nightmare with red eyes. It was full of symbolism, even in its attacks in which it distorts the "visual pattern of dreams[33]" established by Yasuhiko Onishi (art director VFX).

"Toward the end of development, I called the Osaka team several times to ask them to add bosses not initially planned because the scenes seemed insignificant without battles," says Nomura. In particular, he's referring to the climax of the story and a major last-minute change. Asako Suga explains, "We recorded the final voices a month and a half before the deadline." The director, however, was relentless. He had them add a final Dive, as well as change the last boss and even the ending itself: "It's not what we originally planned," he explains, but he nevertheless enacted these changes "for various reasons." This new game led him to "try doing something unique, even if that meant cutting down the epilogue in response." He opted for a shocking revelation like in *Kingdom Hearts Re: coded* instead of a really cool scene. Finally, he had his team add the "payoff"[34] with the Dream Eaters because he thought that "working so hard to raise them deserves a reward" and,

---

33. The "kaleidoscope" effect around the Keyholes in each of the Sleeping Worlds.
34. An epilogue after ending credits.

in particular, "it was a way to show that Sora got the power to open portals to the Sleeping Worlds." Could that be a clue about *Kingdom Hearts III*?

In any case, Nomura was touched by the care and hard work of the Osaka team: "Even if this time the unreasonable demands multiplied, I think that their high level of creativity really shined in this game." Yasue came out on the other side of the development exhausted: "On several occasions, we couldn't even go home because of totally unforeseen bugs. For example, there was one that wouldn't go away, no matter what we did and no matter how many people tried to fix it using any means possible." In spite of that, the experience helped him grow and gave him "a unique enthusiasm"; his words, not mine. Especially because, according to him, they were able to include everything they had planned… except for "several Dream Eaters that were eliminated, to my great disappointment," complains Mamoru Ohashi (planning director), who tried to spare some of the creatures from being cut, "including Queen Buzzerfly, who was miraculously saved to become the boss of a Dive!" he says. I'll conclude with a few fun facts, just because.

— Originally, Rinzler was supposed to face Riku.

— The characters were modeled very precisely and even their tongues were taken into account!

— It was while he was having a bubble tea[35] that Takeshi Fujimoto came up with the atmosphere for the Sleeping Worlds, which hadn't yet been planned out.

— *The Eye of Darkness*, the theme song for the battle against the final boss, was originally intended for a Dive.

— Kinguda Nyan (Meowjesty), the king of the Meow Wows, was created using Mickey Mouse's colors.

— During the credits, the player can control Sora and collect letters to write a code: "A secret message from me," says Nomura.

— In the battle between Riku and Young Xehanort, the latter can control time by making an hourglass appear. This was an idea from

---

35. A blend of hot and iced tea with milk and black, floating tapioca pearls. Bubble tea is very popular in Asia, especially in Taiwan.

Tomokazu Shibata (battle director): "I wanted a battle closely tied to the story," he says.

— At the end of development, Masaru Oka declared that in a future game, he wanted to try writing a scenario (for a world) incorporating musical theater. Could that be a clue about *Kingdom Hearts III*?

The game was released on March 29, 2012, in Japan. Nomura and Yasue succeeded in their incredible challenge: release *Kingdom Hearts 3D: Dream Drop Distance* on the tenth anniversary (OK, off by one day) of *Kingdom Hearts*. Osaka immediately began work on the Western version with the goal of finishing by the summer. No additional content was planned besides the "Drop Speed Down," a new bonus in Dive Mode. The rest was the same. Of course, they also had to do everything that comes with localization, particularly adjusting the interface and menus.

In this regard, Misao Ohara (interface director) had onerous corrections to make: "Sometimes, the names of the Dream Eaters were longer or shorter than expected." **At the same time, voice recording began in April and was less difficult to organize than usual since, besides the main characters,**

⚜ [DROP] > *L'Eminenza Oscura II*

At the end of March 2012, just like every year, Yoichi Wada presented the company's performance for the fiscal year. Square Enix managed to get its head above water, but it was far from making it back to shore. The arcade division perked up, generating around 35 percent of the company's revenues! The games division represented 56 percent, up slightly from the previous year. The company now had three major categories within its Digital Entertainment business:

— <u>MMORPGs</u>. *Final Fantasy XIV* was being revamped and was drawing renewed interest. That was satisfactory while they awaited version 2.0 and *Dragon Quest X*, which had been in the planning phase since 2005 and whose release was imminent. The salvation of the MMORPG category was… *Final Fantasy XI*, which had just celebrated its tenth anniversary. And they thought it was a good idea to throw Tanaka under the bus? (Sigh.)

— <u>SN games</u> (*Social Networking and mobile games*). *Sengoku IXA* generated over 3 billion yen in profits, thus becoming "one of the pillar products of the company," according to Wada, who intended to keep the success going with in-house games like *Final Fantasy Brigade*, which already had over 2 million users. Moreover, the F2P model[36] became their new hobby horse: "It generates enormous amounts of revenue in little time and with smaller teams." He also explained that he had established 10 small teams in order to "reduce as much as possible the creation phase." At the same time, he pushed those who had a successful project to form their own team instead or merging with others. Finally, with the Gameglobe initiative, the president showed an interest in the creation of content by the consumers themselves. An opportunity for the future.

— <u>HD games</u>. The year's two champions in this category were *Final Fantasy XIII–2* (over 2.7 million units sold) and *Deus Ex: Human Revolution* (2.18 million units sold). Both had respectable performance, but were disappointing compared to how they were expected to sell. Wada was increasingly annoyed by the policies of the console manufacturers: "I feel that one of the fundamental causes of the declining trend of the game console market is the delay in implementing new business models. This is regretful," he declared. The new goal was to focus on 10 strong IPs and to develop them as much as possible using new business models, particularly PDLC (*premium download-able content*), which consists of regular releases of extra content to get more money out of players. To conclude, Wada delivered his usual reading of the market, which was clearheaded, to say the least: "The reality is that game development has become so costly and complicated that the whole industry is at a loss." One of the main focuses for the company was the "engine wars." So, from then on, besides the proprietary Luminous Studio (in good hands and set for future AAA games), Square Enix would start using outsourced engines like Unity and Unreal Engine for most of its productions. Naturally, Wada made no mention of the taboo Crystal Tools.

---

36. F2P or "free-to-play." A model that gives free access to an online game, but the game makes its money through small payments made at a virtual store, using real money, where players can buy all sorts of items or upgrades to the game experience.

Wada had pushed back the deadline, but he knew he would have to settle the *Final Fantasy versus XIII* situation before the end of the year. The game had gone through six years of stagnation, communication mistakes, and questionable management methods; essentially, everything wrong with Square Enix. As a result, it was stuck, totally incapable of dealing with changes in the market. The more the publisher tried to respond to the challenges of the day, the deeper they dug their own hole. As the entire industry took off using high-tech tools, the Japanese buried their heads in the sand. To make matters worse, they threw themselves into creating a—amateur—proprietary engine. Refusing to use Unreal Engine 3 in order to avoid paying a 25 percent license fee was beyond dumb (yep, I went there), especially since this put the entire company in a horrible situation. Moreover, it led to them losing the confidence of some of the most faithful video game fans. They went from kings to paupers in less than a decade. Wada was responsible—in spite of himself—for all of it. He was the one making the decisions, the one who up to that point had limited the size of the teams and poorly managed the timing. He's guilty. If the media had found out the true story behind the development of *Final Fantasy versus XIII*, i.e. the completely appalling conditions, it would have been a big scandal. Wada knew that he was in danger and sitting on an ejector seat. So, he had no choice but to find scapegoats and saviors. He used some savvy marketing: "It's not our fault, it's because of the director." First, he had to muzzle the *Versus* director because, as is only natural, he was about to explode. Wada hoped that a little fresh air would do him some good. His goal was then to keep Nomura as far away from the media as possible, especially because, frustrated by a lack of information, they were starting to make things up and share rumors about the game's cancellation.

Nomura spoke again in early 2012. Interestingly, he had changed. The language he used was no longer the same. His way of speaking and responding, his word choice, were totally different. As soon as the subject of *Final Fantasy versus XIII* came up, he became uncomfortable. He stammered and tried to explain implicitly that he wanted to talk about it, but he wasn't permitted to do so. For example, in an interview in March 2012, he said, essentially, "I'm under an NDA, I'm not allowed to talk about it, I don't have a choice." What happened to the guy who puts people in their place, who brushes off annoying questions, who even skillfully uses doublespeak or aggressiveness when journalists go off the beaten path? Who is this robot Nomura being kept silent? The most likely explanation is that someone made him keep quiet. It was a scandalous and very touchy subject for the company, as several other creators have confirmed. This also suggests that the president did what he promised investors he would do, i.e. get a tighter grip on the company. In addition, during the course of the year, the *Final Fantasy versus XIII* team was decimated: it went from 200 to 20. Roberto Ferrari has attested to this. When Nomura asked why the team was being punished like this, they made it clear that he had no choice: *Final Fantasy versus XIII* would become *Final Fantasy XV*. Nomura had to accept the thing for which he'd been preparing himself for a year. So, he asked his boss for a favor: he wanted Hajime Tabata. "He was telling me how interested he was in the project, and he had already proven that he was capable of doing excellent work," Nomura says. However, it wasn't a good time for Tabata who, after the release (with much pain and behind schedule[37]) of *Final Fantasy Type-0*, had started the prototype for a sequel. It was his first real personal project, one near and dear to his heart, *Final Fantasy Type-Next*[38], the code name for a potential *Type-1*, which apparently was to take place in medieval Japan.

Tabata was set on the idea of making a video game for senior citizens and to make it more historically relevant to them. Basically, he didn't want to work on a fantasy game, whether it was based on reality or not. Beyond that, he felt like it was time for him to leave Nomura's shadow and he wanted to stop being the eternal assistant. Wada had screwed things up so badly up to that point that he owed Nomura that much, and so he took Tabata off his project and appointed him co-director

---

37. One year, to be precise, because he had to put it on pause to first finish *The 3rd Birthday*, a project from none other than Nomura. So, when he got back to work on *Final Fantasy XIII Agito* (for which Nomura was creative producer), he managed to get out of *Fabula Nova Crystallis* in order to realize his own vision of *Final Fantasy: Type*. At his age, he found it quite difficult to take orders from someone younger than him, telling him what to put in his games or, more mundanely, telling him to "be more creative."
38. This famous secret video at the end of *Type–0 HD* was supposedly a teaser for this project that he had started about six months previously and that was near and dear to his heart.

4
3
2
1

of *Final Fantasy XV* to relieve Nomura of the daily nitty-gritty while allowing him to continue to have a say in it. Tabata joined the production in late 2012 and saw his project disappear: "Unfortunately, [that project] is now sleeping with the fishes[39]. It would be nice if we could get back to it one day, but…"

[DROP]

At the same time, voice recording began in April and was less difficult to organize than usual since, besides the main characters, the Disney cast was completely filled by the in-house voice actors (except for Leonard Nimoy); no stars this time—not Demi Moore (the original voice of Esmeralda) or any of the actors from *Tron: Legacy*, for example. The worldwide release of *Kingdom Hearts 3D: Dream Drop Distance* marked the end of this special concept of narration. Time to return to "normal" storytelling, or rather, a *(re)Connect*. Third Editions commented to me, "dozens of pages with date after date, that might be tiresome for readers, especially at the end." They have a point, but I'm going to do it anyway.

(RE)CONNECT

2011

June
June 7, 2011. At its pre-E3 conference, Sony unveiled its new portable console, the PlayStation Vita. Nintendo did the same a few hours later with the Wii U.
June 10, 2011. Yoshinori Kitase announced that Square Enix was interested in doing some ports from PSP to PS3. This suggested the possibility of an upcoming release of *Dissidia Final Fantasy, Crisis*

---

39. A turn of phrase that makes references to a quote from *Moby Dick* (and later from *The Godfather*, of course). It has a violent meaning, more or less alluding to murder. Basically, the corpse was thrown in the water.

Core: Final Fantasy VII, or even *Kingdom Hearts: Birth by Sleep* for PlayStation 3.

July

After months of silence, Nomura resurfaced and granted an interview to the Japanese media. In it, he talked about the post-*Kingdom Hearts III* future, revealing that the game would not be a conclusion to the series itself, but instead a conclusion to what he called "the Xehanort saga." Nomura also said he was concerned about the technical limitations of the previous games, suggesting a potential HD re-release. A month later, he revealed that his team was doing "technical tests." Then, he confirmed that with the tenth anniversary approaching he was seriously considering remaking the older games in HD. Finally, he announced that *Kingdom Hearts 3D* would be available to play at the next Tokyo Game Show (September 15-18, 2011).

September

The 12th. During its pre-TGS press conference, Nintendo revealed a few seconds of gameplay from *Kingdom Hearts 3D: Dream Drop Distance* and confirmed that game's compatibility with the Circle Pad Pro.

The 15th. *Kingdom Hearts 3D: Dream Drop Distance* was indeed present at the Square Enix booth in the form of a playable demo. Notably, it allowed players to get to know the game systems and to face off against a boss. There was also a new trailer that was two and a half minutes long and set to an arrangement of *Destati*. It revealed much more about the main points of the game: the Mark of Mastery exam and the alternation between Sora and Riku. It also gave a glimpse of a Dive and introduced Neku Sakuraba (the hero from *Subarashiki Kono Sekai*) and Sora's new outfit. Above all, viewers could see the fluidity of the action and the incredible moves made possible by the new system. The game no longer had Heartless and Nobodies, contrary to what was shown in previous trailers, and instead had a new species of enemies: the Dream Eaters. The trailer also showed that Sora could— apparently—work with them and ride them. The camera then moved to Riku, also dressed in a new outfit and using moves that had never been seen before. Sora appeared to be in Twilight Town, while Riku was in a world inspired by *The Hunchback of Notre Dame*! The trailer

showed that the console's special features were put to good use: apparently, players would be able to "raise" Dream Eaters using augmented reality, and the lower screen interacted with the upper screen. The trailer ended with a first-person view of the moment where Braig loses his heart at "the hand" of Xehanort. However, it seemed players would have to wait until spring 2012 for the final version.

A few days after the TGS, Square Enix made its trailer accessible to all and during an interview, Nomura revealed that development was progressing well and was about 60–70 percent complete.

October

October 20, 2011. On Facebook, someone asked the voice actor for Ansem what his favorite version of Xehanort was. The actor responded, "the next one," hinting at a Western version of *KH 3D* and/or that the localization had already begun.

October 21, 2011. Nintendo modernized its communications and launched a new way to share company news called Nintendo Direct. The news platform offers pre-recorded presentations containing news, trailers, and new game clips. The Nintendo Direct presentation for *Kingdom Hearts 3D: Dream Drop Distance* got the ball rolling by revealing more of the game and focusing on one of the Dream Eaters in particular, a sort of big blue dog who seemed to be the Dream Eater ambassador.

November

November 21, 2011. Square Enix announced that they would add personnel at Eidos Montreal and create Square Enix Montreal, a second studio that would be totally independent from the first, in 2012.

November 29, 2011. A team was being put together to work on a new A-RPG not connected to any license and with a very European style, a sort of cross between *Castlevania* and *Devil May Cry*. What was unusual was that it would use the Unreal Engine, which hadn't happened since *The Last Remnant* (2008). In late November and early December, the Japanese media was worked into a frenzy and revealed two brand-new worlds from *KH 3D*, one after the other.

December

December 16, 2011. Launch of the official website for *Kingdom Hearts 3D: Dream Drop Distance*.

December 17, 2011. At Jump Festa '12, *Dream Drop Distance* made a splash with a new playable demo allowing visitors to play as the two protagonists in the new world taken from *The Three Musketeers*. Conference attendees also got to see a very long (too long) overview trailer (lasting eight minutes) set to multiple brand-new songs (e.g. *La Cloche*, *Ice-Hot Lobster*) and the masterful orchestral version of *Hikari*.

The trailer began with a never-before-seen cutscene "connecting" the game to the others in the series. It revealed that Neku was not the only guest star from *Subarashiki Kono Sekai*: Joshua, Shiki, Rhyme, and Beat would also make appearances. Then, for a good chunk of the video, it featured other cutscenes, notably showing the return of Maleficent and introducing new worlds (*Pinocchio*, *The Three Musketeers*) and allies. About three minutes in, the trailer changed course and revealed gameplay: a Dive, skating down a magical track, new moves with amazing fluidity for both Riku and Sora, and several bosses for each. It also revealed a new world based on *Tron: Legacy* and new systems allowing the player to interact with the lower screen and the Dream Eaters. At four and a half minutes, the trailer refocused on a series of scenes, building to a climax: the return of Lea (Axel in human form), the introduction of a new unknown who looked like a young Xemnas, and the surprising return of Vanitas! The trailer then ended with a true launch window: March 2012.

December 20, 2011. *Kingdom Hearts 3D: Dream Drop Distance* was confirmed for a release in the West.

2012

January

January 18, 2012. Square Enix revealed the release date for *Kingdom Hearts 3D: Dream Drop Distance* in the Japanese market: March 29. There were three editions planned: the regular game, a limited edition with the game and an AR card[40], and finally a collector's bundle with a

---

40. Augmented reality card, giving you new Dream Eaters in the game. A precursor to the amiibo…

Nintendo 3DS sporting a *KH3D* theme and a special AR card. The next day, in the Square Enix online store, there was mention of a *Kingdom Hearts 10th Anniversary Box*. With no explanation.

January 27, 2012. The mysterious *Kingdom Hearts 10th Anniversary Box* turned out to be a collector's edition with *Kingdom Hearts 358/2 Days*, *Kingdom Hearts Re: coded*, and *Kingdom Hearts 3D: Dream Drop Distance*, accompanied by a case for the Nintendo 3DS and a set of 12 postcards. The box set could be purchased for 15,000 yen, or about €200. However, there weren't any images of it yet. Later that day, the official tenth anniversary logo, designed by Nomura, was revealed. It would be used for branding throughout 2012.

February

February 9, 2012. The Japanese cover for *Kingdom Hearts 3D: Dream Drop Distance* was unveiled.

February 16, 2012. *Theatrhythm Final Fantasy* was released in Japan. Unsurprisingly, it was a modest success. The game ultimately sold 500,000 copies worldwide.

February 20, 2012. Fans finally got to see the *Kingdom Hearts 10th Anniversary Box*. As expected, it was a great collector's item.

February 23, 2012. The Square Enix community platform announced a "premiere event" to take place on March 3 at Venus Fort, a shopping center on the artificial island of Odaiba, in Tokyo.

February 25, 2012. The EB Games website listed *Kingdom Hearts 3D: Dream Drop Distance* with a July 1 release date.

March

March 3, 2012. The premiere event turned out to be a veritable sound and light show.

March 28, 2012. A very special day as *Kingdom Hearts* turned ten years old!

March 29, 2012. *Kingdom Hearts 3D: Dream Drop Distance* hit the shelves in Japan and gave a little boost to sales of the Nintendo 3DS, which up to that point had been lackluster. Given the slow start for the console, reaching 213,000 units sold was a strong performance. What's more, the new game immediately rocketed to the top of the sales charts, handily beating *Kid Icarus: Uprising*. *Dream Drop Distance* ultimately sold only around 400,000 copies in Japan. This was a disappointing number given the quality of the game, but it can be explained by the weak sales of its console.

April

April 5, 2012. Through its official Twitter account, Square Enix revealed that *Kingdom Hearts 3D: Dream Drop Distance* would be released on July 31 in the US. A few days later, the European release date was announced: July 20.

May

May 14, 2012. The first trailer in English was released and was nine and a half minutes long! To be perfectly honest, that was too long, especially since it had no sound effects. The result was a feeling of emptiness that became absurd at times. Also, the editing was pretty lame, with scenes strung together without any real logic or structure. Given its length, it contained a number of _spoilers_. To make a long story short, for the first time in the series' history, it was a total failure. That leads me to believe that it was made by Nintendo of America and was never approved by Nomura. The only good thing about it was that it revealed the American release date: July 31, 2012. Also, it was the first time fans got to hear the voice of Ben Diskin, who played the mysterious silver-haired unknown. Two days later, the *Mark of Mastery Edition* was unveiled for the American market. It was a nice collector's edition that included the game, a set of five AR cards, 12 postcards, and a case for the Nintendo 3DS. Its release was set for the same day as the regular edition, July 31.

June

June 2, 2012. The E3 trailer was released in advance. Unsurprisingly, it was a "cut" of the failed trailer. Much more formalized this time, the video lasted four minutes, included the sound effects, and the text on the screen was in English.

June 4, 2012. Nintendo of America launched a video campaign with four videos, shared at a rate of about one every ten days: *Sora & Riku*, *Dream Eaters*, *New Features*, and *New Worlds*. As usual, their artistic style was, shall we say... special.

June 5, 2012. At E3, fans were able to play the demo from Jump Festa '12, which was localized, of course.

June 20, 2012. Square Enix announced on its European website that *Kingdom Hearts 3D: Dream Drop Distance* would only be localized in English, German, and French. Spanish and Italian fans would have to make do with the English version. That decision caused quite a furor.

July

The 7th. Shinji Hashimoto and Yoko Shimomura were present at Japan Expo (in Paris), the biggest trade show in Europe dedicated to Japanese culture. Besides a short presentation about the tenth anniversary and *Kingdom Hearts 3D*, as well as a game signing event, the most interesting part was a brand-new illustration by Tetsuya Nomura created specifically for the event.

The 9th. In a dramatic turn of events, Nintendo Ibérica decided not to distribute the game in Spain. That meant that not only would it not get the benefit of the Nintendo's networks in the country, but it also put a "freeze" on their communications there. Square Enix stepped in to distribute the game itself.

The 17th. The only way to buy *Kingdom Hearts 3D: Dream Drop Distance* would be with a good old-fashioned hard copy. For reasons of intellectual property, Disney blocked legal downloading of the game.

The 20th. The European release of *Kingdom Hearts 3D: Dream Drop Distance*. It sold about 40,000 copies, placing it at the top of the sales charts. However, this was nothing to brag about because no new game had come out in weeks. It fell from the top of the rankings the very next week. Once again, we can thank whoever had the brilliant idea to release the game in the middle of summer vacation. In any case, that was the nail in the coffin for the game, plain and simple, even though it ultimately sold as many units as in Japan, with 300,000 copies. Nintendo of America released its launch trailer and announced an event for the US release.

The 27th. European distribution of *Kingdom Hearts 3D: Dream Drop Distance* was a complete disaster. After a week, Italy was totally out of stock. It says a lot about the lack of interest or care at Nintendo of Europe, or at least in certain countries. Unless, that is, they had trouble communicating with Square Enix…

The 28th. As planned, a launch event took place in New York. It included stations for playing the game, all sorts of goodies, a photo booth, and, most importantly, the opportunity to buy the game three days early.

The 31st. *Kingdom Hearts 3D: Dream Drop Distance* was finally released in the United States and sold over 250,000 copies in the first week (including about 20,000 limited-edition copies). It was a pretty decent performance that put it in second place for sales, just behind *Dragon Quest X* for the Wii and, in particular, ahead of *New Super Mario Bros. 2* for the same console! The following week, the game held onto second place with over 80,000 units sold. Over its entire run, it sold around 900,000 copies. If you add up all sales worldwide, it reached 1.6 million.

August

August 20, 2012. Square Enix launched a mysterious teaser website with a countdown.

August 27, 2012. The website in question turned out to be for the iOS version of *The World Ends With You: Solo Remix*, with graphics recreated in HD, a remixed soundtrack, and, of course, adapted controls. It's hard for me to admit, but it's without a doubt the best version.

THE LEGEND OF
KINGDOM HEARTS

VOLUME 1: CREATION

Genesis of Hearts

CHAPTER VI
THE CALM BEFORE THE STORM

THE NEW hot topic at Square Enix in 2012 was exploring new business models. There was one that over the previous two years had proven to be very promising: browser-based F2P social gaming. The numbers for *Sengoku IXA* and *Final Fantasy Brigade* proved it. So, one of the goals for the year was to double down on them.

DAYBREAK TOWN
[*KH* χ [CHI]: CONCEPT]

Nomura was fielding many requests from higher-ups on this topic. He started looking at it with a small group of trusted advisors, including Tatsuya Kando and Masaru Oka. The idea was to make an F2P social game using the *Kingdom Hearts* universe without betraying it. The game would have Disney worlds, battles, and a scenario. That said, the medium limited their ambitions. Nomura described the game as "a spin-off totally separate from the main story," a standalone title in which the player would create their own Keyblade warrior, a completely customizable avatar. Given the medium, the small team conceived of the game as being entirely (and only) playable using a mouse, whether for moving around, interacting, or fighting. Because of this, the game would lose its "action" side to become a regular turn-based RPG using an ingenious card system similar to that found in *Chain of Memories*, but with a number of original features, including "crafting," as well as the ability to cooperate with other players to beat bosses. Basically, it was to be a simplified, more streamlined MMORPG. The team quickly realized that it would be "difficult to translate the heart and soul of the series into a browser-based game," explains Kando. So, they decided to change the game's visual style to make it a 2D game in a colorful universe with a "childlike" design, which was actually created by Kando himself. Nomura wanted to give the impression of playing "on the pages of a children's storybook." Everything else stemmed from there. The concept for the game then became "the age of fairy tales," with the Disney worlds of the Seven Princesses of Heart being the main destinations. It was a return to the series' roots which, of course, meant a number of things. Because of their lack of experience with browser-based games, they handed off development to "people who know how," according to Nomura, which meant Success Corporation. *Kingdom Hearts for PC Browser* was born. We have little information about the game's development, but that's not really important because it's just a browser-based game not intended to tell much of a story.

MEMORIES IN PIECES
[KH HD I.5 REMIX: DEVELOPMENT]

Starting in spring 2012, the Osaka team gradually began working on *Kingdom Hearts HD I.5 ReMix*[1], a compilation of the first three games constituting the first chronological story arc, i.e., *Kingdom Hearts Final Mix*, *Kingdom Hearts Re: Chain of Memories*, and *Kingdom Hearts 358/2 Days*.

The programmers had already begun laying the groundwork and as they progressed, porting of *KH* and *Re: CoM* proved to be possible; however, the task would not be so easy for *Days*. The initial goal was to make the first two games in HD so that they wouldn't feel like they were 10 years old. To achieve this, a number of modifications were made, starting with replacing old models and redesigning certain backgrounds. A number of backgrounds that handled movement poorly were also fixed. Takashi Fujimoto (art director) explains that, at times, he got a bit carried away: "When I redesigned the princesses' station, I wanted it to be perfect. The resolution was so high that it could have been used in print[2]. However, for memory reasons, I had

---

1. See Volume II to understand the title. And yes, it is indeed written I.5 and not 1.5.
2. The measurement for the resolution of an image is "dots per inch" (dpi). While images on a screen don't require a very high resolution (72 dpi is sufficient), that's not the case for printed products, which require at least 300 dpi.

to compress the texture, and even though people told me it was fine, I wasn't satisfied. Thankfully, Sumio (Nasu) came up with a solution." The textures of the characters, as well as their thumbnail images[3], were also redesigned and then replaced with the goal of "sticking as close as possible to *Kingdom Hearts II*," according to Tohru Yamazaki (character texture director).

However, for Nomura, the idea of remaking the games didn't stop at artistic aspects; he also wanted to "make the controls simpler and more intuitive." The special actions (interactions) were changed to be accessed with the triangle button. The camera was also modified to be more like the camera in *Kingdom Hearts II*. Similarly, Yasue insisted on adding two abilities that would change the gaming experience: the Combo Master, which allows you to keep a combo going even if a hit misses its target, and EXP Zero, an aptly-named ability (that was previously available in *BBS*). EXP Zero gave him some serious headaches: "I couldn't beat a boss, no matter what I did." He had to figure out if this was due to a bug or if it was really related solely to the difficulty. He explains: "We had to adjust things all the way to the end to come up with the right balance and avoid creating bugs (…) That's the danger when you mess with a finished game, there can be unintended consequences." The debugging phase was extremely taxing for everyone, especially for the programmers. Yasue remembers, "As the testers reported bugs, I saw two of our programmers, usually a couple of jokesters, turn into berserkers[4] in the second half of development. It was a little like if their "C++ stamina"[5] was a fury gauge in *Final Fantasy*. They were furiously fixing bugs. As they did so, they gave off a terrifying vibe. When I would go see them, they would scare the crap out of me and I would immediately run away!" he says, laughing.

As for *Days*, initially, Nomura envisioned a true remake like *Re: CoM* was for *Chain of Memories*, but given the time available, he couldn't afford to do that: "That would have required an extra year." So, he decided to incorporate it in the form of a movie composed of cutscenes, both

3. The computer term for little token images.
4. In Norse mythology, a "berserker" is a warrior who enters into a trance while fighting that makes them extra powerful.
5. A reference to the most well-known computer programming language.

the old ones and some new ones: 70 percent of the main story was transformed in this way. "We selected and totally recreated around 100 cutscenes, two hours and 50 minutes in total," says Masaru Oka (cutscene director). They did true remastering, adjusting the graphics, as well as facial expressions and voices so that there would be no noticeable difference between the original material and the additions. Needless to say, that required a lot of work to adapt from the dual-screen setup and revamp the animation. Koji Hamada (animation director) explains that the goal was to "make them as close as possible to *Kingdom Hearts* and *Kingdom Hearts Re: Chain of Memories*," to make everything uniform. His boss, Tatsuya Kando[6] (animation supervisor), says that the hardest part of the remake was probably the change in resolution. Going from a 4:3 aspect ratio (a square-like image) to 16:9 (a rectangular image) means you have to create the "missing" material. For example, the menus "had to be entirely redone, even though they were already in HD," explains Gen Kobayashi (character art director).

That sort of care for visuals wouldn't have made sense without improvements to sound too. Thankfully, Yuki Hirose (sound designer) was on it and managed to work in 5.1 audio[7] across "all real-time sections of *KH* and *KH Re: Chain of Memories*. We also cleaned up and re-recorded the voices for *Days* and, under the supervision of Yoko Shimomura, rearranged the music using real instruments."

Because, of course, they couldn't do a remake without also reworking the OST. However, originally, Nomura didn't ask them to do any such thing. It was Keiji Kawamori (synthesizer operator) who got the idea: "Two seconds after I heard about the plan for a remaster, I figured that it was a good opportunity to redo the music to be more... fitting." He explains that for the first few *Kingdom Hearts*, they used a built-in sound chip[8] because of limitations mostly related to the consoles.

---

6. According to Yasue, with the exception of Kando, the Kingdom Team had almost no involvement in the development process. They just praised the final product. It appears that this time they really did pass the torch.
7. Basically, it's a way of splitting sound in relation to the position of the audience. To "experience" it, it's generally recommended that you have a sound system with five outputs (center, front right, front left, rear right, rear left) and a subwoofer.
8. A sound chip is a built-in circuit that can reproduce a programmed sound from memory. Songs produced with sound chips are called "chiptunes" and are synthesized in real time.

Then, starting with the PSP, they began using streaming audio[9]. He concludes: "I figured that if we were to use our present-day capabilities, fans would love the music as much as the new HD visuals." He then asked Shimomura out to dinner to tell her about his plan: "The first thing that came to mind was that the dinner was expensive," she says mischievously. They eventually agreed that Noda (Hirosato, synthesizer operator) should remaster the music for the three games with help from Yusaku Tsuchiya, a reorchestration specialist, and TaQ, a chord arranger. To make a long story short, starting in September 2012, they re-recorded most of the songs from the three soundtracks at the Tokyo Metropolitan Theatre. It's a fascinating story, but we must move on.

To offer a product in keeping with the times, *KH HD I.5 ReMix* included themes for PS3, trophies, the Japanese voices, the new standard allowing players to skip cutscenes, as well as a Theater Mode allowing players to rewatch them. However, the content didn't change a bit and "there's no new secret movie," as Nomura felt obligated to mention. In regards to the cover art, he says that he took inspiration from his design for the old OST and he created it like the game, as a deluxe remastering. Development was finished in just over a year (in December 2012) and they all came out the other side elated. They all felt the timelessness of the *Kingdom Hearts* series. Yasue says, "I remember how impressed I was back in the day with the battles and particularly how they were connected to the story," and he had that same feeling again 10 years later while working on the remaster. He concludes: "It doesn't matter how technology evolves, the power of the worlds and the narration of a classic never fades, even after many years have passed." I'll let the boss have the final word: "When I saw the final product, I thought it was truly amazing, much better than I was expecting. I am extremely proud of this HD version. Even though the original games are getting on in years, the result gives the impression that they're new and that players can appreciate them just as much as, if not more than, they did before. It's hard to believe that the games are actually 10 years old." From my perspective, I'd like to add that the *Kingdom Hearts* series has always been a decade (or even more) ahead of the rest of the industry and has really understood what you

9. A server with music that provides a database of audio that is often produced by music labels.

need for a great video game. The greatest games are not made with millions of dollars or photorealism, but instead with heart, guts, and talent. Nomura recognizes this: "I want to thank the team of talented and intelligent people who supported me throughout the development of the first few *Kingdom Hearts*. I can still feel their passion and I am proud of them." A poetic way of saying goodbye to them and definitively embracing Osaka as the "new" Kingdom Team.

Starting in early 2013, a portion of the team began working on the localization for the West. The remakes actually had a lot more meaning for these regions since they would finally, 11 years later, get to enjoy all of the additions to the Final Mix version of *Kingdom Hearts*. Yep, it's strange to think about, but most players were still completely unaware of things like the battle against the unknown (Xemnas) and the secret video *[deep dive]*. What's more, Europeans would also finally get to play *Kingdom Hearts Re: Chain of Memories*. On this topic, Kando says, "Since they only got the Game Boy Advance version of *Chain of Memories*, they might be left totally speechless." Incidentally, *KH HD 1.5 ReMix* no longer included dubbing in the other languages for the simple reason that one of the special features of the new version was that the team fixed the lip-synching in Japanese and English. They couldn't reasonably do more than that, so all you French people, stop blubbering about no longer having the voice of Donald Reignoux. Yeah, it's too bad, but such is life. Nomura concludes by asking for forgiveness: "I really want to say sorry to European fans (...) I'm sure that you've always wondered why you couldn't get these versions. I'm truly sorry." Let's let bygones be bygones, Mr. Nomura. Better late than never. And now, it's time for us to *(re)Connect*. If you don't like that, you have two options: either you can go directly to the next section (page 363) or you can write a letter of complaint to the publisher. However, you won't get an answer. We've hired a dog to eat such correspondence.

(RE)CONNECT

2012

September 20, 2012. In an initial trailer, *Kingdom Hearts HD 1.5 ReMix*, a compilation with HD remastered versions of *Kingdom Hearts Final Mix*, *Re: Chain of Memories*, and a *358/2 Days* movie, was announced for the PlayStation 3 at the Tokyo Game Show. The trailer showed significant improvement to visuals, including a change in format to 16:9 widescreen. The trailer ended with a release window: 2013. No more details than that. As a surprise, in a strange video with nothing but text, a second game was revealed. The logo indicated that it was *Kingdom Hearts for PC Browser*.

October

October 3, 2012. Nomura revealed that the formal title for the "Xehanort saga" would be the Dark Seeker Saga. He reminded fans that it would be just the first phase of the *Kingdom Hearts* series! During the same interview, the journalist asked him if he also planned on doing an HD version of *Kingdom Hearts II*. The director, in typical fashion, simply replied, "It would be strange to not do that."

October 30, 2012. Disney acquired Lucasfilm for a cool $4.05 billion. Immediately, *Kingdom Hearts* fans began dreaming of a *Star Wars* and/ or *Indiana Jones* world in the future *Kingdom Hearts III*.

November

November 20, 2012. Nomura indicated that development of *Kingdom Hearts HD 1.5 ReMix* was 80–90 percent complete.

December

December 20, 2012. Square Enix announced that the Japanese version of *Kingdom Hearts HD 1.5 ReMix* would be released on March 14, 2013, for the PlayStation 3.

December 25, 2012. At Jump Festa '13, a new trailer for *Kingdom Hearts HD 1.5 ReMix* was shared, showing a marked difference compared to the graphics from the PlayStation 2 versions. The trailer started by giving an overview of the two games, then focused on the

Kingdom Hearts 358/2 Days "movie" before reminding viewers of the Japanese release date: March 14.

2013

January

January 24, 2013. Jesse McCartney, the voice actor for Roxas, posted a photo of his recording session on Instagram. With it, he included the message, "For all you *Kingdom Hearts* Fans. Recording the next chapter!" A few hours later, likely under pressure from Square Enix, he deleted it. That makes sense: the game had not yet been announced for release in the West.

January 25, 2013. The Japanese packaging for *Kingdom Hearts HD I.5 ReMix* was unveiled.

February

February 20, 2013. *Kingdom Hearts for PC Browser* changed names to become *Kingdom Hearts χ [chi]*. No further information, not even a release window.

February 21, 2013. As part of an advertising campaign, Square Enix made a call for Japanese fans.

February 25, 2013. The release of *Kingdom Hearts HD I.5 ReMix* was confirmed for the United States and Europe. This time, the game would be EFIGS localized[10]. No release date for the time being.

March

March 12, 2013. The list of trophies for *Kingdom Hearts HD I.5 ReMix* was unveiled. It was a new publicity technique that was also a fan favorite and one of the most shared on the internet. The next day, the official website for *Kingdom Hearts χ [chi]* went online, along with a "Memory Theater" page with the videos from the "fan campaign."

The 14th. Release of *Kingdom Hearts HD I.5 ReMix* in Japan. It sold over 130,000 copies, placing it neck and neck with *Sword Art Online: Infinity Moment* (for PlayStation 3) in competing for first place. The next week, it held steady, remaining in the top 10, but couldn't really

---

10. Industry jargon for English, French, Italian, German, and Spanish.

compete with newcomers like *Luigi's Mansion 2* (3DS). In any case, the remake sold over 250,000 units.

The 23rd. At PAX East[11] 2013, fans got to see the first American trailer for *Kingdom Hearts HD 1.5 ReMix*, which was really just a localized version of the Jump Festa '13 trailer.

The 26th. Square Enix announced the departure of its president, Yoichi Wada. The press release was short on details, but it revealed that it was a decision made "in agreement with shareholders."

The 28th. The Walt Disney Company announced that for the first time ever, the D23 Expo would take place in Tokyo, from October 12 to 14.

April

April 3, 2013. To celebrate the tenth anniversary of its merger, Square Enix launched an official website. The next day, the company's new president, Yosuke Matsuda, announced his plans for the future, particularly to "evaluate what's working and what's not working (…) to use resources for anything that brings us success, to completely eliminate anything that does us a disservice." It was a radical statement, but one that rose to the occasion; the previous fiscal year had been a disaster, with a loss of 13 billion yen, the worst performance for Square Enix since… well, since the merger, actually. Happy anniversary!

April 26, 2013. The London office followed the Tokyo office's lead and also organized a campaign focused on fans of *Kingdom Hearts*. The message was short and sweet: "Calling all *Kingdom Hearts* fans! Are you free next Friday (April 26) to come see *Kingdom Hearts HD 1.5 ReMix* and talk about it on camera?"

May

May 7, 2013. Square Enix revealed the Western release dates for *Kingdom Hearts HD 1.5 ReMix:* September 10 for the United States and September 13 for Europe. The first pre-orders would come with a limited-edition art book. The official website was launched on the same day. The same was done for Europe the next day.

---

11. PAX or Penny Arcade Expo, an "alternative" video game trade show split into two editions: Prime (in Seattle) and East (in Boston).

May 16, 2013. A promotional video with testimonials from players was shared on the Web.

May 23, 2013. Just two months after Yoichi Wada resigned, the president of the company's American division, Mike Fischer, assumed responsibility and stepped down. He said that he was leaving "on good terms."

June

June 6, 2013. The E3 trailer for *Kingdom Hearts HD I.5 ReMix* was leaked on the internet. Of course, Square Enix had it taken down very quickly.

June 11, 2013. For its pre-E3 press conference, Sony planned to blow its competitors out of the water with the reveal of the PlayStation 4 and its first several games. However, that big moment wouldn't come until halfway through. Adam Boyes (Sony vice president for third-party relations) played a message from Tetsuya Nomura who humbly apologized for not being able to come (when he was in fact backstage) or announce anything new about *Final Fantasy versus XIII*. All this was done to build anticipation. First, there was the incredible trailer (directed by Nomura himself) for *Final Fantasy versus XIII*, which officially became *Final Fantasy XV*[12]. Then, there was the first teaser for *Kingdom Hearts III*, separated into three parts: a quick recap of the previous games; a cutscene of Sora finding the Master's Defender, Eraqus' Keyblade (inherited by Aqua at the end of *Birth by Sleep*); then a very short extract from the game in Twilight Town showing the abilities of Square Enix's new engine, Luminous Studio. Naturally, it simply concluded with "Now in Development." Plus wild applause from the audience.

Besides the teaser, there was also a trailer for *Kingdom Hearts HD I.5 ReMix* that played off of the theme of memories using a mosaic of images to great effect.

July

July 4, 2013. Hashimoto and Nomura confirmed their participation in the D23 Expo in Tokyo, still planned for October 12 to 14, 2013.

---

12. Looking back, it brings tears to my eyes thinking about what we all missed out on.

They noted that there would be a number of surprises there for fans, including the presence of actors. The next day, Square Enix revealed its first video for *Kingdom Hearts χ [chi]*, simply entitled "gameplay." It actually turned out to be a launch trailer. It gave an overview of everything: the various worlds, interactions with backgrounds, battles, game systems, and even the famous "raid boss" for which you could/should cooperate with other players! While the discerning eye may have already seen a hint of the game's special visuals, most players saw them for the first time in this trailer.

July 7, 2013. Hashimoto and Nomura attended Japan Expo in France. After a presentation on a giant screen of the Coliseum from *Kingdom Hearts Final Mix* and Halloween Town from *Kingdom Hearts Re: Chain of Memories*, accompanied only by Hashimoto, a fairly unusual occurrence, Nomura took the stage. After saying a few words, he started the teaser for *Kingdom Hearts III* and the trailer for *Final Fantasy XV*, then came back to thank the audience, who enthusiastically applauded him. He also decided to do a game signing event that same afternoon. The next day, the open beta version of *Kingdom Hearts χ [chi]* went online.

July 10, 2013. In the United States, a new trailer was released, entitled "*Introduction to* Kingdom Hearts." It was intended for newcomers to the series and was based entirely on *Kingdom Hearts HD I.5 ReMix*. It was the first part of a broader campaign that—for once—was nicely put together.

July 18, 2013. Surprise launch of *Kingdom Hearts χ [chi]*.

July 26, 2013. A promotional video was shared for the limited -edition art book, given for free with preorders of the American version of *Kingdom Hearts HD I.5 ReMix*.

August

August 8, 2013. As part of its Western campaign for *Kingdom Hearts HD I.5 ReMix*, Square Enix Europe shared a second trailer dedicated solely to *Kingdom Hearts Final Mix*.

August 28, 2013. Nomura explained that *Kingdom Hearts χ [chi]* would take on much greater importance than expected and that its story would lead to *Kingdom Hearts III*.

August 30, 2013. Square Enix revealed the third trailer of its campaign, entitled *Combat Vignette*. It was entirely dedicated to *Kingdom Hearts Re: Chain of Memories* and the movie of *358/2 Days*. The publisher took that opportunity to announce two launch events, one in London (on September 6) and the other in Anaheim, California (on September 8).

September
September 10, 2013. Release of *Kingdom Hearts HD I.5 ReMix* in the United States. It reached the top of the sales charts with around 200,000 copies sold. It even managed to beat all of the recently-released sports games (which is a real feat in the US), including *NHL 14*, *Madden NFL 25*, and even *Diablo III* (if you can consider demon slaying a sport). It was an outstanding performance, remaining among the top games, in fifth place, the next week in spite of the sensational arrival of *GTA V* (around 10 million units sold in just the first week). Still, *Kingdom Hearts HD I.5 ReMix* can be proud of its performance, ultimately selling almost a million copies in the US; and let's not forget that it was "just" a compilation. Three days later, the game was released in Europe. It topped the sales charts there too with over 65,000 units sold, which was better than *Diablo III*! It held onto sixth place the next week with 35,000 copies sold. The top spots went to *GTA V* and *PES 2014*. It makes you wonder who made the decision in Europe to release it at the same time as the two heavyweights of the second half of the year... But still, the three remakes together reached around 2 million copies sold. It was unexpected and very comforting: *Kingdom Hearts*, after all those years, was still drawing in fans.

[INTERLUDE] *THE OTHER PROMISE*

We are drawing close to the end of Volume I. The year 2013 was a turning point: it ushered in the "era of *Kingdom Hearts III*," the third and final act. Besides *Kingdom Hearts HD II.5 ReMix*, which marked the end of the second act, all events from this point on are related, whether closely or remotely, to the third episode, for which I have already planned to write another volume. As such, the final pages in

this volume will focus on *Kingdom Hearts III* and *Kingdom Hearts Union χ [Cross]*, as well as *Final Fantasy XV* and *Final Fantasy VII Remake*, because these four productions, as you will see later, are closely related.

As a result, you might think that I could/should stop at 2013, but I've decided to continue and purposely omit certain details. In the end, we'll play a little game where we'll cross-reference the information from the end of this first volume and the start of the future third volume. I'm not putting a gun to your head to make you buy it, but I will say that it is essential for the wording and veracity of the information that we proceed in this manner. For now, I can't exactly tell you the story of the development of *Kingdom Hearts III*. I'll be able to do so once the game comes out.

Thank you for understanding. Now, where were we...

CAVERN OF REMEMBRANCE
[*KH HD II.5 REMIX, KH χ* [CHI]: DEVELOPMENT]

You can't talk about *I.5* without also, of course, talking about *II. 5*. Just after *KH HD I.5 ReMix* was finished, Nomura immediately launched work on the next part, the second chronological story arc, made up of *Kingdom Hearts II Final Mix*, *Kingdom Hearts: Birth by Sleep Final Mix*, and *Kingdom Hearts Re: coded*.

It was déjà vu all over again. The port was again entrusted to Sumio Nasu and Kenro Tsujimoto. They were tasked with doing the same thing, but now with the benefit of experience. The biggest difference was the enormous volume of data to sort through. Yasue explains: "When you talk about conversion to HD, you might think that you just have to press a button and the images will automatically convert on their own, but that's not at all the case." The entire Osaka team and a (very small) portion of the Tokyo team were tasked with patiently adjusting all of the backgrounds, character models, and menus. Almost all of the textures were redesigned by hand: "It's surprising that we had to resort to such a low-tech method, but if we had chosen something else, we would never have gotten the quality we wanted," says Yasue. Then, the programmers converted the new textures created by cleaning up the images using software. The graphic artists then went back over the work to adjust the color saturation in order to maintain Disney's style of "soft" textures. Besides this enormous volume, the other biggest challenge with *Kingdom Hearts II* was the conversion to a 16:9 aspect ratio. The team particularly struggled with the menu, or rather reconstruction of the menu, since they had to, once again, make up for the "missing parts." For *Birth by Sleep*, they had very different challenges. Working off of a PSP game, they had to improve the visual quality of the characters with four times more polygons for their modeling and smoothing of their textures. Same for the sound: Hirose again used 5.1 audio, giving more depth to the background sounds. More generally, he improved the sound of the cutscenes. The music again received deluxe treatment, this time thanks to the Video Game Orchestra in Boston. In terms of gameplay, most changes were in *Birth by Sleep*. The gameplay was reworked for the PS3 controller and the Mirage Arena was stripped of its multi-player mode, even though that was not initially the plan: "There was nothing complicated about it, but we were handling three games at the same time, so we had to make choices," explains Nomura. To fix this, everything was redesigned for single-player mode. The strength of enemies, especially the bosses, was adjusted. Thanks to modified, more powerful AI, the enemies were also faster and more instinctive. Yasue laughs, "Don't worry, Armor of the Master and No Heart will give you a run for your money." And what about *Kingdom Hearts II*? "It was already perfect. Changing anything at all would have risked compromising it. So, we decided to not touch a thing," says Yasue.

[KH χ [CHI]: DEVELOPMENT]

Meanwhile, Nomura was moving forward with his *Kingdom Hearts for PC Browser* project, which had become *Kingdom Hearts χ [chi]*[13]. In response to a request from his team, he introduced Chirithy, a Dream Eater whose role was to guide the player. He explains, "I didn't want a character that would be too strong since it was just supposed

---

13. To learn more about the meaning of the title, you'll have to wait for Volume II.

to accompany. When I started thinking about it, I decided that a cat would be ideal since you never know what they're thinking, but they still stick close to humans. I then drew inspiration from the Scottish Fold, my favorite breed of cat."

The game's script was fleshed out, with very important scenes added that were meant to provide insight into the origins of the *Kingdom Hearts* universe, notably introducing the Foretellers, brand-new enigmatic characters, each with a name related to one of the seven deadly sins. The reason he developed the universe so much is that he was busy writing *Kingdom Hearts III* at the same time and he couldn't resist creating links between the two games. It also gave him the idea of bringing χ to mobile devices in a version that would be easier to access and which would come out at the same time. Because of the exponential evolution of smartphones, the work required became much more complex. As such, they decided to put that project on pause and focus on χ *[chi]*, for which the closed beta, reserved for Yahoo! Japan account owners, made its debut in March 2013. The game was finally made available to all in July and was regularly updated, eventually having a conclusion and introducing several new characters, including Ephemer and Skuld.

[*KH HD II.5 ReMIX*: DEVELOPMENT]

The third and final game in the compilation was *Re: coded*. Nomura decided to give it the same treatment as *358/2 Days* in *I.5*, which is to say that he turned it into a movie; however, there was an important difference between the two: "[The movie *KH 358/2 Days*] explained the battles with text, but many fans were disappointed by that." Nomura took that hard given that he wanted to offer the best version of each of the games in the *HD ReMix*. They messed up. He continues, "Since *Re: coded* didn't have the same volume, we decided to include the battles in the form of videos and to tell the story of the events in the Disney worlds through a narrator, Mickey, who was definitely the best choice since he begins and ends *Re: coded*." This all seems simple, but Yasue has a reality check for us: "I'm sure that players appreciate it, but that sort of work is extremely stressful for the staff (...) The programmers were so tense that they were getting neck pain..."

In June 2014, the re-release was 90 percent of the way through development. There wasn't much left to finish: the cutscenes, as well as the addition of trophies and other bonus features included in *I.5*. In an interview after the release of *KH HD II.5 ReMix*, Nomura joked, "[All of the games], to a certain extent, got remakes; the only one left is *Kingdom Hearts 3D: Dream Drop Distance*. How right he was.

◀ INTERLUDE — (THE TRUE) L'EMINENZA OSCURA II

OK, I know what you're thinking. But if I'm going to follow the patterns of the series, I might as well see it through to the end. This will be my last interlude, I promise. However, I will follow the same pattern in the volume dedicated to *Kingdom Hearts III* because it helps give context and explain the impact on the series.

A major event occurred in 2013. In spite of the "reforms" enacted by Wada, Square Enix was going to the dogs. It reached a critical juncture, the worst point in the company's history. As Wada feared, he was dismissed and replaced by Yosuke Matsuda[14]. The new president had a less eloquent, but more aggressive style. He saw things from a purely economic point of view.

When he took the reins in March, he took stock of the company. The MMORPG category was "stalled." *Dragon Quest X: Mesameshi Itsutsu no Shuzoku Online* had a very poor start. It was the worst selling game in the series' history, with just 367,000 copies sold. Just a trickle on a world scale, in spite of having excellent sales for the genre in Japan. The game ended the year with around 700,000 units sold. Version 2.0 of *Final Fantasy XIV*, dubbed "*A Realm Reborn*," was in the final stages of development with its release imminent (August 2013). The company's HD game category was a disaster. The first test of Square

---

14. In spite of appearances, Yosuke Matsuda was not a "newcomer." He had been a "product" of Square since 1998. After some time at Ernst & Young, one of the most powerful financial auditing firms in the world, he returned to take on a "corporate executive" position. He became CFO in 2004, and then director of Taito when the company was finally absorbed by Square Enix in 2006. He remained in Wada's shadow until 2013, when the shareholders handed him the reins of Square Enix.

Enix's real potential in the West was a failure. The three major releases for the year (while waiting for the Japanese heavy-hitters)—*Sleeping Dogs*, *Hitman: Absolution*, and *Tomb Raider*—performed much worse than expected. The year was saved by the port/remaster of *Dragon Quest VII: Eden no Senshitachi* for the Nintendo 3DS. That said, the game's sales were far from spectacular, with less than a million copies sold in the first week in Japan; that was better than the remakes of *Dragon Quest IV* and *V* for the GBA, but far behind *Dragon Quest VI* for the DS.

In short, fiscal year 2012 was a disaster. Only the social games performed well, with a new major game, *Kaku-San-Sei Million Arthur*. Matsuda concluded that the company would have to focus more on mobile and social gaming in the future (indeed, that explains the many ports and other crappy games they would produce for smartphones). The final verdict could not have been more pessimistic: "From a financial point of view, investment in [HD] game development is being capitalized on the balance sheet over a significant time frame, and investment recovery risk increases. In other words, the investment turnover is low." Since big games are developed over several years, it stands to reason that they don't turn a profit right away. That creates a major cash flow problem, not to mention the fact that the company carries the risk of an "unforeseen" failure. He continued, "We have to create earnings opportunities even before a product is released in order to raise investment turnover of a long-term, large-scale development project." In other words, "early access," pre-orders, demos, prologues, etc. Basically, the origins of a cancer.

"Titles of large-scale development are our flagship titles, showcasing our technologies. We will never lower the flag of such titles (…) It is possible to establish a business model that delivers content in various formats (…) We will promote approaches to raise investment turnover by accelerating earnings opportunities and reducing financial risks." There you go; are you starting to get the message? I'll continue: "A lack of earnings opportunities over a long period of time means, essentially, having no contact with customers during the same period. In these days, it is becoming crucial to strengthen customer relations. Re-examining our approach to long-term, large-scale development is also a step toward building a better customer relationship." There you have it: that all explains what happened next, with DLC all over the place and the aberration that was *Final Fantasy XV Universe*, which saw the methodical deconstruction of the incredibly rich and painstaking work of Nomura (and let's not forget, Nojima too) on its universe, all to extract more or less "bankable" content, including *Kingsglaive: Final Fantasy XV*, which was scalped from the first part of the *Final Fantasy versus XIII* trilogy; the animated series *Brotherhood*, which stole from the game's background to create "promotional" content; and a slew of ridiculous partnerships and DLC, both for the purposes of communications (prostituting the game at that point), as well as, in particular, within the game. I'm sure you noticed the most recent such partnerships as of the writing of this book, *Half-Life* and *The Sims*. Even worse, the scenario was totally rewritten with holes purposely left in it to allow for the creation of "scenario DLC" which, no matter what, required angry players to just shut up and pay up, and there was nothing they could do about it. *Final Fantasy XV* having been an extremely expensive game to produce (much more expensive than the entire *versus XIII* trilogy, I might add), they had to make it profitable as fast as possible given the poor financial health of Square Enix. Becoming totally unrecognizable, it was totally transformed into a first attempt at a "game as a service" in keeping with trends at the time; but we'll come back to that in the volume dedicated to *Kingdom Hearts III*. It was clear that the beautiful creative undertaking, the epic saga in three parts that Nomura had been working on, had been dismembered. Reality again came knocking at the door. Square Enix took control of *Final Fantasy XV*, a numbered episode in the series, to turn it into a product "in keeping with the times" and installed a dutiful soldier, filled with ambition and frustration, to steer the ship. Tabata is cut from the same cloth as Yoshida: they're both producers at heart. They're there to make sure that everything works, willing to turn a creative and artistic work into a big fat marketing product, a patchwork of everything that's worked elsewhere, but turns out badly designed, badly written, and badly executed; in short, bad all around. In the end, it didn't matter: players were dumb (myself included) and they dove head-first into the game thanks to/because of the quality of the graphics, which I must say were good.

Matsuda also knew the crucial importance of the *Kingdom Hearts* license, but he also knew the impetuous character of the series' creator and the nature of the relationship with Disney. So, he decided to take Nomura off of his *FF* project so that he could focus solely on his series. The thing is, this removal from the project, which Nomura was clearly very unhappy about, may have actually been a way to protect him from the inevitable massacre that was coming for his "baby." Matsuda hasn't said much on the subject, Nomura doesn't want to discuss that time in his life, and Tabata will say anything to make himself look good in this sordid affair, which really had nothing to do with him. In any case, we'll try to look on the bright side. Fine, we may have missed out on a great video game. But that being said, I assure you that Nomura hasn't given up and, as we can see from the new design for Riku, he will undoubtedly avenge himself and express all of his fury and genius in *Kingdom Hearts III*, as well as probably in his "*Versus* take two," i.e. *Final Fantasy VII Remake*. All in all, he is now older and wiser and he will prove to the industry that not only was it shameful the way that he was treated, but on top of that, he is far greater than the company for which, in spite of it all, he continues to work.

Still, 2014 was a living nightmare for him. He went totally AWOL and refused to give any interviews. All indications suggested that he had fallen into a depression. Or at least, that's what we can assume from his weight gain and puffy face once he resurfaced that summer. He also spoke in a tone that was less playful and more serious. What's more, he never opened up about what he went through, replying to questions only with a terse "it wasn't my decision" or "it was the company's decision." Long after the fact, he confided that buying his two cats (both Scottish Folds) really helped him get out of what he calls his "depression." End of this long parenthesis. To be continued in the next episode: Volume III. If this guy can't sell it, he better find a new career.

Anyhow, it's time to review numbers and communications.

(RE)CONNECT

2013

September

September 19, 2013. At the Tokyo Game Show, Square Enix showed a new trailer for *Kingdom Hearts χ [chi]*, structured in the same way as the launch trailer, but shorter and more effective. Additionally, while *Kingdom Hearts HD 1.5 ReMix* was already in stores, a final trailer entitled *Remix Vignette* was put online. During a "special talk show" for Square Enix's composers (including Yasunori Mitsuda and Kenji Ito), Yoko Shimomura confirmed that she was working on the original soundtrack for *Kingdom Hearts III*.

October

October 14, 2013. It was time for the *Kingdom Hearts* press conference at the D23 Expo, which *Kingdom Hearts* fans had been impatiently waiting for. And they were not disappointed. First off, Shinji Hashimoto and Tetsuya Nomura were there on stage, along with Miyu Irino, Mamoru Miyano, and Kouki Uchiyama—the *seiyû* for Sora/Vanitas, Riku, and Roxas/Ventus. The event also presented a new trailer for *Kingdom Hearts III*! And the surprises kept coming with the official announcement for *Kingdom Hearts HD II.5 ReMix*, which included *Kingdom Hearts II Final Mix*, *Kingdom Hearts: Birth by Sleep Final Mix*, and the "movie" *Kingdom Hearts Re: coded*, following the same model as *Days* in *1.5*. To top it all off, fans wouldn't have to wait long since the compilation was announced for a 2014 release. Shortly thereafter, the official website was launched.

November

November 28, 2013. *Development Team News #2* (a newsletter about *Kingdom Hearts χ [chi]*) revealed that some serious updates were forthcoming, using Nomura's typical style, i.e., a number of key phrases without any apparent connection: "Five Foretellers, a war for their lands, servants trusted by Chirithy, the final message in the Foreteller's script." This message was accompanied by an image with five silhouettes of characters wearing masks, as well as Chirithy in some sort of flask. Finally, the image's caption read, "The ultimate story will begin

in December 2013." Connecting this enigmatic announcement with Nomura's comments, fans wondered if these "Foretellers" could be linked to the rest of the series. Given the way it was written, the answer was, of course, yes. This got Westerners aching for a localization of the game.

December
December 20, 2013. As every year, Square Enix was present at Jump Festa. For this year's edition, a new trailer for *Kingdom Hearts HD II.5 ReMix* was unveiled. It was set to an orchestral version of *Passion*. The three games looked so amazing that they had everyone longing to play them again. The Kingdom Team had done an incredible makeover. Fans again had to settle for "coming 2014" as a conclusion. The next day, the same trailer became available, but this time dubbed in English, implying that the new compilation would be dual-language just like *I.5*.

2014

January
January 29, 2014. Yoko Shimomura announced the upcoming release of *memória!*, her new solo album, a follow-up to *Drammatica*, which had been released six years prior. As the album's subtitle indicated, it was a new "best of" compilation. The CD was set for a release on March 26.

February
February 22, 2014. Launch of the PlayStation 4 in Japan.

March
March 7, 2014. The official Facebook page for *Kingdom Hearts* asked fans of the series to complete an opinion survey.
March 11, 2014. Nomura confirmed that the voice recording sessions for *Kingdom Hearts HD II.5 ReMix* were complete, implying that the release date would soon be announced.

May

May 17, 2014. Square Enix opened up a new survey for players, this time on the SurveyMonkey website. The survey was entirely dedicated to *Kingdom Hearts HD II.5 ReMix*. Apparently, contact with the community had become important...

In the days that followed, *Kingdom Hearts HD II.5 ReMix* reappeared in numerous Japanese media outlets with new screenshots. Given the timing, many expected an announcement at E3.

June

June 5, 2014. Indeed, at E3, with a spectacular (new) trailer, Square Enix finally revealed the Western release date for *Kingdom Hearts HD II.5 ReMix*: December 2, 2014, for the United States and December 5 for Europe. What's really interesting about the new trailer is that it focused not only on the very narrative side of the compilation's three games, but also on the additions to the *Final Mix* versions, which up to that point had been unavailable for Westerners. Another fun fact: the Japanese learned "their" release date at the same time as everyone else: October 2. Could it be that the lack of communications in the first half of 2014 was tied to something happening behind the scenes? In any case, after the trailer, a new teaser for *Kingdom Hearts III* was shown. This teaser was different in that it didn't show any images from the game; instead, it portrayed a dialog between two drawings in the background, seemingly revealing two new characters.

June 26, 2014. Two years after its iOS release, *The World Ends With You: Solo Remix* was released for Android.

July

July 17, 2014. Fans got to see the packaging for *Kingdom Hearts HD II.5 ReMix*, as well as a beautiful limited edition called *Kingdom Hearts Collector's Pack HD I.5 + II.5 ReMix* which, in addition to the two compilations, came with a *Kingdom Hearts Music Collection* Blu-ray, a *Kingdom Hearts Visual Art Collection* booklet, and an *Anniversary Pack* code to use in *Kingdom Hearts χ [chi]* to get free potions and ethers. The deluxe edition, in a magnificent black and gold box and apparently exclusive to Japan, would come out at the same time as the regular edition for the modest sum of 14,000 yen (about €110). That

same day, *Kingdom Hearts χ [chi]* celebrated its first birthday. For the occasion, its creator released a brand-new illustration of Sora, Riku, Kairi, and a Chirithy.

July 23, 2014. It was time for the West to discover its limited edition. Unsurprisingly, it was nothing like the Japanese version. Still, the Americans and Europeans got an exclusive item: a pin with Sora and Mickey, as well as the logo for the compilation. Cool, a pin!

August

August 18, 2014. In an interview given to a Spanish website, Tai Yasue revealed that like *I.5*, *Kingdom Hearts HD II.5 ReMix* would not support any of the dubbing used in older versions of the games. So, once again, no voices in French, German, Spanish, or Italian. This again caused a mini-scandal. A petition was created to express the dissatisfaction of European fans who again felt slighted. However, Nomura and Yasue had already explained why…

August 28, 2014. At Gamescom, Square Enix revealed a new trailer reviewing all of the "new features," which were in fact the additions made to the *Final Mix* versions. Of course, they were still unknown to Western audiences. They included battles against Roxas and Lingering Will, as well as the Cavern of Remembrance in *Kingdom Hearts II*, Armor of the Master, Monstro, and No Heart in *Birth by Sleep*, etc.

August 30, 2014. As was done for *I.5*, the community managers at Square Enix USA again launched a campaign centered on players' memories. An event was planned for September 6 in Los Angeles. It was to be a memorable day, with the goal of producing enough images to create a video.

September

September 3, 2014. Square Enix released the final trailer for *Kingdom Hearts HD II.5 ReMix*, entirely in Japanese. The goal was to remind the Japanese audience that they would get the different *Final Mix* versions in their native language (instead of with the English voices as in the past).

September 11, 2014. The magazine *Dengeki* revealed that a new scene "connecting" *Kingdom Hearts Re: coded* to *Kingdom Hearts χ [chi]* had been added.

September 18, 2014. Square Enix put out a press release to announce that Tetsuya Nomura would no longer work on production of *Final Fantasy XV*. Hajime Tabata became the sole captain on board. Nomura's ouster was explained thusly: "He will now be able to concentrate on *Kingdom Hearts III*." That same day, Square Enix Europe did damage control by clarifying that *Final Fantasy XV* would not suffer after Nomura's departure because the game was "in good hands." At the time, people believed this.

September 19, 2014. Square Enix announced the creation of a new subsidiary called Shinra Technologies. It would be a center for cloud gaming[15] R&D located in New York and led by... Yoichi Wada. Would it be another waste of time and money?

September 25, 2014. Nomura avoided the subject of his removal in talking with Japanese media, but stated: "I have received many offers from both inside and outside the company, and I will be responding to those first." Apparently, his departure was forced upon him...

October

October 2, 2014. Release of *Kingdom Hearts HD II.5 ReMix* in Japan. Unsurprisingly, even though the Japanese had sung the praises of *Kingdom Hearts II*, that (still) wasn't reflected in the sales, with the compilation "only" selling 85,000 copies. Nonetheless, this placed it in second place, behind *Dairantou Smash Bros* (*Super Smash Bros.*) for the Nintendo 3DS. It took fourth place the following week, knocked down by the release of *Monster Hunter 4G* for the 3DS, which in its first week alone sold a cool 1.5 million. In the end, fewer than 200,000 copies were sold in the Land of the Rising Sun.

October 8, 2014. At New York Comic Con, Square Enix launched a new trailer entitled *Introducing the Magic*, which just like *Introducing Kingdom Hearts* was intended for newcomers to the series. It was a beautiful video, but the choice of font for its text could have been better. Two days later, the official *Kingdom Hearts* Instagram account was created.

---

15. "Cloud gaming" is a technology allowing you to stream a game. It had a boom in the 2000s and was seen at the time as the future of video gaming.

October 20, 2014. A new "video casting call" was issued for a promotional video with fans, this time in Europe.

November

November 5, 2014. The limited edition announced in July was just the tip of the iceberg. In fact, Square Enix had kept its real Western collector's edition under wraps. While it was much less aesthetically pleasing than the Japanese version, it was nonetheless a good effort. Indeed, on top of the limited (and regular) edition, Square Enix planned a nice little collector's edition with *I.5* and *II.5*, a thirty-page art book, the pin with Mickey and Sora, a SteelBook case[16] with a piece of key art from *Kingdom Hearts II* and—surprise!—an awesome stuffed Heartless. All that for just 99.99 dollars or euros. That's less than a hundred!

November 10, 2014. There was a new development in the Utada vs. Disney feud. Tetsuya Nomura created art for the Hikaru Utada tribute album[17] that was set to come out on December 8 of that year. The *Kingdom Hearts* creator left a message loaded with meaning, but once again it was relatively enigmatic.

November 26, 2014. Still intent on teaching new audiences about the series, Square Enix USA released two new trailers: *Disney Worlds Connect* and *Memorable Disney Characters and Final Fantasy Cameos Worlds Connect*. No need to comment on them: the titles say it all.

November 30, 2014. Geoff Keighley, the "Dorito Pope" and creator of the "Oscars of video games," The Game Awards, announced on Twitter that Tetsuya Nomura would be present at the 2014 edition of the awards, to take place on December 5 in Las Vegas.

December

December 1, 2014. To put on a show before the release of *Kingdom Hearts HD II.5 ReMix*, Square Enix organized a "fan event" in Los Angeles. Yoko Shimomura and Tetsuya Nomura were in attendance. Nomura took the opportunity to unveil a new teaser trailer for *Kingdom Hearts III*.

---

16. A metal case, often a collector's item, included with limited editions.
17. A compilation album with various artists performing the songs of the artist who is the subject of the tribute.

December 2, 2014. Release of *Kingdom Hearts HD II.5 ReMix* in the USA. It was fairly well received, with 320,000 units sold in the first week. This put it in seventh place on the American charts, behind heavy-hitters like *Pokémon Omega Ruby and Alpha Sapphire*, *GTA V* (for PS4), *Super Smash Bros. for Wii U*, and *Call of Duty: Advanced Warfare*. In the end, it sold over 500,000 units. This was a weaker performance than *I.5*.

Three days after the American release, the compilation came out in Europe, where it struggled to reach 120,000 units sold. For example, the British gave it the cold shoulder. In any case, globally, it managed to sell over 1.25 million copies. That was less than *I.5*, but was still a great performance.

December 5, 2014. Square Enix shared the launch trailer for *Kingdom Hearts HD II.5 ReMix* that the company had created with the involvement of fans. In fact, it was more of a documentary than a trailer, a love letter to the series from fans all around the world. One of the coolest things about the video is that the first part was shown to the Osaka team, which then gave its reactions in the second part of the video. A great way to conclude five minutes and 46 seconds of pure bliss. In other news, contrary to what had been announced, Nomura did not attend The Game Awards.

December 25, 2014. *Kingdom Hearts χ [chi]* introduced Ephemera, a brand-new character with a <u>very important</u> role, both for the game and for the series (you'll see).

THE KEY
[KH χ UNCHAINED: DEVELOPMENT]

The end of 2013 was very difficult for Nomura, who saw his baby, ~~Final Fantasy versus XIII~~ Final Fantasy XV, taken away from him. As usual, he buried himself in creative pursuits to keep himself from falling to pieces. While continuing to work on "The Big One" (Kingdom Hearts III), he reactivated the development of a mobile version of Kingdom Hearts χ [chi], which he named Kingdom Hearts Unchained χ [18]. Again, there were many reasons behind the choice of name.

The first order of business was to adapt the game systems: "On a smartphone, you interact by tapping, flicking, or swiping your finger" (The Holy Trinity of touchscreens), he explains, "and that's what I wanted to do initially, like tapping to a rhythm, that sort of thing, but I realized it was a stupid idea." He then began to experiment with different smartphone games and analyze the things that bothered him: "Any process that requires many operations on such a small screen is a problem. I often find that these things can be done with a single touch and I hate things that just waste time." Next, he asked himself where satisfaction comes from. He came to the conclusion that satisfaction is found in the moment where the number of points starts to jump up on the screen, or when the player reaches an achievement and sees their score skyrocket. "In Kingdom Hearts, battling enemies immediately gives you a visible reward [munny, among other things] (...) So, we looked for a way to adapt that to smartphones," he says. That's how they got the idea to reward players if they managed to finish a battle in a single turn. In this way, the concept of the port became "to make the fastest game ever," he says with a big smile. This required a number of adjustments from Kingdom Hearts χ [chi]. Instead of players choosing worlds, they would complete very short levels, one after another, designed to last between one and three minutes, perfect for playing during a daily commute. Along the same lines, the cards were replaced by tapping to make normal hits, as well as a system of medals whose form was better adapted to touchscreens since they could be grabbed

---

18. I think you know what's coming by now: see Volume II.

and dropped into an inventory and then deployed by swiping a medal with your finger toward the heart of the battle. The new battle system was brought about by a test session in the US: "When we had Americans test χ [chi], they thought it was a card game, but that's not true. First impressions are everything, so we decided to change it for the smartphone version," he says. In regards to the content, Unchained χ was completely identical to χ [chi], "but the story is more easily accessible." Indeed, but when you look closer, it's important to note that players have to get through several hundred levels to move forward in the scenario and there is quite a bit to do, since at least 50 additional levels are added every month, in addition to special events, raids against bosses, and all sorts of challenges... At the same time, the rich content constantly pushes players toward microtransactions to improve their characters' appearance and abilities, even though it's totally possible to play the game without spending a single cent. In truth, the game was designed around this insidious model and it relentlessly incites players to pay thanks/due to serious psychological pressure. We can thank Matsuda for this new model at Square Enix...

Even though *Kingdom Hearts Unchained* χ came out on September 3, 2015, there was (not yet) any plan to discontinue χ [chi], which continued to progress to its shocking conclusion in the summer of 2016. Since Tatsuya Kando and Success were busy with the browser-based version, Nomura entrusted the co-director position to Hiroyuki Itô, who had become Kando's right-hand man after Takeshi Arakawa's departure and Tomohiro Hasegawa's "betrayal[19]." Itô had also gained solid experience with games for touchscreen devices, particularly from working on *Subarashiki Kono Sekai: Solo Remix* (the iOS version) and *Final Fantasy All the Bravest*, a horrifically bad game that was churned out in three months to "satisfy management," even though the initial idea (from Nomura) was quite good. There's also the fact that the travesty was developed by BitGroove Inc., a startup specializing in smartphone games and led by industry veteran Kouji

19. At the time of the "divorce," nearly all of Nomura's team followed him as he started new adventures. For example, this was the case for Roberto Ferrari, Tatsuya Kando, etc. Tomohiro Hasegawa, however, remained on *Final Fantasy XV* working on art direction alongside Yusuke Naora until the latter left Square Enix to work as a freelancer. Hasegawa was thus promoted out of necessity and actually did pretty excellent work on *FFXV*.

Murata[20]. So, naturally, Square Enix turned to BitGroove again to develop *Unchained χ*.

Once again, the West had been left out in the cold. Fans of *Kingdom Hearts* there had long been begging for *χ [chi]*, even though it was a browser-based game. As usual, they felt neglected in comparison to their Japanese counterparts. On its own, that's not a big deal, as long as the plot doesn't have an impact on the main story of the series. Alas, because of Nomura's obsession with always connecting everything together, *χ [chi]* soon became a key piece of the puzzle. This is another reason why the smartphone version was created and why Nomura accelerated the localization process to make *Unchained χ* available to Americans, around seven months after the original version. On the other hand, Europe (and about a hundred other countries) had to wait until summer 2016, close to a year after the release of the Japanese version.

(RE)CONNECT

2015

January
January 15, 2015. Chikao Otsuka, the Japanese voice of Master Xehanort, passed away from coronary artery disease at the age of 85.

January 29, 2015. Thanks to a new update, players learned more about the character Chirithy (or rather, their species). It turns out the Chirithy are actually Dream Eaters. This raised many questions about Daybreak Town. Could it be a dream? Unless the truth was to be found elsewhere…

February
February 26, 2015. A Theater Mode was added to *Kingdom Hearts χ [chi]*. The story was starting to become increasingly important.

---

20. A sound expert who has been in the video game industry since the 1980s, working for Jaleco, Capcom, Konami, and Namco before getting into the systems themselves. He was involved in creating musical items for children and then founded BitGroove in 2011.

February 27, 2015. Leonard Nimoy, who will always be known as Mr. Spock, but who also happened to be the American voice of Master Xehanort, passed away due to chronic obstructive pulmonary disease, which he had developed from having been a smoker 30 years earlier. He was 83 years old at the time of his death. Master Xehanort was left voiceless, with both his Japanese and American actors having passed away.

April

April 14, 2015. Nomura revealed his plans for the next D23 Expo, to take place in Tokyo on November 3. He would be providing new information on *Kingdom Hearts III* apparently, as well as on a game made for smartphones.

April 23, 2015. Square Enix announced that it would have a press conference at the next E3. That hadn't happened since… well, a long time (ever). This implied a big line-up and probably a new trailer for *Kingdom Hearts III*.

May

May 11, 2015. The hashtag #ChiToTheWest appeared on Twitter. Fans immediately began dreaming of a localization of *Kingdom Hearts χ [chi]*.

May 12, 2015. Damn Nomura. His statement a month earlier had been deceptive. Square Enix revealed the existence of *Kingdom Hearts Unchained χ* , a port of *Kingdom Hearts χ [chi]* for smartphones. Its release for iOS and Android phones was set for 2015. The next day, in an interview with *Famitsu*, Nomura revealed that there would be many changes from *χ [chi]* brought about after tests performed in the US, implying that the new game would be released in the West. The same day, a teaser website was made public.

June

June 9, 2015. On its Facebook page, Square Enix asked fans for their opinions about the series and its future.

June 15, 2015. A date to remember. At its pre-E3 press conference, Sony again tried to make a splash with announcements, including for *Shenmue III*; the release of a phantom of the video game industry, *The*

Last Guardian; and a demo of *Uncharted 4: A Thief's End*. However, the climax of the event again involved Square Enix. After revealing *World of Final Fantasy* for the PlayStation 4 and PlayStation Vita, the enthralled audience learned of the existence of the unicorn of video games, *Final Fantasy VII Remake*. Produced by Yoshinori Kitase, written by Kazushige Nojima, and directed by... Tetsuya Nomura. This last announcement was followed by a huge explosion of joy, both from the audience and in thousands of homes around the world where gamers were watching the showcase live over the internet.

The next day, Square Enix held its own press conference, as planned, and added to the excitement with announcements that included *NieR: Automata*, as well as a new trailer for *Kingdom Hearts III* that made a real impact. In addition, *Kingdom Hearts Unchained χ* was confirmed for release in the West. No more details than that.

June 25, 2015. In an interview with Japanese media, Tetsuya Nomura revealed that a *Kingdom Hearts* fan event would take place at the next D23 Expo in Tokyo on November 3. This time, his announcement wasn't a red herring.

July

July 1, 2015. Disney announced the merger of its Consumer Products and Interactive Media segments. The new entity, called DCPI, was to be led by the two presidents of the merged business units, Leslie Ferraro and Jimmy Pitaro.

August

August 6, 2015. *Kingdom Hearts Unchained χ* was announced for a September release in Japan.

August 17, 2015. At the American D23 Expo, Jimmy Pitaro, co-president of Disney's new DCPI, announced that *Kingdom Hearts* had sold over 21 million games worldwide.

September

September 3, 2015. Release of *Kingdom Hearts Unchained χ* in Japan.

September 8, 2015. Always on the lookout for a scoop, fans discovered the LinkedIn profile of Richard W. VanDeventer, an American game designer who claimed to have worked on a game called *Kingdom Hearts 2.9*.

DIGITAL DOMINATION
[KH HD II.8: DEVELOPMENT]

Remember? In March 2013, when Matsuda assumed his new duties, he decreed a new direction for the company, requiring that its big games include extra content, and more specifically, that they do so in <u>advance</u>. Apparently, Nomura didn't really have a choice and had to adhere to the new rules for his *Kingdom Hearts III*. However, as always, he used his incredible imagination to do something better and he succeeded in giving meaning to the extra content. It took the form of *Kingdom Hearts II.8 Final Chapter Prologue*[21], the third and final HD compilation.

It was an idea that had actually been lingering in his mind for quite some time (well before the reign of Matsuda). Once he started working seriously on writing *Kingdom Hearts III*, he quickly realized that "the content was far too rich and there was far too much of it." So, he broke it up into pieces to create *Kingdom Hearts 3D: Dream Drop Distance* and *Kingdom Hearts 0.2: Birth by Sleep — A Fragmentary Passage*, which he more or less "announced" at the end of *Birth by Sleep*. An "episode," as he called it, that he had long been planning to create, he says. Could it be that he had already planned out everything in 2009[22]? It seems so. In any case, once again, he proved his remarkable creativity. After the secret movies and the playable secret episode, this was his follow-up in the form of a (playable) prologue. It was really a technical demo that gave a

21. To find out the meaning of this unpronounceable name, see Volume II.
22. See page 282.

preview of the "technology used in *Kingdom Hearts III*," notably a new way of using light[23].

Besides that, *0.2* was above all a way to give a preview of the future systems, notably Situation Command, an evolution of the Reaction Command from *Kingdom Hearts II* combined with the Command Styles from *Birth by Sleep*, of which one of the particularities was "offering the player multiple options within a limited amount of time," according to Nomura. Basically, lots of freedom and gameplay that was even more vigorous. Similarly, the forms of magic, besides their incredible beauty, changed significantly to adapt not only to enemies, but also to the environment, as Yasue confirms: "For example, Blizzard creates a path of ice on the ground allowing the character to slide" and adds an extra way of playing. It was a new approach that came from *Final Fantasy versus XIII* in which Nomura, way back in 2010, planned to have real interaction between the backgrounds and the effects of spells. In regards to the backgrounds, because of the story, everything took place in the Realm of Darkness; however, just like in the Realm of Light, that didn't mean that everything was the same: "I wanted Disney worlds consumed by the Darkness and that had fused together," says Nomura. Level design changed to be much more vertical, following a trend started in *Kingdom Hearts 3D: Dream Drop Distance* with its Flowmotion. And, guess what? It was the centerpiece of this compilation. A magical transition.

Originally designed for the special characteristics of the Nintendo 3DS, it had to be significantly revised and corrected for a more, shall we say, conventional console. Starting with its gameplay. According to Nomura, this was an enormous challenge: "The Link with the Spirits and Reality Shift are normally controlled by interacting with the lower screen of the 3DS." Initially, they planned to replace the lower screen with the touch pad of the DualShock 4 controller, but they weren't happy with the results of their tests. They then decided to go back to the good old buttons with a system of combinations that were sophisticated, but ultimately worked quite naturally. While the content didn't

---

23. One of the special characteristics of the series is that it has never lit the characters in order to maintain the soft textures that are so typical of Disney designs. So, this was a new development that would give rise to the "Kingdom Shader," which I will cover in detail in the appropriate volume.

change, several aspects were adjusted. Particularly, the AI of enemies was made more powerful and the game time before each Drop was made longer. In addition, several Dream Eaters made an appearance in response to a request from the boss, and their interaction with the player was changed. Also of note, a significant improvement was made to visuals and speed was increased, with it becoming the first game in the series to move entirely at 60 frames per second. What's more, it was one of only a few PS4 games to achieve this. So is that why this compilation wasn't released for the PlayStation 3? No; there were two good reasons why: "Given that the next game [*Kingdom Hearts III*] would be for PlayStation 4 and that this compilation was to be its prologue, it seemed an obvious choice to make the compilation for the same console," explains Nomura. That makes sense. The other reason has to do with the technology used by *Kingdom Hearts 0.2*, which was far too modern and used too much memory for the older generation of console.

The same technology was also used to create the cutscenes in *Kingdom Hearts χ Back Cover*. Following the pattern of *Days* and *Re: coded*, it was the movie in this compilation. Even though it was shorter (about 80 minutes long) than the previous two movies, it had the advantage of offering brand-new content, created from scratch: "The cast, the character models, the script. It was all original!" Nomura touts. In other words, they had to create a lot of content, even though it was really more of a rewrite of *Kingdom Hearts χ [chi]* from a different perspective. The director explains: "While the χ[24] series is from the player's point of view on the events leading up to the Keyblade War, *Back Cover* focuses solely on the Foretellers and their motives."

The movie also revealed new characters like the Master of Masters, for whom the Foretellers were Padawans[25]. To not ruin the surprise about the Master of Masters and Luxu (the sixth disciple), Nomura made sure to dress them in the usual black hoods, creating an implicit link with the rest of the series. This also led to special work being done

24. It's interesting that Nomura considers χ to be a series. When he said this, he was in fact working on *Kingdom Hearts Union χ [Cross]*, the follow-up to *Unchained χ*, announced a few months after.
25. The name for apprentices in the *Star Wars* universe.

on their body language and their voices to compensate for their lack of faces… and thus mouths. That certainly simplifies lip-synching, but it makes it exceedingly difficult to develop a character's personality. That's one of the things (in addition to the unusual or even eccentric personality of the Master of Masters) that led Nomura to totally exaggerate the Master's voice, relying specifically on the talent of his voice actors (Tomokazu Sugita[26] in Japanese and Ray Chase in English). Also in regards to dubbing, Nomura explains that everything was carefully planned. While the actors may sometimes give the impression that they're improvising, it's not so. One exception was the scene of dialog between the Master of Masters and Aced (Subaru Kimura[27] in Japanese, Travis Willingham in English), which was so natural that everyone broke down laughing; so, they kept it. *Back Cover* was, in any case, a technical tour de force that was thrilling to watch because it had so much to offer (particularly battle scenes reminiscent of *Final Fantasy VII Advent Children*; surprise, surprise). It also served as a teaser for the cutscenes to be found in *Kingdom Hearts III*. It got fans dreaming about the end and the battle against the final boss.

(RE)CONNECT

Since there's not much to say about the development of *Kingdom Hearts HD I.5 + II.5 ReMix*, the ultimate compilation that brought together *I.5* and *II.5* for the PS4, I have purposely added it to this final *(re)Connect*, which simultaneously concludes the story of the development of the *Kingdom Hearts* series. That is, until the conclusion and, in particular, the next game.

---

26. Sugita has had an incredible career as a *seiyū (say me)* for animated media and video games. Among others, he was the voice of Joseph Joestar in *JoJo's Bizarre Adventure*, but he also played Dias (*Star Ocean: The Second Story*), King (*Final Fantasy Type–0*), and Chrom (*Fire Emblem Awakening*). His American counterpart, Ray Chase, was the voice of none other than… Noctis (*Final Fantasy XV*).
27. Kimura is best-known as the voice of Takeshi in the series *Doraemon*, but he is not a stranger to Square Enix, in particular having played Beat in *Subarashiki Kono Sekai* (*The World Ends With You*). As for Willingham, he did the voice of… Guile (*Street Fighter*). He is also a Square Enix regular, having played Yodai in *The World Ends With You* and Roy Mustang in *Fullmetal Alchemist*.

2015

September

September 15, 2015. For its pre-TGS press conference, Sony invited many producers to come present their games on stage. Among them was Shinji Hashimoto who, after again presenting *World of Final Fantasy* and showing the first trailers for *Star Ocean V: Integrity and Faithlessness* and *SaGa: Scarlet Grace*, unveiled a trailer for... a new *Kingdom Hearts*? *Kingdom Hearts 3D: Dream Drop Distance*? In HD? That's what it looked like; but that wasn't all. There was a new title using χ; it was called *Kingdom Hearts χ Back Cover*. It gave some substantial information using key phrases and, in particular, a new stage showing animal heads... those from the masks of the Foretellers in χ! Still, there was one final surprise: *Kingdom Hearts 0.2 Birth by Sleep — A Fragmentary Passage*, which showed Aqua from behind in the Realm of Darkness. Thus, the compilation presented had three components, just like *I.5* and *II.5*. It was dubbed *Kingdom Hearts HD II.8 Final Chapter Prologue* and was set for release in 2016. That same day, Square Enix launched the game's official website. Also at the TGS, Square Enix unveiled a new, very short teaser trailer for *Kingdom Hearts III*, a "cut" of the E3 trailer, as well as a reminder of the existence of *Kingdom Hearts Unchained χ*.

December

December 18, 2015. A little more was revealed about *Kingdom Hearts HD II.8 Final Chapter Prologue* in a new trailer, this time with dubbing. Notably, it showed *Kingdom Hearts: Dream Drop Distance HD* at its best and a new cutscene with unusual graphics for the characters, who lost their soft textures, but became more realistic and "visually appealing." Fans also discovered that the title had lost its "3D" and gained an "HD" instead. Unlike the trailer from the TGS, the new trailer no longer gave a release date; it simply said "Now in Development." A bad sign?

2016

January

January 5, 2016. Japanese magazine *Famitsu* talked with developers to hear about their plans for 2016; among them was Tetsuya Nomura. Besides discussing *World of Final Fantasy* (for which he was creative producer) and *Kingdom Hearts HD II.8 Final Chapter Prologue*, he explained that *Kingdom Hearts III* and *Final Fantasy VII Remake* were in development.

Square Enix announced the closing of Shinra Technologies. This came after the company's failure to secure third-party funding and 2 billion yen (about $17 million) in cumulative losses. In other words, it was an expensive venture with no takers. Yoichi Wada was fired for good.

March

March 3, 2016. Players of *Kingdom Hearts Unchained χ* met Skuld, a new female character who seemed to be important.

April

April 4, 2016. The official US release date for *Kingdom Hearts Unchained χ* was announced: April 7, 2016. Three days from then. To celebrate, Nomura made a black and white drawing of Ephemera, Skuld, and Chirithy.

April 7, 2016. Release of *Kingdom Hearts Unchained χ* in the United States. That same day, an update to *Kingdom Hearts χ [chi]* revealed an important new development in the story. However, it was announced that the game would be shut down in September.

April 25, 2016. At PAX East 2016, the producer of *Kingdom Hearts Unchained χ*, Hironori Okayama, granted an interview to the website *Gamer Escape*[28] in which he revealed many details. For example, he said that the Japanese version already had 500 stages and the American version had about 250. Their goal was to create 50 more each month and to create more partnerships, like the one with *Zootopia* to begin May 2.

---

28. *Gamer Escape* is an amateur website, but it has very close ties to Square Enix since it has maintained the wiki for *Final Fantasy XI* for years.

April 28, 2016. Square Enix announced *Kingdom Hearts Concert —First Breath —*, which would have three spectacular performances: August 11 in Tokyo, August 27 in Aichi, and August 28 in Osaka. But that's not all: *Kingdom Hearts Orchestra World Tour* was set to take place in 2017, beginning on March 10 in Tokyo before moving on to France, the UK, China, the US, and more. According to Nomura, who was heavily involved, it seems that it was more of a show than just a concert. In any case, Nomura said that, in his view, it was just as important as the games.

May

May 11, 2016. In a press release, Square Enix revealed that *Kingdom Hearts Unchained χ* had been downloaded over 2 million times in the United States.

June

June 8, 2016. A week before E3, *Kingdom Hearts Unchained χ* was finally confirmed for release in the European market. However, no release date was provided. That same day, American actor Michael Johnston (known for his role in *Teen Wolf*) revealed that he would be the voice of Ephemera in *Kingdom Hearts χ Back Cover* as part of the upcoming *II.8* compilation.

June 14, 2016. At E3 2016, Square Enix revealed a new trailer for *Kingdom Hearts HD II.8 Final Chapter Prologue*, which was astutely divided into three parts. First, *Kingdom Hearts: Dream Drop Distance HD*, which looked so much like the *I.5* and *II.5* remakes that it appeared that it had never been made for the 3DS. The second part was dedicated to *Kingdom Hearts 0.2*, which showed the game in action and displayed the new lighting. It was amazing. The very last shot appeared to reveal the return of Terra! The third and final part showed what *χ Back Cover* looked like. It seemed to be the movie of this compilation and got the same visual treatment as *0.2*. In any case, it appeared to have a very exciting story connected to the rest of the series. And the best part of all: the compilation was given a release window of December 2016 and for the first time it would be a global release! Since the company likes to pile on the surprises, *DDD HD* and *0.2* were available to play at the Square Enix booth. In addition, a new

trailer for *Kingdom Hearts Unchained χ* revealed new worlds and a scenario with greater importance. What's interesting is that it was a response to *χ Back Cover*.

Tai Yasue, who was in attendance at the expo, gave numerous interviews and said that a *Final Fantasy* world was not at all an option for *Kingdom Hearts*; however, a PS4 version of *I.5* and *II.5* was not out of the question. That said, he clarified that this was not an announcement, just a possibility. Yasue also said that production of *II.8* had zero impact on the development of *Kingdom Hearts III* because both games were being created at the same time and, in a way, *II.8* was needed to test the new technology.

June 16, 2016. *Kingdom Hearts Unchained χ* had a surprise release on the very same day as its announcement in 105 countries simultaneously! To celebrate the occasion, a new Aqua-themed medal was revealed.

July

July 7, 2016. The end of *Kingdom Hearts χ [chi]* was approaching. The most recent "episode" included the start of the Keyblade War and introduced the Master of Masters' sixth disciple, Luxu.

July 21, 2016. *Kingdom Hearts χ [chi]* celebrated its third birthday. It had totally exceptional longevity for a browser-based game, proving that it was much more than that. As he did every year, Nomura created a new illustration. This time, it showed Sora, Kairi, and Riku sporting new outfits (their *Kingdom Hearts III* outfits?). What's more, Kairi's get-up looked like Ava's mask from *χ*; why? Behind the three main characters stood Ephemera, Skuld, Chirithy, and… Ventus. What the heck was he doing there? As usual, Nomura wanted his creation to grab people's attention. Well played. He certainly got my attention.

August

August 11, 2016. The *First Breath* concert indeed turned out to be more than just a concert. In the first performance, actors Ryotaro Okiayu (Terra) and Iku Nakahara (Naminé) accompanied the music by reciting a few lines from the games, then delivered a totally new dialog… one between Lingering Will and Naminé that, in a way, served as an introduction to *0.2*.

August 22, 2016. As a bit of a joke, *Kingdom Hearts Unchained χ* announced an event based on *The Jungle Book*, the world that Nomura had tried to add to every episode in the series but never got the permission to do so from Disney. The joke didn't survive long past August 22, but still!

August 25, 2016. The final episode of *Kingdom Hearts χ [chi]* was released. That meant the climax of the story and the final battle.

August 29, 2016. As always, Nomura didn't know how to stop. He added a secret ending to *Kingdom Hearts χ [chi]* called *Special Episode*, leaving the door open to a continuation of the story...

August 31, 2016. *Kingdom Hearts Unchained χ* got caught up to the scenario of *Kingdom Hearts χ [chi]*. Nomura let fans know that a second season was already planned and that Maleficent had been included in the Special Episode and Ventus in the third-anniversary drawing for a reason.

September

September 3, 2016. *Kingdom Hearts Unchained χ* celebrated its first anniversary. Once again, Nomura created an illustration in black and white that was enigmatic if nothing else. It showed Ephemera, Skuld, Ventus, and two other silhouettes. Could the number five again be important?

September 13, 2016. At Sony's pre-TGS press conference, the logo for *Kingdom Hearts HD II.8 Final Chapter Prologue* was revealed, along with a release date: January 12. During the conference, Square Enix posted a new trailer online that took fans by surprise and revealed much more about the two new components of the compilation, *0.2* and *χ Back Cover*, in addition to being accompanied by a new remix of Utada's *Simple & Clean* called *Ray of Hope*. The US release date was confirmed as January 24, 2017. It would essentially be a global release date, but Japan would still get to experience the game first, about 10 days ahead of everyone else. It was almost laughable. That same day, fans got to see the game's packaging and the official website confirmed that a free piece of DLC would be made available after the release. Nomura confirmed that the final compilation would support 4K and would thus be compatible with the PlayStation 4 Pro.

October

October 6, 2016. A limited edition, similar to the one for *II.5*, was revealed for *Kingdom Hearts HD II.8 Final Chapter Prologue*. And it came with a new pin…

October 25, 2016. The global release of *World of Final Fantasy*. It's hard to know the game's true sales figures. It sold about 800,000 physical copies. However, the number of PC and digital copies sold remains a mystery. That said, we can reasonably assume that it sold over a million given that Square Enix has planned a sequel.

October 27, 2016. Surprising though it may seem (likely a question of timing), Square Enix's plans for the fifteenth anniversary of *Kingdom Hearts* were revealed at the Paris Games Week, a French "mini-E3." Shinji Hashimoto was in attendance at the event and played a trailer. It was for *Kingdom Hearts HD I.5 + II.5 ReMix*! As the name indicated, it was a fusion of the two PlayStation 3 compilations, but this time for PlayStation 4. No difference in the content. Instead, the game had improved resolution, moving up to 1080p, in addition to offering each episode at 60 frames per second! It was THE ultimate version. The announcement struck like a lightning bolt, already giving the release dates for all regions: March 9 for Japan, March 28 for the United States, and March 31 for Europe.

On top of that, the French audience got to see the incredible opening of *Kingdom Hearts 0.2 Birth by Sleep — A fragmentary passage* and two new images from *Kingdom Hearts III*. Finally, there was the reveal of a piece of DLC for *World of Final Fantasy*: the "Champion Summon: Sora." As the name suggests, Sora got his own medal (what do you know?) that could be used to summon him. He thus became one of the "champions," the characters in the *Final Fantasy* universe that could be called in as reinforcements during a battle. No date was announced other than a very vague "winter."

That same day, the official website for *Kingdom Hearts HD I.5 + II.5 ReMix* went online.

November

November 4, 2016. Square Enix announced that there had been 5 million downloads of *Kingdom Hearts Unchained χ*. While it remained F2P, it was an unexpected hit.

November 11, 2016. After the uproar in Spain and Italy with *Kingdom Hearts 3D: Dream Drop Distance*, Shinji Hashimoto, during an appearance at Lucca Comics & Games[29], confirmed that the HD version would indeed be translated into Spanish and Italian.

November 23, 2016. The *Kingdom Hearts* concert was a big success. Because of strong demand, the concert's organizer, La Fée Sauvage[30], announced four additional dates for the *Kingdom Hearts Orchestra World Tour*.

December

December 8, 2016. The launch trailer for *Kingdom Hearts HD II.8 Final Chapter Prologue* was released in English. Fans were again stunned when they saw *0.2* in action. They also had their curiosity piqued as they saw more of *χ Back Cover*.

The next day, Sony and Square Enix announced "PlayStation 4 *Kingdom Hearts 15th Anniversary Edition*." As its name indicated, it was a limited-edition PS4 with a *Kingdom Hearts* theme. It was both understated and highly attractive. Its release was set for January 12, 2017, with a price of 38,980 yen (around $350).

December 9, 2016. The Sora DLC for *World of Final Fantasy* was also announced for release on January 12, 2017.

December 17, 2016. Square Enix put little effort into producing a trailer barely 30 seconds long to remind people of the upcoming release of *Kingdom Hearts HD I.5 + II.5 ReMix*.

December 30, 2016. After working on *Final Fantasy versus XIII*, then *Final Fantasy VII Remake*, Roberto Ferrari said that he wanted to work on *Kingdom Hearts*. Maybe one day?

2017

January

Kingdom Hearts took over the Shinjuku train station from January 9 to 15 with an exhibition featuring its "Memorial Stained Glass Clock."

---

29. The largest comics festival in Europe and the second largest in the world after Japan's Comiket.
30. A French concert organizer that specializes in Japanese artists.

The clock was enormous—two meters in diameter—with a face made of stained glass. It was surrounded by 12 smaller circles of stained glass, each one representing a specific stage in a specific game. Next to the clock was a promotional video screen displaying a one-hour loop of video and a countdown to the release of *Kingdom Hearts HD II.8 Final Chapter Prologue*.

January 10, 2017. In an interview, Nomura admitted that he wasn't thinking about coming out with a "complete package" with *Kingdom Hearts HD I.5 + II.5 ReMix* and *Kingdom Hearts HD II.8 Final Chapter Prologue*. However, he was planning on putting out an exclusive box for storing the two collections side by side.

January 12, 2017. *Kingdom Hearts HD II.8 Final Chapter Prologue* hit the shelves in Japan. Unsurprisingly, it immediately reached the top spot on the charts with 138,000 copies sold in the first week, putting it ahead of *New Dangan Ronpa V3: Minna no Koroshiai Shin Gakki*. The next week, it fell to fourth place because of *Gravity Rush 2* (PS4), *Yoshi's Wooly World* (3DS), and *Valkyria: Azure Revolution* (PS4). In Japan, it ultimately did not sell more than 250,000 units. That's not much.

January 24, 2017. *Kingdom Hearts HD II.8 Final Chapter Prologue* was released everywhere else in the world and came in second place on the charts with 200,000 copies sold in the US and around 100,000 in Europe. It was a difficult time to be released since it had to compete with *Resident Evil VII*, the new sensation from Capcom. For a, shall we say, fairer comparison, the compilation beat sales of *Tales of Berseria* and *Yakuza Zero*, which also came out that same week. Despite the main game's lack of appeal (*KH: DDD HD*), it performed decently, although well below the series' usual level, failing to sell even a million copies throughout its entire run. However, there remains a major unknown bit of information: how were the compilation's digital sales?

January 26, 2017. The usual Proud Mode was added to *Kingdom Hearts Unchained χ* .

January 27, 2017. Just as Nomura had announced two weeks earlier, Square Enix revealed on its online store that fans could get a superb box to hold *Kingdom Hearts HD II.8 Final Chapter Prologue* and *Kingdom Hearts HD I.5 + II.5 ReMix*.

January 31, 2017. *Final Fantasy VII* turned 20 years old. To celebrate, Nomura had an image created with the *Kingdom Hearts III* rendering engine showing Sora facing The Mysterious Tower, a nod to the image of Cloud facing the ShinRa tower.

February

February 9, 2017. Announcement of a limited edition of *Kingdom Hearts HD I.5 + II.5 ReMix*, exclusively for the Square Enix Online Store. And guess what it came with. That's right, another pin.

February 23, 2017. For all preorders of the digital edition of *Kingdom Hearts HD I.5 + II.5 ReMix* through the PSN, players would receive a gorgeous, exclusive PS4 background.

March

March 8, 2017. Square Enix released a video devoted to gameplay showing the improved graphics in *Kingdom Hearts II Final Mix* and *Birth by Sleep Final Mix*. The next day, the same was done for *Kingdom Hearts Final Mix* and *Kingdom Hearts Re: Chain of Memories*. It was a surprisingly effective campaign: you can't get simpler than this to really encourage players to get (back) into the series.

March 9, 2017. Release of *Kingdom Hearts HD I.5 + II.5 ReMix* in Japan. It sold 65,000 units and took second place, behind *Ghost Recon: Wildlands*, but ahead of *The Legend of Zelda: Breath of the Wild* in its second week of sales. Two factors help give more context to this number: 1. The (too) recent release of *II.8*. 2. It was a difficult time for all PS4 games because the Switch, Nintendo's hit new console, had just come out. Finally, there was the fact that it was a re-release of re-releases. Only "some fans, but not enough of them," were willing to keep shelling out money; meanwhile, those who had not yet gotten to know the series were spending their money on the Switch. In the end, it sold about 150,000 physical copies. We don't have access to the PSN numbers.

To celebrate the release of *Kingdom Hearts HD I.5 + II.5 ReMix*, and also the fifteenth anniversary of the series, Square Enix launched a mini-website called Memorial Music Box.

It didn't take long for fans to start complaining about annoying bugs like bosses that were much too difficult or crashes. The 60 frames per

second caused big problems. Square Enix responded quite quickly and promised a patch ASAP.

March 10, 2017. A second season of *Kingdom Hearts Unchained χ* was announced. At the same time, the game would change names to become *Kingdom Hearts: Union χ [Cross]*. In addition to continuing the story, new features would be added, including multi-player quests and the ability to create a team, allowing up to six players to work together. The game would have a basic communication system using emoticons and speech bubbles. Also, there would be a Theater Mode giving access to all of the previously seen cutscenes. Basically, it was a new and improved *Unchained χ* . That same day, to go with the announcement, a trailer was released, with a big surprise at the end: Ventus. The question was, how could that be? Surely one of the many mysteries to come in season two.

March 17, 2017. Patch 1.02 was released to correct a series of bugs encountered in *Kingdom Hearts HD I.5 + II.5 ReMix*. On June 12, another patch (1.03) added the ability to view all of the videos in Theater Mode and a brand-new scene was added to the *Kingdom Hearts 358/2 Days* movie. A final patch (1.04) was released on June 23 to correct a number of bugs that had survived the previous patches.

March 22, 2017. *Kingdom Hearts Unchained χ* officially became *Kingdom Hearts: Union χ [Cross]* in Japan.

March 23, 2017. The official Twitter account for *Kingdom Hearts* reassured Western players that patch 1.02 would be available the very same day as the game's release both in the United States and in Europe. What a relief.

March 28, 2017. *Kingdom Hearts* celebrated its fifteenth birthday with the American release of *Kingdom Hearts HD I.5 + II.5 ReMix*. It managed to reach second place on the charts with a little under 150,000 copies sold, ahead of *The Legend of Zelda: Breath of the Wild*, which had already been out for around a month. In the end, it sold over 500,000 units in the region. Once again, we don't have the numbers for online sales. Indeed, it's very annoying.

Three days later, the game hit the shelves in Europe, selling 65,000 copies. This time, it fell just behind *Mass Effect: Andromeda* (PS4), but still ahead of *The Legend of Zelda: Breath of the Wild*. If you add up all sales of <u>physical</u> copies, *Kingdom Hearts HD I.5 + II.5 ReMix* still managed to pass the one million mark, selling about 1.2 million units. We can imagine that PSN sales hit at least the 300,000 mark, but again, we don't know for sure.

As for the rest, well, you know: to be continued soon!

A

THE LEGEND OF
KINGDOM HEARTS

VOLUME 1: CREATION

Genesis of Hearts

CONCLUSION — PASSION

T ETSUYA Nomura was born on October 8, 1970. He grew up in the south of the island of Shikoku in a city located in the delta of the Kagami River with a castle perched above it. From its forests, to its beaches, to its limestone cave, and of course its various capes jutting out into the Pacific, Nomura's hometown is heaven on earth. It was like the Destiny Islands for the young man, who felt restless and dreamed of adventure and becoming an artist. His life has been marked by the many people he has met along the way. He became a protégé to several important creators who "connected" with his heart and soul so that he would never lose sight of how yesterday's principles can guide the way tomorrow too. Having gone through his own Mark of Mastery exam over a decade, he ultimately became the Master of his own destiny: an exceptional architect. Through great selflessness, ingenuity, and cleverness, he was able to convince the biggest entertainment empire in the world to yield to his genius, giving rise to one of the greatest works of our time; indeed, one of the greatest because it is much more than a video game…

… but we'll get into that in the next volume. I'm sure you've realized by now that things weren't supposed to happen this way. This first volume has always been the first chapter. Still, given my way of story-telling, there was no way I could leave out anecdotes and details; I had to produce a written work as rich as the series itself. Indeed, *Kingdom Hearts* is unique and deserves such high regard, if only for the men and women who created it. This book is dedicated to them. To their hard work, to their ingenuity, to their humanity, to their genius. To their hearts.

This first volume ends here, but the book shall carry on. Coming up next, we will talk about the game systems; how the story is told in a unique way; I will give more details on the creation of the series' universe and its connection to our collective unconscious; and finally, of course, a proper analysis of the story told, and how it's told, with a final deeper reading of the text. That means I have a lot in store for you, that is, unless I wake up to find that this was all just a dream, or I lose my memory before then.

Thank you, from the bottom of my heart, for playing along with me. I'll see you again soon to take on new adventures!

Jay

Better known by his pseudonym "Jay," Georges Grouard is the founder of the world's first magazine dedicated entirely to role-playing games: *Gameplay RPG*. Before that, Jay gained valuable experience by climbing the writing career ladder. He was a journalist, editor-in-chief, then editorial director, and finally the boss of his own media company, through which he published the magazine *Background*. He has devoted his life to "genre" video games and today he continues working in the industry on many different projects.

THE LEGEND OF

KINGDOM HEARTS

VOLUME 1: CREATION

Genesis of Hearts

ACKNOWLEDGMENTS

THE PEOPLE I'D LIKE TO THANK

Emiko Yamamoto and Shinji Hashimoto, because without them, none of this would have been possible.

Tetsuya Nomura and his many team members for… For everything. For the beauty of these people. And for their Heart. I hope that I've been worthy of "connecting" with them.

Hironobu Sakaguchi, for giving Nomura a kick in the butt at the right time and pushing him to truly reveal his talent.

My friend and favorite gaming partner Val, for reviewing my work and giving many good comments. You'll be in my heart always, brother.

My friend Jun (yes, he's Japanese). It helps to have a friend like you when writing a book about a Japanese game, especially so that I don't undercut the messages of Japanese speakers.

My friend Pierre, for his knowledge of music and his flexibility after all the times I've said, "yeah, let's go see *Black Panther*" (which we still haven't seen).

My friend Tom, who did nothing, but this way everyone is included and no one gets jealous.

Thank you to all of you readers for reading this book (in its entirety), and for putting up with the many (re)Connects, my at-times questionable humor, and especially my neuroses.

THE PEOPLE I'D NOT LIKE TO THANK

My editor, Mehdi, because he pushed me to censor myself and I hate that. But I thank him for everything else. Firstly, for the opportunity. Then, for agreeing to my methodology. For trusting me and giving a lot of ground on his own way of seeing things, and for listening to my suggestions. And, above all, I tip my hat to him for having managed to tame the beast.

My family, who provided no support other than coming to bother me with mundane stuff that's more annoying than anything else, not understanding the solitude that an author needs. No, I can't do a drawing and review a chapter for the thirty-sixth time all at once. And I definitely can't answer a boring question while I'm busy developing a brilliant idea. Anyway, thanks for your patience and for tolerating me. And for everything else.

The M Team: you know who you are. They came quite regularly to distract me. No thanks for you.

Finally, I do not thank myself. At all. For burdening myself with absurd challenges, sleepless nights, and my damned compulsion to re-read my work 40 times over and rewrite everything because "no, that's shit." For writing a first chapter that became a first volume, thus requiring me to write a second volume that my old bones would rather I had done without. As such, my body would like to join me in writing an angry letter to my deadbeat brain.

Including for the excessive tobacco consumption brought about by my work habits. Because, indeed, writing leads to smoking. It's psychological. Now, it's time for me to pass out. Please do not disturb me until I have my next stroke.

Finally, a word of advice: NEVER agree to write a book. It sounds cool at first, but in reality, it's not cool at all.

THE LEGEND OF
KINGDOM HEARTS

VOLUME 1: CREATION

Genesis of Hearts

TABLE OF CONTENTS

As I said on page 81, in each chapter, most of the subheadings are references to song titles from the soundtracks for games, mainly *Kingdom Hearts*, of course. Since Yoko Shimomura tends to give the names of some of her compositions in other languages, you'll also find a translation of those.

The idea behind this system is that, if you want, while you read a section, you can listen to the corresponding song if you own copies of the soundtracks; if not, you can go online and create a playlist. That's up to you.

✍

CHAPTER II — THE KINGDOM   63

CHAPTER III — THE TWIN   81

CHAPTER IV.5 — THE RULE OF (THE) THREES PART 2 237

Also available from Third Éditions :

Legal submission for copyright: December 2019
Printed in the European Union by Grafo